RELIGIOUS THINKING FROM
CHILDHOOD TO ADOLESCENCE

TO

JEAN, KIRSTY AND ALASDAIR

CONTENTS

PREFACE   *page* xi

1. THE PROBLEMS OF RELIGIOUS THINKING   1
   The Role of the Intellect   2
   The Nature of Religious Thinking   3
   The Problem of the Content of Religious Teaching   5
   Psychology, Research and Religion   8

2. THINKING AND ITS APPLICATION TO RELIGION   10
   The Materials of Thinking   11
   The Materials of Religious Thinking   13
   The Processes of Thinking and Abilities in Thinking   19
   The Processes of Religious Thinking and Abilities in Religious
      Thinking   22
   Motives for Thinking   30
   Motives for Religious Thinking   31

3. A RESEARCH APPROACH TO THE PROBLEMS
   OF RELIGIOUS THINKING   34
   Possible Methods of Research Available   34
   The Research Procedure   36
   The Final Sample   39
   Two Problems Implicit in the Methods Used   44
   Methods of Scoring and Evaluating the Results   48
   Age Divisions and Children's Names   49

4. OPERATIONAL THINKING ABOUT RELIGIOUS
   STORIES   51
   Intuitive Religious Thinking   52
   Intermediate between Intuitive and Concrete Religious
      Thinking   54
   Concrete Religious Thinking   55
   Intermediate Concrete-Abstract Religious Thinking   58
   Abstract Religious Thinking   60
   Sequences of Thought   62
   Individual Differences   64
   Logical and Theological Thinking   66

5. CONCEPTS OF THE BIBLE   68
   Concepts of What Kind of Book?   69

vii

Concepts of How the Bible came to be Written   *page* 73
Concepts of the Bible as True   75
Concepts of the Relevance and Possible Recurrence of
  Biblical Experience   80
General Comments on Bible Concepts   84

6. THE IDENTITY AND NATURE OF THE DIVINE   87
  The Deity Visualised   88
  Concepts of Divine Communication   93
  Concepts of the Divine Presence   95
  General Comment on Developing Concepts of the Divine
    Identity   99

7. GOD'S ACTIVITY IN THE NATURAL WORLD   102
  The Burning Bush Event   104
  The Waters Divided   107
  Stone into Bread and Water into Wine   112
  Artificialism   113

8. THE HOLINESS OF GOD   116
  The Fear of Looking upon God   117
  The Nature of the Holy Ground   121
  General Comments on Concepts of the Holy   124

9. GOD'S CONCERN FOR MEN   128
  Concepts of Divine Love   129
  Concepts of Divine Justice   135

10. GOD'S CONCERN FOR MEN (continued)   143
  Group Moral Judgments   143
  Concepts of the Chosen Nation   148
  General Comments on God's Concern for Men Concepts   152

11. JESUS AND THE PROBLEM OF EVIL   156
  The Person of Christ   157
  Concepts of Christ's Moral Righteousness   162
  The Temptations   166
  Concepts of Evil   172
  General Comments on Concepts of Jesus and the Problem of
    Evil   174

12. CONCEPTS OF PRAYER   177
  To Whom are Prayers Addressed?   178
  The Content of Prayers   178
    (1) Altruistic Prayers   179
    (2) Prayers for Self   181
    (3) Prayers in Illness and Physical Danger   182
    (4) Set Prayers   183

CONTENTS

Concepts of Efficacious Prayer   *page* 184
Concepts of Unanswered Prayer   188
General Comments on Concepts of Prayer   190

13. CONCEPTS OF THE CHURCH   194
    Aspects of Church Liked and Disliked   194
    The Nature of the Church   199
    Adult Motives for Churchgoing   202
    The Helpfulness of Churchgoing   204
    General Comments on Concepts of the Church   207

14. THE INFLUENCE OF CHURCH, HOME AND
    OTHER FACTORS UPON RELIGIOUS THINKING   209
    Church or Sunday School Attendance   210
    Parental Support   211
    Religious Behaviour   212
    Sex Differences   213
    Familiarity with Bible Material   214
    Some Examples of Individual Pupils   215

15. SOME IMPLICATIONS FOR RELIGIOUS
    EDUCATION   220
    Religious Thinking in Terms of the Bible Stories used—Moses
      and the Burning Bush, The Crossing of the Red Sea, The
      Temptation of Jesus, 'They Must Know the Bible Argu-
      ment'   220
    The More General Implications for Religious Education   224
      (1) The Need to Examine Concepts Involved in Understand-
          ing Material Chosen for any Given Age Group   224
      (2) The Limits of Understanding Imposed by the Various
          Levels of Operational Thinking   226
      (3) The Need for a More Child-Centred Religious Education   227
    The Religious Characteristics of the Young Child   230
    Religious Education with Younger Children   232
    The Religious Characteristics of the Late Junior and Pre-
      Adolescent   234
    Religious Education of Late Juniors and Pre-Adolescents   237
    The Religious Characteristics of Adolescents   239
    The Religious Education of Adolescents   241
      (1) The Problem of Literalism and Authoritarianism   242
      (2) The Problem of 'Two Worlds'   242
      (3) The Problem of Old Testament Teaching   243
      (4) The Problem of Biblical Relevance   244
      (5) Practical Implications for the Secondary School   244

APPENDIX A
    The Picture and Story Religious Thinking Test, Interview
    Blank, Pictures and Story Text   247

ix

CONTENTS

APPENDIX B
A Brief Description of the Guttman Scalogram Method Applied to the Evaluation of Pupils' Responses. A Note on the Reliability and Validity of the Picture and Story Religious Thinking Test   *page* 260

APPENDIX C
A Glossary of Terms for American Readers   264

BIBLIOGRAPHY   266

INDEX OF SUBJECTS   272

INDEX OF NAMES   275

PREFACE

THIS book has emerged from a piece of research carried out in the last few years, but it has also stemmed from a much longer period of concern for the effectiveness of religious education. The book is designed as a descriptive account of how school pupils think about religion and the content of their thoughts as they are taught religion. Based upon research, the purpose of the book is largely diagnostic, so that teachers, parents, clergy and all who are involved in religious education may see more clearly its problems and opportunities. In a later volume to follow this one, the more positive answers to the problems raised will be explored, under the title *Readiness for Religion: A Basis for Developmental Religious Education*. I am keenly aware that no simple answers are possible, but some answers emerge more readily when based upon a true appreciation of the problems. To know what a child is able to grasp intellectually is a surer foundation for education than to know only what adults feel the child ought to grasp. This, briefly, is my aim in producing this volume.

Behind any author's efforts numerous contributors are concealed, without perhaps achieving mention in the official index. This book is no exception. I owe a great debt to the Rev. H. A. Hamilton and many other colleagues with whom I served on the staff of Westhill Training College, for evoking and sustaining my interest in religious education. I am indebted to Professor E. A. Peel and Professor C. H. Dobinson for great help during the research; to Professor M. D. Vernon, Dr. D. Bruce and Dr. R. Curnow for guidance on statistical procedures; to my brother Robert Goldman for designing and drawing the series of projection pictures; to the late Dr. I Gurland for many keen insights in the first stages of the research; to some forty experts in psychology, theology and education who helped to assess the results of the tests; to local education authorities, Directors of Education, and head teachers in one Midland area and two areas in the South of England, for allowing me to interview children in their schools; to the Esther Lawrence Fund, the Dorothy A. Cadbury Trust and the Geraldine Cadbury Trust for the financial assistance which made the research possible; to the several hundred school-

xi

children who made the greatest contribution of all by their patient good-natured participation in the tests; to Mrs. B. Vowles for checking the manuscript and compiling the indices.

All these contributed to the making of this book, but not to its errors and immaturities, for which I alone am responsible.

RONALD GOLDMAN

The Department of Education,
The University,
Reading.

Chapter One

THE PROBLEMS OF RELIGIOUS THINKING

'KING SOLOMON must have been fond of animals, because he had many wives and one thousand porcupines.' The child who made this statement is not only somewhat defective in terms of sex education, but he also reveals one of the problems of childish thinking. We can all quote 'howlers' of this kind made by children as they try to understand their world. This is especially so when the child attempts to explore the complex world of religion. Arnold Gesell (Gesell and Ilg, 1946) quotes a discussion between an older and a younger child. The younger child is firmly convinced that Pontius Pilate is a tree, because they say in church that 'Jesus suffered under Pontius Pilate'. The older child argues persuasively that he is a man, not a tree, until the younger one concedes the point. Still puzzled he says grudgingly, 'Well, if he is a man he's a very pontius man.' We could go on to quote children's malversions of the Lord's Prayer, such as 'Harold be thy name', or the six-year-old praying:

> Thy deliberately faith I full,
> Faith against almighty worship God,
> And faith all unto you,
> Faith against thy holy prayer.[1]

We recognise these statements, not as blasphemies, but as rather amusing examples of children's misconceptions. All too frequently, however, we fail to recognise them as symptoms of the child's real difficulties in thinking, and as indicators of the serious limitations experienced by the young in making intellectual interpretations of experience. The truth is that when faced with complex problems of thinking, children try to make as much sense of them as possible. The above examples illustrate the struggle to make sense of what appears to be nonsense to the child. There are pure verbal mistakes, confusions due to wrong associations of words and errors which enter into any parrotlike repetition where there is no insight into the meaning of a passage.

[1] An extract taken from a recording, the full text of which is in *Studies in Education: First Years in School*, London, Evans Bros., 1963, pp. 203–4.

1

In many areas of knowledge such as Mathematics, History, Geography and English Comprehension, a great deal of work has been done in the last thirty years on children's thinking. Led by that prolific writer and investigator Professor J. Piaget, large numbers of researchers in many countries have helped us to understand the growth of thinking, the structures and sequences of thought and the limits of understanding demonstrated by pupils at varying ages. Experiments tend to show how valuable children's misunderstandings can be in indicating the problems of thinking they face, and the kind of curriculum content in a subject that can and cannot be coped with. Some of these investigations will be outlined and discussed later. I mention them now because when I first encountered them it occurred to me how valuable it would be to apply similar research to the religious thinking of children and adolescents.

Here then is an account of the methods I used and the results which emerged from the research. It is an attempt to understand the modes and patterns of thinking, which the young bring to bear upon the religious teaching to which they are continually exposed in school, church and family. This teaching, of course, is far from systematic and its haphazard presentation is certainly affected by the conflicting views about religion voiced by the adult world. Even so, children are daily faced with the Bible, the Church and with religious practices and activities, sometimes as in school where they participate and sometimes when the children are interested spectators. Confronted by the existence of religion, by adults who appear to believe in it and who wish to teach them about it, children nobly attempt to understand as much of it as they find possible to understand.

THE ROLE OF THE INTELLECT

The central focus in this book is upon the child's intellectual struggle to comprehend the central ideas expressed and implied in religious teaching. This focus upon the intellect is chosen because teaching involves the communication of ideas in such a way as they can be grasped intellectually by the learner. Religious teaching is not exempt from this necessity to communicate at a meaningful level, even though we must clearly recognise that understanding may be emotional as well as intellectual. Religion is not a mere intellectual exercise, a philosophical puzzle to be put together in an orderly rational manner. At this rational level, there is a parallel between the teaching of mathematics and the teaching of religion, but it is a limited parallel. In the last resort, religion is a mystery and speaks of matters and experiences which are not easily communicable. Some religious experiences are so profound and personal and mysterious that it is

2

doubtful if they are communicable at all, except through the emotional language of the arts.

It is unrealistic to minimise the role of the emotions in religious understanding, for the feeling element in religion is of great importance. Indeed, truths which come from emotionally identifying ourselves with certain experiences are usually more compelling than those truths demonstrated by logic. The one may gain by being willing to be absorbed by the truth so that it is seen from the inside; the other, while objective, is distant and encounters the truth only from the outside. In short, arguments for the existence of God remain intellectual exercises unless linked with an act of faith.

The Existential writers and dramatists such as Kierkegaard, Pascal, Sartre, Heidegger, Camus and Marcel, past and present, religious and atheistic, have revolted against an exclusively scientific approach to knowledge and recall us to the sensitive world of feeling, wonder and unique personal experience which is at the heart of all religious knowledge. This dual aspect of knowing must be stressed by the teacher when he considers the methods and aims of religious education.

Nevertheless, the teacher's major task is to communicate truths on an intellectual plane, whereby thinking is engaged at as high a level as the ability of the pupil will allow. Religious truth must be compelling intellectually, not only emotionally, and to hide behind emotional appeals and to avoid answering or even raising intellectual problems about religion, is both dishonest and ultimately destructive of religion. If this is so, we return to the problems which the intellectual development of the growing child and adolescent raises. What is the nature of a child's religious thinking? How does he form concepts of God, of the Church, of moral rightness? Are there sequences or patterns of religious thought to be discerned with increasing chronological and mental age? What limits of religious understanding are imposed by age, immature experience, attitudes of parents, and many other factors? Does Biblical material of certain types assist or impede clarity of thought or level of insight into their religious truths? Are there ages or stages of what we might call 'religious readiness' in the growing young person, when the mind can more readily understand certain religious truths? Can a programme of religious education be devised which is suited to patterns of intellectual development?

THE NATURE OF RELIGIOUS THINKING

Before we can face these questions with any confidence we must try to understand what religious thinking is and what it is not. The view I maintain throughout this book is that religious thinking is no different in mode and method from non-religious thinking. Religious thinking is a shortened form of expressing the activity of thinking directed towards religion, not a term meaning separate rationality. William James (1902) expresses this vividly:

There is religious fear, religious love, religious awe, religious joy and so forth. But religious love is only man's natural emotion of love directed to a religious object; religious fear is only the ordinary fear . . . the common quaking of the human breast, in so far as the notion of divine retribution may arouse it; religious awe is the same organic thrill which we feel in a forest at twilight, or in a mountain gorge, only this time it comes over us at the thought of our supernatural relations . . . (p. 28).

James asserts categorically that there is therefore no religious instinct in man. J. J. Smith (1941) puts it more succinctly:

A child is non-religious at birth as he is non-moral, non-aesthetic, non-thinking. He inherits none of these qualities in a functional form but acquires them gradually through experience.

Not all writers would agree with this extreme view. Basil Yeaxlee (1939), for example, argues that religion is more than an acquired habit of mind and writes of it as 'an innate capacity', on a par with the speaking, fighting and building capacities of man. Yet in describing religion as 'a power of response' and in subsequent discussion in his book, Yeaxlee leaves us in no doubt that for him religion is the total reaction of a man to his experiences rather than a separately identifiable drive or instinct. All this discussion in no way assumes that religion is not a natural expression of man's basic needs; it merely means that there is no one need or drive. Rather, religion is the fulfilment of the entire man, of which his intellect is a part.

When we say that religious thinking is thinking directed towards religion, it is clear that the term religion requires definition. As there are some known fifty or more definitions of religion, I put forward William James's clear definition. Religion, says James, is 'the feelings, the acts and experiences of individual men . . . so far as they apprehend themselves to stand in relation to whatever they may consider the divine'. This divine in our own culture is interpreted in terms of diety, and more specifically in terms of the Christian concept of God as love, revealed most fully in the historic fact of the Incarnation. On this definition, religious thinking is thinking directed towards the nature of God, his relationships with men in history, his dealings with men today, his revelation of himself through the inspired literature of the Bible and through the person of Jesus Christ. It follows that the content of religious thinking will be concerned in our society with concepts involving these ideas. We can see that these ideas and the language in which they are expressed are very adult. The Bible itself is a book for adults and theology is a mature adult activity. Yet there is no doubt that the child from a very early age is forming a series of religious concepts and developing a theology, a frame of reference, which is continually changing as he thinks about God and His activities in the world. This picture of infantile theologians may appear to be ludicrous at first until we remember that all children are infantile mathematicians, assimilating and interpreting the world of quantity, all are infantile poets and artists, expressing creatively their apprehension of what is beautiful, and all are infantile moralists, forming mores or rules based upon their experiences of danger, adult authority, social pressures and later altruism. These are accompanied by crude expressions of number, art and ethics which indicate gross misunderstandings and distortions due to the child's egocentric nature. In religion this is true also in the early stages of development, and there is plainly a long period of apprenticeship, experimentation and searching in childhood religion which must precede adult religious thinking.

THE PROBLEM OF THE CONTENT OF
RELIGIOUS TEACHING

Given a long period of development, as in other areas of life, what then should we offer the growing child in terms of religious teaching? If religious teaching has to have a content what shall the content be and what assumptions can we make about the child's thinking, when we choose certain material as suitable for a certain age?

It is salutary to take a brief look at some of the material suggested as appropriate intellectual diet for the young in religious education. In Britain, the various churches and the day schools are involved in religious teaching. Each group puts forward programmes and syllabuses designed to suggest to teachers material which can with benefit be taught to the various ages of pupils. More particularly in England and Wales, since the passing of the 1944 Education Act, religious teaching in state schools is based upon the Agreed Syllabuses. They are so called because they are the result of an agreement between the Protestant Churches, the teachers and the local education authority. These syllabuses have served a useful function in our state system during the last twenty years or more, despite the fact that many teachers, untrained in the teaching of the subject, have misunderstood and misused them. They were sincere attempts to formulate teaching material suitable for the full age range of the state school population. One of the earliest and most widely used syllabuses, the Cambridgeshire (revised in 1949), specifically states, 'No attempt should be made to present religious ideas which are beyond the child's power of apprehension'. The problem, in stating this intention, is to know what is within the child's apprehension, for some of the material suggested in the Cambridgeshire syllabus would appear to be beyond the age group for which it is suggested. For example, the story of the Exodus is recommended for the seven to nine year olds. Does the child have a sufficiently formed concept of time to understand this series of events at all sensibly, apart from understanding them at a religious level?

Again, the Cambridgeshire syllabus, in keeping with many others, commends stories about babies in the Bible, specifically including the baby Jesus, the baby Moses, and the Call of the child Samuel. Apart from the religious truths or value of these stories, and the intellectual problems they present, many writers have since questioned the wisdom of this approach for the six year olds. They stress the need of young children to identify themselves not with the weak and the helpless, but with, for example, Jesus as a strong elder brother. Many syllabuses recommend the parables of Jesus as suitable for children from the age of five years onwards. D. Ainsworth (1961) in research on this very problem writes: 'In the light of Piaget's work, the young child's understanding of the parables is questionable. Since the significance of the parable is abstract rather than concrete, is it possible that the child will understand this before he has reached the formal stage in his development?' Her answer to this question is that only the beginnings of understanding the simplest parables appeared by the age of ten.

The West Riding Syllabus (1947) suggests stories such as the Call of Samuel and Jacob's vision at Bethel can be used with the three to seven year olds to show *'in an obvious way* how God taught that the spiritual world is within us and about us always'. That this idea of omnipresence is interpreted so egocentrically by the young child as to completely distort reality is brought out by Bovet (1928) and Piaget (1929). The Call of Samuel is cited by Thorburn (1946) as a story entirely misunderstood by six year olds of above average intelligence.

The Durham Syllabus (1946) suggests that children of nine to ten years old are ready to understand the story of Christ's temptations at the level of Jesus rejecting 'all suggestions of using the methods of a magician, resolving to win men only by love and persuasion'. A more recent syllabus, Bristol (1960) recommends the Temptations of Jesus for the six year old. It is doubtful whether even the highly intelligent ten year old has the experience and insight into relationships to understand the idea put forward in the Durham syllabus, apart from the intellectual problem posed by abstract propositional thinking.

While infancy and childhood are difficult periods for which to provide religious syllabuses, one would have thought that the sections providing material for the secondary schools would have been more acceptable and less open to criticism. Yet there is evidence by K. Hyde (1963), D. S. Wright (1962) and J. W. Daines (1962) to suggest that not only the sections recommending material for Modern schools, but those for the Grammar schools also, appear to be frequently unsuitable. Harold Loukes (1961) in an investigation into what secondary modern pupils in their last year at school thought about the subject of Religious Knowledge, reports most of them 'find their lessons on the Bible childish and irrelevant'. A survey by the University of Sheffield Institute of Education (1961) into the attainments of secondary modern school leavers in religious knowledge, after ten years of being taught under Agreed Syllabuses, shows results are so poor and so disturbing that there is a call for a complete revision of existing syllabuses. The investigators say that most of the Agreed Syllabuses do not appear to be suited to their purpose; they require not only drastic revision but frequent revisions. They make the further comment,

The main survey clearly indicates that religious education in schools is making little impact on children and that their knowledge of the Old Testament in particular is extremely limited. This suggests that increased research is needed into both the content and the methods of religious education.

While criticisms of this kind can easily be made against many of the syllabuses, it must in fairness be pointed out that some local authorities have experimented with material and attempted to produce a psychological rather than a biblical framework. Gordon Hewitt (1963) in discussing the significance of my own research mentions several such syllabuses, which have made a brave attempt to present their content suggestions in the light of the child's needs. The major problem, however, still remains. What are children's needs and capacities where religion is concerned? Upon what assumptions about religious thinking in childhood and adolescence should reforms of syllabus material be based? Are the assumptions we are making at the moment testable or verifiable in any way as a guide to our planning? There is a dearth of factual information from research relevant to this particular problem. In the chapters which follow the research will be reviewed, leading to a detailed presentation of pupils' religious thinking. Meanwhile, a brief discussion of the role of research in our understanding of religion would appear to be necessary.

PSYCHOLOGY, RESEARCH AND RELIGION

The methods used in the researches to be reviewed are psychological, and there is some resistance on the part of teachers and clergy to the application of psychological research to the field of religion. The Psychology of Religion as an accepted discipline has never really flourished and has produced only intermittent research during the sixty years of its existence. Much of its writings are philosophical rather than psychological, relating the findings of psychology in other fields to religion, rather than describing first hand investigations into religion itself. The reasons for the lack of interest in this subject are many and are outlined clearly by G. W. Allport (1951) and Michael Argyle (1958). There are two major reasons which should be noted here as relevant to our future discussion.

The first reaction to the application of psychological research to the understanding of religion, is expressed in the fear that psychology will be used to attack or undermine the validity of religious belief. Psychologists such as Leuba (1921) thought that by showing religious phenomena to be a natural, that is, a primitive activity of man, religion would thereby be seen to be based upon false premises. This fear is also linked in the minds of many with the depth psychologists and especially with the attack upon religion made by Freud. The more positive attitude of Jung to religion is frequently unknown, and only the charges of religion as infantile regression are remembered. On the first point, it must be stated very firmly that psychology is not anti-religion, although many psychologists have not been religious believers, but it is a neutral discipline which endeavours to observe objectively, and to describe and assess the data which it observes. Psychology is not concerned with judgment values, nor with the rightness and wrongness of belief. Concerning depth psychology, Flugel (1945) writing of the psycho-analysts, makes several cogent points about the relation between psychology and religion. Flugel suggests that psychology shows religion to be extremely significant by demonstrating the fundamental nature and infantile origin of the needs underlying religion. He shows too that mainly higher types of emotional attitudes are involved in religious experience, and although pointing out that religion 'can exercise a severe crippling and inhibiting effect upon the human mind, by fostering irrational anxiety and guilt, and by hampering the free play of the intellect', he makes it clear that he refers here only to the cruder expressions of religion. Flugel reiterates many times that psychology can neither prove nor disprove the validity of religious belief.

The second objection to psychology as applied to religion can be seen in the view that religion, not only in the last resort but in the

8

first resort, is neither analysable nor measurable in the statistical and quantitative manner which research methods demand. This is a legitimate viewpoint, but if applied to all human behaviour, would invalidate the findings of psychology, sociology and the human sciences generally, for it is religion as a human phenomenon only which can be investigated. Michael Argyle, in discussing this problem, states, 'It is commonly assumed that human behaviour is lawful and that it can be predicted by means of psychological laws, and explained in terms of psychological processes'. These laws are based upon descriptive research assessed and presented statistically. This is the way in which laws of human behaviour are formulated, as hypotheses based upon factually observed data. If then the activity of thinking as one aspect of human behaviour is suitable for investigation based upon quantitative measurement and statistical analysis, then by our definition, religious thinking is also. Religious thinking, not as a separate or sacred rationality, but as thinking directed towards religion, of how man thinks about the existence and activity of the divine, is therefore a valid field for research.

Argyle, in common with other writers, concludes that psychological research can tell us nothing about the truth, validity or usefulness of religious phenomena, but the results of such research may be relevant to religion in many ways. Religion may use the information yielded by research to bring about conditions which help people to become religious. This is particularly applicable in the field of religious education. To know what factors affect the religious development of children and adolescents is of great importance to the educator, and may help him more effectively to present religious truths in such a way that the young may both understand and accept them.

Chapter Two

THINKING AND ITS APPLICATION TO RELIGION

I HAVE defined religious thinking as thinking directed towards religion. This does not differ in mode and method from thinking directed to other phenomena. Our first task would seem to be to examine what we mean by thinking in its many aspects and then to see how this relates to the field of religion.

'Thinking', writes Peel (1960, p. 11), 'is part of what goes on inside the mind, in between sense-perception and effective action.' He notes that the child 'begins his intellectual life with no *a priori* notions of the world about him. These notions have to be learned or instructed on the basis of simple sensation and movements of infancy . . . thought is internalised consistent action' (pp. 7–8). Later, Peel stresses, thinking may occur without immediate sensory stimulus and may not even lead to effective external action.

Essential ingredients of thinking as a psychological mechanism are outlined clearly by D. H. Russell (1956, p. 8). He prefers not to use the word 'idea' since it is a generic term involving images, percepts, concepts and generalisations of thought. First, there are the materials of thinking. These are sensations of the outside world which are selected by perception and stored in memories or images, gradually formed into concepts, as categories of thought about groups of objects. Second, come motives for thinking. These are the feelings, needs, attitudes and habits of thought acquired earlier, often at an emotional level, which help initiate and determine the direction of thinking. Later formed sophisticated sentiments could be included here. Third, there are the processes of thinking. These are patterns of activity seen in selecting, eliminating, searching, manipulating and organising, beginning with crude undirected thinking through to inductive thinking, problem-solving and critical and creative thinking. Fourth, abilities in thinking, which are the habits, techniques and guides to thinking which can be acquired and developed at least to some extent, by children and by others who desire to improve their thinking. We might add that the effectiveness of these acquired abilities is of necessity limited by natural ability, the range and complexity 'ceiling' of which a person is capable at any

10

given time. This, in fact, is the emerging of what Hebb (1948) distinguishes as Intelligence 'B', that is the innate ability of a person (Intelligence 'A') affected by experience and learning.

For our purpose the materials of thinking, the processes of thinking and the abilities in thinking first will be discussed and, later, motivational aspects of thinking.

THE MATERIALS OF THINKING

The raw material of thinking is sensation which is selected and then perceptualised. A percept may be defined as a personal and immediate interpretation of a sensation or sensations. Language may play a part in this by the fixing of a name, as a sound symbol, in the mind of the young child. The round rubbery bright red object which bounces is called 'a ball', but the firm round green object does not bounce and the child discovers it can be eaten. This he learns to symbolise as an 'apple'. There is evidence by Smoke (1935), Heidbreder (1946) and Hurlock (1956) that animals, as well as children, appear to perceptualise and conceptualise before language ability emerges. Or rather in some situations animals appear to behave as though they had developed perceptual and conceptual thinking.

In an interesting discussion on concepts, Bruner, Goodnow and Austin (1956) suggest that the next step in thinking emerges from the necessary pressure of existence. 'To save ourselves from madness, once differentiation (perceptual ability) has occurred we cease making specific responses to specific objects. We form categories or concepts about groups of objects.' In the early stages these categories, or concepts, are at the perceptual level of concrete sensation, for example, a man. Later, a more abstract level of conceptualising occurs, for example Whigs and Tories, although some concrete and illustrative ingredients still remain. So men have to invent categories to make sense of the world and not be overwhelmed by the variety of sensory experience. Conceptualising thus makes more sense by reducing the complexity of experience, by simplifying it, by making identification easier, by reducing the need for constant learning, by providing expectancy levels in behaviour and by later providing us with the ability to relate not only particular experiences together but classes of experience also.

D. H. Russell (1956) supports this view of conceptual thinking. 'The concept, of course, is usually organised as a result of a group of related sensations, percepts and images with a label attached to them. The label is practically always a verbal symbol or symbols. The child's concepts reflect his understanding of the world. They assist him to classify his experience and give meaning to them'

(p. 68). The terms 'generalisation' and 'abstraction' in relation to conceptual thinking are frequently used. When categories are formed a person tends to 'abstract' or 'take from' groups of objects those qualities which are like and unlike. Those which are like are held together in the mind and other unlike aspects are discarded. He then generalises the 'like' aspects in terms of the common characteristics he has discovered. Both an abstracting and a generalising activity appear to be necessary in concept formation. Bartlett (1958) has suggested that 'active search' is a necessary part of the abstraction process where the mind tries out a hypothesis to see if the points of similarity fit the requirements.

Thinking then appears to be formed from a sequence of sensation, perceptualising and finally the forming of concepts. In most of the previous illustrations, the sensation of a round object is identified and named so that a ball is perceived. It is then seen as different from other round objects and to possess certain common characteristics such as spherical shape, bounciness, and a play object. Thus concepts or categories are formed.

Since the forming of religious concepts is of central importance in understanding a child's development of religious thinking, it is useful to elaborate W. E. Vinacke's (1952) summary of what characterises concepts. These characteristics are set out below.

a. Concepts are not direct sensory data but something resulting from elaboration, combination and interpretation of sensory data.
b. Concepts depend upon the previous experience of the organism.
c. Concepts are responses which tie together, or link, or combine discrete sensory experiences.
d. It may be inferred that such ties or links are symbolic in nature, the same response standing for a variety of data. This response is usually a word.
e. On the side of internal processes of the organism, concepts represent selective factors.

Vinacke outlines two problems in conceptualising very relevant to religious thinking. The first problem is how can we explain and describe the development of the child to form and use concepts. Can we trace with age the unfolding and elaboration of a concept and the conditions which influence this development? On this problem a great deal is still unknown. The answer is inconclusive to the question of whether a general function of conceptualising exists. The suggestion emerges that children are more limited in forming concepts as compared with adults because of their limits of experience and knowledge. Verbal problems make research difficult.

On the second problem Vinacke is more hopeful in terms of research. This is the educational problem of what concepts or pattern of concepts characterise the various stages in the development of children's thinking and behaving. Here, much more is known. 'Concepts tend to change with age, become more numerous, more complex and more logical. It has been tentatively ascertained that children acquire concepts in a definite order' (Vinacke 1952, p.28). This is what Bruner calls 'the problem of orderliness of encounter' with factors that go to make a concept.

Specifically relating this problem to childhood Reichard, Schneider and Rapaport (1944) suggest three levels of concepts emerge in children. These are:

(i) Concretistic, (ii) Functional and (iii) Conceptual.

At the first level, non-essential features of objects make for faulty concepts. At the second level, concepts are formed by evaluating the use or value of certain aspects. At the third level, accurate concepts are formed based on abstract and relational properties of objects. Summarising the discussion on research into concept development in terms of the general agreement, D. H. Russell (p. 249) writes that concepts 'seem to move along a continuum from simple to complex, from concrete to abstract, from undifferentiated to differentiated, from discrete to organised, from egocentric to more social'. He adds that modern research suggests there are no sharp breaks but a continuum in the forming of concepts. In addition E. B. Hurlock (1956) writing in terms of 'patterns of development in children's concepts' states that the time needed to develop concepts and the level of development attained will depend partly on the child's intelligence and partly upon his opportunities for learning. Changes occur with age, gradually rather than in definite stages, from concrete to abstract, vague to clear, inexact to definite, from simple to complex levels, and from the general to the specific. Finally, R. J. Havighurst (1933), while agreeing with these observations, remarks that 'by the time the child is ready for school he already has a store of several hundred concepts —mainly simple ones, such as roundness, sweetness, animal, dog, food, anger and love. . . . During the period of middle childhood the individual forms several thousand concepts. . . . As he grows older and stores up concepts he becomes able to form new concepts on the vicarious experiences afforded by reading, or hearing lectures, or seeing movies.'

THE MATERIALS OF RELIGIOUS THINKING

We shall now apply the foregoing discussion to the question of what are the materials of religious thinking? Thinking applied to religion appears to have the same ingredients and the same pattern, with one major distinction. That distinction is evident at the outset of the

13

child's life, in terms of sensation. Religious percepts and concepts are not based upon direct sensory data, but are formed from other perceptions and conceptions of experience. The mystics, who claim to have direct sensations of the divine, are exceptions, but as they are extremely rare cases, rarer in adolescence and practically unknown in childhood, we shall not explore their significance here.[1]

Clearly religion and life in the early years are so interwoven they are indistinguishable. The child has his first sensory experience of the material world in which things and people are at first undifferentiated. He then forms general percepts and concepts based upon these experiences, symbolising them, first in images and later, when he learns to use language, in verbal images or words. The whole structure of religious thinking is therefore based upon what Havighurst calls 'vicarious' experience. There are no definite religious sensations and perceptions, separate from the child's other sensations and perceptions. Religious thinking is the process of generalising from various experiences, previous perceptions and already held concepts to an interpretative concept of the activity and nature of the divine. Because of this it is not possible to supply specific first steps in the religious experience of the young child, other than by enriching his general experience.

This is reflected in the literature of religion, especially in the Bible, where the language is almost entirely based upon analogy and metaphor, inferring from other non-religious experience the nature of the divine and supporting such concepts upon previously acquired concepts. The beginning of the 23rd Psalm makes this secondary use of concepts obvious.

> The Lord is my shepherd; I shall not want.
> He maketh me to lie down in green pastures;
> He leadeth me beside the still waters.

Here, the whole concept of God as a personal and caring God is based upon the analogy of the function of a shepherd caring for his sheep. For the child to grasp this concept in any way, he must have some concept of sheep-farming. To see it clearly he must know something of the conditions of the Palestinian sheep-farmer (this psalm would have a limited application if based upon experience in Westmorland or Australia), the heat and need for water, the barren soil and the constant moves from pasture to pasture. Many adults, of course, do not make this transition in analogy completely, but they have sufficient experience of the sensory, perceptual and conceptual

---

[1] The reader wishing to pursue this line of thought might consult James (1902, pp. 379–429) or any other standard work on the Psychology of Religion.

factors upon which the analogy is based to grasp, even if partially, the religious concepts involved.

Religious thinking is, therefore, dependent upon understanding the original experience upon which the analogy or metaphor is based. When the child hears 'God is a father', we are pursuing certain concepts of fatherhood which the child has experienced directly. But children, we know, have varied experiences of their fathers. Deprived, deserted, cruelly treated, beaten, or hostile children will have different foundations upon which the inference is built. J. W. D. Smith (1949, p. 2) supports this in maintaining that 'The term "God" is best used sparingly and for the young child should not be pressed on the child's attention. The experience which corresponds with the term is far more important than the mere word.'

Once formed, these religious concepts are very dependent upon general experience, verbal association and verbal interpretation. It is inevitable, as in other areas of learning, that the labels are used without the substance of the concept being attained. M. C. Serra (1952) further emphasises 'the more direct the experience on which the concept is built, the greater will be the individual's knowledge and understanding of that concept. . . . Concepts that can be traced back only to verbal language or to symbols acquired through language result in mere verbalism' (p. 276). The danger of verbalising in religious thinking, which may be used to manipulate words which are not understood, is as real as in the young child manipulating number symbols in calculation without having formal concepts of quantity or seriation, as E. M. Churchill has shown (1958).

We may use the concept of God as an illustration, which in itself is composed of many varied concepts such as concepts of power, omnipresence, authority, justice and goodness, and parallel Vinacke's summary of concepts in religious terms.

a. Concepts of God are not direct sensory data but something resulting from the elaboration, combination and interpretation of sensory data such as 'my father', 'my home', 'the natural world'.

b. Concepts of God depend upon the previous experience of the child, not merely in naming the data of this experience but in understanding its component and significant features such as an experience of a father's role in relation to the child.

c. Concepts of God are responses which tie together or link, or combine discrete sensory experiences such as 'father is strong, big, all-powerful, cares for me, punishes me, earns money for me. God is like that and judges and cares for all children'. Or 'God is a big Daddy up in the sky'.

d. It may be inferred that such ties or links are symbolic in nature, the same response standing for a variety of data. This response 'God' is usually a word. It is a word which perhaps unifies all experience of what is thought to be best in human relationships such as love, trust and faithfulness. It may, of course, equally be a word symbolising all that is worst in human relationships, such as anger, deceit, unpredictability and arbitrary punishment.

e. On the side of internal processes in the child, concepts of God represent selective factors, as for example, when God is identified with good and not evil, with something sacred, special and holy. This selective process may lead too readily to a division between the religious and non-religious, between sacred and secular, which is a purely artificial and frequently infantile division, an impediment to achieving higher concepts of divine omnipresence, omniscience and omnipotence.

On the two problems raised by Vinacke little is known on the first in relation to religion. We could, however, work out a theoretical construct of how a religious concept is formed, again using a concept of God as an example. The table opposite shows in chart form the complexity of this concept. The base of the chart represents the child's current concept of God and the generalisations made about His nature, power and activity which the child has developed through the years. The columns above the base show the process by which this growing concept of God is fed, by at first fairly primitive experiences and ideas, gradually becoming more refined and complex. The 'Intellectual' aspects begin with sensations of the physical world and around this period percepts are being formed, objects named and recognised, and differentiation of data begins. These primitive percepts develop into crude concepts as the child tries to make sense of his world, and in the next stages more advanced perception of life leads on to more advanced concepts. These concepts include the natural world, home, parents, school, other adults, including teachers, and not least a clearer concept of self as socialisation increases. Upon these more advanced concepts are based. These are the foundation for religious analogy, fantasised at the emotional level in the young child but later intellectualised and consisting of such concepts as causality, power, purpose and authority. Then follow concepts of supernatural activity, animistic concepts, powers and limits of adults as deities merging into a paternalised God. Many of these appear to rest upon concepts of Jesus and move over into God as divine father.

Intellectual processes, however, do not continue unaffected by the other areas of human experience. Concepts are formed with emotional overtones and this is particularly true of religious concepts. Ideas may be seen intellectually, but the Junior child soon begins to inquire about the truth or falsity of these ideas as part of his emotional growth. Intellectual concepts of fatherhood, of love and security, of punishment, of care for others, all stem from early emotional experiences especially in the home. This is depicted in the 'Emotional' column showing the growth from crude emotional experiences to the

A THEORETICAL STRUCTURE OF A CHILD'S CONCEPT OF GOD

Verbal	Intellectual	Emotional	Moral	Aesthetic
Simple vocabulary	Sensory activity *Percepts* of physical world, parents, the self, etc.	Sensory activity *Crude feelings* of security and insecurity	*Self* gratifications and safety	Undifferentiated sensations
Simple religious stories and associations	*Primitive* concepts of above as generalisation and differentiation occurs. Concepts expressed as fantasies	*Feelings more differentiated* and specific to situations and objects: Love and awe	*Conformity to external imposed* authority	becoming more differentiated as objects and persons are imagined in *fantasy and play*.
Stories of believers and heroes, of Jesus and God.	*More advanced percepts* of above as child becomes less egocentric and more socialised. *More advanced concepts* as operational thinking develops— concepts of	*Growth of social control* as more frustration-demands are made. *Disillusionment* experiences with parents. Ambivalence of dependence and independence. Projection of needs upon God. *Attitudes*—develop ± to self, adults, society, God.	*Conformity to peer groups and mores.*	fear, awe, respect, wonder, admiration, identification.
Systematic religious teachings about God, Jesus, the Bible, Church. Theological language	the Natural world / creation personal and cosmic / Parental powers & limits — supernatural activity / power & purpose / Authority — Holy Spirit / Inspiration / Dependence — Jesus, Church, Holy associations	*Sentiments formed* ± becoming more complex as concepts develop. *Specific sentiments* ± attached to religious persons, objects, symbols and institutions	*Beginnings of personal morals* based upon human or superhuman values	*Specific aesthetic experiences* of the beautiful ± as seen in 'the holy' and 'the other'.

Concept of God ±

Person, power, authority, love, justice, holiness, wisdom, activity, presence of God

formation of attitudes, then combining ideas and emotions into sentiments. Here we see the process of identification and imitation, fantasy and play, as well as the beginnings of acceptance or rejection of intellectual concepts being formed.

Moral and aesthetic development are no less important, fusing intellectual concepts of what is 'good' and 'beautiful' with feelings. Clearly, this development depends again upon the cruder feelings of fear, respect and admiration of the young child directed towards the physical and personal world. Some writers would suggest that the sensation of primitive fear, refined into awe, is the most basic ingredient of religious experience.

Verbalisms, depicted in the left column, also affect religious concept development. Verbal or language elements, which at first are meaningless sounds, help the child to attach meaning to objects and develop specific memories. There soon develops not only a more refined and graded language, but also a religious language, which is actually earlier in the child's experience than specific religious experience, stemming from stories told by adults. Later, these may become religious teaching stories from the Bible, about 'special' religious people and events. Particular words are seen as having 'special' significance, such as Jesus, God, holy, church and many others. Most of these words and stories appear to be poorly assimilated, as we shall see, and often distort or seriously impair the child's natural patterns of thought, by which he attempts to apprehend the idea of God.

The chart is naturally over-simplified. The proportion of each column will differ considerably from one child to another, for some approach religion more emotionally and others more intellectually. Others, again, find the aesthetic a more dominant feature, and there is evidence to show that morality plays an obsessively dominant role in many children's religious development. We should also note that the proportion of intellectual, emotional, verbal, moral and aesthetic ingredients may not remain the same throughout a single child's development, since certain aspects will tend to grow or recede in importance as experience varies. The process of development should also be seen as not only vertical, but also horizontal, with a constant interchange and interfusion of feelings, morality, aesthetics and language with thinking. We may also note that a concept of deity may be extremely diversified, and to the onlooker, may be a blend of many apparent inconsistencies, even though they are felt to be consistent by the child.

The second problem raised by Vinacke in terms of ages and stages of developing concepts is the one to which my own research has been addressed and will form the main substance of later chapters.

THE PROCESSES OF THINKING AND ABILITIES IN THINKING

The quality of percepts and concepts of any person depends upon the abilities of that person. These abilities in action reveal both natural capacity and the effect of experience and education. In turn, the processes of thinking used in interpreting any experience, learning from it and proceeding to higher levels of thinking, are dependent upon ability, both natural and acquired. That there is progression in conceptualising has been assumed in their presentation of research by D. H. Russell, Hurlock and Havighurst. What particular form or forms, what particular sequence or pattern, such progression takes is difficult to generalise upon. Such terms as 'from vague to clear', 'from concrete to abstract' and 'from simple to complex' mean something in terms of progression but are somewhat indefinite and general.

We are indebted to Piaget for providing a structure of developmental thinking which enables us to understand more fully the processes of thinking, which children and adolescents use in their selection, search, manipulation and organisation of their experiences. As this structure is set out by Piaget himself in various volumes (1953) and with Inhelder (1958), and Berlyne (1957) and Peel (1960) have delineated its essentials clearly, only the briefest outline is given here. This can be supplemented by examining the full criteria used in a later section for assessing the responses of children and adolescents to Biblical story material.

The mechanism of thought, including concept formation, is that of discerning relationships between separate objects, events, experiences or facts. There is discernible three levels, suggests Piaget, in this process of relation finding and co-ordinating; the levels of intuitive, concrete and propositional thinking. In the discussion of these levels or stages of thinking ages are used only approximately and may, in fact, be more appropriately thought of in terms of mental ages rather than chronological ages.

The first two years of life is named by Piaget as the period of sensori-motor intelligence. It is simply the time during which the child co-ordinates perceptive and motor functions and works out an elementary behaviour pattern for dealing with external objects. It involves the process of differentiation of one object from another and learning that they exist outside the child's own perceptual field. Towards the end of this time language develops and provides verbal symbols by which experiences are retained in the mind. This is the basic element of the process of memorising and relating past and present experiences together.

19

Intuitive, or pre-operational thinking, the first stage in overt relation finding, extends from about two years to seven years. By 'operational' Piaget means the following (1953, p. 8),

Psychologically, operations are actions which are internalisable, reversible, and co-ordinated into systems characterised by laws which apply to the system as a whole. They are actions, since they are carried out on objects before being performed on symbols. They are internalisable, since they can also be carried out in thought without losing the original character of actions. They are reversible as against simple actions which are irreversible. In this way the operations of combining can be inverted immediately after the operation of dissociating, whereas the act of writing from left to right cannot be inverted to one of writing from right to left without a new habit being acquired differing from the first. Finally, since operations do not exist in isolation they are connected in the form of structured wholes.

At the intuitive stage the child cannot think operationally. The development of language makes 'representation formation' possible and the internalisation of actions into thoughts begins to occur. Thinking is transductive, that is, inferring a particular fact from another particular fact. Isolated features of a problem only are seen, and understanding is limited by attention to one aspect of a situation which the child thinks is central, and is thus misled. In the same situation the child finds it difficult to relate one problem to another and cannot see that a partial solution only creates new problems. There is little systematic thinking, the pattern of thought in a given situation being partial, fragmented and inconsistent. The major disability in thinking here is that thought is not reversible. An inconsistency cannot be seen for what it is since the child cannot work backward but only forward in his thinking. Later in this period, systematic thinking is attempted but it breaks down. More than one feature of a situation may be considered, but attempts to relate differing facts are not too successful. Judgments are uncertain. Reversibility is often tried but frequently ends in confusion.

The second stage which Piaget calls concrete operations, from approximately seven to eleven years, is when inductive and deductive logic, limited to concrete situations, actions, visual and sensory data is used. This represents a major breakthrough in thinking. Data is correctly classified, systematic thinking is now evident and two or more aspects of a situation can be put together. With concrete data reversibility is evident, and the child concentrates upon relating things visibly or tangibly present. The limitations of this stage can be seen in the child's judgments on verbal problems and problem situations in terms of their content and often egocentrically in terms of his own experience. There is little extension or generalisation from one concrete field to another. Later there appears to be an in-between stage where attempts at abstract and propositional thinking are made, not too successfully, due to concrete or tangible data interfering with the relation finding.

The final stage of propositional thinking, termed by Piaget formal operations, is when the capacity to think hypothetically and deductively is achieved. The data of thinking now changes and situations are seen in terms of propositions, which may be logically true or false and these can be tested out in thought. Logical thinking is now possible in symbolic and abstract terms. Incompatibility of certain facts with an hypothesis is clearly seen. The thinker will often start with an hypothesis and work from this, rather than begin with facts. Reasoning is reversible in terms of propositions, and reasoning by implication is also evident.

It must not be thought that once a child achieves a certain level of thinking he functions always at that level. There are frequent regressions, as in adults, to simpler modes of thinking where the problem is too great or the thinker is tired or poorly motivated. There is also evidence to show that the child performs at different levels in differing subjects or areas, depending upon his experience and the extent to which he is motivated.

It is evident that two factors more than any other limit the child at the early stages of thinking in this structure. The first is what Piaget calls 'egocentricity' but which other writers, such as Inhelder, prefer to call uni-directional thinking. The other factor, evident at all levels but particularly at the level of concrete operations, is the important limitation imposed by 'concretisation' of thinking. Both these factors are clearly recognisable in children's responses to religious problems and set severe limits to levels of understanding in religious thinking.

Piaget's work has been criticised by many psychologists, among them V. Hazlitt (1930), who criticised him for using terms such as logical and pre-logical. Since that time, however, Piaget has refined both his nomenclature and his structure of thinking. Other criticisms have been justifiably made of Piaget's poor sampling and lack of statistical sophistication. While it is true that sampling may be criticised, verification of his structure of development of thinking, although not the ages he cites, have been carried out in this country with British children. Lunzer lists these researches, among them those applied to Mathematical thinking (Churchill, 1958), Scientific thinking (Lovell, 1961) and Logical thinking related to Historical Prose (Lodwick, 1958). This latter is included in Peel's survey of four researches (1959) including in addition haptic perception, children's spatial relationships in drawing and moral judgment.

Most of these studies substantiate the general stages posited by Piaget in operational thinking. Many suggest that mental age is a more important variable than chronological age. Most researches tend to reproduce experiments of scientific and quantitative data. Only a few, such as Lodwick, tackle the much harder field involving non-scientific and qualitative data. Among these is Coltham (1960) investigating children's understanding of terms frequently used in the teaching of history. Another by Jahoda, within a context wider than Piaget's, investigates the development of concepts concerned with geographical and space judgments. As much as biblical teaching is dependent upon space-time concepts these studies are very relevant.

Most of this research appears to have been done with children rather than with adolescents and with situations which involve visual material, as in arithmetic, mathematcs and science. Peel, in a more recent study (1961) comments that problems of thinking associated with verbal comprehension are of central importance to education. He therefore took a sample of children aged nine to fifteen years (late childhood to early adolescence) and investigated their levels of understanding of two prose passages, each setting out logical problems of a similar nature. Elsewhere (1959) he suggests that there is little evidence of children's capacity to set up possibilities to account for events in a story, as opposed to mere describing, before the age of thirteen years. The child is reluctant to go outside the story to examine possible explanations in terms other than those found in the story data. This is also very evident in relation to Bible stories where there is a powerful prestige factor at work in limiting judgment to the data of the biblical story under discussion. In both the stories used by Peel, he finds the maturer judgment not emerging until about 13 : 5 to 13 : 8 chronologically and mentally not until about 14 : 8 to 15 : 0. There are degrees of propositional thinking to be seen. Pupils as young as 11–12 years show a capacity to think propositionally, but only at first in terms of partial elements in a story and circumstantially. There appear to be further steps before incompatible elements are seen and explanations calling upon other experiences influence judgments. It may be noted here that as story-telling forms the most widely used method in religious education, the implications of these insights are far-reaching.

THE PROCESSES OF RELIGIOUS THINKING AND ABILITIES IN RELIGIOUS THINKING

Little application of the processes of thinking has been made to religion. It is evident at once, however, that the crudities and confusions of much that is seen in children's religious concepts can be accounted for in terms of pre-operational limitations, and even by the later limits set by concretisation of data. G. Jahoda (1951) quoting

Piaget, remarks that 'thought is very largely sense tied, hence the high level abstractions abounding in religion are well above the mental horizon of the small child'. D. Ainsworth's work (1961) on parables is also appropriate to mention here. Taking a group of six to ten year olds she points out the difficulties caused by parables due to their demand for propositional thinking. 'It is likely', she concludes, 'that until nine or ten years of age, any story heard by a child will probably be interpreted literally, and that the details of the text and incidents of the story will be of paramount importance to the child.' This is interesting corroboration of Lodwick's and Peel's findings. J. G. Kenwrick (1949) using Spearman's concepts of education of relations and correlates as criteria, reports that with eleven and twelve year olds the power to recognise the relevance of an idea to new situations is greatly limited. He discovered a high percentage of failure in understanding the relevance of such widely accepted parables as the Good Samaritan. M. E. Hebron (1957) finds that the majority of 'C' stream pupils in Secondary Modern schools reach their twelfth year of mental age during the third year of their secondary school course. This age is commonly recognised, she reports, through the work of Piaget 'as the level of mental maturity necessary for generalisation with some degree of abstraction'. This must therefore considerably limit their grasp of religious ideas. Much earlier Beiswanger (1930) found that of 63 Old Testament stories recommended for children six to nine years of age very few could be understood and little religious value could be discovered by children before nine years. These and other researchers infer that the limits are not only the limits of experience, but are limits of process or structured thought. For children before 10 years old or later maturational development has not arrived at the point where the complexity of thinking demanded by religion can be coped with at a satisfactory intellectual level.

Many of those who suggest the possibility of religious developmental stages have little or no experimental data upon which to base their assumptions. Theodor Reik (1955), for example, draws from his psychoanalytic experience and discusses three stages in a child's developing view of prayer. He talks of the stage of magic—'My will be done'; the stage between magic and religion—'My will be done, because I am God'; and the stage of religion—'My will be done, if it be God's will.'

Another is P. E. Johnson (1957) who uses theological terms, borrowed principally from Martin Buber, and posits four stages of religious thinking in terms of relationships. These are the relationships of I–Me, I–It, I–We, and I–Thou. The first is the relationship of the Mind to the Body, and shows the beginnings of self identity.

The second is the relationship of the self to the environment of things. The third relationship is that of self to group life, and finally the relationship matures into the self confronted by God. Johnson envisages the child's spiritual growth as a series of concentric circles or relationships each one encompassing the previous ones.

The only clearly defined series of religious stages based upon sound research appears to be that of E. Harms (1944). Because he felt the intellectual content of religion to be only a small ingredient of religious experience he devised non-verbal methods for exploring religion in the child. Taking a large sample of children from three years up to early adolescence he asked the children to imagine God or 'the highest being they thought to exist'. He then asked them to draw or paint what they imagined. In criticism of this method we could cite J. E. Johnson (1961) who found six year olds very reticent in drawing pictures of God. The children taken by Harms were further asked to write any comments on the back of the picture, or with younger children, their spoken comments were written for them by the teacher. In the 3–6 year group 800 children's pictures were evaluated; from 7–12 years a similar number; and more than 4,000 were assessed for those above 12 years of age. No attempt was made to evaluate the results in terms of the religious background or the ability of the children and we have no information of the sampling taken other than that they were children from both private and state schools in the United States.

From his analysis Harms claimed to discern a threefold structure of development.

Stage 1. (3–6 years) The fairy tale stage of religion.
Stage 2. (7–12 years) The realistic stage.
Stage 3. (12+ years) The individualistic stage.

The first stage showed greater uniformity than later stages, portraying God as a king, as a 'Daddy of all children', living in a house resting on clouds, or made of clouds, or as a cloud in the form of an animal floating in the sky with GOD written upon it. All these pictures are commented on in fairy tale language and as fantasised experience. God is in the same category as dragons and giants, all are regarded as equally valid, and God is only different in so far as he is greater and bigger and held accordingly in greater awe by the child. At the realistic stage, approximating roughly to our Junior age range, Harms claims that the greater emotional stability of these years is reflected in the pictures. The child is more able to adapt himself to institutional religion and he is much more realistic in his portrayal. Symbols appear and God as a father, even with angels or saints, is not shown in mystical fashion but as a human figure in real life. Children in the individualistic stage in adolescence show a wide variety of interpretations from the conventional to the creative and mystical.

In discussing the implication for religious education (p. 5) Harms suggests that religious teaching for the younger child is too rational in attempting to make him 'understand' God. Adults are often misled by the apparently profound questions asked in infancy and childhood. Rational and instructional ideas should be delayed because 'the entire religious development of the child has a much slower tempo than the development of any other field of his experience'. This, we would assume, is a natural accompaniment of recognising religious experience as secondary and dependent upon the development of many other concepts before religious concepts can develop. R. M. Loomba (1944), a research worker in India, reported similar findings to Harms, showing a gradual transition with increasing age 'from a religion of pure externals to one of the inner life'. He reports earlier deification of parents, gradually broadening out to portray a man in general, all-knowing and all-powerful, who made the sun, moon and stars. At about seven years the child's more realistic ideas of the natural world no longer attribute time, wind, sun and other physical phenomena to the personal power of God.

Basil Yeaxlee (1939) also supports the Harms 3-stage structure, not from direct experimental data of religious expression but from Ruth Griffiths' (1935) work on Imagination. Her work is of parallel interest since in play children from three to seven years in London and Brisbane revealed much religious expression. Before three years is thought of as a pre-religious stage in which the child is absorbing basic intellectual and emotional patterns. From three to seven years is the age of fantasy (similar in Harm's 'fairy-tale' stage) followed by the post-7 years stage of realism, the continuous questioning, 'Is it true?' In these stages the major emphases, says Yeaxlee, are for the first three years emotional knowing, from three to seven years it is mainly fantasied knowing (a blend in play form of emotion and intellect) and from seven years onwards it is predominantly intellectual knowing; early adolescence being the period of intellectual exploration and of the formation of the religious sentiment.

Gesell and Ilg (1946) in their studies of the child from five to ten years summarise interesting reactions. The five year old, they suggest, is innocent of causal and logical relationships and his views are strongly tinged with animisms. Clouds move because God pushes them; when God blows it is windy. At six years Gesell and Ilg report that the child more easily grasps the idea of God as the creator of the world, of animals and of beautiful things. Prayers become important and a certain awe enters into worship. The seven year olds they report as becoming more sceptical and are leaving behind a naïve view of

God. Such questions arise as 'Can you see heaven?', 'Does God live in a house?', 'How can God be everywhere, and see everywhere?' These observations, however, like many from the Yale Clinic of Child Development are rather generalised and appear to present too simplified a picture in terms of a given year age group.

There are many related researches in which religion is not the direct subject for investigation, but where views on God are involved. Anthony's (1940) study of the child's discovery of death reflects fear of God 'who has taken away' a pet or a parent, and reveals concepts related to the child's slow discovery of the impermanence of life. Unfortunately, the nature of the research makes the sampling of children rather untypical since all the children involved scored I.Q.s of 130 and above.

Finally, Piaget (1929) yields extremely stimulating material in his investigations into how the child thinks of the natural world. His work on physical causality (1930) is interesting and shows the function of animism in children's religious development. In the former work, however, Piaget examines what he terms 'Artificialism' in the life of the child. Artificialism he defines as the child's tendency to 'regard things as the product of human creation'. By human he means both the idea of God seen as a powerful man, and the power of human beings, to whom the child attributes divine qualities.

Piaget suggests that the child explains the origin of sun and moon, clouds, the sky, storms and rivers, in roughly three stages. First, origins are attributed to human or divine agency, as for example, when the six year old sees the sun as originating in God, who lit a fire in the sky with a match. This, Piaget terms 'mythological artificialism', extending roughly from four to seven years of age. Then comes an intermediate stage when a natural explanation is joined with an artificial solution as, for example, when the child suggests that the sun and moon are due to the condensation of clouds, but these clouds originate from God or from the smoke from men's houses. This is the stage, about seven to ten years, referred to as 'technical artificialism'. Finally, there is the stage where human and divine activity are seen as having no connection with these origins and they are conceived in purely natural terms, which a child may reach some time after approximately ten years of age. In a concluding chapter on the meaning and origins of child artificialism, Piaget discusses the role of religious education as a stimulant to the child's interest in artificial solutions. He suggests that artificialism is a natural stage in the child's view of the world. 'We have been struck by the fact that the majority of children only bring in God against their will, as it were, and not until they can find nothing else to bring forward. The religious instruction imparted to the children between the ages of four and seven years often appears as something foreign to the child's natural thought.' He concludes, 'The child's real religion, at any rate during the first years, is quite definitely anything but the over-elaborated religion with which he is plied'. If I understand Piaget aright, he suggests that the child naturally sees the origin of things as due to man or God, because both are seen by the child as interchangeable, both being all-powerful and all-knowing. As, however, man's limitations are seen in the increasing fallibility of parents, and his operational thinking begins to grow as he looks at the physical world, artificialist reasons gradually lose their cogency. At last artificialism is renounced altogether as improbable and unsatisfactory. At the same time physical cause and effect is recognised with the beginnings of formal operational thinking. Piaget does not suggest this, but it is a permissible addendum to say that during this final logical-scientific stage the child may return to an artificialism of a higher and refined nature with God posited as a first cause, and as an immanent divine law within a universe acting according to preconceived scientific laws.

The first stage of mythological artificialism receives some support from my own limited research. But it does not substantiate Piaget's second stage, when, in fact, the Junior child may become more artificialist in a mythological sense than the Infant child, even if it is more refined, and a definite theological artificialism is apparent. There seems to be a tendency in the child to use dual methods of looking at the world, which are not seen by the child as contradictory. One is theological and allows for supernatural interventions especially when thinking of Biblical events, and the other is artificialist-scientific, gradually giving way to 'natural' explanations. A major problem of religious education is to bring these separate worlds together so that when the scientific view gains ascendancy the theological view is not invalidated in the child's experience.

Ruth Griffiths (1935) suggests that the period up to three or four years is the major period of animism and magic. This gives place at about five years to finding an explanation for all things in the power of God, who is conceived as omnipotent in the sense of having complete control of natural forces. All events of the universe are dependent upon divine or human will. This obviously supports Piaget's general assertion about artificialism.

Most of our discussion so far has been related to children. There are a number of interesting studies concerning adolescents and their religious ideas, concepts, beliefs and attitudes. A few span late childhood and early adolescence.

F. E. Morton (1944), using a sample from nine to ten years found that the commonest ideas of God are descriptive and at the early age tend to be more anthropomorphic. At nine boys appear to be more anthropomorphic than girls, although this conclusion may be due to limited sampling. Ideas of God as Love and Spirit, and more abstract concepts, appear to increase with age. O. Kupky earlier (1928), although revealing many reservations about anthropomorphisms, posited three stages of concepts of God.

(1) Picturing God as someone or something actually seen.
(2) God conceived in a definite role as King, Lord, Father, or the embodiment of experience.
(3) The real core of the concept, the imageless, formless, experience of God.

Although D. Mathias (1943) studied the relationship between ideas of God in twelve to fifteen year olds and their moral conduct, the first part of his investigation is relevant to our discussion. He found that 68 per cent of the sample scored high in belief in God, belief tending to increase with chronological age and mental ability. God is seen as all-powerful, and seeing God as someone on whom one is dependent decreased with age. God is seen as personal at all ages but His love quality is an increasing concept with age. Using Mathias' method Walker (1950) in Scotland found with Secondary school pupils aged eleven to fourteen that seven major aspects tended to make up a God concept—God as omnipotent, fearful, impersonal, just, loving, mysterious and dependable.

R. S. Dawes (1954) found among Secondary school pupils that three concepts of God were predominant:

(i) His powerfulness,
(ii) His concern for the individual expressed in Fatherhood, and
(iii) His activity as creator.

He further found that these concepts retained their adequacy with age and the 'role' concept of God becomes more symbolic and abstract.

An early work by R. G. Bose (1929) on children's concepts, ranging from eight to eighteen years, presents some curious findings. While he finds considerable vagueness and confusion about a large number of religious words and finds better understanding of concrete terms such as Christmas, Sunday and Church, he finds only slight progression in understanding with age. He reports that eight to twelve year olds seemed to understand as well as thirteen to fifteen year olds. Not surprisingly, in the light of this, he finds only a slight relationship between mental age and level of understanding. He finds also that family habits and worship, and church attendance of the pupils, appears to have no significant influence upon developing levels of understanding. One would suspect here some fault in the nature of the questions in the tests, or faulty sampling.

K. Hyde (1963), whose work on attitudes we shall discuss later, found that in testing large numbers of secondary school pupils a rapid drop in crude anthropomorphic ideas was observable with age and only seemed to be retained where there was least mental ability. J. Bradshaw (1949) found not only higher concepts were more fully understood by girls, but with both sexes, there was an increase with age in the ability to think abstractly and to picture God as non-material.

The University of Sheffield Institute of Education presented the results of a group of teachers' investigation into the attainments of fourteen to fifteen year olds in secondary schools (1961). They found widespread ignorance of religion, even of some of the religious festivals; arrangement of events in chronological order for Old Testament and New Testament was poor, many pupils had no concept of what was a prophet and only 20 per cent Secondary Modern and 30 per cent of Secondary Grammar pupils could name prophets. 'One significant result of the survey', they report, 'was to supply evidence that for many children there was little correlation between the factual knowledge gained through education and a faith by which to live.'

F. H. Hilliard (1959) discovered that up to the beginning of adolescence the majority of children believe that God upholds the moral law by rewarding good behaviour. At the same time God's punishment for wrongdoing is doubted. With the growth of more critical reasoning adolescents begin to abandon both concepts.

U. Nagle (1934) whose research was confined to twelve to sixteen year old Roman Catholic boys, concludes that at twelve years thinking is usually unproductive of adult ideas, with some anthropomorphic concepts lingering on. Fourteen years shows more imaginative thinking, but conflicts now occur and growing uncertainty is evident. As a result of this his thinking turns more inwards. At fifteen years the intellectual difficulties grow and temptations, many of them sexual, have to be faced realistically. By sixteen years Nagle reports the worst period over and more time is given to reconciling scientific and religious notions emerging from wider reading.

In general, Kuhlen and Arnold (1944) do not substantiate this from a sample of 12, 15 and 18 year olds, and do not register adolescence as a period of generally increased religious doubts and intellectual problems, although they did find that Roman Catholic adolescents tended to 'wonder about' fewer beliefs than non-Catholics. Between the twelve and eighteen year old groups they found greater tolerance about religious belief and practice, a discarding of crude ideas and beliefs, and an increased tendency to wonder specifically about death, heaven and hell.

Michael Argyle (1958) in summarising research into adolescent religious development suggests that intellectual doubts start at a mental age of twelve years, followed by emotional stress. By sixteen years these conflicts appear to be resolved either by conversion to religion or by a decision to abandon the religion of childhood. The sum total of these researchers seem to indicate several interesting features of religious thinking. First, there is general agreement of a gradual increase in quality of thinking in terms of religious ideas and concepts accepted. Secondly, a change in concepts and general ability is reflected in religious thinking between about ten and thirteen years of age. The lack of agreement about a precise age appears to stem from the fact that differing concepts were investigated. Thirdly, a few of the researchers specifically support the Piagetian description of the development of operational thinking in religious terms, especially the consecutive stages of concrete and formal operations. Finally, those researchers who have made estimates of children's mental ability, on the whole indicate that this ability and religious thinking are fairly closely related.

MOTIVES FOR THINKING

Affective behaviour influences thinking and especially the formation of concepts. Emotions are dynamically related to man's deepest needs and inevitably influence the selection of particular sensations. The Gestalt school of psychology has emphasised the role of motivation in perception; we see what we wish to see, learn what we wish to learn and this process of selection is continuous at both an intellectual and an emotional level.

We have already mentioned the egocentric nature of the child. In early life he is merely a bundle of appetites requiring satisfaction, and his egocentricity gradually moves in emphasis to more subtle forms. The child becomes capable of play but only parallel play and the exploitive manipulation of playmates; only after many years does he become capable of reciprocal relationships and true friendship. This emotional egocentricity, sometimes loosely called selfish behaviour, strongly influences perceptual and conceptual activity. Unidirectional thinking, or egocentricity, is but one symptom among many of the child's inability to think flexibly in a wider context. Unidirectional thought is contained by limited experience, the dominance of the senses and resulting maturational limitations. What Piaget sometimes calls the period of intuitive thinking, is seen in the simple quantitative problem of conservation of quantity. Because a liquid or a substance, such as clay, appears to be larger, it *is* larger to the child at this stage. The egocentricity of the eye deceives the mind or rather the egocentricity of the mind deceives the eye and even adults exposed to modern packaging methods are not immune from this self-deception in thinking.

The crystallisation of emotion, negative and positive, in regard to particular objects, classes of objects, persons or experiences, soon hardens into attitudes. An attitude may be defined as an enduring organisation of motivational, emotional, perceptual and cognitive processes with respect to some aspect of the individual's world. A belief is an enduring organisation of perceptions and cognitions about some aspect of the individual's world. The difference between belief and attitude is seen when we regard beliefs as the cognitive embodiment of attitudes. Together, beliefs and attitudes, help us to work within a frame of reference, an area of meaning, by which life is interpreted and problems solved. This involves a mind-set or prejudgment towards an object, person or situation which is often called prejudice. All beliefs, by definition, involve prejudice. Racial, national, religious, educational prejudices, to name only a few, influence a person's judgments considerably and involve his attitudes and beliefs. Since attitude is not a direct concern of this present book we have only briefly delineated its essential elements.

MOTIVES FOR RELIGIOUS THINKING

Because religion is fundamentally a pattern of belief, and not an intellectual formula, the emotional aspect of religious thinking is of great importance. Whilst theoretically it is quite possible to have well developed concepts about certain subjects in which we disbelieve, in practice it is rarely possible, since negative emotional behaviour interferes with our thinking. The influence of racial prejudice, attitudes to the other sex, beliefs about the authority of the Bible, for example, may lead quite intelligent persons to the most astonishing conclusions, in defiance of a great deal of evidence against their point of view. Further, the amount of intellectual effort we are prepared to expend on a subject will depend upon the level of our interest or motivation in relation to that subject. This is not merely a quantitative matter but also a qualitative one, and may account for the many varied levels of insight on any one subject seen in a single one year age group in school.

We should clearly recognise this influence on religious thinking. Researchers reveal that motivation is dependent upon the attitudes of pupils to religion and to the subject of religious teaching in church and school. This is further dependent upon the attitudes of the pupil's family, and especially of his parents. Social psychology reveals that group attitudes, especially in adolescence, affect individual attitudes and levels of aspiration. A great deal of work has been done on the relationship of religious attitudes to other factors, especially in America, and we shall here sample a few of those most relevant to the problems of religious thinking. Most of this research by its dependence on questionnaires and other written techniques is confined to the adolescent and student population, who are not only more more mature, but capable of reflecting upon their experience in sufficiently abstract and propositional terms.

In America Thurstone and Chave (1929) developed their attitude scale, dealing with attitudes to Church. This scale has been adapted and used many times. In England, W. Glassey (1945) found among Secondary Grammar school pupils that as the pupils moved up the school their attitudes expressed towards religion became less favourable. He also found, as many other investigators have done, that the attitudes of girls to religion are much more favourable than boys.

K. Hyde (1963) drew up an attitude scale and applied it to 2,500 pupils in secondary schools in Birmingham and then compared the results with their religious concepts. His results clearly indicate that conceptual growth appeared to take place only where there was a degree of religious interest. Where children lacked interest no increase in scores with age was observed. He noted also that lower interest was observable more in senior than in junior forms, more in Secondary Modern than in Secondary Grammar, and more in boys than in girls. Rixon (1959), Daines (1949) and others support some of these findings.

In a study of sixth form boys in Grammar schools, D. S. Wright (1962) found in general a serious and searching attitude towards religion. The religious influence of the school appeared to be small, but that of parents tended to be great, upon the boys' religious beliefs. A later work of Daines (1962) with teachers in training, reflect similar findings of positive attitudes towards religion. These, of course, are investigations only of the top 5 to 10 per cent of the population in terms of ability.

The importance of home and parental influence upon various aspects of religious behaviour is brought out by many studies. Here the attitude of parents to religion appears to be the most important factor. Newcomb and Svehla (1937) found a 0·6 correlation between attitudes of children and their parents in 548 cases when both parents and children were tested on the Thurstone scales. G. Gorer (1955) found that the religious practices of parents affected whether they taught their children to pray, but had little effect on whether they sent them to Sunday School. E. Chesser (1956) discovered that about half the married women in his sample imposed their own church-going habits on their children, the rest either sent them more than they went themselves (25 per cent) or less often (16 per cent).

The major problem posed by research is that about the time when more abstract thinking becomes possible, and so more religious insights can be seen, many adolescents appear to lose interest in religion or develop more negative attitudes to religion. This appears to be less of a problem with brighter and girl pupils. It is a problem to which we shall return in our concluding chapter.

Chapter Three

A RESEARCH APPROACH TO THE
PROBLEMS OF RELIGIOUS THINKING

IT is evident from the research reviewed in Chapter Two that there is still very little known about children's religious thinking, the formation of religious concepts and what possible sequences, patterns or stages can be discovered throughout the whole age range of the day-school population. As all these aspects are important in the construction of religious education syllabuses and the selection of suitable material for varying ages and abilities, an investigation was designed concerned with the following problems. The first purpose of the research was to ascertain a variety of religious concepts which are central to any understanding of religious stories and activities from the age of six years to the end of the seventeenth year. The second was to discover what sequences, if any, exist by which the pupils' levels of understanding progress in religious thinking. The third purpose was to evaluate the logical processes used by children and adolescents at varying stages of development, taking Piaget's schema of the development of operational thinking as a comparative guide. Finally, the intention was to examine what factors may influence religious thinking, especially the influence of home, the religious affiliation of child and parents, chronological age and mental ability.

POSSIBLE METHODS OF RESEARCH AVAILABLE

From the many possible psychological research methods available it was at once clear that some methods were more appropriate to the purposes outlined above than others. The age range of six to seventeen years chosen, and the attempt to discover changes in religious thinking over this wide age range, meant that a standardised procedure should be such as to be suitable for both the young child in Infant school and the sixth form pupil in a Secondary Grammar school. The content of any test should be neither too difficult for the former nor too childish for the latter. This eliminated at once the possibility of written responses, or even the construction of multiple choice tests, which involve reading skills, since poor literacy attainments would interfere with true responses. The choice, therefore, had to be made between taking a very large sample from a smaller and older age group of perhaps late Juniors and the Secondary school pupils, using written response tests as the basis, or a smaller sample large enough to form a representative sample of the whole school population, and here using a more personal interview method.

The clinical interview method was chosen for several reasons. First, problems of literacy were eliminated although the problem of verbalisms and language still remained. This problem will be discussed in detail later. Second, research based upon written responses such as questionnaires and various multiple-choice item tests in relation to religion have been fairly frequent recently, and yield interesting, but limited results. Those limitations are due to two factors. One is that responses are usually brief and in the nature of a written test it is impossible to explore answers at depth, as in an interview. A learned response may be an adequate one in a written test. For example, to the question: 'What is special about a Church?' a child may answer a stock response: 'It's the House of God.' It is possible in a written test to provide some alternative follow-up questions and a number of choices made from previous pilot tests, but in the interview situation it is possible to follow up question after question to a considerable depth. A simple: 'How do you mean?' or: 'What makes you think so?' (the question 'Why?' is usually, an inappropriate question to ask) may elicit many types of response as, for example: 'God lives there', 'He built it', 'It's His land', 'It's where Jesus was crucified', 'It's where God meets with people', 'It's where God was born' and many others. This makes for wider differentiation of response, reveals obscurities, explores them, and gives a more accurate picture in depth of a child's concept. The other limitation in written responses, especially in matters relating to religion, is that they may be elicited due to the child's desire to impress adult authority, or simply to conceal true opinions in case they are unacceptable. These non-typical responses can be minimised by various assurances to the testee, often the assurance of anonymity, by disguising the purpose of the test, or by duplicating items in different form as a cross-check on consistency. While this problem still remains in an interview, it is possible, by projective methods and other means, to overcome these difficulties in relatively more effective ways.

The clinical interview method was chosen for the third reason, because it was felt that motivation is helped by a personal interview, if rapport is suitably established, interest evoked from the start and a friendly, interested adult conducts the discussion. Even the usually inarticulate and introverted child can feel flattered by the importance of being asked to help an adult. The point could be raised that this might work contrarily in adolescents, if hostile attitudes are felt towards authority, but again it is the stereotype of the 'bossy', authoritarian, unsympathetic, unfriendly adult against whom adolescents react. Written tests are usually administered as group tests and personal rapport is not easily established.

The fourth reason why an interview method was used was the question of fatigue; the limit of a written test is usually forty minutes at the outside for adolescents and shorter than this for children. On the other hand an interview can be stopped at any time, if constructed in such a way as to allow for frequent breaks at the first signs of fatigue. In an interview this is more flexibly arranged than in a written test.

Since much of the data to be evaluated was similar in nature to the problems used by Piaget the clinical-interview used frequently by Piaget served as a model, and a technique was developed to apply to individual pupils. Some thought was given to the possibility of using children's drawings as a method of evaluating religious thinking, as did Harms (1944) and Johnson (1961) and Coltham (1960), who used this method in investigating children's understanding of historical terms, but this was rejected on the grounds that only a rather narrow range of thinking would be possible by this method, and that it would be a method not acceptable to older adolescents as perhaps a rather childish activity. It was felt that this also made for problems of subjective evaluation, already particularly evident in religious interpretation. Some pictorial method, however, was used as part of the procedure. The steps by which the investigation was designed, tried out and administered are set out below.

THE RESEARCH PROCEDURE

Five simple pictures, pen and ink drawings, were devised and eight scripture stories, used widely at all ages in many Agreed Syllabuses, were discussed with some 60 pupils, some individually and some in small groups. The ages were 6, 9, 13 and 16 years of age.

The pictures were devised to act as a projective device. Each picture had four parallel copies so that the one appropriate to the size and sex of the child interviewed could be used. The pictures were of a child entering church with a man and woman, a child sitting in a church looking at an altar, a child looking at a picture of Christ, a child kneeling down and praying at a bedside, and a child looking at a mutilated Bible. The figures in the picture were deliberately designed as 'neutral' showing no expression, few features and often the face of the child was hidden, only the back of the head being visible. This was necessary to eliminate responses suggested by factors in the picture and not 'projected'.

36

Initially it was thought possible to secure stories from the children looking at the pictures, followed by certain standard questions. This was rejected on several grounds. First, the time taken in relating stories was considerable. Second, the interpretations of the pictures in story form were so diverse that comparative evaluation would be difficult and perhaps of very limited value. Third, it was a device not acceptable to many adolescents. It was found that when the situations in the picture were structured for the child: 'This shows a boy going into church with his parents to attend some kind of service' followed by standard questions, a great deal of more relevant data was gained.

The scripture stories used in these preliminary interviews were: Moses and the Burning Bush, the Crossing of the Red Sea, the Call of the Child Samuel, King Ahab and Naboth's Vineyard, Jesus in the Temple as a boy, the healing of blind Bartimaeus, the Temptations of Jesus and the Resurrection appearance on the road to Emmaus. These were read in simplified versions to the children and a fairly free discussion took place on the various problems of each story. The child was encouraged to voice difficulties about the stories and explore points of interest. Because of problems of time, not every child discussed every story, most of them discussing five stories each. Close attention was paid to verbal and linguistic difficulties of the children in these discussions.

A second series of preliminary discussions was held later, after difficulties due to language problems, ambiguities and other verbal problems were eliminated and a more systematic discussion of each picture and story was devised. Twenty-seven children were taken at random from the registers of two Infant, three Junior and three Secondary schools. Class teachers supplied chronological age at the time of the discussion and rated each child as below average, average or above average in school performance. Otherwise no further information was solicited.

From the results of the preliminary discussion it was found that the pictures tended to reveal the following concepts. Concepts of the Church, describing its nature, its purpose and the motivation of attenders; concepts of prayer, involving prayer content, the purpose of praying, failure in prayer and God's presence in prayer; concepts of the Bible, its uniqueness, its nature and its origins. The picture of a child looking at a picture of Christ was found to be too ambiguous and was rejected. Of the rest, three pictures were chosen as the basis for evoking responses involving the three groups of concepts noted above. These three, used with a series of standardised questions were, a child entering church with adults, a child praying alone and a child looking at a mutilated Bible.

An examination of responses to the eight Bible stories showed that six major groups of concepts were involved. These were concepts of God, His nature, power and holiness; concepts of individual man's relationship with God, his guilt, fears, trust, expectation, the demands of divine love and justice, and how the divine communicates with man; concepts of group man in relation to God, group salvation and destiny, judgment on groups of men, the demands of divine love and justice; concepts of Jesus, his humanity, his power, his relationship with God; concepts of miracle, God's power over nature, divine intervention and appearance; concepts of biblical authority, the interpreting of the Bible, its authority and relevance. Three of the eight stories were selected because they provided the widest range of responses involving the largest number of concepts. Those selected were Moses and the Burning Bush, the Crossing of the Red Sea and the Temptations of Jesus.

The three stories finally chosen were not therefore the result of mere arbitrary choice. It was found, for example, that concepts of divine communication were evoked equally well in the story of the Burning Bush as in the Call of the boy Samuel, that concepts of divine justice were stimulated in the crossing of the Red Sea incident as in the Naboth story, and that whatever story of Jesus was used practically all the same concepts were used in each one. The temptations narrative raises most of the major concepts and at the same time is in parabolic form. Another consideration in the choice was their possible use with differing age groups. The Burning Bush story is frequently recommended by syllabuses for Infants as one of 'the stories Jesus heard as a boy' (among them Durham, Manchester and Bristol) and many more recommend it for early Juniors. The Exodus, in which the crossing of the Red Sea is an integral part, is recommended for Juniors by almost all syllabuses (Cambridge, Berkshire, West Riding, Sheffield, Middlesex, Carlisle, Westmorland and Cumberland, Surrey and the L.C.C.). The temptations of Jesus are recommended for secondary schools by most syllabuses (Berkshire, Cambridge, Carlisle, Sheffield, Manchester, Surrey, West Riding and the L.C.C.) but frequently this is recommended for Juniors and occasionally for Infants (Bristol, 1960). This variation among syllabus planners is an indication of the uncertainty of criteria by which to judge what is suitable material for a given age.

A criticism could be made that out of the wealth of biblical material available two out of three stories are concerned with Moses and one with Jesus. It should be pointed out, however, that Moses and Jesus are the two dominant figures in the Bible representing salvation at two different levels, in the events associated with them. In addition it can be seen that the questions raised by each story go far beyond the story itself and appear to reflect concepts about many other areas of the Bible in the child's mind. Finally, it can be said that the stories selected are among those most used in current Agreed Syllabuses.

A further relevant criticism is that all three stories have been depicted vividly in the cinema and on television, in such a way as to predispose pupils to a more literal interpretation of these stories. At the time of writing this could be said of most of the well-known historical incidents depicted in biblical narrative. Certainly, not only films and television, but film strips, books, reproduction of great religious paintings and most other material may influence religious thinking. We are concerned, in this research, with testing children's concepts and logic in relation to religious stories and experiences which are formed by the total influence impinging upon the child's life, not merely the results of teaching by school and Church.

The test of three pictures and three stories, having been devised as the basis for a standardised interview, was then administered to a pilot sample of twenty pupils ranging from the ages of 6 : 4 to 16 : 7, of varying mental ability and religious backgrounds. The test was modified in the light of the pilot sample results and a system for scoring the responses objectively was devised. The final form of the test can be seen, in the pictures and story texts, in Appendix A. Interviews of the final sample pupils only took place in schools where a private room could be provided so that no interruptions would be experienced and a continuous period of discussion was possible. In a few secondary schools the head teacher felt it necessary to obtain permission from parents. On no occasion was permission refused.

THE FINAL SAMPLE

The stages in the construction of the interview procedure were first, preliminary discussions with 60 children aged 6, 9, 13 and 16 years of age designated as 'average' ability by the schools. Further discussion followed with 27 children from 6 to 16 years designated as below average, average and above average by the schools. A picture and story interview procedure was then devised upon these discussions. This was applied to a pilot sample of 20 children tested for intelligence by the investigator with a C.A. range of 6 : 4 to 16 : 7 and a M.A. range of 6 : 4 to 18 : 0. The procedure and content of the test was then revised in the light of the pilot sample results and scoring methods explored. Finally, the revised procedure was administered to the final sample of 200 school pupils.

Since the composition of the sample had to be representative of that part of the school population normally exposed to religions education under the specifications of the 1944 Education Act, a random sample of the entire school population was not feasible. The largest sample possible in the limits of time and finance available was 200 pupils, since the smallest number to give a typical cross-section of each year's age group was felt to be 20. Under the terms of the defined population it was necessary that all pupils interviewed should be in state schools. Children of parents who were Roman Catholics, Jews, negroes or of foreign extraction, even if naturalised and their children born in this country, were excluded as a source of possible bias to the sample. Similarly, all children whose parents withdrew their children from school assembly and religious instruction for various reasons were excluded. There is one exception, in the 7–8 year group who was included by error, whose parents were agnostics and invoked the 'conscience' clause. This information, however, was only forthcoming after the final results were compiled. Although it slightly weakens the composition of the sample, this one case makes an interesting individual study.

The number of variables in such a sample of pupils are so many that a stratified sample was necessary, but the problems of selection, due to lack of information, meant that strictly speaking a stratified random sample was not possible. The method used, however, was as near to a stratified random sample as could be made, with the avoidance of various biases.

DISTRIBUTION BY AGE AND SEX

Year	Age Range	Chron. Age Mean Average	Sex distribution
6	6:1–7:0	6:6	10 boys & 10 girls
7	7:1–7:11	7:6	ditto
8	8:1–8:11	8:6½	ditto
9	9:2–9:11	9:7	ditto
10	10:1–11:0	10:6	ditto
11	11:2–11:10	11:6½	ditto
12	12:1–12:11	12:6½	ditto
13	13:1–13:11	13:5½	ditto
14	14:1–14:11	14:7½	ditto
15+	15:3–17:11	16:6½	ditto

Each year age group was stratified in such a way as to be comparable with every other year age group, in order to observe a possible increase in 'levels of understanding' and growing concepts. These 'strata' included sex, age, intelligence, religious allegiance, and religious behaviour.

The age group 5 to 6 year olds was not included in the final sample on evidence from experience in the preliminary discussions and the pilot sample interviews with the younger children. Problems of establishing rapport with children new to school life were considerable and much more time than was available would have been necessary. On the face value of responses of the 6 year olds it was evident that the quality of thinking below this range would not be sufficiently differentiated from the 6 year group as to merit the inclusion of a 5 year group. Further difficulties, due to the limited stay of the 5 to 6 year old in school were the lack of information about the home and social background of the child available to the teacher and therefore to the investigator.

DISTRIBUTION BY ABILITY

Year	IQ Range	S.D.	IQ_x Boys	IQ_x Girls	Total IQ_x
6	77–140	22·50	103·7	105·3	104·5
7	79–132	20·62	103·9	107·5	105·7
8	79–146	19·34	103·6	109·4	106·5
9	76–140	21·86	109·2	106·8	108·0
10	78–144	19·02	104·0	107·2	105·7
11	77–140	20·88	108·4	107·9	108·1
12	78–140	19·30	104·6	107·9	106·25
13	76–140	19·30	107·1	104·1	105·9
14	76–140	19·30	104·9	106·3	105·6
15	91–140 ⎫				
16	104–140 ⎬		118·55	119·8	119·1
17	110–137 ⎭				
	TOTAL IQ_x incl.	15–17	106·77	108·24	107·5
	„ „ excl. „		105·46	106·95	106·2

Here the 15–17 year old age range constitutes the main sampling problem. The variable of 'after leaving school influence' would predominate in a selection of adolescents representing the normal curve of the distribution of intelligence, since practically all those of lowest ability left school at the first opportunity. The lowest IQ noted in this age range remaining at school was 91, a few at 103 to 105 and the rest 'superior'. This, however, is to be expected since mostly those capable of profiting from Further Education in an academic sense tend to stay on. It must be made clear therefore that the 15+ sample is included but does not meet the requirement of 'typicality'. An inspection of the table 'Distribution by Ability' shows that there is a slightly superior mean average score of girls' intelligence quotients over boys, but this is not statistically significant.

In brief, the mean IQ's meet statistical requirements in respect of distribution within each year and between mean average IQ's each year. As some of the Infant and Junior portions of the school population had been tested by the Sleight Non-Verbal Intelligence Test this was used for estimating mental age with pupils up to 10 years of age. Beyond this age pupils had been tested by various Moray House and N.F.E.R. tests and the highest IQ was taken as typical of each pupil. The criterion of mental age was recognised as only approximate and no pupil was selected as part of the sample where the school's estimate of his ability differed appreciably from that achieved in tests.

RELIGIOUS DENOMINATION ANALYSIS

Year	6	7	8	9	10	11	12	13	14	15–17	Totals
Ch. of England	9	9	9	9	9	9	8	9	9	10	90
Free Church	4	4	4	4	4	4	5	5	5	3	42
Gospel Sect	1	1	2	2	1	2	2	1	1	1	14
Nothing	6	6	5	5	6	5	5	5	5	6	54
										TOTAL	200

It was clearly necessary to provide a controlled proportion in each year age group of the various church and non-church allegiances possible. It was also evident that of attenders at Sunday School or Church the largest group would be Church of England, the next largest the Free Churches and the smallest would be the Gospel sects, such as Pentecostal, Adventist and Salvationist churches. Roman Catholics are not included since they would normally be in separate schools or be withdrawn from religious instruction in state schools. The crude numbers of attenders would appear to be in excess of all estimates (see Argyle and Hyde) of the proportion of children connected with the churches. This sample, for example, suggests 20 per cent of children are connected with the Free Churches when Hyde estimates approximately 15 per cent in 1954. These crude figures, however, conceal wide differences of frequency of attendance. 'Nothing' is the term given to a child who goes nowhere at present, has not been to church or Sunday School for over a year and who has neither parent a churchgoer. This is a rather stringent requirement for this category. Figures for attenders may conceal the fact that a child calls himself Church of England, but only goes at Easter and is to all purposes a very marginal member.

A major problem in attempting to control the variable of church or Sunday School attendance is the fact that from 11 years onwards there is a recognisable trend (Argyle) of declining attendance. If this decline were to be reproduced in the sample it would introduce variable factors, hence the attendance proportions have been kept as constant as possible. No attempt will be made to generalise the results in terms of denominations since the numbers of each denomination are too small as separate samples and too many other variables are involved.

From biographical details—information from the items on the final page of the tested headed 'Church Connections'—scores of religious behaviour were made. These reflected frequency of attendance at church or Sunday School, parental support for such attendance, and frequency of reading the bible and praying on the part of each pupil. The results of this demonstrated that the sample was typical, in terms of what is known about religious behaviour from the various surveys available. From an assessment of fathers' occupations the sample appeared also to be typical of the socio-economic distribution of the population.

SAMPLING OF SCHOOLS AND CLASSES

Year	No. of schools	No. of classes
6	4	6
7	5	7
8	2	5
9	7	13
10	6	9
11	7	15
12	9	17
13	6	15
14	7	14
15 plus	5	20

Finally, it was important in Primary ages to have a variety of classes, since each class teacher generally takes Religious Education with her class. The influence of one teacher should not therefore predominate in any year sample. Where Secondary schools are concerned, it is important to have a wide variety of schools, if the influence of one teacher is to be avoided, since Religious Education is a specialist subject and most classes may be taught by one teacher. This, however, is minimised by the fact that even in a Grammar school there will be one Religious Education specialist teacher, but on average a quarter of the staff will do some religious teaching.

TWO PROBLEMS IMPLICIT IN THE METHODS USED

Two problems arise from the methods applied in this research. The first problem concerns the pictures used and to what extent we can support the view that the pupils 'projected' themselves into the picture situations. Before we can answer this clearly we must first examine the assumptions upon which projective techniques are based. The two major assumptions are first, that the individual will tend to 'project his characteristic modes of response into such a task', and second that they are disguised in their purpose, 'thereby reducing the chances that the subject can deliberately create a desired impression' (Anastasi, 1955, p. 17). Referring specifically to attitude testing, where projective techniques are sometimes used, she elaborates . . . 'It is expected that the test materials will serve as a sort of screen upon which the subject projects his characteristic ideas, attitudes, aspirations, fears, worries, aggressions and the like' (p. 599).

The Thematic Apperception Test, (Murray 1943) is perhaps the most well-known picture projection test. Anastasi, commenting on this test of 19 picture cards about each of which the subject is asked to tell a story, writes: 'Most of the pictures in each of these sets contain a character with whom the subject can identify himself' (p. 605). The test adapted for children employs pictures of animals on the assumption that young children identify themselves sufficiently with the picture characters. Bellak (1951) suggests that: 'A further assumption absolutely necessary for the interpretation of material of the Thematic Apperception Test is the hypothesis of psychological determinism as a special case of the law of causality; namely, that everything said or written as a response, like all other psychological productions, has a dynamic cause and meaning.'

A list of advantages and disadvantages of projection techniques is drawn up by J. E. Bell (1948). The advantages, he notes are several. Firstly, the disguised nature of such a test minimises deception. We may note that this is important on a subject so emotionally charged as religion. Secondly, rapport with the subject is often more easily gained. In this instance I began the interview with pictures because of children's natural interest in visual material. It also serves as a 'warming up' section preceding the Scripture material. Thirdly, it is especially advantageous when used with children but less useful with adults who usually recognise its purpose. One comment here concerns the 15 year groups upwards, who were clearly conscious of the device, but tended to accept it with interest and good humour. 'You really want to know what *I* think, don't you?' said a few. Fourthly, it is good for those with verbal limitations. This advantage does not apply to our situation although I have already pointed out the advantage of purely oral responses for those with literacy limitations. Finally, it may stimulate responses by a visual setting of a situation for the less imaginative and least intelligent. This is particularly important with our sample which contains very young children and the lowest intelligence group in every age capable of profiting from normal schooling. It is especially so where most of the questions are essentially abstract; for example, 'What is a church?' is related to the child's experience rather than raised as an abstraction. The disadvantages, however, had to be looked at frankly and overcome as far as possible.

Firstly, the administration and scoring is often not completely standardised and therefore may prove to be subjective evaluation. In this case administration is completely standardised, as also is scoring, which is subject to the same tests as the biblical material, in requiring agreement at a sufficiently high level with independent judges. This disadvantage is more evident with freely told stories. In our situation the pictures are used as projection devices in the answering of a completely standardised set of questions. The subjective element is also reduced by a verbatim account of the pupils' responses being scaled on the agreed criteria of scoring with an independent judge. Secondly, norms are often said to be lacking or based on only vaguely described populations. This is a valid criticism of many projection tests such as the Rorschach and other personality testing devices. Our sampling is of such a nature that it presumes a normal cross-section of the school population within certain defined limits. Norms, however, of religious judgment are indeed lacking and any scoring, based on any method where religion is concerned, is open to this criticism. Thirdly, scorer reliability is said to be poor. This is really a different way of putting previously mentioned criticisms. In our case there is high scoring reliability between the investigator and independent judges in all the picture items. Finally, validity is often said to be lacking or not available in a sufficiently rigorous manner. Our test of validity is, 'Do the pictures really test what we wish to test, namely, levels of understanding in concepts of Church, Prayer and the Bible?' Checks were therefore devised to test validity, as for example how the religious behaviour assessed for each pupil compared with projection judgments of the pupil.

To this summary we can add that in the projection pictures used in our investigation there is only one figure, deliberately arranged as such, with which the pupil can possibly identify and upon whom projection can occur. For comments on this problem see Jackson (1952). The results in general appear to support the view that the picture items assisted the pupils to project their characteristic modes of response into the picture situations sufficiently to reveal concepts of church, prayer and bible.

The second problem implicit in the methods used in this research is the difficult one of verbalism. There are several aspects of this problem which are relevant, including the view that children may hold concepts but cannot express them adequately due to poor verbal ability or personality difficulties. How far is the test merely one of verbal facility? There is the further point that some children may have linguistic fluency and poor concepts, but their verbal flow conveys insight of a level higher than the level they actually possess. How far can the child convey a higher ability than he actually possesses? There are, finally, children who for various reasons wish to supply answers which are acceptable to the investigator. How far can the child consciously deceive?

The question of deception, conscious or unconscious, was faced in the construction of the interview. First of all, by establishing good rapport and by stressing the fact that the questions were not a test for getting marks—'there are no right or wrong answers'—and all that was required was what the pupil thought, a conscious emphasis was made to minimise this factor. Secondly, the probing nature of the interview with its follow-up questions such as 'What makes you think so?' or 'How do you mean?' or 'I don't understand; can you put that in another way?' penetrates the glib answer to the reasons behind the verbalisms. It is true that these reasons are couched in language, but it was discovered frequently that what looked like an advanced concept at first, when reduced to its essential rational elements was in reality very limited and childish. Thirdly, answers were assessed in terms of their content meaning, so that crudely expressed ideas were scored at the same level of insight as the same idea expressed in a verbally polished manner. On this question of deception, Piaget (1929) typified five types of reaction revealed by clinical interview as answers at random, romancing answers, suggested conviction answers, liberated conviction answers and spontaneous conviction answers. The two latter are sought for by any interviewer who seeks to liberate ideas about problems already thought through or to evoke spontaneous thought about a problem obviously new to the child. The child who is unmotivated or cannot understand the questions will tend to provide random answers by mere association of words and here the problem is to motivate the child or to rephrase the question in such a way as to make it intelligible. The romantic and the suggested conviction answers are the deceptive answers and the methodology outlined above was evolved to meet these.

This raises the further question of adult teaching and the child repeating with real conviction what he has been taught. Here again, the scoring criteria would appear to penetrate this and the questioning in depth sought to constrain the child to go beyond what is learnt at the school level from adults and to justify the statements he makes.

This whole matter is discussed very fully by Piaget (1929) in his introduction to *The Child's Concept of the World*. In conclusion (p. 32) he points out that 'if all the children of the same mental age arrive at the same conception of a given phenomenon, in defiance of the variations in their personal circumstances, their experience and the conversation they have overheard etc., this may be regarded as a prime guarantee of the originality of the conviction.' Whilst I consider this a somewhat sweeping generalisation, if 'most' for 'all' is substituted the argument would appear to be a valid one. Piaget makes the further point that as the child's convictions (here he appears to mean 'concepts') evolve to higher levels with age a sudden disappearance of concepts is not evident, but combinations or compromises of the new with the old takes place. Elsewhere, he describes this as the process of assimilation and accommodation. The fact that this process is visible with responses from numbers of children in sequence of age and ability, would seem to argue either the rather fantastic view that children develop their ability to provide deceptive answers with increasing age in a uniformly rational manner so as to provide a scoring sequence, or that, in fact, the responses on the whole are valid 'liberated' or 'spontaneous' modes of thinking.

Far more difficult is the whole question of the problem of the child who has formulated concepts and behaves according to them, but cannot express them adequately in words. Our survey of research in Chapter Two has indicated that this is possible, from the work of Smoke, Kuenne, Heidbreder and Hull. However, Hunter and Bartlett (1948) found that 'inability to verbalise a concept was complete before the age of five years'. R. Beard (1960) summing up this problem, writes, 'In recognising the existence of other conceptual schemas than verbal ones the importance of verbal concepts should not be under-estimated. The child's ultimate representation of the world is in the form, chiefly, of verbal concepts and these can be examined and corrected through social interaction . . . it is through verbal concepts that the child builds an accurate picture of his environment.'

This comment is very appropriate where religious concepts are concerned. As these are based upon inferences and interpretations of direct experience, and as much of this is based upon analogy and metaphor, verbal representation must play a major role. There would appear to be a growth of verbal ability (and linguistic ability to express it), intelligence and concept formation in a related pattern. In the realm of religious thinking levels of understanding and the ability to verbalise them will tend to interpenetrate each other, especially with the advent of schooling. There will, naturally, be variations due to personality differences, but this is a problem common to all testing situations dependent upon language ability. In our test examples, it should be pointed out that they were deliberately designed in 'situations' or 'action' settings, both in picture and story form, to assist the normally inhibited and verbally limited child.

METHODS OF SCORING AND EVALUATING THE RESULTS

Once the responses of the children to the questions were put down verbatim, these were assessed on an agreed scale of theological concepts by some forty independent experts theologically trained. Five questions were also assessed for logic, or levels of operational thought achieved, and these were scored by independent experts conversant with Piaget's levels of operational thinking. A surprisingly high level of agreement was reached between the scoring of different assessors, the lowest achieving a coefficient of correlation product-moment of 0·73 and the highest 0·94.

The scores on all questions were then scaled by means of the Guttman Scalogram method. Where the scaling achieved a coefficient of reproductibility of something in the nature of 70 per cent or above, this was taken as the indication of changes in concepts at certain points and the sequences of religious thinking. This method is briefly outlined in Appendix B, and discussed by E. A. Peel (1959).

Although 'objectivity' in scoring on agreed criteria is the aim the problem of differing theological views and interpretation arises at once. D. Mathias (1943) recognising this problem that, for example, some religious thinkers would rate fear as a necessary and rightful ingredient in a child's religion, or theologians in a literalist tradition would score some young children's biblical insights high, had the following pertinent observation to make:

Since there are varying viewpoints on the validity and value of the different concepts of God, the author has exercised the privilege of setting up a certain standard. He has assumed that too much dependence on God and excessive fear of God are not wholesome for the individual. . . . It is believed that to conceive of God as a person is not as desirable as to think of Him in terms of a spirit . . . to conceive of God as all powerful and mysterious is wholesome, and that justice and love ideas of God are desirable attitudes. (p. 41)

In this study I have consulted expert and independent judges and fully disclosed all criteria used in assessing pupils' answers. All criteria for scoring the test are based upon the current theological approach of biblical theology, interpreted from a central-to-liberal position. The view is held that Scripture is the inspired but not the infallible Word of God, transmitted or revealed to fallible men, who at times have only partially grasped and communicated the truth revealed to them; that to discover 'The Word' within the words we must approach the Bible with what methods literary and historical criticism can supply; that any part of the Bible must be evaluated in the light of the highest revelation and that this implies the view that God has progressively revealed Himself to men through the centuries. Although the concept of progressive revelation as it was first conceived is naïve, and does not fit the facts of biblical chronology, yet I suggest that it is a concept, which when modified and not seen as an 'automatic' progression of insight, is a necessary and rational frame of reference by which the Bible, and especially the Old Testament can be understood. Further, it is suggested that these assumptions are implicit in the formation of all Agreed Syllabuses and the effectiveness of insight in religious thinking should be assessed by criteria based upon these assumptions.

There will be those who differ radically in their theology from the above statements and in their case this research will have little to offer. It would be pertinent, however, to ask what possible criteria could be used in assessing the pupil's responses which offers a valid alternative? It is likely that if such criteria from, say a 'conservative' view of biblical theology were offered, then not only the assessing criteria but the whole nature of the questions and the interview procedure would have to be radically changed.

AGE DIVISIONS AND CHILDREN'S NAMES

In the ensuing chapters, we shall be discussing the sequences of religious thinking and the ages when the various stages appear to begin and end. Some caution is necessary at this point, since the ages at which certain levels of religious thinking appear to be reached are only very approximate. The ages, usually, although not invariably, will be seen more in terms of mental age than chronological age. The ages cited at which various stages appear to begin, are only rough indicators of apparent boundaries of thinking from one level to another. They are approximations of what we would term 'areas of probability', when the majority of pupils appear to move from one conceptual level to another. The sequence of thinking, or the order of level of understanding, is of greater importance than the ages at which the boundaries of thought appear to fall. For practical purposes, however, the age boundaries are used as a rough guide to indicate the general trends apparent at various school levels. This caution only applies to the age boundaries discussed, but the ages of

individual pupils given in many examples are the mental and chronological ages of each individual pupil at the time of testing.

It must also be stressed that when age boundaries are cited, as
they are frequently, this is to indicate where most pupils change their
thinking from one level to another. But even if this 'most' means
80 per cent of the children these still leave 20 per cent who are exceptions. These are frequently the dull or backward pupils who may only
attain the suggested conceptual levels much later than the normal or
above average pupil. This time-lag for the dull and backward is a
natural assumption we make in all school subjects and we would
expect the same to be true in religious thinking. On the whole this is
so, but there are interesting and surprising exceptions where the
occasional child of well below average ability will perhaps surpass
his brighter peers in religious insight. Examples of this and possible
explanations are discussed at the end of Chapter Fourteen.

The children's names quoted in all examples given are fictitious,
but all other details given are authentic, the responses being taken
verbatim from the records of the interviews.

Chapter Four

OPERATIONAL THINKING ABOUT
RELIGIOUS STORIES

BEFORE we examine the content of the pupil's religious thinking, it will be useful to see what are the major characteristics of religious thinking during childhood and adolescence in terms of the processes and structures of thought in more detail. Maturational limitations and sheer inexperience will obviously restrict thinking among younger children. We have already noted two characteristics, such as egocentric thinking and concretisms. But these are only symptoms of many other factors which affect the child's judgments about religious matters.

In Chapter Two we described Piaget's outline of the development of operational thinking. The first period of sensori-motor intelligence need not concern us here since there is no data, in specifically religious terms, available. We are interested more in the subsequent stages of development, namely intuitive or pre-operational thinking, concrete thinking and propositional thinking. These are very relevant to the years of schooling.

To see whether Piaget's three stages could be applied to the realm of religious thinking, I selected five questions from the Bible stories in *The Picture and Story Religious Thinking Test,*[1] and the responses to these were scored independently by those psychologically trained and conversant with Piaget's ideas. These questions were:

S1 : Q2. 'Why was Moses afraid to look at God?'
S1 : Q4. 'Why do you think the ground, on which Moses stood, was holy?'
S1 : Q5. 'How would you explain the bush burning, but not being burnt?'
S2 : Q5. 'How would you explain the dividing of the waters of the Red Sea?'
S3 : Q2. 'Why wouldn't Jesus turn the stone into bread?'

They were chosen because the discussion of each question with each child revealed the possibilities of checking the child's mode of thinking by Piagetian methods. We shall see how the three stages can be observed quite clearly in the pupil's answer to the questions. The reader should bear in mind that our concern in this chapter is with

[1] See Appendix A.
51

the structure and process of the child's thought, not with his theological insights, which will be discussed in detail in subsequent chapters. We shall here focus upon the characteristic features of the pupil's thinking rather than upon the content.

INTUITIVE RELIGIOUS THINKING

Intuitive, often termed Pre-operational, thinking has several important characteristics. The child thinks transductively, inferring a particular fact from another particular fact. This is because only an isolated part of a problem is seen and the child is off-centre in his thinking because of absorption in unessentials. What may be central in an incident to an adult may be relegated to an obscure and unimportant detail to the child, while what are obscure and unimportant details for the adult are often seen by the child as of the greatest importance. The child can only deal with one problem at a time, and will therefore oversimplify a situation because otherwise it would be too complex for him. This leads to unsystematic and fragmentary thinking, which in turn leads to illogical and inconsistent conclusions because all the evidence has not been considered. But the major disability is the lack of reversibility of thought, the inability to work back from an inconsistency to check on the evidence in the light of conclusions reached.

We shall now consider some pupils' answers to illustrate these characteristics from the Burning Bush story. The first question was: 'Why was Moses afraid to look at God?' When the child answers, 'God had a funny face' he is introducing an irrelevancy and centring his thinking only upon this. 'Funny', in this context, means horrid or horrible, not 'humorous'. Similarly, the child who says 'Moses was frightened of the rough voice', and another who answers 'It was because he hadn't spoken politely to God' reveal the same problem. This latter is a clear case of transductive thinking, from one particular aspect to another, with no clear evidence to support the inference. To the second question, 'Why do you think the ground on which Moses stood was holy?' one answer was 'Because there was grass on it.' The warning notices in public parks perhaps is the associated off-centre ideas, or the experience of young children being allowed to run about on grass with their shoes off. Here is a strong egocentric element. Another child introduces a curious literalism by saying, 'He was standing on a ho.' Discussion revealed that the child had fastened upon the first syllable of 'holy' and she described this 'ho' quality as 'nice, hard ground'. Literalisms abounded at this stage and are in themselves indications of oversimplified thinking. A refinement of this is the reply, 'It was hot ground. It would burn his shoes.' A good example of irreversible logic is seen in the statement, 'God wanted a friend and because God had his shoes off, they'd be friends (i.e. God and Moses)'.

A third question from the Burning Bush story was concerned with the miraculous element, 'How would you explain the bush burning, but not being burnt?' An alternative form of the question was 'How do you think such a thing could happen?' A child who sees only the one aspect of the problem, the bush on fire, answers: 'I think Jesus saw the bush burning and some men put it out by water.' In discussion he adds: 'Some bad men or boys came and lit it again. The flowers, leaves and branches weren't burnt because they were up high.' Here he seizes upon another single aspect and his reasoning switches to deal with this, not relating it to his first statement. Another sees a problem, but repeats it in another form without solution: 'God made the bush. No one else was there to make it. He'd keep the bush alive.' Here is an irrelevancy that God was obliged to keep the bush alive as its creator, but the child does not say how. A briefer reply was: 'God made it happen' and when pressed further the boy said: 'Well, he just did.'

In the Exodus story, interesting answers at the intuitive level are seen to the question: 'How do you explain the dividing of the waters of the Red Sea?' One child centres upon the irrelevancy of the colour. 'The man ran past the blue sea and the white sea. The blue sea went on one side and the white sea the other side.' When asked how the sea was divided, this aspect was dropped and the child replies 'Moses done it.' Similar to this is the child who centres upon the magical act, and this alone provides him with a satisfactory answer, 'God did it. He would magic it.' A variant of this merely describes or repeats, 'It was a miracle. God told Moses to put his hand out. It was magic.' The focus is upon the single feature of an extraordinary happening, and this is not evidence of propositional thinking about God's power.

Finally, there was the temptation of Jesus' question: 'If he was hungry, why wouldn't Jesus turn the stone into bread?' A child provides differing answers switching from one reason to another when questioned further, 'Because God was invisible. (Q) Jesus didn't want any bread. (Q) He didn't like bread anyway.' Another concentrates irrelevantly on the manners of the devil, reflecting a small child's egocentric concerns, 'The bad man wouldn't let him go. The bad man didn't say please.' Unsystematic thought can be seen in the statement, 'Jesus didn't want anything to eat. Anyway, it would be dry. Jesus didn't like the devil.' One can see here the child shuttling, unsystematically, from one aspect of the problem to another, without relating them together.

INTERMEDIATE BETWEEN INTUITIVE AND CONCRETE RELIGIOUS THINKING

Before children move out of the limitations of intuitive thinking they appear to pass through an intermediate stage where they are striving to break out of their limitations, because they are clearly unsatisfactory to them. At this time children attempt to think operationally but fail to achieve the levels necessary. Because transductive thinking leads to obvious mistakes, inductive and deductive logic is attempted. It is, however, faulty and breaks down for various reasons. The child attempts to classify, for example, but the complex material usually baffles him. His efforts to relate one feature of a situation to another are unsuccessful. He is uncertain in his judgments and although he develops the beginnings of systematic thought, it is crude and faulty thinking. Attempts are also being made at this stage to check his thinking, by reversing his thought, but again he is too inexperienced to do this with any accuracy. Nevertheless, it is an important point to achieve when the child sees the necessity of a different process of thinking, even though he has not developed enough skills or insights to execute it.

An example of inefficient classifying can be seen in the child's answers to 'Why was Moses afraid to look at God?' which was 'Because God wears a beard and Moses doesn't like beards.' This attempt to relate more than one aspect of the situation, God wearing a beard and Moses' alleged dislike of beards, breaks down simply because the fact that Moses had not yet looked at God is missed. Another boy puts Moses' fear down to the fact that God 'might kill Moses for making the bush on fire', an obvious attempt to relate two features of the story unsuccessfully.

Typical of this period is the circular argument such as the answer to 'why was the ground, on which Moses stood, holy?' Here the child states, 'It was holy because it said it was. *Why? Because God blessed it. Why did God bless it?* Because it was holy!' Again, this is an unsuccessful attempt to be systematic, as is the following reply, 'It was holy because God made it. *Doesn't God make all ground?* Yes, but this was made specially, because God made it holy, and people won't be allowed to tread on it.' Many answers to this question dealt with the surface of the ground being smooth or rough or muddy, showing attempts to provide a reasonable explanation but failing to do so. The children are evidently discontented with purely intuitive answers but do not know how to get beyond them. The explanations of the burning bush follow a similar pattern. 'The leaves were too strong to burn. They hadn't been burned before,' or 'It was raining and God sent the wet,' showing the children's attempts to

54

relate their own experience to the situation but they are unable to incorporate the major problem. One girl says irrelevantly, 'It's in a different country. There ain't no houses like we've got. *How does that make a difference?* Well, it's different bushes. There weren't no sticks on the bush.' This is a very good illustration of intermediate thinking, a near successful attempt to systematise the thought.

Vivid illustrations of the child's intermediate position can be seen in answers to 'How do you explain the dividing of the waters of the Red Sea?' One child says, 'God did it. He was in the middle of it. *How would God do it?* If he was in the middle he'd push his arms and legs up and force the water open. *Would they see him?* No. *Wouldn't the Israelites fall over God when crossing over?* No, he'd be under the water and sand. *If he was underneath, how would he keep the waters apart?* I don't know.' This child attempts a system but it breaks down in confusion and he cannot advance an alternative one. It is certainly concrete, but does not quite attain an operational level. Here is another random attempt to form a system. 'It couldn't. Moses' arm wasn't long enough to stretch right over the sea. Moses sailed over in a boat. *There were no boats there.* Well, Moses kept pushing the water back with his hands. *How do you mean?* No, it wouldn't work. He built a wall on each side.' A similar idea is voiced by another child, 'God reached down with his hands and scooped out the water.' A relevant possibility is seen but it ignores the possibility of water flowing back and is still contained by a single centring of thought.

Finally, the answers to 'Why wouldn't Jesus turn the stone into bread?' are most revealing of this stage. 'Because he said not to eat bread alone. *How do you mean?* They should have something else like cheese and something to drink.' This literalism is based on association of ideas, relating one idea to another, not successfully. Another child interprets 'Not by bread alone' in terms of having company when you eat. Yet another child says, 'The devil wouldn't let him have it, if he did make it into bread.' There is no evidence for this, but it is an attempted system. A curious generalisation can be seen in the response, 'The devil tells lies. *How do you mean?* Well, if Jesus turned stones into bread, he'd have nothing left to walk on.'

CONCRETE RELIGIOUS THINKING

I am using concrete religious thinking here as an abbreviated form to indicate concrete 'operational' thinking. It is true that much thinking at an earlier stage is concretistic but this stage is characterised by operational thinking where the 'operations' are limited by concrete elements. Successful inductive and deductive logic is now employed, but its scope is limited to concrete situations, visual experience and sensory data. Classifying can be made with more success than error, and systematic thinking, where two or more facts can be related, now takes place. There is no extension, however, or generalisation from one concrete field to another. The child is able to reverse his thinking and therefore is capable, to some extent, of checking the results of thinking. One interesting feature of this stage is that although they deal with many verbal problems, children will judge them purely in terms of their content, and often egocentrically, that is solely in the light of their own experience. The concrete elements dominate the child's thinking, limiting thought frequently to those features visibly or tangibly present in a situation.

The clear system where several aspects are related, but confined to concrete relations, is seen in answer to 'Why was Moses afraid to look at God?' Children at this stage see God as a man or a power threatening specific action, sometimes because a specific wrong has been mentioned and punishment is feared because of it. For example, 'Moses thought God would chase him out of the holy ground, because Moses hadn't taken off his shoes.' Another, slight variant of this, is 'Moses hadn't been going to Church or anything like that. *Why should that make him afraid to look at God?* God wouldn't like him any more and not make him go up to heaven.' An interesting sidelight on her moral concept of God can be seen when this same girl then states: 'Moses hadn't prayed, and God wouldn't forgive him if he had done anything wrong.' Most other answers at this stage tend to centre upon the light or fire as the source of Moses' fears. 'Because it was a ball of fire. He thought it was coming nearer. It might burn him,' says one child. Another says, 'It was the bright light and to look at it might blind him.' Both these answers illustrate the child's focus upon specific and concrete features of the story.

The ground on which Moses stood is seen as holy at this stage, because the child says there has been concrete physical contact with 'the holy'. This can be seen in the answer: 'It was where God was standing. *How did that make it holy?* Because the holy would go down through God's feet into the ground and make it holy.' Or simply, 'God was there. His face and his angel was there. *How did that make it holy?* Something very good had happened there, like the place where Jesus was born.' This concrete element may also be seen in the answer: 'It was where God was speaking to Moses' where the child means it to be speech in a physical human sense. Some children also make associations, correctly related, with other places and so deduce the special character of the place where Moses was. 'It was like a graveyard and you had to tread carefully,' or 'It was like a Church: you've got to be very quiet.'

Explanations of the burning bush at this stage are dominated by concrete elements. God actively arranges that the bush is unburnt by covering it with protective material of some kind such as 'iron stuff', 'watery stuff' or something like God's wings or an angel's hand. Another concrete explanation is a crudely devised concept of space, for example, 'The real fire was behind it and shone through it and it looked as if it were alight.' Another example of the same kind is 'The fire was all round it and it looked as if it were burning.' A little cruder, but systematic and relating a number of factors is the answer, 'It was a light from an electric torch, or a stick with flames on it held up by an angel.'

Physical explanations which are feasible in a concrete sense and which, from the child's view, successfully meet the facts can be seen in answers to how the Red Sea waters were divided. 'God stretches his spirit over the water and that divides it.' Subsequent discussion of this answer shows that the child thinks of spirit, not as abstract, but as physical, rather like a piece of elastic. More physical is the assertation that 'God's palms (of his hands) were pushing them apart. You couldn't see them because they were invisible. When the Israelites were through he took his hands away and the waters flooded back.' Sometimes, it is the sea which is animised, as in the answer, 'God told the sea to part. *Has the sea got ears so it can hear?* No. *Is it alive so it hears God?* Oh yes, it can go one way or go another way. *How do we know a thing is alive?* Because it moves.' This animistic view is a physical interpretation which can only be explained in physical terms by the child.

This level of thinking is also evident in relation to the question of why Jesus did not turn the stone into bread. 'God said he must not eat. *Why was that?* Because Jesus had a lot of work to do.' This answer shows concrete action and concrete authoritative command. Another type of answer was 'Because Jesus didn't want to show off.' The child is limited by his egocentric view of childhood, but what is interesting is that when this reason was examined in relation to Jesus turning the water into wine, there was no extension or generalisation to this other situation. Many children when faced with a contrast of Jesus being willing to turn water into wine, but unwilling to turn stone into bread, gave as their explanation that water after all was 'runny' liquid, but stone was hard and had no similarity to bread. A final example is of interest. 'He thought the devil might take the magic away. Jesus might have it hidden, and if Jesus used it, the devil would know where it was and take it one night.' This is a well thought out, systematised, but concrete operation of thought.

INTERMEDIATE CONCRETE-ABSTRACT RELIGIOUS THINKING

There is evidence that no sudden change in thinking occurs with the onset of adolescence, nor with transition from one type of school to another. Change there is from a concrete to a more abstract mode of thought, but it is a gradual change and the change-over appears in what may be identified as an intermediate stage of thinking. At this stage, more advanced inductive and deductive logic is employed and a move towards a more abstract level of thought is evident. It is, however, still distracted by concrete elements in the situation which the pupil seems unable to shake off. One way of seeing this attempt at abstract thinking is in the pupil's desire to deal with propositions or verbal statements and to consider hypotheses. These attempts are limited by distractions of concrete elements. The pupil may also go outside a story and use other experience to consider a possible hypothesis or explanation. This is an indication of his unwillingness to be contained by the concrete elements or by the narrative itself. Even so, his attempts have only limited success, since again tangible or concrete data tend to interfere with a clear perception of how propositions are related to each other.

The attempt to break away from concrete elements can be seen in reasons advanced for Moses' fear of looking at God. At the previous stage children cited a specific wrongdoing as the basis of Moses' fear. Here the concrete wrong gives place to a generalised statement, 'Perhaps he had done evil things. *How would that make him afraid?* He would be ashamed to look at God.' But this proposition is somewhat diluted by the later statement by the same child. 'Moses was afraid because all the names God mentioned were great people. *How would this affect Moses?* Well, Moses had killed a man.' This also illustrates the ability to go outside the story and the need to form a hypothesis. The general ideas of Moses' unworthiness is put forward as a propositional statement but often for a concrete reason such as 'he smelled of the sheep'. One girl expressly states 'I'd be scared. *Why?* God is good and if I'd done something wrong I wouldn't like to face him.' Another attempted proposition was 'It'd be hard to describe it to other people and Moses would want to keep it a secret and wouldn't look at it.' Some expressed the same idea adding, 'Moses didn't want to be laughed at by people who wouldn't believe him.'

At this stage a variety of reasons is given to explain what made the ground holy and the beginnings of propositional thought emerge. 'Taking off your shoes is a sign of respect; it was a tradition in those days.' The holiness is explained, as in the previous concrete stage, by some children as due to the fact that God spoke there, but the answers show clearly that divine speech here is not envisaged as physical. It is not so abstract, however, as the idea that this was 'a moment of truth' for Moses.

The interpretations of the miraculous provide splendid illustrations of this tension in the child's mind between the concrete and the abstract, resulting in an intermediate mode of thought. In the burning bush story an attempt is made to redeem the materialistic idea by spiritualising or symbolising action, but still with concrete elements impeding the thought. For example, the flame is not a 'real' flame but some kind of holy, non-burning flame. Some children create a barrier between the fire and the surface of the bush, not of water or physical substance, but a semi-physical essence of a transparent nature; 'so you can see through it,' says one child. The symbolic element is seen in replies which show that the child believes God changed himself into the bush or into flame, and so the material element is transcended in some way. Others see the light from the bush as a physical reflection of God or an angel, another semi-physical interpretation. Of a propositional character is the frequent answer, 'Probably God did a miracle. *How do you mean?* It's something God and Jesus can do which ordinary people can't do, and can't understand.'

The miraculous in terms of the Red Sea dividing, again is semi-physical. 'It was a miracle. *How do you mean?* It could have been the way Moses waved his hand. God told him that if he had faith, it would save them.' Concrete elements of magic restrict this proposition. Animistic ideas are further developed to a higher level, as in the answer, 'He told the waves to part and they obeyed. *Were the waves alive?* No. *Well, how could they hear and obey God?* God can do anything!' The hypothesis is assumed, that all creation must obey the creator, but limited by concrete elements. Some children advance the hypothesis of a wind blowing in two directions, such as 'Water is liquid and would easily move, but the wind wouldn't be strong enough to knock over human beings.' Another boy is not so certain and argues with himself. 'They might be sheltered from the wind by the waves. No. That's a contradiction. I don't know.'

The temptation of Jesus to turn stone into bread at this stage is met at a similar level. 'Jesus was trying to prove he could live without food. *How was that?* His father would look after him. He went into the desert to think and not do miracles.' A good propositional idea but limited by the concrete concern for the food element. Another child says, 'It would only have been showing off and he wasn't the kind of person to show off.' When asked if turning the water into wine at a wedding, which this girl said did happen, wasn't showing off, she replied, 'Yes, but that's different. He was helping someone'.

ABSTRACT RELIGIOUS THINKING

'Abstract' here is used to indicate what Piaget calls 'formal operational thinking', and it is the final stage when the capacity to think hypothetically and deductively, without the impediment of concrete-elements, is achieved. The mode of thinking changes from situations to verbal propositions. Thinking is now possible in symbolic or abstract terms. Consistent thinking, in which incompatible elements can be seen, is also achieved, and hypotheses can be tried out experimentally in thought, and posited, rejected or accepted in the light of reason. It is obvious that reversibility operates at a propositional level and the implications of a statement can be explored and traced back to the original argument. The pupil can therefore start with a theory and work back to the facts, which considerably widens the scope of his thinking.

There is clearly a wide difference in quality between the pupil who has just entered this stage and the older adolescent who has become accustomed to this mode of thought over a period of years. They share, however, the same characteristic of having achieved a liberation from concrete limitations. Consequently in answer to Moses' fear, the general proposition is frequently made that Moses shared with all men a general sense of sin or unworthiness, which made him hesitate to look at God. 'God is holy and the world is sinful.' Sometimes this is stated specifically as 'The awesomeness and almightiness of God would make Moses feel like a worm in comparison.' A girl who has just achieved the abstract stage puts it a little more crudely, 'Moses might be frightened because God was great. He'd never followed him before', but the essence is there. More advanced is the view that Moses like most people of his day, 'would have a primitive feeling of awe'. The critical examination of an hypothesis is well illustrated by one pupil's answers to why the ground was holy, when he said, 'Can God have a greater degree of presence? I'm not sure. Wasn't it supposed to be the Lord's mountain? Wasn't it a volcano and what they couldn't understand they called holy, something dangerous to be left alone?' Answers also range from the simple proposition, 'Everywhere is holy where people believe and worship God,' to the ingenious hypothesis, 'The presence of God would hallow it like a magnetic field. The magnetic field is everywhere but the pole is in one spot. God is concentrated there.'

The burning bush, at this stage, is now seen mainly as an internal phenomenon, such as the view, 'Instead of God appearing as a person he came in the bush. It seemed to be to his eyes, but it wasn't really. *How do you mean?* He could have imagined it in his mind.' The hypotheses at this stage may be entirely natural explanations such as 'a mirage; Moses was exhausted and started seeing things', or supernatural, such as the theory of 'continuous replacement of matter'. Some accept the story by saying, 'It can't be explained on rational grounds', arguing that there is not enough data on which to form a judgment, a very sophisticated advance in thinking.

The division between natural and supernatural explanations, with sometimes a fusion of both, is seen vividly in the Red Sea story by pupils at this stage. Natural explanations can be seen in the many hypotheses of tides, tidal waves, earthquakes and similar events. Here is one example, 'It's been proved that at a special time the sea does part. It gets very shallow. *How do you mean?* At a special time of the year, only once a year. *Did God do it?* No, they just got there at the right time. God had nothing to do with the sea, but he knew about it and got them there at the right time.' There are a few who advance the same idea but maintain it was just a coincidence and a divine agency at work is rejected. The supernatural explanations can be seen in the following proposition, 'The seas opened and there was a big path. *How did it happen?* Perhaps a path came up and rose up out of the water. God made it happen. *How?* If God makes things, He can create things as he wants.' A fusion of natural and supernatural can be seen in such answers as the wind theory expressed by a boy. '*How could it be a wind?* It was God's force. *How did he use it?* He'd just move it, remove the forces keeping the water there, such as gravity, or put another force that pushed it back.' More sophisticated is the statement, 'All things are possible with God. It quite literally happened. It's a comparatively simple thing for God to do, if we can build atomic power stations. *How would God do it?* He might take away the kinetic energy of the molecules on the surface area of the water and a sheet of ice would form to keep the waters back.' Most pupils who support a natural explanation support the expressed view, 'God must have had something to do with it as the controller of Nature.'

Propositional consistency can be seen in replies, at this stage, to the problem of the temptations. Jesus would not turn stone into bread 'because that would be using the power for his own good. If he didn't use it for some better purpose, he'd no right to go out and preach'. This relates several propositions together and the implications beyond the story are followed. Similarly, 'To obey the devil would be to acknowledge the devil as your master. It would be breaking the first commandment.' It requires, of course, this level of operational thinking to perceive the parabolic nature of the story, which a few older pupils were able to see, as in the answer, 'Jesus lives by the Word of God. *What does that mean?* You have faith in him and he will provide all your needs.' Others see the whole incident as basically abstract,

'He had gone to the desert to sort his own thoughts out, and God gave him this test. It was his own conscience, to see if he would give in or go on.'

SEQUENCES OF THOUGHT

An analysis of results when scored on the three major stages of thinking (and two intermediate stages) outlined above, substantiates very clearly the view put forward by Piaget that there is a continuum of thinking which follows an 'operational' sequence. When applied to thinking about religion, in the Bible stories chosen, this threefold sequence is very evident. It is noticeable when the pupils are arranged in order of chronological age, more noticeable when they are arranged in order of mental age and very marked when the pupil order follows the total score order.[1]

When each pupil's highest operational score is taken and the totals analysed the sequences are even more marked, and when the mean average score for each pupil is taken the results score very significantly.[2] We can therefore say with confidence that there is a sequence or pattern through which children appear to pass, at varying speeds, which closely corresponds, in religious thinking, to an intuitive stage, a concrete operational stage and a formal or abstract operational stage. The presence of intermediate stages is also evident but they are not clearly definable since they overlap the main sections.

It is not only difficult but it may also lead to an over-simplification if we stated the ages at which these three major stages tend to occur in their religious thinking. Children's experiences in the field of religion are so varied and personal, that inferences from a sample of 200 must be drawn with caution. The important fact established is that children appear to pass through this sequence of stages in their development. Nevertheless, with this caution in mind it is useful to recognise that some general indications of ages at which the boundaries of thinking are passed are available from our results.

The end of intuitive thinking and the beginnings of the concrete operational stage, on the five questions from Bible stories just discussed, is within the general age range suggested by Piaget. Taking mental age as the more accurate indicator of boundaries between the different stages pupils seem to achieve the concrete stage between 6 : 6 and 8 : 10. The problem which appeared to be solved earliest at

[1] The respective coefficients of reproducibility are 63·3 per cent, 68·2 per cent and 78 per cent. For explanations of the significance of these figures see Appendix B.

[2] On highest scores the coefficients of reproducibility are for chronological age 65·6 per cent, for mental age 73·5 per cent and for total scores 80·5 per cent. On mean average scores the coefficients of reproducibility are for chronological age 74·5 per cent and for mental age 80·5 per cent.

the concrete level was the nature of the burning bush miracle. The problem surmounted at the latest age at the concrete level appears to be the problem from the temptations of Jesus. To solve this even at a crude concrete level pupils had to be almost nine mental years. The differing ages at which intuitive thinking is left behind can perhaps be accounted for by the varying difficulties posed by the different questions, the stone-turning-to-bread-temptation being of greater complexity than the bush-burning-but-not-being-burnt. Other factors in causing differing levels of difficulty could be problems of verbal comprehension, unfamiliarity with the experiences depicted in the stories and inexperience in facing such problems.

A similar range of mental age is observable where the concrete stage changes over into the formal or abstract stage of thinking. The boundary appears to be between about 13 : 5 and 14 : 2, the earliest being evident in the burning bush story again. Three of the problems, Moses' fear of looking at God, the dividing of the Red Sea and the stone to bread temptation all show the same boundary of 14 : 2 as the transition from concrete to formal operations. There is evidence from one story that the intermediate stage, when propositional thinking is attempted but is held back by concrete elements, may begin about 12 : 8. This range of 13 : 5 to 14 : 2 (M.A.) for the beginnings of religious thinking at a formal operational level, is very much later than that suggested by Piaget. His estimates, however, appertain mostly to data involving an understanding of the physical world of the child. This finding on the beginnings of propositional thinking substantiates Peel's finding (1961) reported earlier, 'that there is little evidence of children's capacity to set up possibilities to account for events in stories, as opposed to mere describing, before the age of 13 plus'. Peel's further evidence, gathered in New Jersey, on story data, yields a general boundary of intermediate hypothetical thinking from a mean average age of about 13 : 1 which only yields to the highest level of hypothetical thinking between a mean average mental age of 14 : 8 to 15 : 0. The ages in his sample differ, as in mine, with the variety of story data involved.

This delayed development could be an indication of two related factors in religious development. First, it could substantiate the theory put forward in our first chapter that religious thinking is secondary, dependent as it is upon the enriching of general experience, before religious language can be understood. In this area of the child's development then, a time lag appears to be a necessary delay, while he acquires enough knowledge of life to make sense of the analogy and metaphor so basic to religious stories. This draws our attention to the fact that inference by analogy and metaphor, as in parables, requires some level of propositional thinking before the child can deal with it. The second factor in delayed arrival at the formal operational level in religious thinking may be a confusion in the child's mind about religious matters due to poor or premature teaching, so that in being called upon too soon to deal with data which is beyond his comprehension, the child clings longer to concrete modes of thinking because he can do no other. As in other subjects, children who find concepts too difficult will tend to crystallise their thinking too quickly and be satisfied for too long with crude and inadequate forms of thoughts. This is not only true of methods of thinking in relation to a given range of experience, but it is also true in relation to the content of religious thought, as we shall see at a later point in this book.

To sum up, we can say that in religious thinking, the stages reached in terms of mental age are very approximately:

Up to about 7/8 years: Pre-operational intuitive thought.
About 7/8 to 13/14 years: Concrete operational thought.
13/14 years onwards: Formal (abstract) operational thought.

These age boundaries are very approximate and should not be regarded as fixed or the results of maturational limitations. It may be that with the avoidance of premature material and the introduction of a programme designed to stretch the child's thinking in relation to religion these age boundaries could be lowered. The impact of experience upon the child's levels of thought was discussed some time ago by Susan Isaacs (1945) in describing her work at the Malting House School, but the whole issue has been raised more recently by Professor J. McV. Hunt (1961) in the United States. How we can enrich a child's environment, in such a way as to lead him beyond his immaturities of religious thought, I shall discuss in the last chapter, and in more practical detail in another volume.[1]

INDIVIDUAL DIFFERENCES

Our last section gave the sequences and the approximate mental ages when most children appear to pass through the three stages of religious thinking. Yet there is a vast range of individual differences. These differences are twofold in character. First, there is the difference of speed, some children being far ahead of others of approximately the same age, others being backward when compared with their peers. Then secondly, there are different levels of response any individual child will make to varying problems. As Lodwick (1958) discovered in terms of problems posed by history stories there is a variation within each child's responses from item to item.

[1] *Readiness for Religion: A Basis for Developmental Religious Education* (1965).

On the first difference between peers our results show roughly that mental age will indicate a child's possible place on the sequence of religious thinking, and that what we loosely call intelligence will be an important factor in determining the mode of thinking used by the child. A more intelligent child has more ability to call upon, in religion as in other areas of experience, and we would expect him to do better. But religious development is dependent upon a complexity of factors and for this reason a child of lower mental age may surpass a child of higher mental age. This is why the correlation between mental age and levels of thinking is far from perfect. In some cases chronological age, and the fact of wider experience, would appear to be a decisive factor. More important still are factors such as attendance at church or Sunday school, habits of prayer or Bible reading and attitudes of the parents to religion.

The second kind of individual difference can be seen in a fairly large minority of pupils. In our five story problems, most children were fairly consistent in the level of their religious thinking attained in each story, varying their score from question to question only by a point or so. Even so, many children are inconsistent from question to question, a few showing a very wide range of response, a child achieving some level of concrete operations on one question then falling back to a crude intuitive level on another. This uneven development may be due to the varied content of the different problems posed in terms of the vocabulary used, the concepts involved, familiarity with the stories and the ideas within the stories. It is obvious that a child will find some stories harder to think about than other stories, not only because of the intrinsic difficulties but also because of varied experience and motivation.

Here are a few examples of both kinds of individual differences. Colin, aged 8 : 9 with a mental age of 7 : 5, a regular attender at a Church of England Sunday school, backward in day school. On two questions he attains concrete operations, on two he only achieves an intermediate level between intuitive and concrete thinking, but on one question he attains formal operations. Mental age is not important in Colin's case, but church attendance obviously is. Conversely the case of Cynthia shows two possible factors at work. Cynthia has militantly agnostic parents, no church connections, and at the chronological age of 7 : 5 has a mental age of 8 : 0. She scores well ahead of her peers with two concrete operational responses, one intermediate between intuitive and concrete, and one intermediate concrete to formal operational response. Her range is considerable from intuitive almost to formal level. Her better performance would be best explained in terms of her mental ability, or the impact of freshness of most of the stories heightening her interest and motivation.

Stephen, on the other hand, at 7 : 8 has a mental age of 8 : 7, is a regular attender at a Free Church Sunday school and has fairly consistent responses of intermediate concrete to formal operations, with one exception at a concrete level only. Both his mental ability and his church attendance might account for his higher levels of thinking. Again, by contrast, William at 11 : 9 with a mental age of 11 : 10, also a Free Church regular weekly Sunday school attender, has two intuitive responses, two concrete operational responses and one intermediate between them. Here is a case where attendance, though regular at church, may be enforced and motivation is low. About the same age, a girl Lesley, 11 : 5 with a mental age of 10 : 7 who goes nowhere and has no religious support from parents, achieves one formal operational response, three intermediate concrete to formal and one intuitive response, a very good average for a non-attender.

Christopher, a Grammar schoolboy, aged 14 : 5 and a mental age of 17 : 6, a regular Church of England attender, confirmed and a choirboy, attains five formal operational responses, with an absolutely consistent level of thinking. Contrast with this Theresa, a regular Free Church weekly attender, aged 16 : 1 with a mental age of 17 : 1, who achieves two formal operations, one intermediate, one concrete and one intermediate intuitive to concrete operations.

These are only a few examples, but they should be sufficient to illustrate the uneven power of thinking exercised by many pupils.

LOGICAL AND THEOLOGICAL THINKING

From our findings so far we have seen that religious thinking employs the same modes and methods as thinking applied to other fields. The child tries to think as systematically, consistently and operationally as his own development and the religious material with which he is presented will allow. The methods of thinking, of course, cannot be divorced from its content and it is interesting to see that when the five questions were evaluated by psychologists on an 'operational' scale and quite independently evaluated by theologically trained scorers on a theological scale, there was a very high correlation between the two sets of scores.[1] The lowest correlations were to be seen in responses to the questions, 'How would you explain the bush burning?' and 'How would you explain the dividing of the waters of the Red Sea?' Both these questions involve, on the theological assessment, concepts of miracle where non-rational factors may exercise a stronger influence on thinking than in the other questions. Here we are dealing with belief as much as with intellectual

[1] The coefficients of correlation (product-moment) ranged from 0·78 to 0·89.

judgments. Nevertheless, even in these questions there is a significant agreement between the way in which the intellectual patterns of development occur.

This supports the view that theologic and logic are closely related. Once the act of faith is made in terms of believing in God, logical forms are used in much the same way as in other areas of experience. While there is a continuous fusion between intellect and emotion, between fact and faith, in the child's religious development, he is only able to form a theological view of his world, at a level which his current stage of 'operational' thinking will allow. The child's theologic is determined by his normal thought processes, and he applies these normal processes to the nature, activity and power of God, to his notions of what kind of book is the Bible, what is the Church, how prayer operates and many other religious problems. We shall see in detail how this affects the level of the child's religious thinking in subsequent chapters, especially in terms of the limitations imposed. The implications of this fact are very far reaching for religious education.

One fact must be faced from our analysis of 'operational' religious thinking. It is clear that because the forms of thought used by children are childish and immature, children's religious ideas and their concepts will also be childish and immature. We should not expect anything other than this. What is disturbing is that the childish immaturities continue so long into adolescence. A great deal of religious thinking is propositional and therefore can only be dealt with at a formal operational level of thought, to be intellectually satisfying. If 13 to 14 is the mental age at which this level in religious thinking is generally achieved, a great deal of time and effort may be wasted by the instruction in ideas which are beyond the comprehension of the child. The problem, however, is not quite so extreme when we see that the mental age of 13 to 14, mentioned as a boundary between concrete and abstract thinking, may perhaps be lowered with better teaching. This better teaching will avoid instruction in ideas far too difficult for the child to grasp; it will seek not to reinforce crude immaturities but to wean the child away from them; and, while allowing a child's religion to be childish, will prepare him for a more critical and rational approach to religion with which to face the years of adolescence.

Chapter Five

CONCEPTS OF THE BIBLE

THE Bible is the major source book of religious teaching in our culture. It provides stories from the myths, legends and historical narratives of the Hebrew people; it contains the poetry and song of this deeply religious nation; it shows the dramatic conflict between prophets and rulers; it attains a climax of conflict and consummation in the New Testament narrative of Jesus Christ and in the beginnings of Christianity in the growth of the Early Church. The Bible is the documentation of a revealed religion and is largely a description of how revelations of the divine came to men and what these encounters between God and man revealed. Two words are commonly used to describe what the Bible is in terms of its religious value. The first is 'inspired' and the second is 'unique'. Many differing interpretations are placed on the meanings of biblical inspiration and uniqueness. A small minority tends to represent a biblio-centric viewpoint and to regard the Scriptures as directly inspired by God, holding that its authority lies in the words themselves. Inspiration is almost regarded by this group as infallibility, and the Bible is true because it claims to be true. That claim is authoritative because it stems directly from God. At the other extreme is another small minority who would interpret these words in a very liberal manner, seeing the Bible as one of the sources of religious truth but as essentially a man-made account of his own search for God, inspired indirectly by the divine and containing a unique account of this search of one particular nation.

In between these two extremes the current view of biblical theology, to which the majority of Bible scholars would subscribe, occupies a middle position. It does not subscribe to the infallibility of scripture but places it in an important central position, and while utilising critical modern scholarship has tended to react against much of the analytical criticism of the past fifty years.

The church, when drawing up its education programmes, and local education authority syllabus committees generally, have tended to reflect this central position in assuming that much Bible material should be used in the religious education of children. Irrespective of what the child is able to understand in terms of the Bible's inspiration and uniqueness, it is invariably assumed that from an early age,

68

with careful selection, the child ought to be exposed to the Bible's content, the amount increasing with the growing years. Before we go on to examine children's capacity to understand the Bible's message, it is important to know how the Bible as a book is regarded by children generally. For this general appraisal and intellectual judgment of the nature, authority, truth and relevance of scripture on the part of children, will inevitably colour what they accept and think about its content. Certainly, the Bible is seen from an early age as an important book, used in church and school, read at all kinds of religious services (sometimes in a special voice and in a highly artificial manner) and to the child the adult world appears to respect and revere it. Even parents no longer accepting the Bible's truth will hesitate to criticise it before their children. We shall see now what concepts the child has formed about the Bible and what ideas he has acquired from the adult assumptions about the scriptures to which he has been continually exposed.

CONCEPTS OF WHAT KIND OF BOOK?

One of the three pictures shown to the children was designed to evoke the concept behind the question, 'What kind of book is the Bible?'[1] The picture is one of a child looking at a mutilated Bible and it was explained that a younger child had torn it and scribbled all over it. There was a fairly common response by children of all ages to this situation, this usually being one of condemning the child responsible for having done such a dreadful thing. A few said it was naughty because no book should be treated in this way, but most conveyed real concern that it was the Bible particularly that had been damaged. All children showed in these discussions that they regarded the Bible as a special kind of book, many of them using the words 'different' and others naming it 'holy'. When these children were asked why it is different and holy, when compared with other books, a very frequent reply was 'It's about God and Jesus.' The words 'different', 'special' and 'holy' were used almost interchangeably in the child's vocabulary, and the Bible is seen as unique generally because it deals with God, Jesus or other people classified in the child's mind as 'holy'. This, however, is fairly clearly circular reasoning since it was also evident from discussion that the children regarded these as holy because they were in the Bible. An example of this very vague concept is seen in Harold's replies (C.A. 10 : 2), 'It's naughty for the boy's small brother to have done that. *Why?* It's all about stories of Jesus and God. *Why shouldn't you do that to such*

[1] See Appendix A. Picture 3 and the questions under headings P.3. Q.1, Q2, and Q.3.

stories? The Bible guards you, sort of. It's special. *How is it special?* It's stories about Jesus. *There are other books about Jesus.* The Bible are all true stories about Jesus. It's holy. *How do you mean, holy?* It's stories about God.' Since its association with God and Jesus was almost universal the reasons behind the uniform response were of greater interest. An analysis of these differing responses led to the building up, with age and the growth of insight, of concepts of the Bible.

The significance of the Bible is seen by younger children to be its physical nature or its associated use. 'It's a big book and it's got small print.' 'It's got a lot of teeny print and it's got no pictures in it.' 'It's big and black and holy.' 'It's a church book and you take it to church.' 'It's got commandments and psalms in it.' 'It's what the Vicar reads from.' One seven year old complained, 'You can't see the writing; it's so small you can't read it.' A six year old said it was special 'because you have to take it to the church. It's got a blue top on and you take it to church.' When asked why it was called the Holy Bible, she replied, 'It's got holy in it. *How do you mean?* People get stones and chuck it at the book,' so revealing the simple association with 'holes'. Another older child says, 'It's read on Sunday and Sunday was holy so they call it Holy Bible.' These very limited views tend to be common and continue until about M.A. 10 : 1 (C.A. 9 : 8).

The next step appears to be where these external factors of appearance, print and usage are left behind and the concept now centres upon the Bible as the only completely true book, the oldest book or a book from which we learn about God and Jesus. Attention has moved to the content but insight is very limited and the generalisations made are very sweeping. For example, when children say the Bible is a true book, they are extremely vague. Timothy, for example. 'The Bible is a sort of true word, it tells the truth. That's why it's special. *Are there any other true books?* Oh yes, a cookery book is true. *Then how is the Bible different from these?* The Bible's got Jesus' name in it. God himself printed his own name in it.' He falls back on a fairly magical explanation. Another boy is more precise. 'It's all about God, it's stories about him. *Are there other books about God?* Yes, but the Bible's thicker. *Why do they call it Holy Bible?* It's true. Everything in it is true. They are what happened, what really happened to God.' Here we can see a firmly established literalism of the Bible operating. A slightly more selective answer from a nine year old girl is, 'A lot of it's about people who have done good things. *How do you mean?* Some of it's about Jesus and the disciples.'

As a teaching book many children revere it, some not necessarily because of its content, but simply because it is taught from. 'You learn about Jesus in it and you know he's with you all the time.'

'It teaches you all about God, Jesus and his disciples. *Why is it called Holy Bible?* There are religious things inside it. *How do you mean? What is true about God.*' Fred, aged 6 : 7 but with an IQ of 131 says, 'It's a good book. It tells you how to be holy. *How do you mean, holy?* It tells you what God does. It's a good book to read. *Are there other books about God?* No, none 'cept fiction. The Bible is true stories. *Why is it called Holy Bible?* 'Cause it *is* holy. It tells you about God. *I have some other books about God.* The Bible tells you *more* stories about God than other books.' This is interesting because it reveals a quantitative judgment. Occasionally, there is an appeal to age. 'It's got things in it that people did a long time ago. *Is it different from a history book?* Yes, some of it's about before Jesus was born, like David. *There are other books about David.* The Bible's holy, and it's usually very old.' Rose, aged 10 : 4 (M.A. 11 : 8) says, 'The Bible is before Jesus. It's got an Old Testament (emphasis on "old") nearly from the very beginning of the world.' These kind of concepts for most children continue until about M.A. 13 : 1 (C.A. 12 : 6).

The next stage refines formerly held ideas and now we see the development of concepts dependent upon insight into the teaching content in terms of how the Bible helps people and how the Bible is true because it is based on eye-witness accounts. Compared with other books now it has more truth and religious meaning in it. Here are some examples. 'It's a special thing you worship to God with and read about people who've done good. It tells you what to do and what not to do. *Why is it chosen for worship?* It's one thing which has come from the past.' A little more mature expression of this is, 'You learn a lot of things from the Bible you can't get from other books. *How do you mean?* It can help you to grow up if you read it regularly. If he's particularly Christian he might want to be a vicar, someone who works in the Church.' On the truth of the Bible based upon eye-witness accounts one girl puts it, 'It's not a story book. It's about true things about God. *Are there other true books about God?* Yes, but in the Bible the prophets passed it on all the way through.' Another more precisely says, 'It's the Jesus' followers' words and what Jesus taught them. *I have a book about the followers of Jesus.* Your book wasn't written by the apostles themselves and the Bible was. They saw it all.' And another, 'Luke wrote about God and Jesus. He was alive with Jesus and was one of his followers.' A girl says, 'In the Bible you get the actual words spoken by Jesus.' A thirteen year old boy of average intelligence, with no church connections, says: 'It is treated, to most people, as the best book in the world. (Q) The stories are more exciting to people who believe. (Q) It's got more books in one book. It's all made up from true stories of what has happened, and it's in every home. There are so many versions of it.'

These types of answers continue to approximately 14 : 8 (M.A. 16 : 7) and tend to represent the final concepts of most Secondary Modern school leavers.

Finally, the book is seen as an original source book of religion through revelation, based upon concepts of its origins and its importance in man's struggle for truth. The emphasis is now placed upon its spiritual meaning and significance. This is expressed in various ways. Tom aged 11 : 5 (his M.A. is 14 : 2) says: 'It's God's Word. *How do you mean?* It's how Christianity came to the world. It's God's message to his people. *I have other books about Christianity. Is the Bible different?* No, it isn't. All religious books are important.' Another boy, Christopher, at 14 (M.A. 15·0) says, 'It's a history of the people who formed the religion. It's the original book about this religion.' A qualified version of this is given by a thirteen year old Grammar school girl, 'It tells all about different men who believed in God and what happened to them, not as history. It's about belief in God, not pure history.' A Grammar school boy put it in this way, 'The Bible is the original one written by the true followers of God. It's like God talking to us through the Bible.' A literal minded 16 year old says, 'It's God's direct word to man. Christ tells us to search the Scriptures. *How do you mean, direct word?* It was given to his prophets and elders to write down. God must tell them, to inspire them to write. *What about other religious books?* The Bible is directly inspired by God and the others were maybe helped by God, but they only put their own thoughts on paper.' Another boy about the same age says, 'It tells the story of God being on the earth and his saving of us. In this way it has become a sacred emblem of God.' A very intelligent boy says forthrightly, 'It's a holy book, but you've got to find the meaning for yourself. *How is it holy?* It's supposed to be the Word of God, like the ten commandments in it. He didn't speak direct. He spoke it through writers.' An intending science specialist says, 'Physically, it isn't different. It's the contents. It's the whole essence of the Christian faith, the words directly or indirectly of God. *Other religious books?* They were written by people using the Bible as a source book.'

We can see the development of concepts about the Bible, moving from ideas limited by physical ideas of size, colour, print and its external uses, into some limited insight into an old, venerated, literally true document which is important because it is used as a teaching book; then it is seen as helpful in personal living and finally it is seen as the summation of man's spiritual experience as he meets God in history. We shall understand the content of this development more fully when we have examined how children think the Bible originated.

CONCEPTS OF HOW THE BIBLE CAME TO BE WRITTEN

A question of importance was: 'How did the Bible come to be written?' which was supplemented by questions such as, 'Why would anyone want to write it?' designed to see what concepts children had about Bible authorship and the motives of such authors on writing the scriptures.[1] Three different qualities of concepts emerged clearly with the increasing age and ability of children.

First, the Bible is regarded as having been written by God or Jesus by one powerful person or a very religious man. It is, at this stage, seen as a unitary composition, and this limitation may be due to the rather magical associations of the Bible, or limitations of knowledge that some books can be written by a number of authors. Six year olds, for example, say: 'Jesus thought of the stories and God wrote them down', or 'God did it, on his typewriter.' Another six year old says, 'God. *Why did he do it?* So people could read it. *Why did he want people to read it?* To learn at school and the writing.' A seven year old replies: 'Jesus; he came down from the sky and wrote it with his pen.' Another seven year old says, 'Jesus—I mean God. *Why would he want to write it?* To send it to little children so that they can read it. It helps them to read and write.' The answer may be a human regarded by the child as important enough to do such a holy task, such as 'A king or a queen', 'The vicar 'cause he loves God and Jesus and 'cause Bibles are in his church.' The child who answers seriously, 'Enid Blyton' is probably thinking of her Bible books and not Miss Blyton as a prolific author. Misled by associations one child asks, 'It was someone called Christopher, wasn't it? *Why?* For people to learn prayers.' Perhaps the association here is with the Christopher Robin poem. Another replies, 'A very religious man like Stephen, who wanted to be forgiven.' Sometimes it is a disciple or an old wise man or 'people who found old tablets of stone' but in the end only one of them is responsible. An eight year old boy Colin (IQ 105) says, 'One man did it, one who was very good at writing stories. *How did he get the stories?* He was probably taught them in a classroom as a little boy. *Why would he want to write them down?* The man liked the stories.'

A nine year old refines this, but its unitary concept is essentially the same, 'A man in Jesus' time wrote about what Jesus did. After the man died, the book was found, copied and circulated.' An older boy (11 years) with an M.A. of 9 : 7 says, 'It was someone who believed a lot in God and started to write about him, and all the stories. *How so?* He picked them up in his mind when he was praying or lying

[1] See Appendix A, question P.3: Q.4.

in bed. *Why should he want to write them down?* He would know God
would love him for writing the stories.' This stage goes on for most
children until about M.A. 9 : 7 and chronologically just over nine
years, although some children continue even later. An example of
this is Harry, C.A. 8 : 10 (M.A. 10 : 11) who maintains 'God or Jesus
wrote it', and Fred aged C.A. 11 : 8 (M.A. 11 : 5), 'God would have.
He could have wrote it with a pen on parchment and then some other
people copied it, so it's like a Bible today. It was translated. It could
have been in French or anything.'

A second stage in the children's thinking moves on to some concepts of multiple authorship, based upon eye-witness accounts or an
oral tradition, but these ideas are frequently confused. Here is a ten
year old's reply, 'By a man who knows all the things Jesus did and
writ it down in a book. He didn't write it all. Another man wrote the
first part. One man couldn't be everywhere Jesus went.' Sometimes
the answer is very general, such as 'People who lived in Palestine
where God and Jesus were', or more specific, in terms of 'disciples
and prophets'. There is a frequent confusion of the Old and New
testaments, sometimes 'Christians' writing the Old Testament. Here
are some typical responses. Maurice 13 : 10 (M.A. 11 : 5), 'When
they heard what Jesus did the priests in the Church wrote it in a big
book. *Who were these priests?* They were his disciples and they saw
what he did. The disciples wrote all the Bible and the monks copied
it later.' Ronald 12 : 2 (M.A. 11 : 5), 'It was religious people who believed in God. They saw things happen at the time. I don't know the
names of any of them.' Dick 13 : 0 (M.A. 12 : 1), 'The disciples of
Jesus, like Mark. They was with God when it happened. It was like
a diary each day. The prophets and Moses wrote the rest. The Old
Testament is much older and people saw what Moses did and wrote
it like diaries.'

Diary reporting gives way to a more sophisticated view, but still
confused, as for example, Bill aged 11 : 6 (M.A. 12 : 5), 'By the
Greeks who translated it out of Hebrew. The Hebrews wrote it. The
Babylonians rescued them from the Phoenicians. They (the Hebrews)
wrote The Old Testament. The New Testament was written by S.
John, S. Mark, S. Luke and S. Matthew, some of God's followers.'
And Alyson 14 : 10 (M.A. 13 : 8), 'It was first written on long pieces
of paper by rabbis and scribes and S. Luke—he wrote the Gospel and
Acts. Some saw it happen and others heard stories from others.' This
stage continued roughly until about 14½ years and a mental age of
about 15 : 8, until the confusions are resolved and concepts of multiple
authorship are seen clearly.

Another characteristic of this final stage is that inspiration rather
than accuracy is the major characteristic inherent in a multiple

authorship view. Here are some examples. Janet aged 13 : 2 but with a mental age of 16 : 6 says, 'Priests and scribes of long ago have gathered stories and put them together in one book. (Q) Followers of Jesus in the New Testament first wrote the stories and in the Old Testament some people who were well known wrote them down. They only put down what had happened before they lived, mostly from people who *had* seen it.' A fifth former in Grammar school says, 'It's a collection of Pharisees who wrote it for the good of the people. They collected all the books into one and made a complete book. They were never written by one person, even one book wasn't. The stories were handed down verbally and then they were written down.' He adds, 'The Old Testament involved miraculous stories of eating up enemies by fire. The New Testament is more readable and shows how to treat enemies differently. The Old Testament is much more difficult, and there's more of it.' One sixth former comments, 'Many Old Testament documents were administrative rather than religious documents . . . the scribes were guided, putting down what God wanted them to. They wouldn't have put down blasphemy. They were God-fearing Jews.' Others specifically mention the possible fallibility of the Bible record. 'The people who wrote it are inspired, not the Bible.' 'In my own view half of it can't be true; half of it is legend. It's true but the basic details can't be true if it depends on oral tradition.'

We can therefore see in these three stages a progression of concepts from a book with unitary authorship, to a book of multiple authorship but some real confusion about the origins of stories and leading to a multiple authorship view without confusions, which also shows an awareness of the Bible as a fallible record as well as an inspired one. What is interesting is the approximate similarity of the first stage age boundary with that of the first stage of concepts about what kind of book the Bible is. Up to approximately ten years the child's view is that the Bible is a special thick, black, holy book with tiny print and obscure language which God, Jesus or a powerful person wrote, not for any particular religious purpose but for other reasons. Only after this age does insight into the religious nature of the scriptures begin to develop.

CONCEPTS OF THE BIBLE AS TRUE

Concepts of what kind of book the Bible is and how it came to be written, appear to be related to what degree children think the Bible to be true. From replies in previous sections we have seen how many children have themselves used the word 'true' to describe an essential characteristic of the scriptures. It is evident that children do not appear to question the veracity of the biblical record and up to a fairly late stage in their development use the term 'true' in a very literal sense. This naturally limits their insights where what is literally true cannot be distinguished from what is true symbolically. To know how the child responds to the Bible in terms of its truth is of great importance to the educator. With this in mind the pupils were asked, after each Bible story discussion had been completed, 'Do you think this story really happened?' To clarify the quality of the simple affirmative or negative replies further questions were asked such as 'Is all of it or part of it true?' and 'What makes you think so?'[1] Incorporated as a check, a further question was put during discussion of the Exodus story. 'Is everything in the Bible true?'[2] We shall now examine the children's ideas on these questions in detail.

On the simple assertions positive and negative about the Bible's truth a few pupils said none of the stories really happened at all. It was striking that these seven children were all six years old and of low mental ability. The inference can fairly be made that these children were unable to understand the question or merely made random answers. These children apart, the rest could be described in various ways. There were those with a basic literal level where all three stories were accepted as literally true. There were the near-literalists who accepted two stories in this way but felt doubt about one of them. There were those partly critical of two of the three stories, accepting them only with critical reservations. Finally, there were pupils who were fully critical of all the stories and rejected them as literally true. The story showing the most literal responses was the Temptations of Jesus. Since few pupils recognised it as a parable, it is presumably more credible as it stands than the two Old Testament stories. This interpretation would include the devil as an actual person, Jesus going up literally to the pinnacle of the temple and onto the summit of a high mountain. The age 'boundaries' of literalism can be seen from the table on the opposite page.

'Full literalism' is where all three stories are accepted as literally true, and 'full or near-literalism' is where two out of the three stories are so accepted. It will be seen that the majority are literalist (58·9 per cent) or near literalist (80 per cent) up to almost 13 years of age, the percentages falling after this but still with sizeable proportions remaining literalists. The major swing does not appear to be until 15 years. In terms of mental age the divisions are much more marked. From this table, three stages seem to emerge fairly clearly in terms of chronological age—a basic literal stage (up to about 12 : 11), an intermediate partly critical stage (from about 12 : 11 to about 14 : 11),

[1] See Appendix A, questions S.1 : Q.7, S.2 : Q.6, and S.3 : Q.6.
[2] See Appendix A, question S.2 : Q.7.

and a fully critical stage from 15 years onwards. If some 57 per cent are full or near literalists until the end of their fourteenth year this may be an indication of the state of most pupils leaving their Secondary Modern school. The sudden drop to 15 per cent from this time onwards may be because our sample of pupils from 15 to 17 years were those staying on at school, possessing a significantly higher level of ability and perhaps more used to active exercises in critical thinking. The true picture of the middle-adolescent population may not show this sharp drop. It may indicate why so many adolescents reject religion as childish, since they hold on to childishly literal views of the Bible until they are no longer tenable and then abandon them, perhaps suddenly during an emotional or intellectual disturbance.

PERCENTAGES OF LITERALISM ON COMBINED STORY RESULTS

	Age groupings	Full literalism	Full or Near-literalism
Chron. Age	Up to 12:11	58·9%	80·0%
	13:0–14:11	30·0%	57·5%
	15:0 on	5·0%	15·0%
Mental Age	Up to 12:5	60·0%	83·3%
	12:5–17:6	35:0%	55·0%
	17:6 on	5:0%	25·0%

A closer examination of the children's answers gives a much clearer idea, not only of what they think about the truth of the Bible, but also their reasons for thinking so. Three stages can be very clearly seen in the development of concepts.

The first stage shows irrelevant and sometimes repetitious answers by the younger children leading into acceptance of the Bible as authoritatively true because of God being the writer or because of the assurance of adults. Examples of purely repetitious or irrelevant answers can be seen in typical responses, such as, 'It's true. I just know it is,' 'Everyone knows it's true,' 'It's there so it must be true.' Answers using external authority can be seen in the following replies, 'It's in the Bible and the Bible is true,' 'It's written down, so it must be true,' 'My mother says it is,' 'The vicar tells us it is,' 'It's an old story and wouldn't have lasted if it was untrue,' 'Everyone believes it or tells the stories,' and 'God (or Jesus) writ it and they don't tell lies.' Chronologically this stage appears to extend to about 10½ years of age (M.A. approximately 11 : 0) and many of these answers reflect the normal assumptions of Primary school children. The authority of the adult world is still highly regarded, and the child at this stage over-simplifies 'truth' in terms of its immoral opposite, the telling of lies.

It is shocking to the children who voice this objection frequently that God or Jesus should be associated with lies. This is the response of the pious literalist who cannot admit that the Bible record may be inconsistent or fallible, because he fears once you begin questioning a little you cannot stop and the whole authority of the Bible is undermined. Reverence for the printed word, of course, is not restricted to childhood but there is a wholehearted and uncritical character about this childhood respect which is not reproduced in adult life.

The second stage may be described as concepts of authority stemming from God, or Jesus, not as the writer of the stories but as the originator of the action in the stories. God, at this stage, is seen as all powerful and the stories must be true because God is associated with them and the deity can do anything. Typical answers are, 'It must be true 'cause God and Jesus are in it,' 'All stories about God are true,' 'God can do that sort of thing and he was there,' 'It's the sort of normal thing God would do.' A few express the view that 'It sounds true; it's put in a convincing way; the words sound right,' but are unable to explain this further. One boy with a mental age of 12 : 7 says, 'If the stories were wrong or untrue, God would stop letting everyone know.' A rather naïve view of the Burning Bush is taken by Mary aged fourteen, with a mental age of 10 : 9, who says, 'It's been proved by people going over there to see the place where it's supposed to happen.' She accepts all of the temptation as true because, 'It seems real enough. The places where it happened are real.' This stage for most children appears up to about the age of 12½ (mental age of 13 : 0).

Finally a stage can be seen where the story is accepted as authentic because it is somehow based upon eye-witness accounts, or it is true because it is consistent with other sources or one's own inner experience. The later levels of this stage obviously indicate quite advanced thinking and the development of a critical approach to the scriptures. Up to this stage most children accept all of the stories as true, but after this it is apparent that the children are beginning to question certain literal elements of the story. Some examples of the authority of eye-witnesses can be seen in responses to the Old Testament stories, 'Moses wrote it down as soon as it happened', and in relation to the Temptations, 'Jesus told his disciples and they writ it.' A more general reply is this, 'People saw it happen, it got passed down by word of mouth and then it was put in the Bible.'

The consistency reasons can be illustrated from the following examples, 'It's the sort of thing that could happen to a believer. Moses was a holy man, a believer. It could happen to him.' Conversely the occasional child says, 'None of it is true. It's too unusual to happen', but more pupils say 'It is so unusual a thing, who'd want to invent it?

It's not the sort of thing people would make up.' In the Temptation story many replies were of the kind, 'It's normal or human to be tempted. Jesus was a man, so he'd be tempted.' A much more advanced argument of consistency is expressed in the answer, 'It's not so true historically, but it may be in a deeper sense, perhaps parabolically', or in the Exodus story, 'It explains how Moses came to lead his people out. If that sort of thing hadn't happened, the slaves would never be free', and in the Temptation story, 'It's a parable to teach all men how to overcome evil; all four Gospel writers wrote it down.'

The check question dealing with 'Is everything in the Bible true?' reveals the same stages as in the previous question, the answers being of similar content and quality. It is of interest to see the answers to a supplementary question, asked if the child expressed a negative to everything in the Bible being true. If the child said 'No', the question put was, 'How can we tell what is true and not true in the Bible?' First stage replies were, 'Some are holy and some are not. The Old Testament didn't happen, but the New Testament did' (here presumably because Jesus appears in one but not in the other) and 'Jesus told the people before us which were true and untrue.' Second stage replies, still authoritative because Jesus or God are associated, tend to be similar to 'If Jesus or God's in it we know it's true. Wrong parts may be bad print' and, 'God tells you in your mind. Most things you can't understand are not true.' Stage three answers allow for error and begin to use 'true' in a relative rather than a moral sense. 'There are only a few parts which aren't true, like in Ruth, Solomon was wise. The scientists have proved it all from old scrolls in these jars. Some bits got altered through the ages to make it more sensible.' 'The parables aren't true, they are only used to illustrate meaning. All the rest is true.' 'You have to think what things could happen. Like if someone said he's swum the Atlantic, you wouldn't expect it to happen.' 'Where there's poetic licence and things are added for dramatic effect.'

To sum up, concepts of the authority of the Bible as 'true' in relation to all three stories tend to show belief in it because of external authority. 'God, or Jesus wrote it,' 'It's written down,' 'My mummy, the vicar, or teacher said it's true,' about M.A. 11 : 0 (C.A. 10 : 6). It is true after this age for most pupils because its subject matter is God and Jesus, or the words themselves sound true. Only later at about M.A. 15 : 0 (C.A. 14 : 0) is it true because it is based upon eyewitness accounts or its consistency with other sources. At this time pupils tend to see its authority in terms of how it speaks to human experience, not in terms of externally induced authority. This is roughly substantiated by crude Yes/No answers which reveal a basic literal stage to about C.A. 12 : 11, an intermediate, partly critical, stage from about 12 : 11 to 14 : 11 and a fully critical stage about C.A. 15 : 0 onwards. Qualitative answers tend to show a slackening of literalism by the twelfth year. It is probably that they are becoming critical about certain aspects of the Bible some time before they consciously recognise their own emerging criticisms.

Acceptance of the written word, of course, is not confined to the Bible since there is a fairly wide conviction, not limited to school pupils, that the printed word is true because it has attained the prestige of being printed. When to this is added the weight of associations with God, divine authority and many adults, it is not surprising that literalism persists until well into the secondary school years. Is it because the beginnings of criticism of the Bible comes in the early, difficult years of adolescence, that pupils will swing to an extremely critical position towards the end of their secondary schooling? Do they become hostile to religion because they recognise childish patterns of thinking as inadequate and are not offered a satisfactory intellectual alternative to literalism? Loukes (1961) discovered among secondary school leavers frequent complaints of 'childish' religious and biblical teaching.

CONCEPTS OF THE RELEVANCE AND POSSIBLE RECURRENCE OF BIBLICAL EXPERIENCE

One aim of religious education is to help children to see the personal relevance of what is being taught. Unless religion is understood as a continuing experience and perceived as an interpretation of contemporary life, it will be relegated to the past and although of interest will be regarded as irrelevant to normal living. There is no conflict between seeing the Bible as a unique religious book and the attempt to interpret it in terms of contemporary experience. As M. V. C. Jeffreys (1955) has written, 'Religious truth is normal experience understood at full depth; what makes truth religious is not that it relates to some abnormal field of thought and feeling, but that it goes to the roots of the experience which it interprets.' Much of the Bible, especially in the Gospels, is unique and many historical events can never occur again. Even so, the Bible speaks of underlying religious truth which is normal experience understood at full depth at any age and in any society. If this were not so, it would remain merely a series of documents of interest only to the historian and antiquarian. It is therefore of importance to understand how relevant to modern times the child considers biblical experiences to be. Does he view Bible incidents as only relevant to the past, or can he grasp the idea of continuing truths so that the eternal spiritual issues presented by the Bible are also seen as contemporary?

After each story was discussed, I asked questions designed to evaluate the possible relevance for the child concerned and to discover what transfer, if any, from biblical to present times occurred in his thinking.[1] After the Burning Bush story 'If it happened in Bible times could it happen now?' was asked and the reasons for the child's answers were explored. Following the Exodus story the question posed was, 'Could this story happen today in real life' with the elaboration that it would have to be different people and places, naturally. The reasons for the child's answers were again discussed, with an additional question if the child answered 'No', 'Why did it happen in Bible times but not now?' The Temptations as a continuing experience was explored by the final question, 'Is the devil still about today, telling people to do wrong?'

Although greater value is to be gained from examining the pupils' reasons for saying 'Yes' or 'No' the plain 'Yes' and 'No' answers to these questions are of interest. These were as follows:

Story	Yes	No	Unsure
The Burning Bush	110	87	3
Crossing the Red Sea	108	90	2
The Temptations	137	62	1

The proportion of those in the first two stories is very much larger than in the third story of those who find it difficult to see any relevance for today. The third story is, however, easier to see as relevant since even the youngest child knows what it is to be tempted to do wrong. The form of the question also tends to clarify the issue for the child ('Is the devil still about today, tempting us to do wrong?') in a way, perhaps, that the other two questions do not. 'Could it happen today?' is a much more general question. In addition, the Old Testament stories may be more remote in time and experience, although chronologically the young child's known confusion about historical sequence may cancel this out.

By a graded scoring device I was able to assess each child's consistency and arrived at the following figures.

Those consistently seeing relevance in all stories	74 ⎱ Relevance for	
Those seeing relevance in two stories	41 ⎰ today view	
Those seeing relevance in only one story	52 ⎱ Isolation in	
Those seeing all the stories as isolated in history	33 ⎰ time view	

If the first two and last two are grouped together we can conveniently term the 115 children, who saw relevance in two or three stories, as

[1] See Appendix A, questions S.1: Q.8B, S.2: Q.8A and S.3: Q.5A.

the 'Relevant for today' group, and the 85 children, who saw no or little relevance, as the 'Isolation in History' group. There was a clear division between the mental ages of both groups, most children having to attain a mental age 13 : 0 to move from the 'Isolation in History' view to that of the 'Relevance for today' view. We must accept this age boundary with caution, since given different biblical stories the result will vary. There is sufficient evidence here, however, to suggest that between 12 and 13 years of age the tendency to relate the stories to today will be evident and a greater willingness to admit their possible recurrence with different people and at differing times.

We now turn to the reasons behind the simple answers and three stages emerge in the quality of answers. The first is where the children firmly isolate the incidents in history and answers here give such reasons as, 'It was in the olden days,' 'They dressed differently and it was a different part of the world' and 'God (or Jesus) isn't alive now. He's gone back to heaven,' 'God is dead; his miracles have wasted and he doesn't do it now. He's dead up in the sky and he lives all over the world.' 'He doesn't want to. He might be running out of breath.' The child who gave the last answer does concede that God 'could speak to someone from the tops of trees.' One child says it would happen now but doesn't because, 'If we was good then God could come down and speak to us. But we're not good.' In the Burning Bush story one child replies, 'Moses was one of God's sons. He has none living now.' Concerning the Temptations, answers at this stage to the question of the devil being alive and active today show a similar 'isolation' view. 'He died of old age.' 'He was killed by God because he was evil.' 'He was put in a lion's den and eaten.' 'He was caught by the Romans and crucified by Jesus.' 'He's up in the sky. He's a giant.' Slightly better answers are, 'He's just left us alone. He doesn't bother us now because God stopped him, by punishing him,' 'It doesn't want to do it all the time, not every day, but he comes back occasionally,' and 'He would make the world unhappy. The world is happier now.' This stage, where clearly Bible experience is very remote, is firmly established until about $9\frac{1}{2}$ years (M.A. 10 : 0) but continues for many children after these ages.

There then appears an intermediate stage where most children make erroneous attempts to explain differences, and sometimes, the similarities between ancient and modern times. For some, God is willing and able to intervene again but he is available only for a sufficient reason. Here are some examples. 'More people believe in God and Jesus now.' 'We don't need it now. We've got the Bible and we can see his message in other ways.' 'He doesn't need prophets. There are so many priests now and they know.' Of the Burning Bush, there are several specific comments, 'There are more people about now and less lonely places,' and 'I've never heard of anyone now seeing God.' In the Crossing of the Sea, salvation is seen as limited to certain features, as in the responses, 'It could happen once in a million years. But there are no slaves now,' and 'There are no refugees. If there are we all give money and God needn't help.' At this stage many children say God could do it, although such an action might be arbitrary or haphazard, 'It could be but there aren't many slaves today and people don't want to get out of a country very often.' 'God can do anything, but it's not likely now.' 'The beavers could still dig all through and block the sides up.' And the charmingly naïve reason, 'The people in those days could have believed it. Today the world is so big people wouldn't believe it.' Whereas in the previous stage those children who could see the devil still active express it in crude magical terms ('He casts a spell over you and tells you to do wrong,' 'He scares people at night and tells them wrong things'), at this stage evil is only seen in spectacular activities, such as in murder or crime. Some examples are, 'That little girl was murdered. He tells in people's minds to do evil,' and 'He's in some people's minds, like murderers and thieves. *What about other people?* No, most people believe in God.'

In the third stage, more realistic differences and similarities between ancient and modern times are voiced. The event, unless it is unique, shows some consistency of recurrence in the child's mind. This stage tends to begin about 12½ years (M.A. 13 : 2) thus supporting the generalisation about the emerging of a 'relevance for today' concept about this time. Here are some typical answers: 'There are so many believers in God now; God feels speaking through prayer is enough.' The opposite is expressed, but the same level is apparent in the reply: 'People seem more cynical now . . . They might hear God speaking to them but not see the bush like that,' 'There'd be no burning bush,' says another girl, 'but God can still talk to men.' And the thoroughly consistent boy who says, 'If it happened once it would happen again. God is still alive and his power is everlasting.' Some modern equivalent to the burning bush episode is possible, say many children, 'People still have visions or dreams,' and 'If God wanted a man to do a job, a very religious man with courage, it probably would.' One sixth former says, 'How people see God will alter with the age in which it happens,' and another, 'Why should God stop his activities among men a thousand years ago?' Temptation at this stage becomes something normal in everyday life, not confined to the spectacular sinners. 'It's thought in people, two voices good and bad.' 'If you see a wallet and pick it up, there's a voice saying, "Keep it," in your mind.' Expressed in a more sophisticated manner are the replies: 'There are evil urges in people which give satisfaction and wealth. God gives us a free hand to let us do what we want,' and 'In the sense that man always fights with himself.'

These three stages of isolationist reasons up to about M.A. 10 : 0, intermediate confused views up to about M.A. 13 : 2 and a final stage of seeing genuine relevance of the stories for today after M.A. 13 : 2, are very clear in the Burning Bush story, and in the Temptations story. They are evident, though not so clearly, in the Crossing of the Red Sea insights. Perhaps they are more limited because of the physical problems of the dividing of the sea and it is not surprising that this concrete element would fix its significance more securely to a given place and time as a unique event.

Two factors appear to be at work here in the children's religious thinking. The first is the limitation of relation finding, in children not yet achieving formal operational thinking. The relating of a story and its significance to an entirely different group of people and a different society calls for abstract qualities of thought. It involves also a transfer of learning from ancient to modern, Palestinian to British, and rural to urban conditions, which is difficult for many adults to achieve. There is, however, the second factor at work, namely the quality of teaching which may try to bridge this gap of time, space and experience in the child's mind but may equally be a 'straight' presentation of stories without any attempt to relate them in a relevant manner. It would appear that there are difficulties imposed both by the natural development of the child and the confused teaching he receives, which may make the period of 12 to 13 mental years as the period when potentially he can see biblical material as relevant, speaking of ideas, situations and experiences not limited to a holy period of history, to holy people wearing special holy clothes, in a holy land far away. Many pupils well into adolescence do betray a tendency to isolate Biblical events in much the same way as a fly is trapped in amber, sealed off from the outside world. Relevance is not some additive to a religious lesson, achieved by a vague modern parallel. It only comes from a thorough-going assumption, made continually explicit, that we learn about Bible events because they speak of ordinary experience understood at full depth, in human and spiritual terms, common to both ancient and modern times.

GENERAL COMMENTS ON BIBLE CONCEPTS

The picture of how the pupil thinks about the nature of the Bible, its origins, its veracity and its relevance can be seen fairly clearly from the concepts we have just examined. For the young child until the late-Junior years are attained, it is a book of almost magical veneration, with a special exterior appearance and point, written by

God himself or a powerful adult, unwaveringly true in every point because of their holy origins, but relating to matters of long ago and far away because God has died or returned to heaven and abdicated from responsibility. These crude ideas move on towards venerating the Bible as an ancient and true book because it contains holy stories about God and Jesus and because adults teach from it. It is a book written by several people but the Old and New Testaments are confused but still literally accurate. While many pupils see it as still talking of past things a few are moving towards the view that the Bible speaks truths relevant for today. By the second year of secondary education real insights are emerging. The Bible now is a helpful book containing truths which are consistent with our own experience, the idea of its multiple authorship can be embraced without confusion and some pupils are just leaving behind their childish literalism and beginning to see the Bible as inspired but fallible. While most at this age begin to see Bible-experience as relevant to today, the connection is still very tenuous and impeded by an unwillingness to appear critical of the holy book. These views persist for most Secondary Modern school leavers and only appear to progress to a higher realistic level among those of higher ability in Grammar schools. It is evident that no real awareness of the nature of the Bible is grasped until well into the secondary school course, and even here the Bible is regarded as authoritative in a strongly literal sense. It appears that pupils are not often aware of the possibility of a critical but reverent approach to Scripture. Concepts of the nature and authorship of the Bible are extremely confused until middle-adolescence.

There would appear to be a need for parts of the religious education syllabus to deal with the whole approach to the Bible as 'true', as 'inspired', and as 'revelation'. There is every reason why this should be provided for late Juniors or early Secondary school pupils in a suitable form, and not left to the sixth form Grammar school discussion group. There is a need for children, as they enter into a more detailed study of biblical history, especially the Old Testament, to have a clearer frame of reference within which they can interpret what they read.

All concepts discussed are impeded by a natural literalism from which the adolescent is achieving some liberation. But the child's literalism regarding the Bible may be protracted far too long by teachers and clergy who fear to introduce critical ideas about the Bible to the young. Trained as many of these are in the modern critical approach of biblical theology, they often fail to communicate these ideas in the classroom or pulpit. When they talk about the Bible they may behave as disguised literalists and nourish childish misconceptions by telling stories straight, without illuminating comment. In such cases the Word may be lost in the words. As Richard Acland (1963) has pointed out, we may be sacrificing whole generations of children to literalism due to the fear of rousing the antagonism of a small but noisy minority of those who can only accept the literal truth of the Bible themselves. The teaching of religion should be aimed to make children think about the Bible, not to engender a passive acceptance, which may quickly collapse because it has no firm rational foundation.

Chapter Six

THE IDENTITY AND NATURE OF THE DIVINE

IT is inevitable in Christianity, an incarnational religion which emphasises the personal nature of God and uses human analogies such as 'Father' to describe the deity, that children and adults will think of the divine in human terms. The tendency to attribute human form and personality to God is known as anthropomorphic thinking. Some have asserted that Christianity is essentially an anthropomorphic and a materialistic religion, in the sense that the spiritual and the material are inseparable. We have already seen that other investigators, especially Piaget, have noted the tendency in young children to anthropomorphise the deity. This is a natural result of egocentric thinking where only human and childhood experiences are known. It also stems from what Bovet describes as the need of the child 'to parentalise the deity', once he discovers that his human parents are not infallible nor possessed of divine qualities, as he had previously imagined. Piaget's examples of what he calls artificialist explanations of the natural world illustrate this tendency. The sun's beginnings are caused by God lighting a fire in the sky with a match and the clouds originate from God's breath.

Although children refine their anthropomorphisms it is evident that they do not altogether outgrow them and they take them forward into adult life. For this reason we cannot, and on theological grounds should not, distinguish between anthropomorphic and non-anthropomorphic concepts of God, for this would be an unreal division, as though one is childish and crude, and the other is adult and refined. From the evidence we shall examine in this chapter, however, a real distinction can be made between anthropomorphism of a crudely physical kind, and that which sees the divine as possessing all that is highest and noblest in human life. The one at the childish level thinks of God only in human terms limited in a human sense, and the other, more maturely, thinks of God not only as superhuman but suprahuman, where human analogies about the divine nature are made with the clear recognition that they are only analogies. The limitation of the child is to take the analogy for a fact, and indeed, the language of religion may encourage him in this. The

Bible itself, especially in the myths and legends of the Old Testament shows this first level of crude anthropomorphisms. The growth of biblical literature can be said to reveal emerging ideas about the identity and nature of God. Although the concept of progressive revelation is not very fashionable these days but there is no denying the growth and refining of ideas as one moves through what Noah, Abraham, Moses, Elijah, Deutero-Isaiah and Paul claimed to be the nature of God. It is obvious that in many places there are regressions to cruder ideas in the Bible and progressive revelation must not be confused with a smooth escalator type of ascending truths. But when we have made allowances for these regressions there still remains a growth in the scriptures from a lower to a higher form of anthropomorphic thinking.

One other feature should be mentioned, and that is the problem of children in perceiving the spiritual in a material world. The transcendance of God is probably easier for the child to conceptualise about than the immanence of the divine. As we shall see, the child's early ideas of omniprescence are strikingly materialistic and physical. 'Spiritual', in contrast to material, is not a good word to use, because in a metaphysical and theological sense the one interpenetrates the other. I use it, for want of a better word, to mean ideas of a non-physical and spiritual nature. It is obvious that children will be limited in understanding religion at a spiritual level until they have achieved methods of thinking at the formal operational level, when the limitations of concretising experience are left behind and propositional thinking emerges. This is very evident in their concepts about the identity and nature of the divine, as we shall now see.

THE DEITY VISUALISED[1]

When shown a picture of a child kneeling down beside a bed, pupils were told that here was someone of their own age praying alone. In discussion more than 90 per cent of the pupils said the child in the picture was praying to God, the remainder suggested Jesus, a very small number mentioning the Holy Spirit. The children were then told that most people when they pray have a picture or an idea of God in their minds, and asked, 'What is the picture or idea of God the child in the picture has when he is praying?' The question was slightly altered where children replied that they prayed to Jesus or to the Holy Spirit, although it is evident that most younger children confused the identity of God and Jesus frequently.

A sequence of answers would be seen ranging from gross materialistic and crude anthropomorphic thinking to the view that God is

[1] See Appendix A; questions P.2: Q.4, S.1: Q.3 and S.1: Q.4.

unseeable because of his spiritual nature. To the younger child, God is seen in purely physical and human terms. Morgan, a backward six year old, supplies a vivid action picture: 'He's a man up in the sky. He chucks down all the water and it rains.' Leona aged 6 : 5 (M.A. 6 : 0) says, 'A nice person who will like you. He has a cloak and long hair, a beard and short trousers. He'd look pretty and his face'd look old.' This answer is fairly common at this age with slight variations, as is Penelope's answer (age 6 : 8, M.A. 6 : 4), 'He wears a long dress, long hair and sometimes he don't have no shoes on him.' The similarity of these answers shows a marked tendency to clothe God in Palestinian garments and when Jesus is described the same responses could be made interchangeable with those about God, as for example, Denise aged 6 : 6 (M.A. 5 : 10), 'He wears different clothes, all white, like shawls. His face would be different, like every face is different, different coloured eyes. He might look as though he wore glasses.' Occasionally God and Jesus are seen together as says Peter aged 8 years (M.A. 9 : 1), 'He'd see like a man with long hair with a cloak on and blue eyes. Jesus might be with him and they'd be sitting up in heaven.' Heaven, as 'a place up there' is a frequent locality in the child's thinking where he envisages God to be. Although the responses given so far have been those of younger pupils they could equally be those of much older children up to and beyond ten years of age. The major emphasis in these answers is the emphasis upon outward appearance and physical attributes.

Still at this stage, with external appearance as the main focus, come answers showing more concern for some special attitude which might make God different in some way. This might be some 'holy' activity, as in Tim's reply (C.A. 7 : 9 and M.A. 9 : 4), 'He'd have a shirt like, and a rag round his head, maybe with a stick. He'd be kind and he'd be praying.' This is seen in a much older boy. Jason aged 12 : 11 (M.A. 10 : 1), 'He'd look like a father. *How do you mean?* A man with a beard, clad in a robe, a nice person. His face would be kind. He might be healing someone in heaven.' Again God and Jesus are synonymous and the child even points this out, as does Catherine aged 10 : 8 (M.A. 10 : 6), 'He'd have little children sitting on his knee. He'd be a kind man with a beard like Jesus did, and clothes like Jesus.' Annabel aged 11 (M.A. 10 : 7) specifically says she'd see Jesus. 'Him looking after her and all the children and people on earth. He'd have medium height, a white shawl over his head and a long robe of white, a beard and hands clasped in prayer over his tummy.' These kinds of anthropomorphic responses tend to continue for most children until about 10 : 6 chronologically and 10 : 11 in terms of mental age. Many pupils, of course, continue with these ideas until much older.

The change in quality of thinking about this aspect of the deity can be described as a move from a human to a superhuman emphasis. Later this is symbolised in spirit or ghost form and later still God's invisible nature is emphasised. Some of the answers are almost identical with the previous stage but there are subtle changes of emphasis as when comparisons with Jesus are made. 'He's like Jesus, with a kind face and with peace in his eyes' or 'Like Jesus doing miracles with his disciples.' Here there is a change to Jesus as a very superior kind of man, if not superhuman. The move towards what we might call supernal elements in a description of God, can be seen in a human figure accompanied or surrounded by powerful portents signifying a greater than human status. These portents may include angels, clouds, light from heaven, dead people in the sky sitting in glory and other details. Kenny, aged 11 : 8 (M.A. 11 : 0) is interesting, 'I see a man with his arms out and a round thing over his head, shining. He'd be about 30 years old, with a beard and clad in white garments. I see him above me in the air.' Josephine, aged 11 : 4 (M.A. 11 : 0) after a conventional human Palestinian description of God adds, 'He'd be a holy person, living up in heaven and not on earth. He's very very very old and wise.' Age and perhaps beardedness, may be identical in the child's mind with wisdom. We must not forget that in these days when a child mentions thirty, he may regard this age as very old. Martha, aged 12 : 9 (M.A. 11 : 8) says, 'She'd see a man with a beard, an old kind gentleman, dressed in a gown. He'd be standing in the clouds, with lots of glory around.' This glory is described by Harry aged 9 : 8 (M.A. 11 : 11) in detail, 'He's sitting in heaven in all his glory, on the throne, with angels around him, wearing a white satin robe with S. John and S. Peter on the left and right hand. There'd be people what's dead playing golden harps all round.' Sally aged 11 : 5 (M.A. 12 : 5) says, 'A wonderful man sitting on a throne of clouds with angels round him, and the sun glittering. A man who teaches what is true. He doesn't seem real because he's too good to be real.' Sometimes this is formalised as in the simple statement, 'He'd see the trinity, like you see in a stained glass window', or the anthropomorphism is expressed as partially human and partially supernatural, 'A piece of sky or something, maybe a cloud with a face on it. God is the sky.'

This leads into a later stage, which we cannot clearly identify in terms of age, where symbolic representation of God is common. It tends to occur with older pupils since there is an element of abstraction about the thinking, even though human features are still present. For example, 'A gigantic person with a cloak all over the world, looking down on it and making sure everything is all right', and 'God he pictures as everything. A kind of ghost or holy ghost.' One boy aged 14 (M.A. 13 : 4) says God to him is 'like Jesus in ghostly form'. This boy, like others when questioned, thinks of the spiritual in terms of a ghostlike transparency which is adaptable to all shapes and objects. Another boy expresses this as 'God can look like an ordinary person. He can really look like anything and everything.' One boy sees him as 'A shepherd dressed in white, with a sheep in his hands', another as 'A loving man, knocking on the heart of a person', a third as 'A king sitting on a throne with Jesus beside him.' One girl suggests he would be in the shape of a dove or 'a ghostlike person, not a clear shape, but a spirit'. Finally, older and more able pupils tend to reject a visualised concept. 'You can't describe God because he can't be seen. There's just an empty space or spirit', and instead God is 'An idea or feeling of fatherliness' or 'An idea of love.' The occasional answer may be symbolic and at an abstract level, such as, 'Light, because God is supposed to be a perfect being!'

In the story of the Burning Bush there is striking corroboration of the stages seen in the previous question, in answer to the query, 'Supposing Moses had got over his fear and had looked at God, what do you think he would have seen?' Most children give the same quality of answers as their visualised concepts of deity thought of as they pray, but there are some variations due to the differing context of each question.

The grossly anthropomorphic concepts are revealed when Moses is thought to have seen a full human figure, even though some of it would be obscured by the bush. Sometimes, it is an angel who is seen, but the angel is entirely human in concept despite conventional robes, wings or halo. In these answers a clear division can be seen between humanised answers and symbolised answers at about 12 : 0 chronologically and 12 : 6 in terms of mental age. This age indicates the beginning of God seen as a shadow, a cloud, a flame, a dove, or a bright piercing light. Although a human element, such as a face, may appear in these symbols, nevertheless God has appeared in symbolic form superhuman rather than human. Thereafter the answers again become very similar to prayer visualisation of the deity. Mary aged 12 : 8 (M.A. 16 : 10) is fairly typical. 'Moses could have seen a man like himself. It says in the Bible, God made man in his own image. Or a fierce animal. God can take the shape of anything he wants. Or it could be a dove, the sign of the holy spirit, to show that the holy spirit is gentle.'

The Burning Bush discussion did lead naturally to the question, 'Why should God be invisible?' put to those who maintained God could not be visualised because by nature he was unseen. The answers to this ranged from rather simple and ingenuous reasons such as, 'To give people a surprise when they get to heaven', or 'They might die of fright if they saw him', to those with more insight such as 'God is spiritual and is immanent in all things, so he cannot be seen as the things themselves', or 'He would not be held in awe if he were seen', or again, 'Believing in God is a matter of faith, so God should not be seen. If he were seen there would be no need for faith.'

A criticism could well be made that the questions, discussed here under 'The Deity Visualised' are weighted questions, implying to the pupil, by the phrasing used, that God was to be seen in some way. I feel that there is some substance in this criticism, but that it is in fact a criticism of the story and of the conceptual level of Mosaic religion. The story itself specifically states Moses being afraid to 'look at God' implying that God was there to look at, and in some way to be seen. Despite this criticism we can say that the sequences of thought in these two series of answers show a clear development in three stages. There is a first stage of visualising God in human and physical terms, with sometimes special human features, such as gentleness or kindness. This goes on until between 10 and 11 years of age. An intermediate stage of human and anthropomorphic ideas with some attempt to break away from these limitations, by introducing supernatural elements, is then seen. From 12 years onwards (M.A. 12 : 6) this gives way to symbolising God's appearance leading on to a more abstract and spiritual conception. Spiritual is thought of in semiphysical terms at first, as some kind of transparency or ghostlike quality before this is supplanted by a concept of a non-visual kind and the deity is thought of solely in terms of his qualities of love, goodness or justice. Although this is sometimes thought of in human terms, such as a father, it is clearly recognised only as an analogy. The sequences here confirm generally, with more elaboration of the middle stage, the research of O. Kupky (1928).[1]

Much of this sequence can be discerned in various other questions discussed with the children. As we shall see later in more detail, God is thought to have feet when he makes the ground on which Moses stood holy. God is similarly thought to have arms and legs when he divided the waters of the Red Sea with them, or to have human breath, although of enormously greater power, when he blows the waters apart. These are not symbolic in the child's mind but plainly statements of physical fact beyond which the child cannot progress because of his concrete limitations and difficulty in spiritualising experience in more abstract terms. This is clearly demonstrated in our next section.

CONCEPTS OF DIVINE COMMUNICATION

The Bible is continually using the following type of saying: 'And God spoke unto Moses and said . . .' It is not surprising, therefore, that children who think of God in physical and human terms should extend their thinking in a similar manner to the way in which the divine communicates with men. It may be that something of the opposite influence occurs, namely that because God is depicted frequently as speaking like one man to another, this suggests or reinforces anthropomorphic concepts of God. Whichever aspect influences the other, it is of interest to see how children think not only about how God is identified but how communication between the divine and the human occurs. Naturally, young children will be very literal at first and interpret 'God spoke' in a physical auditory manner. Of greater interest, however, is how children develop from this point and when they change their thinking on this problem. It is a problem, and remains a problem, for many adults, but children are at first unaware of the existence of such a problem. There is a simple, naïve and unhesitating assumption that God speaks as man to man.

This can be seen in the answers to the question, 'If Moses had been deaf, do you think he would have heard God calling him?' The pupils are then asked to give reasons for their answer and to say whether or not any people nearby might have heard God speaking to Moses. This last point is important as a check on the quality of their thinking.

Three stages in their concepts of divine communication appear in the children's thinking. The first is where they interpret God speaking solely in terms of material, physical and external explanations. It is man-to-man talk, human voice speaking to human ear, and if Moses were deaf this would obviously limit or prohibit communication. At this stage there are the children who state firmly: 'No, he couldn't hear. Deaf people can't hear. It would be no use God talking to him.' There are also the children who say, 'Yes' and give as a reason that God would make him hear in some other way. When we examine God's solutions to Moses' deafness, we find that they are physical solutions, such as, 'God would shout louder in a great big voice' or 'God would make him a deaf aid like wires coming down from the sky into his ears', or again, 'God would speak and Moses would lip read him.' Many children, also at this stage say that God would cure Moses of his deafness. Peter, aged nine, for example, says, 'He'd use his magic and make him hear, cure him. *Would Moses then be able to hear just God's voice or other things?* Oh, Moses'd hear everything like birds singing and sheep calling each other. Then when God had finished speaking Moses would go deaf again.' This clearly indicates the physical limitations in his thinking and, as all other children at this stage assert, if there had been other people present who were not deaf they would all certainly have heard God speaking to Moses. But most children, especially the younger ones, see deafness as an insuperable barrier to communication, like the six year old making an unconscious pun, 'He wouldn't 'cause Moses suffered from a diar-ear!' It is clear then that these children cannot dissociate divine communication from human speaking, and crude physical anthropomorphic ideas seriously limit understanding. Most children do not get beyond this until at least 8 years of age (M.A. 9 : 4).

There then follows an intermediate stage with some attempts at non-physical explanations but 'the others' pose a problem which the pupils cannot consistently resolve. Lillian aged 9 : 3 (M.A. 11 : 7) says, 'Only Moses could hear inside of him', but people near by couldn't hear 'because God spoke in a quiet voice'. George aged 9 : 8 (M.A. 13 : 6) is quite certain that the other people could not hear God speaking because 'He was saying it into Moses' soul', but on the other hand sees it necessary to have Moses cured of deafness before God can make himself heard. Rose at 9 : 11 (M.A. 10 : 0) rather similarly feels that God would have to cure Moses' deafness, but is feeling after a less physical solution in the second question, 'No, they wouldn't hear. Moses was a holy man and p'raps the man next to him wasn't . . . He wouldn't hear because he hadn't received the Holy Spirit, or God spoke in a soft voice so only Moses could hear him.' In contrast, Jeffrey aged 10 : 4 (M.A. 9 : 7) says adamantly, 'No, deaf people can't hear at all.' But regarding other non-deaf people present at the time, they couldn't hear either, 'because Moses is a holy man and they wouldn't be holy. Only holy people hear God.' This boy obviously is finding simple materialistic explanations unsatisfactory, but because he cannot shake them off will produce inconsistencies in his thinking. It is very evident that this intermediate stage lasts until midway between 11 and 12 years of age (M.A. about 12 : 1).

The final stage is the resolution of the problem of 'the others' in a consistent manner because concepts of divine communication are now non-material, non-physical and based upon an inward experience. Typical answers are, 'Yes, Moses would hear in his mind, like telepathy. *Would other people nearby hear?* No, it was only in Moses' mind', and 'Yes, but it was only to Moses. The others might see him talk to himself, but they'd hear nothing.' It is of interest to note that not all of these pupils would explain the Burning Bush entirely as a mirage or a subjective experience. They would go as far as saying that the voice was an internal act, but many would still say the bush burning had objective reality and other people would have seen it even if they could hear no voice.

These three stages can be said to correspond roughly with first, pre-operational and concrete operations, second, intermediate to formal operations and the final stage, full formal operational thinking. There is an interesting similarity with the 'God visualised' concepts in that the mental age of 12 to 13 years appears to be required before the pupils can get beyond physical anthropomorphisms in visualising the deity and also the limitations of God having only a physical voice by which he can communicate with his people. We have already noted in Chapter Four the age of 13 years as being the approximate age when religious thinking becomes fully operational in a formal sense. We shall see in many other items how this age, 12 to 13 years, seems to be a crucial time in religious conceptual growth.

CONCEPTS OF THE DIVINE PRESENCE

Children do appear to have a real sense of the omnipresence of God and in certain questions of the test this fact was especially evident.[1] We must not forget, however, that this may be in the beginning only a transfer from how they imagine their parents to be omnipotent, omniscient and omnipresent. The young child stealing biscuits from the kitchen may be uneasy that the all-seeing parental eye may be watching. After much cautious experimentation the child learns that his assumptions are incorrect; nevertheless, it is important to note that this may be a natural assumption on the part of the child which he later transfers to God, in his need to parentalise the deity. One of the most vivid pictures I ever saw painted by a child, was one in response to the question, 'What is God like?' It showed an enormous eye peering over the edge of a plain, occupying almost the entire horizon and gazing balefully at a tiny house.

If this conviction is emotionally based the intellectual concepts which support it are already apparent by the time a child begins school. To assess how children think of this presence and the basis of their judgment of the fact of a divine presence, a question was asked as the pupils looked at the picture of a child at prayer. The question was 'Is God in the room with the child?' It was varied if the child was praying to Jesus or to the Holy Spirit, and all answers were followed up for reasons behind the answer, such as, 'How does the boy know that God is in the room with him?'

The vast majority of children gave 'Yes' answers and a sequence of ideas could be traced in two stages. The first stage sees the children preoccupied with physical and crude ideas of the omnipotence of God, and the reasons advanced for believing this are materialistic

[1] See Appendix A, questions P.2: Q.5 and S.1: Q.4.

evidence of hearing a voice, feeling a touch or some visual evidence is experienced. Authoritarian reasons are also advanced at this stage for knowing God to be present. Here are some typical answers of younger children. 'He sees him when he goes up to bed, in one of the rooms.' 'He'd feel God breathe, with his breath on his face.' 'He's invisible. *How does the boy know he's there?* Something touches him; God does, anywhere.' 'Every time he prays God comes down from heaven. *If lots of boys and girls pray does God come down to them all?* Yes, he is busy at night coming down and listening to everyone's prayers.'

A six year old girl of average intelligence is convinced God is there. To explain why she never sees him she says, 'He's at the back of the little girl. If she turns round he flies round to the front.' Perhaps the eight year old has certain hospital television programmes in mind when she answers, 'His spirit only is in the room. The night angel hears our prayers and tells God when the day angel comes on duty.' Authoritarian answers from adults are advanced, such as the minister, parents, teachers, the Church or the Bible say so and this is sufficient reason. 'God's supposed to be everywhere. *How does he know that?* A person at church has told him about it', or 'Perhaps God told her in her prayers' and 'He keeps her from danger when she's asleep.' Still in this stage are responses such as this one: 'He knows God goes to everyone who is good. He knows God is all over the world. He's praying and he's good, so God is there', and this answer, 'She can hear him because she is praying, so she knows he's there.'

This type of answer, still rooted in material considerations and authoritarian judgments is evident in most children up to about 13 years (M.A. 13 : 5). After this time reasons are decreasingly materialistic and increasingly based upon faith, belief and logic and the divine presence is inferred rather than experienced directly as an external voice, touch or vision. After 13 years most children find it unnecessary and inappropriate to support their convictions with physical evidence. A frequent answer is that God's presence is known because the child thinks of him, is praying to him or is felt in a mystical manner such as a feeling of peace, safety or happiness. 'God gets closer and closer the harder you think about him.' 'He's no incentive if he didn't know. He'd feel his presence and be at peace.' 'She believes God is everywhere and in everyone, and when she prays she believes that he hears her.' 'Sometimes it's hard and that's where faith comes in.' 'I don't feel it myself. I don't know. There must be a God, and he must be there.' 'It's through faith and proved from experience. *How do you mean?* She's known God was there through relying upon him.' Again, it is interesting that 13 years appears to be the time when anthropomorphic elements tend to be left behind and a higher theological concept occurs.

The smaller number of children who say that God is not in the room with the praying child, because he is in heaven or in the sky, were asked, 'How could God hear the prayers?' These answers, too small in number to be scaled, do nevertheless show a sequence. First, there are the crudely physical answers such as, 'The boy would have to shout louder,' 'God puts some ear things on and an electric wire goes down invisibly to her room', and 'God could hear 'cause he is listening ever so hard.' Then come answers which show that a divine intermediary is there. 'No, he's up in heaven listening, it's like a telephone exchange. *How do you mean?* 'It's the same as being in Church, God's near the altar and the prayers go up to him. But he's not in the room. He might have an angel in there if it's a special prayer . . .' 'No, not actually in the room, but in heaven. He'd know the boy was praying because God's spirit was in the room.' Finally come reasons of divine omniscience such as 'No, he's supposed to know everything in our minds and bodies. I think he does', and 'No, he doesn't hear them as we hear. He's in her mind and knows what she is thinking. He's with her but not beside her.' For all these pupils, their answers solve the problem of how God may be in more places at once and although we cannot generalise on a statistical basis the quality of these reasons improves with age. These 'No' answers seem to correspond closely with concepts of divine communication, showing the problem, as it were in reverse.

In the Burning Bush story, many children think of the ground where Moses stood as holy because God was there. Here we shall focus upon how the children think of God's presence there, not their ideas of the holy. An examination of these replies reveals a range of concepts from a crude anthropomorphic level to a spiritualised presence. We have already quoted, 'It was where God was standing. *How did this make it holy?* Because the holy would go down through God's feet into the ground and make it holy.' This is not merely a clear indication of concrete operational thought, but a splendid example of a crude anthropomorphism. Advanced as the reason why Moses should take off his shoes, presumably because only direct contact with the skin can receive the holy power, the child sees the deity present in physical human terms. Children who give this type of answer, tend to reply to a supplementary question: 'Is God everywhere?' with a negative, because God can only be physically in one place at once. This results in some confusion, when a further question is asked, 'Is everywhere holy or just special places?' Many children, as a verbalism, may reply that God is everywhere but only special places are holy because that is where he was physically at some time. This shows an attempt to think of God in two ways, one as an all pervasive presence, but also in human terms limited to one place at a time. A six year old (IQ 77) says, 'Yes, God's everywhere. *How do you mean?* He's with everyone, he follows us. *Suppose there are two of us together and we have to separate, can he be with both of us?* No, he follows us one at a time. *What about the 300 children in school?* He takes turn following them all.' A 7 year old says, 'He's in one place, but holding your hand wherever you go. *How many people are there in the world?* About 200. *Does he hold all their hands?* No, not all at the same time.' Some children are plainly ambivalent and see no contradictions, as Desmond aged 8 : 9 (M.A. 7 : 5), 'God was on the ground himself, standing on it. *How do you mean?* He was there with his feet on it. *Is God everywhere?* Yes. *Is everywhere holy or just special places?* Yes, everywhere's holy 'cause God's there. *Is this ground holy?* Yes, 'cause he stood on it once. He's here and in heaven.' Andy aged 8 : 6 (M.A. 7 : 6) on the other hand is consistent, 'God was on that ground. *How do you mean?* Touching it. *Is God everywhere?* No, not all the time. He can't be. *Is everywhere holy or just special places?* Just special places because one of Jesus' disciples or Jesus have been there, or God himself. *Is this ground holy?* No, of course not. One of Jesus' disciples hasn't been here yet.' Keith aged 8 : 11 (M.A. 10 : 0) is puzzled and thinking aloud, 'God was standing there on that ground as well as Moses. *Did God touch it with his feet?* No. God was sort of floating. God doesn't have feet!'

There is also some confusion about where God lives because some children state the ground where Moses was, was holy because it was where he lived. In discussion children state God lives everywhere, but this is usually a verbalism, because they cannot envisage such a disembodied existence and frequently lapse into this type of thinking, 'This ground here isn't holy because he doesn't live here. *You said he lives everywhere.* Well, he lives nearly everywhere!' A curious remnant of this omnipresence in a physical sense continues with Delia aged 14 : 3 (M.A. 15 : 4), 'God was there. It was there that he saw God. *The story says Moses didn't look.* Well, he knew God was there in the body. *Is God everywhere?* Yes, he's everywhere as a feeling but not in the body.'

Further replies of this nature are shown in the fact that not only is God regarded as having a body, but it was also the place where God spoke with a physical voice, so that God is seen at this stage of religious thinking in essentially human terms. Not only has he physical attributes but logic leads to the conclusion by one boy (M.A. 11 :1) that God cannot do the miracles he once did because 'God was new then. He's old, in a way, and not so strong now.' These limitations in thinking, because of physical attributes, in God's nature reflected both in his presence with individual people and universally with mankind, do not give way to higher concepts until about 12 : 3 in terms of mental age. This age is consistent with our other findings set out in this chapter in terms of the deity visualised and the ways by which the deity communicates with men. 12 to 13 years seems again to represent the breakthrough for most pupils into less anthropomorphic concepts which reveal the potential for more spiritual, non-physical insights.

GENERAL COMMENT ON DEVELOPING CONCEPTS OF THE DIVINE IDENTITY

A remarkably consistent picture of the child's developing thinking emerges from the answers we have considered above. It is not only internally consistent for most children, but it is also consistent with what we know about the problems of egocentric and concrete thinking of children in the primary schools. Their natural tendency is to deal with abstractions as concrete as they are able and they are limited emotionally by restricted experience of human life and their constant misunderstanding of the complexity of human relationships. It is no wonder that these limitations will seriously affect their religious understanding. Added to this, the language of the Bible and the authoritative weight of scripture reinforce the physical interpretations children will make about the nature of God. Where the Bible narrative states that God can be seen, he has feet and hands, he breathes, he speaks, and behaves generally in human terms, the child will naturally accept these statements, translate them to a concrete level in a literal fashion and use them in the light of his egocentric needs. Moreover, the limits of a child's experience must naturally lead him to make judgments about human life on a superficial, external and often physical basis, until such time as the more subtle aspects of human relationships and qualities are appreciated. These limits joined with a restricted process of concrete operations, would appear to combine in religious thinking of a strong anthropomorphic tendency, quite apart from the factor of religious teaching which may tend to anthropomorphise the person of God, until such time as the child attains mature judgments in other areas of life. This is not to suggest that the Bible must be abandoned, but that where it is used there must be a constant attempt to help the child beyond his crudities into a fuller non-physical understanding.

The decisive age of twelve to thirteen may not represent the natural division between crude and higher thinking about God's nature. It is possible that sensitive education, consistent with the child's needs, might help children to attain higher concepts earlier than this. For the brighter child this may be possible, but for average or backward children, it is doubtful whether they could respond very much earlier than the ages suggested because of the difficulties of thinking imposed by religious problems.

The picture of God reflected by Infant children is very crudely physical of a man, with the physical characteristics of a human being, clad in clothes, usually Palestinian, invariably bearded and fairly old. He speaks in physical tones, often with a harsh and loud voice. He lives remotely in heaven, situated in the sky and when he visits the earth it is for a specific purpose in a physical form. His presence is known by physical contact and his acceptance of omnipresence is only a verbalism. In some ways this picture resembles more the Greek deities and the myths of Genesis than the Christian view of God. The Junior child tends to relinquish some of these cruder immaturities but is still strongly anthropomorphic, thinking of God as a superman but still a man, with special magic qualities of power, and with supernatural signs to symbolise this power. God still speaks with a physical voice but later there is some confusion about methods of divine communication, as simple explanations are seen to be unsatisfactory. God is seen as present in human life by the Junior child but the confusion between physical presence and omnipresence still persists. The first two years of Secondary schooling are still an extension of the Junior years, something of an intermediate stage during which the pupils are seeking to resolve their former childish and too simple concepts of God. Thereafter the physical limitations are left behind and the deity is thought of symbolically and abstractedly, but with occasional anthropomorphic traces still apparent. God is unseen and unseeable because he is non-physical in nature. Where adolescents use human terms to describe God they are on the whole regarded as analogies, not to be understood literally. Divine communication is now regarded as non-physical, in terms of telepathy, thoughts, or the operation of conscience. God's omnipresence is possible in spiritual terms because God is not limited by physical immobility. These problems are not resolved but a more consistent conceptualisation is now possible. Many adolescents, especially those backward or disinterested in religion, tend to retain cruder anthropomorphic thinking much longer than the twelfth and thirteenth years. Where there are intellectual limitations it is obvious that this must also be so due to the continuation of concrete elements in religious thinking longer than with the average pupil.

We shall be dealing with concepts of Jesus in a later chapter, but it is useful to recall here that there is real confusion in the child's mind about God and Jesus, in many cases the names being interchangeable as the child uses them. Jesus as a God-man, and God envisaged in terms of the human Jesus are not two distinct pictures.

An analogy of two pictures superimposed one upon the other, with a resulting blurred effect, is perhaps a fair representation of how the child thinks. Certainly ideas of the historic Jesus reinforce and perhaps perpetuate anthropomorphic thinking about the divine. The sequence of concepts here is far from clear, but in general terms we can observe that the young child sees Jesus and God as identical, Jesus having the same human characteristics as God, and his powers are those of God, the relationship being rather of a master magician and his apprentice. At an intermediate stage the confusion clears a little and the separate identities of God and Jesus are recognised. There follows after this a third stage with some understanding of Jesus as more than human, in terms of his mission and his unique relationship with God beginning to emerge. With young children we should perhaps minimise the first stage, stressing the separate identity of God and Jesus, leaving the third stage until adolescence when the necessary powers of propositional thinking have developed enough to cope with the rather abstract issues involved. This will be discussed more fully in Chapter Eleven.

Chapter Seven

GOD'S ACTIVITY IN THE NATURAL WORLD

A DEITY seen in human and physical times would be active in the natural world in rather a different way to a deity not limited to physical modes of activity. By the natural world, I mean the world of nature, of plants and trees, sea and mountain and the physical composition of the universe. The natural world is here seen in contrast to the human world, which is the subject of a later chapter. The world of nature and the world of man are of course closely related and in the larger sense the natural world is not only the living context of humanity but man is an expression of the natural world, as one of its creatures. Nevertheless, some kind of division for the purpose of discussion is both necessary and useful. When viewing this natural world, therefore, it is of interest to see how children and adolescents conceive the activity of the divine. Very few, until middle adolescence, appear to doubt the existence of God. Most believe that God has been active in the past and a large number see him as still active today. Very young children tend to express a crude theism, namely that God having created the world long ago washed his hands of it and retired to heaven to watch from a distance what was going to happen. Certainly, many of these children appear to think that this retirement was no later than the ascension of Jesus and with this event God cut down his activity on earth. Others, the vast majority, appear to have a more moderate concept that God was especially active in a physical sense during Bible times, fairly active up to modern times but not very active today. Older and more intelligent pupils do tend to argue for consistency and would believe that the Bible is a dramatised account, with a theological interpretation, of normal events we still experience. This is, however, true only of the upper range of our age group. It has been discussed in detail elsewhere in this book.

Our focus here is upon what the child thinks to be God's power and his activity in the natural world in Bible times. About this fact few pupils have any doubts, but of course their concepts of the activity of the divine differ as their concepts of the nature of the deity differ. It is possible to discern a sequence of concepts with increasing insights of the way in which God behaves within the natural world he has created.

The natural scientist tries to understand the world of nature by formulating laws, which are not the immutable forces many non-scientific laymen think them to be, but are more in the form of hypotheses advanced to account for as many of the facts as possible. These laws may give way to others as better hypotheses are advanced and are seen to account for more of the facts. On the other hand, the theologian, beginning with a concept of God as the creative first cause of the natural world may accept the laws of the natural scientist as not a necessary contradiction of a theological interpretation. Questions obviously arise where apparent miracle occurs, unaccountable in terms of natural law, where the divine is said to intervene in a manner contrary to natural laws. This, of course, is the centre of the old controversy between science and religion, still perpetuated by these who so revere the Bible narrative as to regard it not only a revelation of spiritual truth but also a text book of supernatural law. To the literalist it is no problem that an axe head should float, a river should turn into blood, and water should obey the direct command of God contrary to normal happening. So great is the authority of the words of the Bible to them they would as readily accept that Jonah swallowed the whale as that the whale swallowed Jonah if the Bible said so. That the book of Jonah is a vivid allegory of the Exile of the nation and a divine call to a new mission for them is lost, because there are no intellectual problems if God is believed to be able and willing to use the natural world in such a manner. There are many adults who do not subscribe to this extreme view, but who would nevertheless be reluctant to try to explain biblical miracle, lest they merely explain it away. This reluctance is certainly experienced by many teachers when children ask questions about biblical narrative which contains miracle or miraculous elements.

My object here is not to enter into this controversy but only to take note of it and to see that children, who at first see no problems, do grow to a point of tension where they must accept or resolve the existence of miracle. How and when this occurs in the child's religious development is important and it was my intention to pose questions and discuss them so that some description of this development was possible. For this purpose, in each of the biblical stories, an explanation was asked of the pupil about how such an event could happen. These questions were, 'How would you explain the bush burning and yet not being burned?', 'How would you explain the dividing of the waters of the Red Sea and the temptation to turn stone into bread?'[1] some of the children's answers quoted below have already been used

[1] See Appendix A, questions S.1: Q.5, S.2: Q.5 and S.3: Q.4B.

when we were examining levels of operational thinking. Here they are reviewed on their theological value, in terms of levels of religious insight they attain.

THE BURNING BUSH EVENT

This story can be and has been interpreted in different ways. The most widely held is that a bush caught in a shaft of sunlight stimulated a vision or experience of God at the time Moses was meditating upon the troubles of his people. But other interpretations are possible, and no one knows the true explanation or indeed, the validity of the description we have. However, given the story as it stands our task is to see how responses occurred in terms of theological insight to the question. These range from crude materialistic ideas and simple magic to advanced views of a vision and a spiritual experience.

A sequence of concepts in three stages could be seen from the children's answers. The first is crudely materialistic, where God intervenes by changing, manipulating or constructing the bush in a special way as a means of attracting Moses' attention or playing 'pretend' in some childish way. These kinds of answers are up to about nine years of age. Here are some examples. Massey aged 7 : 8 (M.A. 6 : 1) says, 'Someone threw a fag or a match down. *How do you explain the bush not burning?* God might be behind throwing water over it.' Jill aged 8 : 11 (M.A. 7 : 0) answers, 'It wasn't really burnt. It looked as though it was. Someone pretended it was going to burn. It was Jesus. *What did he do?* When no one was looking he pretended it burnt with a piece of paper.' Rather similar is Pat's reply, aged 8 : 7 (M.A. 8 : 6), 'God was inside the bush and he was holding the fire up on sticks from inside. The sticks were burning and it looked as though the bush were on fire, but it weren't.' Even a very bright child Rose aged 8 : 7 (M.A. 12 : 6), says, 'It might have been imitation flames like bits of red paper stuck on the bush.' Nathan aged 6 :10 (M.A. 7 : 9) says, 'It might have been some brown iron over the branches which God might have put there.' Similarly Leona aged 6 : 5 (M.A. 6 : 0), 'The leaves were all strong. They hadn't been burned before. They were very very strong.' An exception is the little girl aged 6 : 6 (M.A. 6 : 4) who states flatly, 'Moses was telling a lie.'

Still at this first physical stage we see children using miracle itself as an explanation. It has no problems for them because God is a master magician and can do anything. Miracle and magic appear to be the same to these children, as in the answers, 'God didn't want to kill that bush. *What happened?* He done a miracle. God made it happen. He magicked it', and 'The bush is magic done by God', and 'He put a spell on it, a spell like water chucked on a bush.' Other physical answers are common, sometimes with God as the agent, sometimes not. Tina aged 6 : 6 (M.A. 5 : 8) used distance as an explanation, 'The fire was a way off from the bush, so it couldn't burn it.' Again distance is used, rather differently, by Denise aged 6 : 6 (M.A. 5 : 10), 'It could have been above the bush and then the bush couldn't have been burnt.' Jenny aged 7 : 1 (M.A. 5 : 10) says, 'God didn't make it burn. He put water on it because he didn't want the boy Moses to get burnt.' Rather ruefully Billy aged 6 : 9 (M.A. 7 : 10) says, 'God made it so the fire couldn't burn any bushes or flowers. *How do you mean?* It was probably an experiment. My brother made an experiment and made me drink it.' Lester, aged 8 : 2 (M.A. 8 : 1) remarks : 'Green can't burn very easily. God might make it very green to stop it burning.' Large numbers of children use this green idea as an explanation. An older girl 9 : 8 (M.A. 10 : 6) put it graphically, 'God was stopping the flame burning it. *How do you mean?* The spirit was there over the bush and it can't be burnt so it stopped the flames. *How?* The spirit is a kind of watery stuff like water and paste and other things.'

The second stage for most children from about nine years onwards, is a period of intermediate thinking in the sense that semi-physical explanations are used. The most frequent of these show God in some way interposing himself in some special way between the bush and the flames. Or semi-magical explanations are advanced, in that God commands the bush or touched it with power in some way, or creates a special holy bush of some kind. The first type of answer is seen in Rose's ideas, 'Because Jesus put a holy spirit on it and it wouldn't burn. *How do you mean?* It was a real flame but the holy spirit stopped it. *How?* 'Cause God was by the bush and he'd block the way. The fire couldn't reach the bush when he was there.' Rose is 9 : 11 (M.A. 10 : 0). The semi-magical type can be seen in the two following examples. Peter aged 8 : 6 (M.A. 9 : 1) says, 'God might have put his magic on it and say, "Don't burn the bushes." *Who would God talk to?* The bush. *Did it have ears to hear him?* No, but the bush would hear and obey him; with the magic on it, it could.' Jenny aged 11 : 5 (M.A. 9 : 7) is more dramatic, 'When God's feet went off the ground the flames went off when he floated in the air. *How do you mean?* God got his hand out and said, 'Bush, stop burning' and it went away. It was a real burning flame.'

A third stage very clearly occurs about eleven years of age (M.A. 11 : 5) when most pupils see the phenomenon of the burning bush as non-physical, which later moves into symbolism, mirage, hallucination and thus an inner experience of illumination. The dividing line is what one might call the level of nuministic response, when the flame or the bush is thought of as mysteriously spiritual and non-material. This is expressed in various ways, at first expressed with material lapses but moving on to a less material emphasis. Alice aged 10 : 4 (M.A. 11 : 8) says, 'God made it not burn and he can do anything. It might not be flames, but something like flames, but holy, to attract Moses to go over there', while Andrew (M.A. 11 : 8) says, 'The flames would probably be God, flames that didn't burn.' Peggy aged 10 : 6 (M.A. 13 : 5) talks of 'holy flames so nothing could be scorched. *How do you mean?* They were God's flames. He blessed the flames so they burned but not in the usual way.' The numinous is vividly expressed by Lesley, aged 9 : 11 (M.A. 13 : 5), 'God was in it and he was holy and the bush couldn't burn. God's holy spirit was there and stopped it being burnt. The holy spirit is better than any other spirit. *How didn't it burn?* Because God was there and an angel. The spirit spread all round the bush and protected it.'

These give way to more symbolic answers such as Sheena's, aged 9 : 9 (M.A. 13 : 0), 'Maybe it was a light, reddish looking, like a fire. It might come from Jesus in the bush or the angel', and Fred's, aged 14 : 5 (M.A. 14 : 2), 'It would be a brilliant light but no heat, similar to a light bulb. The light was God. He was in the centre but the light was so bright he couldn't be seen.' Alice aged only 10 : 11 but with a high IQ (M.A. 15 : 8) says, 'It was a flame of goodness, not a burning flame . . . God put it there. There are flames of holiness everywhere but he made Moses see this one. Usually they are unseen.' God is frequently thought of as coming *in* the light and *as* the light. Many suggest this is not indications of the glory of God, but the sunlight. For example, Celia, aged 13 : 5 (M.A. 13 : 1), 'It was one of God's miracles. *How do you mean?* The flames weren't real burning flames. They only seemed to be there. It might have been the sun in a certain direction making it look like flames', and Polly, aged 13 : 5 (M.A. 15 : 3), 'It sounds impossible, doesn't it? It could have been the sunlight shining on it. I've been told that and it sounds reasonable enough.' Also, among the older or more able pupils imagination or hallucination are common explanations. Belinda aged 15 : 3 (M.A. 13 : 2) says, 'They weren't real flames. When Moses heard God say take his shoes off, he thought he saw God's face. I think he imagined what he saw, not God speaking.' Hilda, aged 12 : 7 (M.A. 15 : 7) says, 'It was a real bush, but it was a vision, not a real fire.' A sixth former from a rather fundamentalist sect says, 'God created matter and could keep a thing burning indefinitely. He could replace matter continuously as it burned. Or God could have created an illusion or a vision in Moses. *Which explanation do you prefer?* I'd prefer the first, the miraculous.' But in contrast another sixth former prefers the vision, 'There wasn't really a fire. It was a mirage in Moses' thought. It may even have been started by looking at the sun. It's something

106

that could have happened. Moses must have been given a message by God to help the Israelites as he did.'

In brief, we can say that up to about nine years there is a very anthropomorphic way of explaining the situation with God intervening in a rather human manner, altering natural laws of growth by magical means or protecting the bush by water or iron or similar substance. Then come semi-physical explanations, where God still intervenes actively in the natural world by sheer commanding power of a more spiritual kind. Finally from about eleven years onwards the explanations become entirely non-physical, when the light or flame is not real and merely symbolise the presence of God, this later giving way to the experience largely based upon an internal encounter with God, as it were, in Moses' mind. The external details of the story then became unimportant and the interest is focused upon the spiritual encounter with truth. These later insights are very evident among older and more able pupils but very many are content with lesser insights.

THE WATERS DIVIDED

The view is taken here that this story is part of the Hebrew legend to explain the beginnings of Hebrew religion in the Covenant. This is the dramatised act of salvation which convinces Israel of the God of Moses. Some startling natural event occurred which, combined with the defeat of a powerful enemy and human ingenuity, is interpreted in theological terms. Oral tradition, fallible reporting and the long gap of time before it was written down account for the version we now have. The answers of children range from crude, unrealistic belief and materialistic theology to a more reasoned acceptance (or, indeed, rejection) on more 'spiritual' theological grounds consistent with the Bible as a whole. This is not a grading from belief to agnosticism, but from crude concepts about God's activity in the natural world to more advanced concepts.

The responses to the questions 'How would you explain the dividing of the waters of the Red Sea? How do you think such a thing could happen?' resulted in three levels of explanations. The first level shows thinking in terms of irrelevancies or crude physical intervention on the part of God. The second is the intermediate level where God does not directly intervene in a physical manner but influences wind, sun and temperature to secure the specific event. It is manipulation of the elements, sometimes by the powerful word of command. Finally, Nature is not controlled by God in any sense, but normal occurrences, consistent with natural law, were used by God. Elements of coincidence and exaggeration enter into these later judgments. The age ranges approximate to the same conceptual levels as the Burning Bush explanations, although the three stages of the divided sea concepts are grouped somewhat differently.

In the first stage ranging up to 10 : 10 (M.A. 11 : 5) we see three types of answers, but all physical and direct in terms of God's activity. There are the literal answers such as Andrea's (aged 7 : 7 and M.A. 7 : 7), 'God made Moses' hand stretch right over to the other side and water went into two rivers on each side. *How did it happen?* God didn't do it. Moses did it with his arm and when there was one part dry he ran back and did the other side.' Then there are the simple magical-miracle answers, where in spite of long discussion, the child is unable or unwilling to think about possible explanations, because the fact that it is a miracle is enough. Kathy aged 6 : 2 (M.A. 6 : 6) gives a typical response, 'God did it. *What would he do?* He'd magic it. *How?* It were a miracle, that's all. *How would you explain the magic?* God did it with his spell . . .' and so the discussion could go on indefinitely. Roger aged 7 : 6 (M.A. 6 : 11) put it simply as 'God did it 'cause God's a miracle man.' That is enough! And Desmond aged 8 : 9 (M.A. 7 : 5) says, 'It was just a wonderful miracle like someone pulling a curtain down.' Massey aged 7 : 8 says, 'I fink God's magic. Here's a little hand and he says, "Magic, Magic," and it becomes a big hand and the sea parts. The waves go back by magic.' An animistic example is seen in Joan's reply (age 7 : 11, M.A. 10 : 1), 'Well the sea was alive. It can go one way or go another way. *How do we know something is alive?* 'Cause it moves. *Is a motor bike alive?* Yes. *The Sea?* Yes. *A pebble rolling down a hill?* No.'

The rest of the responses of this first stage can be described as crude-concepts of God who is regarded as the controller of Nature, by physical actions or extensions of himself. As the illustrations indicate, these are strongly anthropomorphic explanations. They also include physical explanation involving the use of planks for floating across on, bridges or boats, supplied by Moses or God, or laying grass over the sea. Seventy children in all make this type of response, a considerable proportion of the total number of 100 children before the age of eleven. An example of human artificialism, with divine help, is Leona's reply (age 6 : 5 with M.A. 6 : 0), 'Moses put his hand in the water and all the water swayed away. *How did that happen?* He pushed it this and then that way and it didn't come back again. God told him what to do.' This is near-literalism, but not quite. Jill aged 8 : 11 (M.A. 7 : 0) gives a more explicit artificialist explanation. 'God helped Moses to do it. *How?* He'd share out the water. God would be invisible and no one would see him. He'd wave his hand and push the water back.' She is explicit about divine hands, physical, if unseen. Eyes may be cited as in the response, 'God looked at the waters and they parted. *How did he keep them from flowing back?* Well, he kept one eye on one side, and his other eye on the other.' But David aged 7 : 1 (M.A. 8 : 4) is for more direct intervention. 'God's hands were like this (he puts his hands together) and then like this (he pulls them apart and parallel) and he kept them wide all the time, and the people stepped over them.' Later he adds thoughtfully, 'If it was deep water it would go over the arms, wouldn't it?' Pat, on the other hand, has no doubts at 8 : 7 (M.A. 8 : 6), 'God'd make a dam. They'd see a big pair of hands come down from the sky, nothing else, and scoop out mud and water.' The total body of God in the water, not just hands or arms, is implied by Sally aged 7 : 8 (M.A. 8 : 7), 'God was everywhere and had enough power or holiness in him to make a path across. He was in the waters and could make them part by pushing.' This is made very explicit by Sara aged 9 : 10 (M.A. 8 : 10), 'God was in the middle of it. *How do you mean?* If he was he'd push his arms and legs up and force the water open. *Would they see him?* No. *Would the people have to walk on God?* No, he'd be under the sand and water just pushing his legs and arms up.'

Apart from the use of his limbs and body God is seen as active in other ways. Jason aged 12 : 11 (M.A. 10 : 1) suggests, 'Maybe all the bottom was sand and it all soaks in and part would open. *How?* God'd make it rise from the bottom, bring up the sand and make the water sink in that place. *How would God do that?* He might throw a rock into the water and do it that way.' The idea of building a barrier is put by Grace in a curious form (age 10 : 1, M.A. 10 : 1), 'God could have blocked it by putting big stones in the bottom of the water. *Could they be seen?* No, they were invisible stones. *How did God get them there?* His invisible angels would do it. *Wouldn't the Israelites fall over the stones?* No, because the stones would be all spirit, they would walk through them. *How was it the water couldn't get through then?* Because God was stopping the water by his spirit in the stones.' Ray, aged 12 : 2 (M.A. 11 : 5) is sceptical of water dividing and says, 'God made them some boats and they rowed across.' Many other suggestions of God building bridges, floating rafts or providing other means are made at this stage.

Now comes the intermediate stage where God is conceived as controlling natural forces. This is indirect intervention in the natural world and the control of nature is often made by command. The wind is frequently used as a divine instrument, but the problem of the people being able to stand up in such a fierce wind is either ignored or unresolved. These responses are made by the majority of children after about 10 : 10 (M.A. 11 : 5). Typical of the command idea is Donald's (age 13 : 10, M.A. 12 : 1), 'It was God's power. It told the sea to part. *Has the sea got ears?* No, but everything God asks, they do. It's alive, like people. It makes a noise.' Similar is Frieda (aged 13 : 10, M.A. 12 : 1), 'He made it calm by speaking to it, then telling the water to divide. *Has the water got ears?* No, everything could obey God because he's everywhere. He's in everything, in the water. *How can he be in the water and talk to the water?* He's not actually in the water, but he is everywhere.' Rowena aged 10 : 7 (M.A. 12 : 3) says, 'He made everything, and he commands them like the birds.'

These ideas are frequently made by older backward pupils. The wind hypothesis is proposed by Jay aged 12 : 6 (M.A. 12 : 1), 'He could have sent a very strong wind and pushed the water back. *How would that make it divide on two sides?* He'd send two winds, blowing on each side. *Would they not blow the Israelites over?* I don't know. I'm stuck there.' Roland 12 : 7 (M.A. 12 : 4), 'It were a miracle. He could have made the tide, if it was going one way, to go different ways and make it dry in between *How would he do that?* He'd command it. I dunno how it could obey. He's got some power no one else has got.' In a later question he says, 'They couldn't just think it up. Someone must have been there and others would contradict it if it weren't true.' Priscilla aged 12 : 8 (M.A. 12 : 8) uses tidal wave and wind to explain it, 'God sent a tidal wave. He made a strong wind over that part of the sea. *Wouldn't it blow the Israelites over?* Yes, but they'd force themselves across.' An ingenious explanation is Anis' (aged 13 : 1, M.A. 14 : 1), who says, 'God made it a very very hot day by shining the sun hard. *How did that do it?* Well, the mountain springs might stop, the waters would stop flowing, the rivers went down and the people got across wading. When the Egyptians got there the waters might flow again and the seas be deep and choppy.' One boy 14 : 5 (M.A. 14 : 2) tries a rational explanation and rejects it because it has no biblical support, 'On TV it said there was already a path used for years by traders, like a secret path among the marshes. *Do you think this is the explanation?* No, God sent a wind in each direction which blew the water away. *Would it blow the Israelites off their feet?* No, he protected them with an invisible barrier.' Another merges a miraculous and a rational explanation: Ann aged 12 : 4 (M.A. 13 : 10), 'Maybe a sort of dam God made, which stopped the water flowing. *How?* God can do anything. The Israelites travelled light but the Egyptians wore heavy armour and sank into the sand.' After putting forward the idea of a wind and saying the Israelites would be tough enough to withstand it, Gordon says, 'God controls the whole world, so it's not much to part the sea for a few hours.' Barny, aged 11 : 6 (M.A. 12 : 5) sums up this stage when he says, 'God is the creator of it all and he can do anything with the water, the land, the wind or the whole world.'

Finally, at about 13½ years of age (M.A. 14 : 6) most pupils are changing over to more rational concepts where coincidence and exaggeration are possible and natural explanations sought, which may or may not be consistent with divine providence. God guides men to where natural events help the escape, rather than altering the physical world of nature. Typical of the coincidence view is Polly aged 13 : 5 (M.A. 15 : 3), 'I've heard it was the tide going out. I don't see why it wasn't a coincidence. It was a normal tide. They were just lucky.' To this is often added the weight of the armour and chariots making the Egyptians sink in soft mud and sand. One boy, aged 15 : 9 (M.A. 15 : 11) says openly, 'I don't think it could have divided. The person who first wrote it down could have exaggerated it. The Israelites crossed the sea somehow, and the Egyptians who came after were drowned by some means.' Another advanced an ingenious idea (age 13 : 4 and M.A. 15 : 11), 'Manuscripts found since the Bible say it was the Red Sea, almost a mass of seaweed. Probably God made it support the weight of Israelites but not the weight of the heavy chariots.' But even here there is evidence of God altering the forces of nature as George, aged 16 : 11 (M.A. 16 : 10) says, 'It was God's force. He'd remove the forces keeping the waters there, such as gravity, or put another force which pushed it back. It was a physical force the Israelites could neither see nor feel.' The wind explanation recurs but this time more rationally, in Bridget's answer (age 15 : 7, M.A. 17 : 8), 'The winds were in two directions. A current of air was keeping the water back and wouldn't affect people in the middle. There's peace at the centre of a gale.'

The coincidence of a natural event used by God is expressed by Sandra, aged 12 : 2 (M.A. 17 : 0) a very bright Grammar school pupil: 'I've heard it happens nowadays: the tide rises at two different parts of the shore and leaves the middle dry. It was a natural tide but God got them there at the right time.' Jonathan, aged 15 : 4 (M.A. 17 : 6) similarly, 'It was more of a tidal occurrence or earth tremor. It was a natural wave, it would have happened anyway. God was at the back of it, but not so extraordinarily as in the story. They got across as the tide was turning and the Egyptians were caught. God had something to do with it as the controller of nature.' A fifth former says, 'It was normal in that there was a low tide. God may not work the tides but might put it into Moses' mind the exact time to get there.' A science sixth student in also supporting this view, 'It was a sandbank, or rib of sand'—says of the story, 'the fundamentals are true, not literally, because the details aren't always exact, due to writers wanting it to be more vivid.' A girl in a sixth form favours the tidal wave idea as a natural event, but entirely dismisses divine intervention except for the psychological condition of the pursued, 'He made them more persevering.'

So we can see a rough sequence of concepts occurring from direct intervention of an anthropomorphic kind, to indirect intervention due to manipulation of related natural elements and intervention less direct or not at all, other than in the human condition. This roughly approximates to the conclusions reached by pupils in looking at the Burning Bush event, but it is apparent that the waters dividing tend to continue the miraculous element longer and intervention continues in a physical sense until much later (C.A. 13 : 8 and M.A. 14 : 6) than in the developing ideas of the Burning Bush. In many responses here we can observe the real tension between theological and scientific concepts, which we will discuss in detail later.

STONE INTO BREAD AND WATER INTO WINE

The Temptations narrative leads naturally to a discussion of whether Jesus could have turned the stone into bread if he had tried. Our purpose here is not to discuss the motivation of Jesus in refusing to do this, but to examine what divine powers pupils feel Jesus had, and how far these extend to intervention with natural laws. There is no doubt in most of the pupils' minds that Jesus had the power, conferred by God as the creator, to change the stone into bread. Otherwise, one boy pointed out, it wouldn't have been a real temptation. The point was missed, as with all of them with one or two exceptions, that this was a parable and real stone and real bread were not literally involved, but merely symbolised the temptation of Jesus to become an economic reformer. However, within a literal context, unlimited power over nature was assumed to be possessed by Jesus. The young children see it as magic and 'Jesus would touch it with his magic stick' or cast a spell on the stone. An intermediate group at the top end of the Junior school and early Secondary, see it transformed from stone to bread by the word of command, a slightly more spiritualised concept. Only a few resist the idea that Jesus had the power, saying it was too trivial or, more discerningly, this wasn't the kind of way God worked. The general sequence of development in the first two stages corresponds closely to similar concepts up to thirteen years in the Burning Bush and Dividing of the Sea stories.

Those pupils who discussed the similarity, or otherwise, between this temptation and the turning of water into wine, also showed a similar conceptual development. Practically all children affirmed that Jesus actually turned water into wine, not only because it was to help his friends (in contrast to helping the devil) but, as many younger children pointed out, it was easier because water resembled wine in the first place, more than stone resembled bread. As one child expressed it, both 'water and wine are runny and almost the same

112

liquid'. This naïve and inconsistent view that Jesus possessed un-limited divine power, but would find some substances easier to change than others, continued until the age of about eleven years. A few pupils, older adolescents, resisted the idea that Jesus could do this kind of thing, with stone or water, for the reason that God does not tamper with natural law but prefers to work within it, or for the reason of rational disbelief. Even so, some of the pupils rather curiously accept the possibility of one occurring, but not the other. As we have no details or further evidence of how adolescents in par-ticular view the miracles of Jesus it is difficult to generalise. There are indications, however, that many older and more able pupils, find the healing miracles of Jesus easier to accept than the nature miracles. Yet some of them quote the stilling of the storm as a comparable example of divine control when trying to explain the dividing of the waters in the Exodus story. Only one boy, sixteen years old, pointed out that if Jesus rejected the use of magic and miracle at the begin-ning of his ministry, it was inconsistent of him to use it later on.

ARTIFICIALISM

To summarise this discussion we can say that in both the Exodus stories God is seen by children up to about M.A. 11 : 5 as intervening in materialistic and physical ways, in such a manner as to indicate that magic and miracle are the same in the children's thinking. God must personally intervene and manipulate nature to secure his ends by physical means, and as discussed earlier, in crude anthropomor-phic terms. In the Burning Bush story God sends rain to stop the bush burning, or coats it with iron or interposes His body between the fire and the bush. In the Red Sea incident, God is seen as parting the water with His hands or lying in the water pushing it aside with His body. The most mature view expressed by pupils is that God does not interfere with nature but influences man internally or uses natural occurrences to help man in his distress. In the Red Sea incident, this is very striking as occurring after about M.A. 14 : 6. In between, there appears to be a stage when God manipulates the natural world, not imminently nor in person, but by changes of wind, sun or tem-perature, often as 'the Word', commanding the world as its creator. The Temptations of Jesus story indicates another aspect of this con-ception in two items. Jesus, as God's agent, is almost universally (by all ages) conceived to have the power to change stone into bread. Either he possessed the power himself, or could request God to do it. Similarly most pupils felt that not only could Jesus literally change water into wine, but he did. There is, therefore, a clear concept at all ages of God's power having no limits, at least theoretically.

The Old Testament story items illustrate what was written earlier about what Piaget called Artificialism in the young child. Piaget in his suggestive structure of mythological artificialism (4–7 years), technical artificialism (7–10 years) and non-artificialism thereafter, was addressing himself to the problem of how children conceived of the origins of the sun, moon, stars and clouds. 'Mythological' artificialism he defines as origins being due to human or divine agency, 'technical' artificialism as a fusion of mythological artificialism and explanations, and non-artificialism where natural logical-scientific thinking is found by the child to be the only satisfactory explanation. Where the biblical incidents are concerned, mythological artificialism would appear to be very strong in the youngest groups of 6 and 7 years where, for example, the bush is not really burning because God is inside pushing up bits of lighted paper on sticks, but just as strong up to the mental age of 11 : 5, as for example: 'He (God) magicked it,' 'He put a spell on it, a spell like water chucked on the bush', and 'God was standing there unseen, dividing the fire from the bush.' A similar trend is apparent in the problem of how the sea was divided. It appears from this that the stage of technical artificialism (the second stage) does not come until much later than 7 to 10 years and may even continue as late as 13 years.

Where the natural world is concerned, therefore, it is probable that the Junior school and early Secondary school pupil conceives of it in terms of dualistic systems. One system is theological and incidents such as are narrated in the Bible illustrate how God can and does persistently intervene, sometimes arbitrarily, often personally in a physical sense and occasionally dramatically. The other system is composed of growing logical-scientific concepts where artificialism is gradually being abandoned for a more rational view. There is probably some interpenetration between the two systems, but not a great deal. It would appear that a synthesis of the two systems is one of the major tasks of religious education beginning, perhaps, at the end of the Junior school, and most certainly in the first two years in the Secondary school. This, as we have seen in Chapter Five, is closely linked with what the pupil thinks about the authority and veracity of the Bible.

In the Secondary school the teacher is confronted by many pupils who appear still to equate magic and miracle, and see God as intervening actively, personally and physically in the natural world to achieve His purposes, up to the twelfth year of mental age. After this age, artificialist explanations of biblical incidents tend to diminish but there is confusion and conflict between what is regarded as authoritative in the Bible and what the pupil is beginning to develop as a logico-scientific thought system. That God's power should be limited by himself appears to be a concept quite beyond most school pupils even after a mental age of 15 : 0. For most, the natural world is God's to do what he wishes with, as its Creator, and his power is unlimited and often arbitrary. Faced with this situation some teachers have spoken to me of how they began to introduce critical ideas to their pupils in the later school years, and how many of their pupils expressed both shock and anger that they had been led to continue literal and childish beliefs for so long. This feeling among adolescents is so strong that it is often expressed as 'betrayal' by the adult world. Plainly, therefore, teachers must overcome their fears of disturbing the simple childlike faith of the young, and educate to the realistic possibilities of a belief in a deity who is not in contradiction with their growing logical powers and scientific concepts. This is not to avoid the thorny problem of miracle, nor to seek to explain it away, but to encourage positive and critical thinking in relation to biblical narrative. Some of the anguish felt by adolescents at their betrayal is partly the conditioning they have had about biblical authority and the feelings of guilt engendered thereby when they come to be critical of its truth. This process of literalism seems to continue far too long for the healthy religious development of young people. They may equate religious belief as uncritical childish acceptance and the only valid alternative is to jettison the whole structure as rationally untenable. This process may tend to occur much earlier, and probably less consciously but more emotionally, among less able adolescents as Kenneth Hyde's work (1963) has shown. The problem is not resolved by saying that religion is at its heart irrational and all attempts to understand God must result in limited knowledge. Some methods of presenting the Bible appear to so create misunderstandings that much of it seems to be a real hindrance to the adolescent's religious quest.

Chapter Eight

THE HOLINESS OF GOD

RUDOLF OTTO (1950) in *The Idea of the Holy* has explored the view that primitive man found the deity both fascinating and fearful. His feelings are ambivalent, naturally curious and intrigued by possible contact with the holy, but also repulsed by a dread, which later becomes awe, developing into respect, admiration and worship. The story of the Burning Bush is an interesting biblical example of what Otto calls the numinous, this sense of dread and awe in man. Moses is plainly afraid to look upon God, for who shall look upon the greatness and splendour of the divine, and live? Yet he is drawn, fascinated not merely by the attraction of the bush, but by the presence of the holy. So impressed is Moses by the presence of the divine that he shields his face with his cloak lest he be tempted to look, and removes his shoes as a sign of respect. Here is the numinous, the sacred, the holy, the divine. To be familiar with the holy is a violation which might bring down terrible punishment, for beside its enormous brooding power man is small and insignificant. In the Mosaic stage of Hebrew religion the holy is not equated with the good. Ethical monotheism is still far in the future. God is powerful rather than good, menacing rather than comforting, often unpredictable, arbitrary and angry, somewhat in the moody manner of a powerful Pharaoh. This is anthropomorphic thinking, not about the person and identity of the divine, but about his personality and psychology. Moses was limited by his day and age and undoubtedly shared many of these crude anthropomorphisms, while at the same time lifting his people to a loftier view of God.

It is often said that children are similar to the primitives in their approach to the holy. Certainly, childish fears of the unknown are frequent, not only in general, such as fears of the dark, but in more specific anxieties displayed when entering a large building such as a church. Fear is sometimes expressed that 'there is something there', unpredictable and menacing. It was of interest, therefore, to examine what children thought to be the basis of Moses' fear of the holy and his awe of it, as a reflection of their own sense of the numinous. Two questions were asked in the discussion of the Burning Bush story, to see what concepts emerged.[1] These were, 'Why was Moses afraid to

[1] See Appendix A, questions S.1: Q.2 and S.1: Q.4.

look at God?' and 'Why was the ground, on which Moses stood, holy?' We have already analysed some of the responses to these questions in terms of operational thinking. We shall now see them in the light of their theological significance.

THE FEAR OF LOOKING UPON GOD

In evaluating the pupils' replies to the question of why Moses would not look at God, some supplementary questions were asked later to clarify the assessment of their thinking. These were, 'Should Moses have been afraid to look at God?' and 'Would you, if you'd been Moses, have been afraid to look at God?' A large majority of the pupils said Moses should not and they would not have been afraid to look upon God. Most advanced the reason that now we know God loves us. 'We know better,' and 'Jesus came and told us God isn't like that.' A few older and more intelligent adolescents said they would still be afraid, because God is powerful and to be held in awe, even though we know God is love, revealed in Christ. The almost universal response, frequently in identical words, leads one to suspect the majority of these answers to be verbalisms, and subsequent discussion revealed this to be so. The authentic thinking of the children and adolescents was revealed in the reasons they gave for Moses' fear. These could be divided into three major groups, in a sequence of age and mental ability, shown in the examples which follow.

The younger children up to about eight years of age (M.A. 8 : 4) revealed some irrelevant answers, showing how they had grossly misunderstood the essentials of the story. Such answers were, 'He was afraid God might kill him for setting fire to the bush,' 'Moses didn't like God for telling him to take off his shoes,' and 'Moses loved God and didn't like to see him burn.' Even so, in this type of answer something of the menace of the holy can be seen. The majority of responses, however, up to the age of eight were relevant and clearly revealed fear of God as an unpredictable, threatening presence at a most primitive level, although many of the children are obviously confused and led astray by verbal associations. Typical is Bernard aged 6 : 7 (M.A. 5 : 1), 'He didn't want to. He was frightened of God's voice. It was loud', and Jean aged 6 : 2 (M.A. 5 : 3), 'He was frightened God might kill all his sheep.' Leona aged 6 : 5 (M.A. 6 : 0) says, 'He didn't like God's face. *How do you mean?* 'It's all old and frightening and that.' This child said Moses should have been afraid and she would have been if she'd 'been on God's ground'. Frank aged 6 : 7 (M.A. 8 : 7) said 'Moses thought God did evil things. He thought God might catch him and then hurt him.' Here the menace of the deity is unpredictable. It is again expressed by Lillian aged

7 : 5 (M.A. 9 : 2), 'He was afraid God might do something to Moses. (Q) No. Moses hadn't done no wrong.' Sidney expresses dread (age 7 : 8, M.A. 7 : 7), 'He was afraid he'd see something horrible, something coming down on top of him as though it might murder him.'

Many of these younger children suggested Moses hid his face in his cloak as protection from the flames, but this physical protection is also a defence against a possible sudden venom, as Lester aged 8 : 2 (M.A. 8 : 1), 'He was afraid the bush would hurt him. It would burn him if he came too near God.' Others are worried about God punishing Moses, not because he has come too close or looked upon God, but because he has done wrong in walking on holy ground with his shoes on. Karen aged 6 : 4 (M.A. 8 : 4) expresses this. 'Moses thought God would chase him out of the holy ground, because Moses hadn't taken off his shoes. *Any other reason?* Moses thought God didn't look very nice, frightening', but several older children also advance the same view of impending punishment. Sometimes fear of the unknown is stated simply as shyness or ignorance, as with Lora aged 9 : 6 (M.A. 7 : 3), 'Moses didn't know it was God. You see God had a beard and Moses didn't like beards. He'd never seen God before. *How did he know God had a beard?* Because he had seen it in the Holy Bible.' Sometimes it is because God is angry at Moses' ignorance, as in Joan's response (age 7 : 9, M.A. 10 : 3), 'God might be cross with Moses because the shepherd Moses didn't know God was in the bush and he should have known.'

After this limited stage there develops for most pupils an intermediate stage of concepts about the holy where the dread is still expressed but to a lesser degree. The reasons for Moses' fear are similar to the previous stage but more elaborate and show the deity as more rational and less vindictive. This quality of answer goes on to about 12 : 8 (M.A. 13 : 3). At this stage two categories of answer can be seen, those which emphasise the strange elements of the experience and those which say God's presence awakens a general sense of guilt. The first can be seen in the following answers: Richard aged 9 : 3 (M.A. 8 : 7) said, 'It hadn't happened to him before . . . God was stronger than any other person. He was afraid God might hurt him.' The bright light is often associated with God as fearful, as when Poppy aged 8 : 3 (M.A. 10 : 7) says, 'It might have been because the bright light from the bush was frightening him. He would know God wouldn't hurt him.' The strangeness of the unique events is Daisy's reason (aged 8 : 9, M.A. 10 : 3). 'He'd just seen the bush on fire and it wasn't burnt and there was a voice coming from it and he was frightened.' Daisy added, 'It'd frighten me. It'd be strange hearing and seeing that.' Julie aged 9 : 8 (M.A. 10 : 6) advances the awesomeness of a God of old, 'Because it was his father's father's God, and he was standing on holy ground and anything drastic might happen there.' The unpredictable and possible evil element still lingers on in Allen's reason (age 10 : 2, M.A. 9 : 9), 'He hadn't seen him before and he might have thought it was an evil spirit', and also in Alastair's (age 10 : 7, M.A. 12 : 7), 'He might not be able to believe it was God. He thought it might be an evil spirit. People in these days might gossip about an evil spirit getting into you and he'd be afraid of this happening . . . He'd be more afraid then than he would now.' Malevolence is also expressed by Keith (age 10 : 5, M.A. 10 : 6), 'Not many people have seen God. *How do you mean?* He didn't know any who'd seen God, and Moses thought they all might have been killed.' Keith says of his personal feelings, 'Yes, at first I'd be afraid to look. Nobody says they've seen God 'cept the disciples, and they didn't see God but the spirit of Jesus.' Alice aged 10 : 4 (M.A. 11 : 8) says, 'No one else had seen God and Moses was frightened to be the only person. He didn't know what God would look like.'

The second quality of answer at this intermediate stage, continuing up to the twelfth and thirteenth year, is concerned with guilt feelings aroused by contact with the divine. Lesley aged 9 : 11 (M.A. 13 : 5) reflects a churchgoing pietism in her answer: 'He hadn't been going to Church or anything like that. God wouldn't like him any more and not make him go up to heaven . . . If he hadn't prayed, God wouldn't forgive him if he had done anything wrong.' With great confidence she asserts she would have been unafraid, 'because *I* go to Sunday School'. Keith aged 8 : 11 (M.A. 10 : 0) is more general, 'He was shy and it was a strange voice. *How do you mean?* He thought God was accusing him of doing something wrong.' The malevolence still appears in Harry's reply (age 9 : 8, M.A. 11 : 11), 'He'd done something wrong. Everyone has sinned sometime and he thought God was going to curse him or something terrible.' Rose implicitly states the reason for not looking (age 9 : 11, M.A. 10 : 0), 'Moses might have done some evil and was afraid to look at God 'cause God might not forgive him. *Would you have been afraid to look?* Yes. I might have done wrong and didn't want God to know about it so I wouldn't look at him.' Jan is more explicit about the looking (age 11 : 0, M.A. 13 : 8), 'It might be he was ashamed of himself. He might be afraid to look like you are with a person when you're accused of anything. He knows God's power and feared what he might do.' There is still no concept of feeling unworthy to look upon God because of God's greatness and his awesome nature. This belongs to the next and final stage.

The almighty, awesome nature of God contrasts with man's smallness after the age of 12 : 8 (M.A. 13 : 3) for most pupils. A sense of personal unworthiness in the face of the tremens is later recognised as something not peculiar to Moses but as an experience shared by all. This concept takes some time to mature but once it is arrived at the personal question, 'Would you have been afraid to look?' is answered consistently, 'Yes', because once this aspect of God is known it follows that all his people must feel the same way. 'Moses was no different from other man and no one is supposed to look at God,' says Charles aged 13 : 4 (M.A. 17 : 8) 'and he hadn't the right to look at God.' Adrian aged 14 : 5 (M.A. 16 : 3) puts it this way, 'He wondered what God would look like, and he was afraid to find out. If you think of God as Jesus and it might be different, you wouldn't want to look. Moses would think of God as a spirit.' Roger, in a Secondary Modern school, aged 14 : 11 (M.A. 11 : 8) says, 'He knew God was much higher than him. He was much greater than Moses.' In the same school Diana, aged 14 : 11 (M.A. 13 : 1) says, 'He was ashamed that he'd spoken to God. He hadn't realised it was God. He should have known because everything about God is good and clean and pure.'

The more intelligent adolescents emphasise the awesome aspects more, as does Larry, aged 13 : 2 (M.A. 18 : 4), 'God was a much greater person than himself. There was something over-awing about it . . . God was so great and Moses was like a worm in importance.' Polly aged 13 : 5 (M.A. 15 : 3), says, 'He felt he wasn't fit to. *How do you mean?* He wasn't worthy enough to look at God himself. In those days they felt God was very special and he had to be treated with great care.' A science fifth form boy says, 'He'd be afraid of what he might see . . . He'd have a primitive feeling of awe.' A Grammar school girl, Delia, aged 14 : 3 (M.A. 15 : 4) says, 'God said, "No man shall see God and live." God was holy and the world was sinful. People wouldn't be worthy to look on God.' Barry, aged 14 : 5 (M.A. 17 : 6), puts it more concisely, 'He thought of a person too high and too glorious to look at. Moses was filled with awe and wonder . . . He was afraid of what he might see because he was so devout he couldn't understand. He was afraid of what he couldn't comprehend.' Two very advanced concepts can be quoted, one by a sixth form girl, 'Moses wasn't good enough to look. *Why not?* God was very good and Moses had sinned . . . nothing specially; he was an ordinary sinful man. God was almighty. He'd made all the earth and to think God would come to Moses would overawe him.' The other, finally, is from a sixth form boy, 'The sight of God was too much for human eyes. It's too tremendous a vision. Moses knew this and was afraid. He may have been taught that if a man looked he'd turn into stone or be consumed by divine power. *Would you have been afraid to look?* Yes, anyone would. The circumstances were awesome.'

Fear of the holy is therefore seen in this sequence of the pupils' religious thinking, the major change appearing in the twelfth to the thirteenth year, before which primitive, irrational and specific guilt feelings are attributed to Moses, whereas after this time a concept of God as almighty and man in relation to him develops more realistically. We shall see a similar pattern in examining our next question, and it is interesting to note a very close comparison in terms of age.

THE NATURE OF THE HOLY GROUND

Continuing our examination of how pupils conceptualise 'the numinous', the sense of dread and awe felt in the presence of God, we see that young children fail to see the significance of Moses removing his shoes. Not only is this Eastern custom of respect not understood, but with the very young the experience which prompts such action is only partially grasped. Discussion with groups of children before my test was devised showed that the young use the word 'holy' frequently in relation to religion, describing God, Jesus, the Bible, biblical stories, the church, prayer and other religious experience as 'holy'. Sometimes it is only a verbalism, sometimes it is used as to depict something special or different, without the speciality or difference clearly defined. In the given context of the story of the Burning Bush the word is understood in a hierarchy of meaning which ascends with age. Apart from the misunderstanding of the very young, what makes for holiness is seen in some way, from the youngest to the eldest, to be the hallowing of that place by the divine presence either in the past or during the incident. The differences in the quality of answers can be seen in the varied ways by which the presence of God is conceived and how it mediates the essence of 'the holy'.

We shall now look at the sequence of responses to the question, 'Why was the ground on which Moses stood, holy?' For some younger children, who did not seem to grasp this standard form of question, a simpler form was sometimes used such as 'Why do you think Moses had to take off his shoes?' or 'Why was the ground so important that Moses had to take off his shoes?' Three stages, in terms of sequence of thinking, were evident, but only in times of mental age. For this reason it is mental age which we shall use throughout this section indicating the division between one stage and another. Two children only gave wholly irrelevant answers. Martha aged 7 : 3 (M.A. 6 : 10) said it was 'nice ground, not to be trampled on . . .' and Massey aged 7 : 8 (M.A. 6 : 1) said, 'I can only say he took his shoes off because God wants a friend. God wanted a friend 'cause he didn't have no friends. *How do you mean?* Because he had his shoes off, then they'd be friends.' In a previous answer, Massey had pointed out that God always went barefoot.

The first stage, with these two exceptions, shows much confusion in the child's mind due to focusing upon the nature of the ground or misleading associations and literalisms. Nonetheless most children reflect the sense of the numinous, the undercurrent of awe because of the ground having some contact with the divine power. This can be seen in Leonard's answer (age 6 : 11, M.A. 5 : 9), 'It had holes in it. God had to take his shoes off, so Moses had to.' Here is gross literalism, presumably because the child thinks the ground is so full of holes it is in danger of collapsing and the removal of shoes will lighten the weight of people who walk on it. In further discussion Leonard adds, 'It's God's ground, it's holy, and Moses shouldn't be on there. *How is it God's ground?* He's magic. He lives in the sky and he comes down and walks underground and everywhere you go.' Again, the reasoning may be that if God walks under the ground this may account for the holes (holy ground). This is stated explicitly by Penelope (aged 6 : 8, M.A. 6 : 4), 'If he has his shoes on, the ground might fall down. There's a lot of holes in it, you see, and it wasn't safe.' Jill aged 8 : 11 (M.A. 7 : 0) has the same association of ideas. 'Holy is everywhere, because God was under the ground. He's everywhere.' Many answers indicate children concentrating on the texture of the ground. So Kevan aged 7 : 7 (M.A. 6 : 5) says, 'It was all nice and smooth and it had no stones on it.' *Why should he take his shoes off?* 'God made him to try his feet on the holy ground to see how it feels.' In an effort to define holy ground Bob, aged 7 : 7 (M.A. 7 : 11) says, 'It's soft ground . . . God's only in special places where they are soft.' *Is this ground holy?* 'No, it's made of wood.' Brenda, aged 8 : 4 (M.A. 7 : 10) tries to cope with it differently, 'It was a different place. *How do you mean?* It's got different grass, it's holy grass, that's why he had to take his shoes off. *Is this ground holy?* No, it's in a different country. It's only holy in a special country, Palestine.' There are associations here with the term 'the Holy Land' and possibly park notices, 'Keep off the grass'. Similar to this is Godfrey, aged 8 : 1 (M.A. 8 : 3), 'Because it was holy ground. In Nazareth Jesus used to stand and that was holy.' Again this is merely associative thinking focused upon the word 'stand'. Interesting egocentric answers are Leona's (age 6 : 5, M.A. 6 : 0), 'It was all mud with water and it would spoil his shoes. Holy means it's all wet and muddy', and Henry's (age 8 : 3, M.A. 6 : 8), 'It was hot ground. It would burn his shoes.' Reprimand by adults for careless soiling of shoes may be reflected in these answers.

Still at this stage, but showing associations with God or Jesus, thus making it holy, are such replies as Andrea's (aged 7 : 7, M.A. 7 : 7), 'It was his land. He was in charge of Moses, in his power, because he was on land God made.' When asked, 'Did God make everywhere?' she replied, 'Yes. Everywhere is holy. *Is this ground holy?*

Yes, God made it. *Should we take our shoes off?* No, you'd cut your feet on stones. *What about Moses?* No, there wouldn't be any stones around there.' Some answers indicate it was holy because it belonged to the disciples, or Jesus was buried there (in the time of Moses), or holy because it had flowers and crosses (association with graveyards) and concern lest Moses should trample on the graves. Many children say, as does Billy (age 6 : 9, M.A. 7 : 10), 'Probably it was where God lived. He didn't want any dirt to be on his ground.' Despite the fact that Billy thinks God is everywhere, a place is only holy where he makes his home. In answer to the question, 'Is this place holy?' comes an emphatic, 'No, God wouldn't want this place (the school) to be his home. He could live in a nicer place.' We have already quoted Nathan's vivid reply of the holy power, 'It was near God. He makes it holy. Moses took off his shoes to make himself holy. The holy would go up through his feet and through his body.'

The second stage, beginning about M.A. 8 : 2 and continuing to about M.A. 12 : 3, shows concepts of the holy, dependent upon God being present at that place in a physical sense, in a physical body or speaking with a physical voice. Sometimes it is seen as a holy place because it is the scene of a miracle, in the physical sense, but all answers reflect the immanence of God for that particular incident. The scene of a miracle reason is expressed by Sylvia, aged 8 : 7 (M.A. 11 : 5), 'Because God was holy and God was there. The other bushes were burning but this one wasn't.' Sylvia felt God was everywhere and therefore everywhere was holy. 'Everywhere is holy, but special places, like this (the Burning Bush) are very holy.' Eric, aged 11 : 2 (M.A. 11 : 5), is more precise, 'God was there and performed a deed there by making the bush burn. Maybe he sacrificed a dove there and prayed.' For this reason Eric maintained that only special places were holy, '. . . not where wrong is done as in China where opium smoking takes place.' Rikki, aged 10 : 7 (M.A. 10 : 3) says, 'Something very good happened there, like the place where Jesus was born', while Winifred uses this idea but reverts to the old graveyard association. 'Jesus was there and the bush was holy. That's why it wouldn't burn, although there were flames coming from it and the ground must be holy. Someone might be buried there.' Association with Jesus and feet is made by Norman aged 9 : 10 (M.A. 10 : 1), 'When Jesus said to his disciples, "Take off your shoes" he began to wash their feet. *What's this got to do with the Moses' story?* God said, "Take off your shoes" to Moses. Moses was standing near the bush. *How did it make the ground holy?* 'Cause God was in the burning light.'

Examples of the physical experience of God being present are many. Some are primitive like Netta's (age 6 : 5, M.A. 8 : 2), 'Because

123

God was down on earth on that place. This place isn't holy because God isn't with us here', and Laura's (age 9 : 11, M.A. 8 : 5), 'It was near God. This was where God was standing.' Clive (age 10 : 11, M.A. 8 : 6) isn't sure if it's contact with God's feet on the earth or a place where God prayed that makes it a holy place, but Jerry (age 11 : 5, M.A. 9 : 7) has no uncertainty, producing an ariel landing concept, 'God was on the ground. He is holy and put his feet there when he came down and he made it holy.' David aged 11 : 8 (M.A. 11 : 5) makes it an angel's foot, 'The angel had trodden on it with his foot', but Gerald does bring in the Eastern custom (age 11 : 8, M.A. 11 : 4), 'God was standing on it. He's holy and in those days they used to take off their shoes to go into holy places.' An interesting analogy is made by Joe (age 13 : 10, M.A. 12 : 1), 'It's like when there's a king stands on a carpet, it's special. Well, God stood on that ground.' Sara reverts to a fairly crude idea of ownership, 'God was around that place. It was private. No one was allowed to go in there 'cept the owners. God owned it. It was his private place' (age 9 : 10, M.A. 8 : 10). D'Arcy aged 10 : 5 (M.A. 11 : 3) says only special places are holy, 'places where God has been seen'. Andrew aged 8 : 5 (M.A. 11 : 8) uses a physical analogy but emphasises God's invisibility, 'God had been there and made it holy by standing on it, without anyone seeing.' He also develops a holier by degree concept. 'All places are holy, but certain places are holier than others because God might have been there more.' Poppy uses an important distinction (age 8 : 3, M.A. 10 : 7), 'God was standing on it. It was there, not just his spirit. *Is God standing in other places?* No, he's usually in heaven. *Is God everywhere?* Yes, he's sent his spirit everywhere. *Is this ground holy?* No, it isn't like a church. We don't say prayers here. *Did God say prayers near the Burning Bush?* Oh, God was there, not just his spirit.' The power of the holy is transmitted in another way, suggests Frank aged 6 : 7 (M.A. 8 : 7), 'It was holy 'cause God was near it. *How do you mean?* He was there making the land holy, by looking at it.'

The third stage after about M.A. 12 : 3 reveals most pupils' concepts moving over to a more spiritual non-physical encounter with God, where also the sense of the numinous is much more marked. A few older sixth formers show strong numinous insights, with some imaginative understanding of the reaction a man may feel in a fairly primitive world, or they conceive the holy to be the moment of truth. God's presence may be seen symbolically as does Joyce, aged 14 : 9 (M.A. 12 : 4), 'God was there. *How do you mean?* It was a special place. He was there as the flame', and Max, aged 14 : 10 (M.A. 14 : 1), 'God was near it. It was holy because of the flaming bush. It was a symbol telling Moses it was a place where he shouldn't go.' The place may be seen in terms where God spoke, but in a spiritual manner. So Dianne 14 : 11 (M.A. 13 : 1), 'God was there. He's everywhere but his presence was there insofar as he was speaking to Moses . . . it was a sign of God . . . spiritually in his mind.' Alastair indicates the presence is non-physical to him (age 10 : 10, M.A. 12 : 7) by saying, 'Two people can see God at the same time, because he comes in a vision.' A more mystical concept is expressed by Petula aged 11 : 4 (M.A. 15 : 0), 'The burning bush wasn't actually burning. The glory of God made a light, and it had the power of making the ground to be holy, a place where anything could happen . . . All three were there, the glory, the light and the power.' George 16 : 11 (M.A. 16 : 10) is unsure, 'God was there, but not as a presence—he is everywhere—but specially so, as he is in church. But can he have a greater degree of presence? I'm not sure!' The element of belief is important to Mary aged 12 : 8 (M.A. 16 : 10), 'God was there. God *is* everywhere, yes, everywhere is holy, but not so holy as there. Where God says he is or where we believe he is, that's holy.' A sixth former puts this more succinctly, 'Anywhere people acknowledge the presence of God is holy.' Dennis compares the incident with other Old Testament incidents (age 14 : 4, M.A. 19 : 2), 'God was there. It was something special there as with Jacob at Bethel. God spoke to Moses and Moses was specially chosen to hear in his mind.'

A few sixth formers try to search into the nature of a primitive experience and produce some interesting insights. Barry says, 'Wasn't it supposed to be the Lord's mountain? Wasn't it a volcano? What they couldn't understand, they called it holy, something dangerous to be left alone. Maybe it was Moses' conscience speaking.' Edward suggests a scientific analogy, 'It's the custom in the East to take off his shoes in reverence. *Why was it holy ground?* The presence of God would hallow it. It was like a magnet. The magnet field is everywhere, but the pole is in one spot. *How do you mean?* God concentrated there, although his influence is everywhere.' Deborah advances the subjective aspect of the experience. 'The presence of the Lord was there. The author didn't conceive God the same way as we do, as they thought of him on top of the mountain. It was here Moses *felt* he came into contact with the person of God, even though his presence is everywhere.'

It appears from the above that in order to grasp the essence of Moses' experience most children need to have matured intellectually to just over twelve mental years. Before this age crude anthropomorphic thinking and frequent misunderstanding makes it difficult for pupils to cope intellectually with the meaning of the story. Nevertheless, as in the problem of Moses' fear of looking upon God, there is a continuing sense of the numinous. Childish and primitive fear tends to give way to a sense of awe as God's presence is seen in more spiritual terms.

GENERAL COMMENTS ON CONCEPTS OF THE HOLY

The picture which is formed from the child's ideas of the holy is consistent with the previous evidence of the child's concepts of God, both his identity and nature, and his relations with the physical world. For the Infant child, God is to be feared as an unpredictable and touchy powerful adult, who is to be treated with caution as one treats some adults with caution. God has physical attributes combined with magical powers. This deity can harm, cast spells, punish and generally 'pay back' for what he considers is bad behaviour. There is no moral judgment present other than the fact that what God disapproves of is wrong. Children of this age appear to understand the deity at this level of thought, but alongside this must be set the view expressed by most of them that God is a friend. In a sense, what they attribute to Moses, in terms of fear, could be separate from their own experience, and in theory we could say that they perceived why Moses should be afraid without sharing that experience themselves. It is fairly clear, however, that for younger children at least, God is a friend, is a concept only partially grasped, both intellectually and emotionally. This is not surprising since Infants are at the stage of trying to live with a strange and, to them, unpredictable world of adult authority, when parents, teachers and other powerful figures do the oddest things for no apparent reason at all. Certainly in worship, assurance of the friendly, trusted and abiding presence of God should loom large for Infants. The person of Jesus may be a means of conveying this assurance, as a man God sent to help and heal people. But the natural awe of the child should not be discouraged by an over-simplified intimacy with God, which may only exist in the sentimental attitude of the teacher, and be reproduced as verbalisms in prayers and hymns, but have no firm reality in the child's understanding.

Junior children, as their anthropomorphic tendencies indicate, still see God as a superman, but not so irrational or unpredictable as the younger children see him. Fear appears to moderate into a sense of awe at this magical and powerful presence, which can appear in the world as a clear identity in miracle or any other event. He walks on the ground he has created, owns and sometimes lives on, making special visitations in a physical body or with a physical voice, as the need arises. Nowadays this doesn't happen so often as it did because God is mostly in heaven. Some Juniors think the same rules about divine appearance appertain now as in Bible times, only in modern life he doesn't need to visit us so often. Some confusion about holy places and God's omnipresence exists at this stage and is not often resolved. There is an uneasy, temporary solution reached by some children that although God is everywhere he nevertheless must appear in specific places at specific times as his anthropomorphic self. This view is supported by biblical authority and it again raises the question of whether we should expose children at this stage of their development to stories, especially from the Old Testament, which only reinforce these crude ideas. Guilt feelings about particular wrongs are apparently connected with the fear of God, and the deity is seen as a punisher, an avenger of actions of which he disapproves, although in not the same extremity as conceived by Infant children.

Pupils in the secondary schools appear to continue their Junior school religious concepts of the holy until about their twelfth year, when gradually physical ideas tend to give way from non-physical, material anomalies, to spiritualised ideas of a more consistent kind. An awe of God for his almightiness rather than his readiness to punish or his unpredictable power slowly develops. This beginning of a higher level of religious thought corresponds roughly with the beginnings of formal operational thinking, when propositions and hypotheses about the deity begin to be expressed.

A distinction begins to be made by the brighter and older adolescents, despite the literal authority of the Bible continuing, that a story such as the Burning Bush is a subjective account of a great religious leader's experience at a primitive time, when God was very partially revealed, or only dimly seen by men. It may be that these pupils are reflecting what they have been taught in terms of the successive religious ideas which can be seen in the Bible as a nation's religious quest is unfolded. It may be that some of them are naturally building up such concepts despite their previous literalisms, which had made all parts of the Bible equally true. Whatever the explanation, it is possible that by the age of thirteen to fourteen such concepts become feasible and teaching based upon the development of biblical ideas may provide better religious nourishment than a straightforward chronological treatment of Old Testament events.

Chapter Nine

GOD'S CONCERN FOR MEN

THE Crossing of the Red Sea story is evocative of a variety of concepts of deity. It is ideal for testing out the pupil's concepts of historical perspective and whether or not what he knows about New Testament concepts of God, as taught or demonstrated by Christ, is transferable in making judgments about an Old Testament situation. The evidence seems to indicate that the younger the child the greater the limitations of insight into history, moral judgment and many other aspects which combine to make the pupil distort, misunderstand and misjudge the activity of God in relation to corporate man. It is also evident that before a certain age the social and moral inexperience of children make it impossible to understand the New Testament ethic. It is not surprising, therefore, that little transfer is made until a later age.

In contrast to the question of how God behaves in relation to the natural world, this story raises all the important questions about God's dealings with the world of men. As Christianity is a historical religion, assuming belief that not only does God work through history but also that he actively intervenes in the affairs of men in history, these questions are of central importance. Concepts of divine love and justice, group and individual morality, and the divine purpose for the chosen nation Israel in the setting of world history, are basic to any biblical theology. These concepts are, of course, dependent upon a large number of other concepts. Divine love, for example, rests in the first place upon understanding relationships within a family, problems of favouritism, and concepts of equality and fairness, all involving some elements of propositional thinking. Concretistic thinking will take a child part of the way but will often impede his insights. Concepts of divine justice also involve a large number of related concepts, dependent in turn upon social and emotional maturity, the development of reciprocity in relationships, and many other ingredients. The child will also make moral judgments on people as a group, and because of inexperience and undeveloped moral standards, will reach immature conclusions. Some concept of historical continuity must be developed if the child is to understand the role of Israel in biblical history, especially in terms of a theological interpretation of God's purpose in 'choosing' Israel.

The limitations experienced by children and adolescents in grappling with these extremely complex ideas is often recognised, but we do not know clearly enough what the real nature of these limitations are and the educational problems they create. We shall now look in more detail at how the pupils' concepts on these matters appear to grow, and the kinds of sequence of thinking which seem to emerge. Chronological age appears to be a more important variable in these difficult questions. This is not surprising since many of the judgments are dependent upon certain social and moral experiences having occurred in the life of the child. Moral judgments and emotionally toned concepts of love may be more dependent upon length of life and the development of character than the mental ability to think in a logical or operational manner.

CONCEPTS OF DIVINE LOVE

Questions were designed[1] to see what insight the pupils have into the nature of God's love. To see if they accepted the universalism of divine love, 'Does God love everyone in the world?' was asked. To test the straight 'Yes' or 'No' answer, the further question was put, 'Did he love the men in the Egyptian army?' because it is in the particular example that the universal assertion can be tried out. The reasons for these answers were explored. If the answer was 'No', they were then asked, 'Why did he allow them to be drowned?' and if 'Yes', 'How could he love them and let them drown?' Moral judgments inevitably appear in the answers to these questions, and we shall examine these in more detail in the appropriate section on Divine Justice. Here our concern is how such judgments affect the concepts of divine love held by the pupils.

Two stages of thinking about divine love are clearly indicated, with the majority moving from one stage to the other about the age of 10 : 6 (M.A. 10 : 11). In the first stage the children tend to reject universal love or accept it at only a verbal level, their answers to the various questions being contradictory. Because God can and does act in an arbitrary manner, for children at this stage, the question of the relative moral guilt or innocence of the Egyptians is unrecognised and the destruction of the army is justifiable for various reasons. The divine ove is selective on a group basis, in terms of group label rather than individual worth. We are a long way from Isaiah's view, 'Blessed be Egypt my people, and Assyria the work of my hands, and Israel mine inheritance' (Isaiah xix, 25), where ancient enemies are included in the divine love.

[1] See Appendix A, question S.2: Q.2, A and B.

Here are some examples of rejection of divine love as a universalism. A few are irrelevant or stem from misunderstandings, such as Jenny aged 7 : 1 (M.A. 5 : 10), 'No, God doesn't love everyone. (Q) No, because the Egyptians were naughty, trying to steal the Israelites' money. (Q) They got drowned 'cause they kept on stealing money', and Kevan, aged 7 : 7 (M.A. 6 : 5) who denied universal love and God's love of the Egyptians because, 'They were bad and caught all the people and took them over to Germany. "We'll kill them," they said, and when they were died (the Israelites) they went up to heaven.' The reason for God allowing the Egyptians to drown was given by Kevan that, 'They nearly killed everybody.' Most, however, who reject universal divine love are consistently relevant, in that there is no contradiction because God's love is obviously denied to those who are naughty, wicked and cruel. Leslie expresses it clearly (age 6 : 1, M.A. 5 : 6). God doesn't love everyone in the world, 'because he loves the good and not the naughty. They (the Egyptians) were naughty charging after them.' God let them drown 'because he didn't like them; they were so naughty, fighting and charging'. The reasons for exclusion from divine love include, 'They chased them and were rough and put some in prison,' 'They were cruel and horrible to the Israelites,' 'They were trying to make them do what they didn't want,' 'The Israelites were his friends and the Egyptians weren't. *Why?* Because they was chasing after God's men.' Most children see God allowing the Egyptians to drown as a necessary act of prevention: 'Because they might put the slaves in prison,' 'He wanted Moses to be safe', and 'So the Israelites could be saved.' Some attribute angry or vindictive motives to God, 'He was angry with them,' 'They were naughty; they decided to let them free and then decided not' and 'The Egyptians weren't very nice. I've heard other stories about them how they were cruel. God didn't like them and didn't want them on earth so he let them drown.'

These type of responses are not limited to the younger children. Many older Juniors voice the same ideas, 'If he did like them, God wouldn't bring the water back on them. *Why didn't he like them?* When they captured anyone they made them slaves and work hard' (Vera aged 10 : 3, M.A. 9 : 1). Similar, and beyond the age of the majority of children changing their views, are Gertrude (aged 13 : 5, M.A. 13 : 3) in a Modern school, and Daly (aged 11 : 5, M.A. 14 : 2) at a Grammar school, although Daly does qualify his answer by saying, 'I don't think all the Egyptian soldiers *were* drowned. It was unfair, and no one could take a message back to the ruler.' He affirms, however, that the story is substantially true since 'God wouldn't allow it to be written if it wasn't true.' There are also the pupils who change their minds, such as Robert aged 9 : 6 (M.A. 9 : 0). He at

130

first affirms that God loves everyone. He then denies God's love for the Egyptians, 'Otherwise he would not have let them drown. *Why did he let them drown?* Because they were after the Israelites.' He then saw his contradiction and said, 'No, no, of course not, God doesn't love everyone in the world.' Rather undecided is Poppy aged 8 : 3 (M.A. 10 : 7), 'Yes, God loves everyone, unless someone was very very bad. (Q) Yes, he could have loved the Egyptians. *How could he love them and let them drown?* Oh, yes, I forgot about that. He loved them *until* they got the slaves, and after he didn't love them any more. He drowned them because the King changed his mind.'

The most numerous answers at this stage are from those who indicate a verbal acceptance of universal divine love, but this breaks down as a generalisation when the specific case of the Egyptians is discussed. The reasons are very much the same as those who denied universal love. Some children do see a contradiction between affirming that God loves everyone and then denying that the Egyptians are included but seem unable to solve the problem. All these answers state explicitly or it is implied that God deliberately destroyed the Egyptians as punishment or to prevent further wrong doing. The event is not seen in any way as the result of the Egyptians' own folly. Here are some examples. After assenting that God loved everyone, these pupils say the Egyptians were exceptions: 'No, they weren't on our side. *Why did they drown?* So they wouldn't catch the other men'; 'No, they were cruel. They drowned 'cause God didn't like them; they were so cruel and not kind to other people,' 'No, He couldn't love them or he wouldn't kill them'; 'No, He didn't love them *at the last moment* when they turned bad.' Rowenna aged 10 : 7 (M.A. 12 : 3) produces the inevitable logic, 'If he loved them he wouldn't have let them drown, unless they'd all done wrong.' He let them drown 'to save the people who were innocent and good and believed in him, and to prove to others it was right to believe in him and to follow his servant Moses.' D'Arcy aged 10 : 5 (M.A. 11 : 3) hints at degrees of responsibility but then dismisses it, 'No, the King was after Moses and the slaves. He wanted to kill Moses. *Did God love the soldiers of the Egyptian King?* No, the soldiers followed the King and obeyed his orders to kill.' In trying to resolve the contradiction between asserting God's universal love and the Egyptians not being loved, Betty aged 9 : 10 (M.A. 10 : 11) says, 'God likes the good and tries to make the bad good', but this is no solution to the problem she sees.

Almost 75 per cent of pupils overcome the problem after the age of about 10 : 6 (M.A. 10 : 11) by not only accepting universal divine love as a general assertion but by including the Egyptian within it. God does not cease loving them because they are bad, and punishment or misfortune is seen as compatible with love. Neither is divine prevention of wrong seen or incompatible with God's love. At this stage, the pupils often express the view that death is not the end and that, in a sense, it didn't matter because the Egyptians would go to heaven after their drowning. Two children assert that the Egyptians were not really drowned and others produce varied reasons for resolving the apparent contradiction. Later on, the answers begin to show a much clearer insight into the nature of God's love and its logical implications.

Typical of a consistent answer that God's love does not exclude punishment is Martha's (age 12 : 9, M.A. 11 : 8). 'They drowned because they treated the others cruelly. They deserved it', and Harriet's (age 16 : 4, M.A. 16 : 0), 'The earth is ruled by the will of man and it was the Egyptians' will to go after them, so God . . . (she stops, confused, and then continues) it was because they deserved it.' Meg aged 14 : 9 (M.A. 10 : 9) explains, 'They done wrong and even if he let them drown he forgave them and loved them.' Some say God sends disaster not only as a punishment but as a warning, as does Adrian (age 14 : 5, M.A. 16 : 3), 'Yes, he loved them. Only he knew the King was to blame. He took the army and they were wrong in obeying the King, so God drowned them. (Q) He did it as a warning to tell them how strong he was, and what they were up against.' Christopher aged 14 : 9 (M.A. 13 : 9) puts it similarly under questioning, 'He loved them but they committed a sin in making others work for them. He did it to teach them a lesson. *How could they learn the lesson if they drowned?* It was a lesson and a warning to other people.' Marion aged 11 : 8 (M.A. 15 : 0) is not too definite, 'He might have loved the Egyptians. Not so much as he loved his followers, because the Egyptians didn't believe in him. *How is it he let them drown?* They were chasing his true followers, and he was angry because they kept the Israelites as slaves for so many years.' The question of belief is voiced by Terence, aged 13 : 4 (M.A. 15 : 11), 'Because they chased his people he destroyed them as a punishment. *How could he love them, if he did that?* No, he loved them, but because Pharaoh didn't believe in him, he destroyed the army to persuade Pharaoh.' Priscilla is more contemporary (age 14 : 4, M.A. 14 : 5), 'He loves people today and lets them drown today, but he still loves them.' Kenny aged 13 : 3 (M.A. 14 : 7) puts the heavenly view, 'They'd go to heaven if they were sorry, so it wouldn't really matter.'

Typical of the view that there is no problem because the Egyptians didn't really drown is Lorton's (age 15 : 5, M.A. 15 : 0), 'Yes, God loves all men, but I don't know about the Egyptians. *Why not?* That's the part of the story that doesn't seem correct. God should have slowed them down or stopped them in some other way. *Well, why was it he let them drown?* They didn't drown. *Did the Israelites escape?* Yes, but the sea cleared before the Egyptians got there.' He said later he couldn't accept the sea closing and drowning the Egyptians 'because God wanted all people to be equal and free'. Nina, on the other hand, puts forward an explanation for this, 'I don't think they were drowned. They were cut off and couldn't get across the sea. *How did the story get to be different?* The people who wrote the story put it in. *Why?* They put it in for elaboration, to make it more exciting . . . The Egyptians weren't drowned. It was due to exaggeration. It would be contrary to his nature, if they'd been drowned. They weren't bad enough.' Nina's age is 13 : 2 (M.A. 16 : 6) and she says everything in the Bible is true, 'It's not true literally, but the meaning of it is true.'

This level of answers is consistent, even if a little naïve. Pupils of similar age and ability can be both consistent and realistic, although most of them tend to be the more able pupils. Even so, most answers reflect a concept of God actively intervening in history and taking sides. Some ideas of why Israel was a 'chosen' nation, many of them misguided, enter into some of the explanations, as in Barry's answer (age 11 : 6, M.A. 12 : 5), 'If they were after his chosen race he didn't want them to capture the Israelites,' and Anne's (age 12 : 4, M.A. 13 : 10), 'He wanted the Israelites to escape. He'd promised that they could go back to the promised land.' Dianne aged 14 : 11 (M.A. 13 : 1) explains, 'He was trying to start a new Christian country, where good Christians could be bred from there. The soldiers, he loved them, but it was part of his plan that they should be destroyed, in order for his plan to succeed.' 'I'm not sure if love is the right word,' says Jonathan (age 15 : 4, M.A. 17 : 6), 'God cares for all but loves some more than others, those who believe in him. It was the time when his religion wasn't very strong and it was the case of Moses who would further his religion and the Egyptians who wouldn't.' Hatty in the fifth form of a Grammar school says, 'He'd chosen the Israelites to be his followers. *Why did he let the others be drowned?* There was no other way to get rid of them. If they hadn't done any wrong I'd expect they'd go up to heaven. They were no different from the Israelites.' The effect upon the Israelites is the emphasis of a science fifth form boy. 'He wanted to show the Israelites his power. . .' A sixth form science pupil says, 'Drowning isn't a particularly painful way to die. *Why did he allow them to drown?* He had to because of his plan to let the Israelites survive and the Jewish nation continue.' Yet another stresses the omnipotence of God. 'God has full authority over everyone in the world. If he can kill and give birth and let people die, he will only do it when necessary. If the Israelites hadn't escaped there'd be no Christ and no Christian religion.'

Many pupils at this stage stress that the Egyptians were behaving in such a way, that God had no choice. Peggy aged 10 : 6 (M.A. 13 : 5) puts it, 'He loved them but was sorry about them because they weren't doing the right sort of thing. (Q) He knew they wouldn't improve; even if they did get to know about God, they wouldn't believe in him.' Martin aged 11 : 5 (M.A. 15 : 7) has the same idea. 'They were doing more harm than good. It was to stop them doing any more harm.' Another points out that God was concerned to stop slavery and the Israelites 'had a right to their own freedom'. The cloud with a silver lining is expressed by Loretta, aged 14 : 11 (M.A. 14 : 11), 'Perhaps God thought they weren't really suffering. *How do you mean?* It was a quick and sudden death. They'd done wrong and it was a way of getting them out of this world into heaven. They wouldn't do evil there and be better off.' But even these answers betray severe limitations. Rikki, aged 10 : 7 (M.A. 10 : 3), for example, 'They were evil, and he wanted people to be free. He didn't want to start his work all over again.' And Maureen aged 14 : 10 (M.A. 13 : 8) still hankers after a magical concept, 'He had to save Moses and the Israelites. *How could he love them and let them drown?* That is a contradiction, isn't it? But nobody knows. Maybe God could open the sea and they all came out alive again.'

Finally, a group of older or abler pupils see the incident not as God intervening but as the result of the Egyptians' own folly. So Fiona aged 11 : 10 (M.A. 16 : 7), 'Maybe he didn't mean them to be drowned. But he couldn't help it. He couldn't keep the waters back if they persisted in following the Israelites', rather like a mother watching her baby in a pram roll down the hill onto a busy road. Sandra aged 12 : 2 (M.A. 17 : 0) also says, 'I don't think he let them drown. The sea happened to close at that time.' A younger boy, of average ability, aged 12 : 10 (M.A. 12 : 7) says, 'It was their own fault. They were determined to get the slaves back. God would try to stop them but they would go on and get killed', while Deborah, a sixth former says, 'It's like the plagues isn't it? Did God let them drown? Was it his will that they should drown? I don't blame God for an act that was brought about by the Egyptians through their sins in chasing the Israelites across the sea. I don't agree that God for any reason of partiality or vengeance killed the Egyptians.' This rather mature insight is also elaborated later with this view, 'It was an historical account by a Jew. He'd naturally be delighted. I don't think they all did drown.'

There are many intriguing facets we could explore in these varying views, expressed by the pupils. But two things stand out. The first is that a clear watershed in thinking is evident in the tenth year when the universal love of God achieves more than a verbal level for most children. The second is that almost all see God as intervening in human affairs in such spectacular historical events of the Exodus, yet very few are aware that the narrative is not 'straight' history, but a theological interpretation of history. And certainly there is very little evidence to show that this Old Testament event is judged by a New Testament standard.

CONCEPTS OF DIVINE JUSTICE

Questions about divine love inevitably involve questions of divine justice, which in the child's language and experience approximate to ideas of fairness. Two questions were therefore asked, one specifically about the instance of the drowning of the Egyptians and the other in more general terms.[1] These were 'Was it fair that all the men in the Egyptian army should be drowned?' and 'Can God treat people unfairly?'

The nature of the specific question about the drowning made it difficult to apply the categories of moral judgment worked out by Piaget (1932). 'Authority' and 'constraint', terms used by Piaget, enter into almost every pupil's response. However, by adapting Piaget's structure for our purpose certain patterns of thinking stood out clearly. It was apparent, for example, that in the first instance children were concerned only with retributive justice, where expiation of a wrong is the dominant interest and the severity of punishment has little relation to the actual crime. There then comes an intermediate stage where other considerations begin to enter into the child's concepts of justice, and there appears after this the period of what we might call distributive justice. By distributive justice I mean where justice is seen in terms of equalitarianism, the beginning of a system of 'fair', impartial justice. It should be noted that positive or negative answers to the straightforward question 'Was it fair that all the men in the Egyptian army should be drowned?' do not in themselves indicate concepts of justice. Only a discussion of the reasons for their judgment can inform us about the pupils' conceptual level. A few children would make a judgment but not be able to advance a reason for making it, while another small group showed some confusion and often put forward incomprehensible answers. Typical of these are Kevan aged 7 : 7 (M.A. 6 : 5), 'It was unfair. The leader was drowned first and then the second in command. *How was it unfair?* All the other Israelites weren't drownded', and Nicola aged 8 : 3 (M.A. 8 : 6), 'It was unfair. He wanted them drowned . . . (Q) They weren't going to keep them as slaves as before, they were

[1] See Appendix A, questions S.2: Q.3A, and S.2: Q.3D.

135

going to give them food.' The last answer is inconsistent with the child's assertion and the content of the story. Apart from these kinds of responses three conceptual levels were evident. We shall now examine them in detail with appropriate examples.

The first level is that of retributive justice, where retribution is the sole consideration. We can describe this as based upon the need for vengeance, where punishment is enforced by God as a means of expiating the evil done. In childhood we know that this expiatory type of punishment, the view that bad things have to be paid for, is very common, many children believing, as Piaget points out, in immanent justice and that if misfortune afflicts anyone then they must have sinned. Such, of course, is the burden of the duologues in the book of Job. Sometimes the punishment is arbitrary in its intensity, not graded to the crime or to the amount of guilt. Even if the King and his officers are seen to be responsible, it is fair to a child at this stage that the punishment be meted out to all. Most children are at this stage of conceptual judgment up to almost ten years of age (M.A. 10 : 3). The statements are very simple, based on the view that they have done wrong and deserved drowning as a punishment. No ideas of prevention of future bad behaviour are advanced, as they are at a later stage.

The examples are very similar so only a few need be seen. 'Yes, it was fair. 'Cause sometimes they kill somebody' (Leona aged 6 : 5, M.A. 6 : 0). 'Fair, because it was their fault for chasing after the Israelites' (Leonard aged 6 : 11, M.A. 5 : 9). 'It was fair because the King had said he'd let them go free and then they wouldn't let them go' (Karen, aged 6 : 4, M.A. 8 : 4). 'Yes, they'd been horrible men ... they kept on stealing money' (Jenny aged 7 : 1, M.A. 5 : 10). 'Yes, because they made the slaves obey and would give them the whip' (Andrea aged 7 : 7, M.A. 7 : 7). 'Yes, it was fair. They'd done horrible things to the slaves. They wasn't very nice and whipped them' (Lester aged 8 : 2, M.A. 8 : 1). 'It was fair. They hadn't done what they were told to do by God' (Jill, aged 8 : 11, M.A. 7 : 0). 'It was very fair. The Egyptians were very cruel to the Israelites and some of the slaves got killed' (Geoffrey aged 9 : 8, M.A. 10 : 4). By objective standards of justice, of course, these are very immature judgments. Even on a Mosaic standard it savours of two eyes for one, since drowning a whole army seems rather excessive for the misdemeanours cited. But this is typical of the child's all-or-nothing judgments.

By the mental age of about 10 : 3 a more objective view is beginning to prevail. This is an intermediate stage between retributive and distributive justice, between vengeance and equalitarian justice. Prevention of further acts of evil is the child's concern, and degrees of punishment as there are degrees of responsibility are now beginning dimly to be recognised. In other words, the glimmerings of equalitarianism are evident, namely, that many of the soldiers did not have evil intentions and were even, perhaps, unwilling servants of the King. Yet at this stage the fact that they obeyed orders negatives their good intentions, and the evil result is the main consideration. This being so it is fair that they should all drown. This perplexity is expressed thus by one child: 'I don't know. It was partly the fault of the Egyptians for going together, but God couldn't let part of them get across for they'd attack the Israelites and he wanted to save them', and by another, 'They weren't drowned. *How do you mean? I don't think God would do it. They hadn't done anything really bad. If they had, would God let them drown?* Yes, he would. *Would that have been fair?* Yes.' And again, 'Some of them didn't want to do it, but they were under orders. But if God let only a few get away they'd kill Moses.' D'Arcy aged 10 : 5 (M.A. 11 : 3) says, 'All of them done as the King ordered and they'd kill the slaves as ordered. It was fair to drown them.' Most answers are from this simple preventive viewpoint, 'God didn't want the Israelites to be killed' (Grace aged 10 : 1, M.A. 10 : 11). 'They were going to do more wrong things so Jesus (*sic*) had to stop them' (Eric aged 11 : 2, M.A. 11 : 5). And, 'Moses and his people had already been captured once and they were going to be tortured or killed' (Jenny aged 11 : 5, M.A. 9 : 7).

Distributive justice emerges in the pupils' judgments in this story in the eleventh year (about M.A. 11 : 10). This is indicated by strong elements of equalitarianism and equity, because for justice to be done it must apply to all. Evil results seem to be less important, motive and intention begin the main criteria. Degrees of guilt are recognised and regarded as extenuating circumstances and the real responsibility is seen not to be in the hands of the soldiers. Sometimes, in these answers, a concern for the innocent is seen and also the need to reform, rather than to extinguish, punish or prevent wrongdoers in a specific evil action. The majority of the children at this stage see total annihilation of the soldiers as unfair for one of the reasons stated above, but absolve God of the responsibility. Some express the dilemma God was placed in by the foolish actions of the Egyptians.

First an example of equalitarian thinking. Hazel aged 12 : 3 (M.A. 13 : 3) puts it numerically, 'Yes, it was fair. (Q) Because there was more of them, they'd have easily overcome the Israelites.' In other words, drowning them evened out the numbers more equitably! Relative degrees of guilt are frequently expressed. Brian aged 11 : 6 (M.A. 14 : 5), 'It was not fair. Some may not have killed others and they should live', and Marion aged 11 : 8 (M.A. 15 : 0), 'Only some of them should have been drowned to teach the others a lesson.' Many pupils, among them Basil, aged 11 : 9 (M.A. 13 : 5) claims it was unfair, because, 'They were only doing their job which the King had commanded', and Alison aged 11 : 9 (M.A. 11 : 10), 'Some maybe didn't want to fight the Israelites and the captain made them.' Pharoah is named or implied as the responsible party. Timothy aged 16 : 1 (M.A. 17 : 1) says, 'Only the ringleaders should have been drowned. (Q) In some ways the others deserved it too because they helped.' This boy was obviously undecided about the justice of the drowning, altering his 'Yes' to a 'No'. Later he said God could treat people unfairly 'as he did with the Egyptians when they did wrong'. Fear of being punished is one reason why the soldiers obeyed the ruler, even if their hearts weren't in it. Harold aged 12 : 1 (M.A. 15 : 7) said, 'Some could have agreed with the King, and others not. But they would be killed for disobeying orders (if they objected)', and Martha aged 12 : 9 (M.A. 11 : 8) says, 'They were ordered to capture them, and if they didn't catch them they'd probably be made slaves themselves. Another possible reprisal is seen by Jason, aged 12 : 11 (M.A. 10 : 1), 'The king ordered them to do it and he'd cut off their hands if they disobeyed. They had to do it.' Conscription is another extenuating circumstance, says Anis (age 13 : 1, M.A. 14 : 1), 'Some might be forced into that army and may be good men.' A few express a dilemma. Typical is Fionna, aged 11 : 10 (M.A. 16 : 7), 'I don't know if it was fair. It was partly the fault of the Egyptians for going together, but he couldn't let part of them get across for they'd attack the Israelites and he wanted to save them.' Another is Polly aged 13 : 5 (M.A. 15 : 3), 'It wasn't fair. Surely they all didn't need to go after the Israelites. They could have ambushed the Israelites. *How do you mean?* I don't see the point of drowning a whole army. If they'd only drowned a quarter that would have taught them not to chase Israelites.' Commenting on God's justice she says, 'He may *seem* unfair at the time but it's better for them later.'

The innocents are the concern of several pupils. 'It's unfair. All their families, their mothers and children would have to be looked after' (age 12 : 2, M.A. 12 : 2). And, 'There ought to have been a few saved, not everyone is completely bad. And the horses would be drowned and they aren't bad.' A rather sentimental view is expressed by Hatty (age 15 : 9, M.A. 19 : 3), 'Some of them may not be old. They were too young to die. They'd not had enough time on earth.' George (aged 15 : 9, M.A. 15 : 11) expresses equalitarian views on the excessive nature of the punishment, 'It was unfair for my point of view. They shouldn't have had such harsh punishment', yet he feels God can act unfairly, 'If he wanted to.' Dianne aged 14 : 11 (M.A. 13 : 1), while saying it was unfair feels, 'God must have thought it was fair . . . To kill all those people, they may not all have been sinners or bad. They may have come round to be Christians.' Later she says, 'God could be unfair but he wouldn't. People may *think* he is unfair . . . He only wants what is right for us.' A science sixth former works it out thus: 'Yes, it was fair, otherwise God wouldn't have done it. *Do you think it was fair?* No, it wasn't fair anyone would say. God was interfering purely between themselves and the Israelites . . . No, God can't be unfair. People may not like his justice but he is never unfair in an absolute sense.'

To summarise, we can see retributive justice continuing up to about ten years of age (M.A. 10 : 3) giving way to an intermediate stage of moral judgment, then at about 11 : 4 (M.A. 11 : 10) moving forward into a fuller concept of distributive justice. This would appear to support Piaget's (1932) general outline of sequence in moral thinking, and to generally substantiate his age boundaries. There is some discrepancy of the age at which distributive concepts prevail, Piaget's children appearing to achieve them a little earlier. Apart from sampling and cultural differences there may be two explanations for this. The first is that the universe of thought and the ingredients of the stories used by Piaget involved are not identical with mine. The second may be that the religious story requires a transfer of thinking to a relatively remote situation and this may be yet another illustration of the secondary nature of religious thinking and would account for a time-lag of concept development.

The boundary ages and stages of the judgments just reviewed are substantiated when we examine the pupils' answers to the question, 'Can God treat people unfairly?' and the reasons for their judgment are discussed with the children. It may be argued that this is a weighted question, but the negative form of the question seems less suggestive to the child than 'Is God always fair to everyone?' The item is an attempt to discern insight into divine justice and answers range from crude childish ideas to the refined view that God cannot be unjust, since it would be a contradiction in his nature. Most of the children who reply 'Yes' do so without seeing 'unfairness' as something wrong: it is merely 'paying back' and is plainly at the Mosaic level of an eye for an eye. They see nothing odd or inconsistent in God behaving in this way. This question is intended to reveal ability to generalise about the divine nature and also what the child infers about God from this particular incident in the story of the Exodus. There are three apparent stages in which a sequence of developing concepts can be discerned. First, there is the concept that God is arbitrary and unpredictable in his behaviour and is not bound by moral laws. Then there comes an intermediate stage where God can be unfair. He is kind and tries his best to be as fair as he can, but regretfully may have to be unfair as an occasion demands. Finally, concepts predominate which indicate God cannot be unfair, because

God is bound by his own moral law, since not to be so would be a contradiction in his nature.

A few answers reflect only the child's incapacity to understand the questions or such crude anthropomorphisms as to lead to the reduction of God to human size. For example, 'No, He's not unfair. He didn't want the policeman to catch him. *Could they?* Yes, if he were in this country', and 'Yes, He'd make people naughty.' He could be unfair to them because they were naughty.' Those who give these and similar answers are all six years old, one of them picturing God as being taken by a whim, 'Yes, when he likes. *When does he like?* Oh, once a day if he feels like it.'

Out of 200 children some 88 respond at the level of the first stage where God is seen as behaving rather like a small child. Egocentric experience and limited moral development will lead a child to these conclusions, but how much, may we ask, is reinforced by Bible stories which appear to reflect this crude morality? This stage continues to about 10 : 5 (about 10 : 11 in mental age). Here are some examples in the order of chronological age taken at random. 'Yes, some pray to him and others don't. He treats *nice* people fair' (age 6 : 5, M.A. 6 : 0). 'Yes, when they are unfair to other people God can be unfair to them' (age 6 : 6, M.A. 6 : 6). 'Yes, if people were unfair to him, he'd be unfair back. If they threw jelly in someone's face, throw it back' (age 7 : 0, M.A. 7 : 2). 'Yes, when they're cruel or bad' (age 7 : 9, M.A. 10 : 3). 'Yes, when they do things they shouldn't' (age 7 : 11, M.A. 10 : 1). 'Yes, to not very nice people. He's always fair to to good people' (age 8 : 2, M.A. 8 : 1). 'Yes, like when he drowned all them soldiers, 'cause they were bad' (age 8 : 10, M.A. 10 : 11). 'Yes, He's done it in the Bible' (age 9 : 3, M.A. 8 : 7). 'Yes, but not usually. *When would he be unfair?* If they were bad to him and didn't pray and not go to church' (age 9 : 9, M.A. 13 : 0). 'Yes, when they don't worship him and go drinking' (age 9 : 11, M.A. 13 : 5). This very crude form of divine morality, in terms of wrong for wrong, changes to a higher concept as we have seen soon after ten years of age, but it is important to note some 29 exceptions who retain these crude concepts, some until as late as fifteen years of age.

For most pupils there is an intermediate stage before divine consistency is seen as a necessity. This mid-way position shows concepts of a God reluctantly compelled to be unfair by circumstances. His intention is to be fair, yet exceptional times may demand exceptional measures and plainly, for many pupils, the crossing of the Red Sea is one of these occasions. I list below some typical answers, taken at random. No comment is necessary, since they speak for themselves. 'Yes, in a way. He can do as he likes but he doesn't do it. (Q) He loves people and you're not unfair to people you love' (age 10 : 11,

M.A. 15 : 8). 'No. He's good and kind and made life and nature and everything and I don't think he'd destroy. He might have lost their sight (i.e. blinded them). It was fair if they'd done wrong, like if they stole something he'd paralyse their hand' (age 13 : 1, M.A. 14 : 1). 'Yes, if he wants to. He would if he thought they deserved it' (age 13 : 2, M.A. 18 : 4). 'No. He treats everybody alike. *Was he unfair to the Egyptian soldiers?* Yes, but he was only unfair to a few of them, the good ones' (age 13 : 6, M.A. 14 : 3). 'Yes. The point involved is a principle. A whole country shouldn't be slaves' (age 14 : 4, M.A. 19 : 2). 'Yes, occasionally, but not very often. *When?* If someone who is really a bad person and God punished him in some way and the person went on really bad, then God might cause something unjust to happen, and he might be killed' (age 11 : 8, M.A. 15 : 0). 'If it's his will to do so, yes. If he wants to teach people a lesson' (age 14 : 5, M.A. 17 : 6). A few pupils express some kind of compensation theory, as for example, 'If people are treated badly on this earth, they'll be compensated in the next life, so they wouldn't be unfairly treated. In the long run it wouldn't be unfair.' I have included several answers of those beyond the age boundary of this stage to show how some older pupils still express these intermediate concepts.

The third stage is one of moral consistency in that for God to be unfair would be a contradiction of his nature. This tends to dominate the pupils' thinking from about the age of 12 : 6 (M.A. 13 : 2). Some bring in the fact of God's love, for example, 'No, because he loves all people' (age 12 : 8, M.A. 12 : 8), and 'No, he wouldn't want to. He loves everyone. He may have to be unfair to help others, but he'd always make it up again' (age 12 : 8, M.A. 16 : 10), and also, 'No, He loves them whether they do good or bad' (age 12 : 11, M.A. 11 : 6). The fact that God appears to be unfair is often mentioned. 'No. Some people may think he is but he isn't. *Why not?* He loves everyone. He must be fair to all' (age 13 : 2, M.A. 16 : 6). Sometimes there are rather naïve generalisations, as in this example, 'No, He believes everyone should be treated fair. He likes to be fair. If anyone takes a life God sees they get hanged. If he's fair with one person he must be with another' (age 12 : 7, M.A. 12 : 4). Another cites Jesus, 'No, He's always fair to everyone. When Jesus told the story of the vineyard, they worked different hours and He gave them all the same money. People think he's unfair, but he isn't' (age 13 : 4, M.A. 15 :11). Analogy is used by Audrey aged 13 : 11 (M.A. 12 : 8). 'If he gives one a fair chance, he must do the same for everyone. All are equal. *How do you mean?* We are his children and he's got to look after each one of us. He's like an earthly father, only he's got so many more to look after.' 'God believes in justice and fairness. He thinks it right and only he is perfect,' says Patsy aged 14 : 5 (M.A. 16 : 11).

Statements of this kind continually occur, 'He can do no wrong', 'He is God and God never does anything wrong', and 'Perfection means no flaw and unfairness is a flaw.' Several sixth formers express themselves in this way, 'I'm not sure how you mean "unfair". In one sense the Egyptians didn't believe in him and thought he was just another god. But no, he couldn't prefer one person to another. He cares for us all.' 'He's just and good, because he stands for good in the world.' 'No. He gives people an equal chance and if they get into trouble, it's their own fault. He's fair, just. He's God. We know this from Christ's teaching.' 'We know he is just. *How?* To be the supreme form of Good, he has to be just.' These pupils have reached a high conceptual level and their constant appeal both to reason and to New Testament standards show that they are looking at the Old Testament with some kind of moral yardstick. We shall discuss the significance of this later.

Comparing the specific question of drowning with the more general question of God's fairness, we see that the ages of each conceptual level are roughly comparable.

Was it fair all the Egyptians should be drowned?		*Can God ever be unfair to people?*
Retributive justice—vengeance and punishment (up to 10 years)	Stage 1	God can be unfair, unpredictable and arbitrary (up to 10½ years)
Intermediate with Retributive elements; drowning is a necessary prevention (up to 11½ years)	Stage 2	Intermediate; God sometimes regretfully, is unfair (up to 12½ years)
Distributive justice—all must be treated alike; punishment according to degree of guilt (from 11½ years)	Stage 3	God is always fair, to be consistent with his nature. He only appears to be unfair (from 12½ years)

The parallel stages are fairly similar since they depend upon identical concepts. In general a God who pays back evil for evil will be the kind of deity to demand vengeance (Stage 1), and the kind of God who is consistently just will also be unwilling to condemn whole groups of people because of their group membership. We shall continue this exploration of ideas of justice in the next chapter.

Chapter Ten

GOD'S CONCERN FOR MEN
(*continued*)

IDEAS of right and wrong and their accompanying moral concepts cannot be separated from questions of individual responsibility. Since there can be no responsibility, in terms of moral choice, without the individual freedom to exercise it, when moral judgments are made individual and corporate responsibility must be taken into account. Distinctions between the individual and the group to which he belongs must be made realistically. We consider it immoral for a man to be judged solely as a group member, although conversely we see that an individual must bear some responsibility for what his group does. The tension between these moral ideas can be seen in all parts of the Bible. At first, man and his group are inseparable in moral terms and the tribe stands or falls together. This concept continued for many centuries of the Hebrews' development and one of the functions of the prophets was to awaken the individual conscience to its responsibilities. That poor moral judgments and tribal morality still persisted into New Testament times can be seen in the parable of the Good Samaritan, where Christ pointedly used an alien to represent the one who cares. Since group sympathy or condemnation enters into so many Old Testament narratives, it is of interest to see what kind of moral judgments children formulate in stories they hear from the Bible.

GROUP MORAL JUDGMENTS

Two questions were designed to test out these judgments.[1] The first concerned the Egyptians: 'Were all the Egyptians soldiers bad?' Since a simple 'Yes' or 'No' reply is not very informative about the quality of thinking attained, in discussion the reason for their assertion was usually asked of the children. 'Were all the Egyptian soldiers bad?' may be thought to be a weighted question, but the emphasis was carefully placed upon the word 'all'. Furthermore, from the context of the story and previous discussion with pupils, it was revealed that they thought that the slavery, cruelty and general behaviour of the

[1] See Appendix A, questions S.2: Q.3B and S.2: Q.3C.

Egyptians was unjust. The questions and subsequent discussion, therefore, were designed to evaluate just how much the pupils thought the individual soldiers in the Egyptian army were responsible.

Scaling the answers revealed clearly that moral judgment of the Egyptians as a group fell into three stages. There was first no differentiation made within the group, but judgment went merely with group membership and association. The second stage showed that the children were making some attempt to differentiate, but the judgment was largely quantitative and no concepts of individual degrees of responsibility for evil behaviour in all men are evident. Finally, in the third stage we can see realistic differentiation prevailing, so that in making judgment of the group, qualitative differences of responsibility and motive in each man is seen. At this stage also there are several adolescents who say there is insufficient evidence on which to form a judgment.

In the first stage, up to about eight years of age (M.A. 8 : 4) the group label is the dominating feature. All Egyptians are bad merely because they have the wrong label and belong to a group of people who have done bad things. These younger children do not seem to be able to discriminate in any effective degree in their judgment. A few examples will illustrate this. 'Yes, they were after the other men, going to put them in prison' (age 6 : 2, M.A. 6 : 6). 'Yes, they were horrible men' (age 6 : 5, M.A. 6 : 0). 'Yes, they had guns with them. (Q) All bad people carry guns' (age 6 : 7, M.A. 5 : 1). 'Yes, they were cruel men. They all did cruel things' (age 6 : 10, M.A. 7 : 9). 'Yes, because that was the sea water and that can make you bad. *Were they all naughty?* Yes, it was their fault . . . they weren't friends of God' (age 6 : 11, M.A. 5 : 9). 'Yes, they made the slaves work' (age 7 : 5, M.A. 9 : 2). 'Yes, they tried to capture the Israelites when they'd let them go' (age 7 : 4, M.A. 7 : 1). 'Yes, if they weren't all bad, all the others wouldn't go out with them to kill people. So they were all bad' (age 7 : 7, M.A. 7 : 7). 'Yes, they used to smash all the windows up in towns' (age 7 : 8, M.A. 6 : 1). There is the occasional response revealing ideas of immanent justice as in the reply, 'They wouldn't drown if they weren't bad.' In all answers there is total condemnation of the group and all its members.

Some differentiation appears after eight years (M.A. 8 : 4) where the possibility of a few not being bad is conceded. Some even suggest half of the Egyptians might have been bad and half good, but in all these judgments it is a quantitative matter, a counting of heads, rather than insight into degrees of responsibility. Typical of the 'Most were bad' viewpoint are the following. 'Most of them were bad. (Q) I don't know. *Why do you think some of them must have been good?* Some of them stayed to guard the fort. They didn't fight every time and kill people,' says Lester aged 8 : 2 (M.A. 8 : 1). Poppy is rather vague and totally unrealistic, 'Most were bad, but a few were good. All of them drowned, but they don't have to be bad. They might all have been good, but one day they might be very bad so God drowned them' (age 8 : 3, M.A. 10 : 7). More realistic, and introducing the idea of religious belief is Peter, aged 8 : 6 (M.A. 9 : 1), 'Most of them were wicked. A few believed in the God of Moses. Moses was an Egyptian, but he helped the Israelites. Good and bad Egyptians all drowned.' The dominance of Pharaoh is voiced by Keith aged 8 : 11 (M.A. 10 : 0), 'Most were bad. They were made to be bad. Pharaoh made them and then they were bad. It was their duty to obey,' but he cannot absolve the soldiers from responsibility. This is echoed by Claude aged 9 : 8 (M.A. 13 : 6), 'Most were bad with a few good ones. (Q) Some of them loved people, but the rulers made them to be soldiers.'

Many of these responses do give some qualitative judgments but what decides the judgment is not inner doubts or motives, but the evil result, as in other questions asked about this story. So Dennis, aged 9 : 8 (M.A. 12 : 11) answers, 'Most were bad; a few, perhaps, were not too bad. (Q) Because they probably didn't believe they should go after the Israelites again, once they had let them go', and Julie aged 9 : 8 (M.A. 10 : 6), 'Most Egyptians are bad. In one book it said they were. A few may not have been too keen on having slaves.' An interesting variation is Lawrence's, aged 9 : 9 (M.A. 11 : 5), 'Most of them were bad. (Q) They'd not go after the Israelites if they weren't. They liked war. *What makes you think there were some good ones?* I expect they didn't like war and feared getting killed.' Sara is very definite in terms of proportions, 'About 9 out of 10 were bad. (Q) There may have been some left in the Egyptian camp who didn't want to go after them. All the others wanted to go' (age 9 : 10, M.A. 8 : 10). Vera's distinction between good and bad is very quantitative. '*Why were some good?* Some of the Egyptians didn't hit the slaves so hard' (age 10 : 3, M.A. 9 : 1). 'One or two were good,' says Gordon aged 10 : 5 (M.A. 14 : 6), 'because that seems to happen in every story and I don't see why it shouldn't happen here.' Belief is expressed by Jan aged 11 : 0 (M.A. 13 : 8) as a factor, even though her chronology is inaccurate, 'Some believed in Jesus, but they served their King more faithfully than they served Jesus.' Anis feels that not all the facts are known, 'Most were bad, but a few were good. (Q) We might not be told some stories. A soldier may have saved another life at danger to himself' (age 13 : 1, M.A. 14 : 1). A point of interest in many of these answers is that to resolve the problem of some of the 'good' Egyptians being drowned, the 'good' ones are made to stay at home on guard duty or some similar activity.

Still at stage two, where a quantitative differentiation is made, many pupils will judge the Egyptians on a fifty-fifty basis. Half of them are good and half bad. The reasons they advance to support this judgment are of interest. 'The good ones might have helped Moses to escape. Perhaps some of the good ones stayed behind and didn't get drowned' (age 8 : 10, M.A. 10 : 11). The half who were bad, says Geoffrey, aged 9 : 8 (M.A. 10 : 4) 'were officers who wanted the others to kill. The others were just under command.' Again the resolution of the problem of the innocent is spoken by Alice, 'Half were bad and half were good. Some Egyptians weren't as cruel to the slaves as others were. God didn't let the nice Egyptians go in the army so they'd not drown' (age 10 : 4, M.A. 11 : 8). Most answers propound the view that the element of compulsion accounted for the wicked acts of the Egyptians, although Phyllis inverts the argument (age 12 : 6, M.A. 12 : 1), 'If the Egyptians were all good the King wouldn't have anyone to support him or fight for him.' When Mary says 'God makes men of all sorts, good and bad' (age 12 : 8, M.A. 16 : 10), she is still making a quantitative judgment, since it is not every man being a mixture of good and bad she asserts but that in every group there are good and bad men.

By the age of 13 (M.A. 13 : 8) the more subtle, and more mature, differentiation takes root in the pupil's thinking. At about this time most of them see the leaders as mainly responsible, but together with this grows a concept that all humans are evil to some degree. As for many adolescents this appears to be the general period of increasing personal analysis, this age boundary seems consistent with other aspects of the adolescent's developing social sensitivity. The judgment exercised from this time on appears to move from a quantitative to a qualitative one, and motive is now seen as more important than the result of an action. Typical is Kenny, 'A few were bad and the rest were all right. (Q) The leaders were probably bad and the men below them had to do what they were told' (age 13 : 3, M.A. 14 : 7). Dennis says, 'They'd be a fairly ordinary bunch and they'd be about average' (age 14 : 4, M.A. 19 : 2), and Maureen, 'A few may have been taught to be bad as children. The others would do bad things because they were under orders and not really bad at heart' (age 14 : 10, M.A. 13 : 8). A qualitative example is given by Lorton, aged 15 : 5 (M.A. 15 : 0), 'You can't say. The commanders probably had the wrong intentions, but even they weren't wholly bad,' and Hatty, aged 15 : 9 (M.A. 19 : 3), 'All people are good and bad. Everyone is a mixture of good and evil.' On the specific question Meg, a sixth former, says, 'Not necessarily. We don't know. There's no evidence to prove they were bad or not.'

Alongside group judgments of the Egyptians we should examine those of the Israelites. A question was asked, 'Were all the slaves, the Israelites, good?' and the reasons for their answers were explored in subsequent discussion. Due to scoring problems, the results are less clear than is the case with judgments about the Egyptians, but the same sequence of conceptual development is evident. There are, however, slightly different emphases due to the different content of the question.

The first stage of no differentiation in group judgment from one Israelite to another is identical with judgments about the Egyptians. This stage, however, goes on a year longer, until about nine years (M.A. 9 : 7). This difference occurs also at the later stages, and we shall discuss the possible explanations for this shortly. Meanwhile, it is interesting to see some of the reasons advanced by children at this stage. 'Yes, they were all good people. They believed in God.' 'Yes, they don't kill anybody.' 'Yes, they hadn't got no guns.' 'Yes, they were on the good side and they were all Christians.' 'Yes, because they were slaves.' 'Yes, they were friends of Moses and he was good.' 'Yes, because when the angel came over before they left, all the good ones were asked to put crosses of blood on the door. All the bad ones were killed, and so they didn't escape.' 'Yes, they were poor people. Poor people are always good.' Some of the reasoning here is sound, but is based upon incorrect data, and is often merely associated thinking. The myth of the kind and good poor is an interesting one which occurs many times in answers. It is also intriguing to see what use the child has made of the gruesome Passover story.

The second stage shows that pupils have achieved some kind of differentiation between the Israelites, although the view is firmly held that most of them were good. The reasons are often as inappropriate as in the earlier stage. 'Because of the way they suffered.' 'They won and the good usually win.' 'God saved them. They were God's chosen people, so they must be good.' The few who were thought to be bad were judged so for the following reasons. 'They made a golden calf.' 'Some killed people.' 'They did their work badly.' 'They gave information to the Egyptians.' One boy aged 8 : 11 (M.A. 10 : 6) says, 'They did wrong in the past and had reformed. They must have been bad at the beginning or God wouldn't allow them to go into slavery.' A few showed the beginnings of qualitative insight but not enough to merit a higher conceptual level. 'It's human nature to have an odd one out.' 'There's some bad in every group.' 'Most of them were good after they'd been saved. They learned.'

Real qualitative differentiation begins to prevail in answers about the Israelites from about the age of 14 years (M.A. 15 : 0). At first this is still crudely seen such as 'There must have been a good proportion, 50 per cent of them good, for God to have taken so much trouble with them', but later still after about 15 years the responses correspond to the third stage seen in the group judgments about the Egyptians. 'They were a mixed bag, morally, like any other people.' 'They weren't all saints. They were a mixture. Under oppression they'd tend to be more religious than their masters, as they needed it more.' 'None were good. All were sinners. They were just as sinful as the Egyptians.' A few, as in the other question, pronounce that there is not enough evidence on which to base a judgment.

The age boundaries differ somewhat in the judgments about the Egyptians and the Israelites.

	Egyptians	Israelites
No differentiation:	Up to C.A. 8:0	Up to C.A. 9:2
	M.A. 8:4	M.A. 9:7
Realistic differentiation	From C.A. 13:0	From C.A. 14:0
	M.A. 13:8	M.A. 15:0

Some of this difference may be due to differences in the grouping of scores, but this does not wholly account for the apparent later development of judgment about the Israelites. It is possible that children in listening to stories from the Bible are being asked constantly to identify themselves with the Israelites as God's people and by implication, his favourites. Perhaps the expression 'the children of Israel' helps them to do this and to image the Israelites as helpless, innocent children. This might make them reluctant to attribute faults in a group who obviously receive such divine support. What we might call a group halo effect may be at work, which could effectively delay realistic thinking and distort the pupils' judgment.

To conclude this discussion of moral concepts we can see that when all the scores of answers to all parts of question 3 ('Was it fair that all the men in the Egyptian army should be drowned?' 'Can God treat people unfairly?' and the two group judgments about the badness of the Egyptians and the goodness of the Israelites) are combined, the total scores are scalable. We can deduce from this that the dominant feature in these questions appears to be progress in moral judgment, as applied to the activities of the deity. The divergent age boundaries show that moral judgment has many and varied aspects, some of which we have touched upon, but many of them remain to be investigated.

CONCEPTS OF THE CHOSEN NATION

We have already seen that children tend to be influenced by the special status attributed to Israel as a chosen nation. Although the term is not specifically used in the story told to them during the interviews, the majority of children have heard the word 'chosen' in relation to the Israelites many times. I have put forward the hypothesis that this not only influences judgment in a general sense but creates a halo effect in a specific moral context. It is relevant, therefore, to discover what concepts of chosenness pupils have with increasing age and experience. A question was included in the test asking, 'Why did God want to save the Israelites?'[1]

The results indicate that the concept of chosenness, from a theological evaluation, is very difficult to achieve, dependent as it is upon some sense of history, the development of altruistic motives and many other experiences. It should be also pointed out that many Jews retained restricted and 'childish' concepts of chosenness for a long period of history. The whole problem of accepting Messiah was not only what kind of saviour he was to be, but what was to be the role of Israel in terms of messianic purpose? This is the major issue of the drama played out in the Gospel story, and it is not surprising if the large majority of pupils are unable to grasp these difficult issues, even with the possible advantage of historical hindsight.

Four stages can be seen in the developing concepts of Israel's chosenness. The first is non-conceptual when answers are irrelevant, inadequate and often tautological. This is evident up to about 10 : 8 (M.A. 11 : 4) and there is a diversity of answers. Among them are the following: Kathy says, 'They were all on his side' (age 6 : 2, M.A. 6 : 6), but can only repeat this in discussion. Jean feels Moses is central, 'It was for Moses' sake. Moses liked some of them, the Israelites' (age 6 : 2, M.A. 5 : 3). Karen shares this view, 'The Egyptian king had changed his mind and was naughty. Moses was a nice man' (age 6 : 4, M.A. 8 : 4). Leonard, aged 6 : 11 (M.A. 5 : 9) replies, 'They were his friends. *How do you mean?* Because they made friends with God, they liked God.' Jenny feels that the Israelites were saved 'because they was nice and kind' (age 7 : 1, M.A. 5 : 10). Massey expresses a mutual help relationship, 'He was friends with them. *How do you mean?* They helped God and God helped them' (age 7 : 8, M.A. 6 : 1). 'They were poor,' says another (age 7 : 9, M.A. 7 : 10). 'They had no money and he was sorry for them.' The virtue of the Israelites is frequently expressed. 'They were good people. They helped God' (age 7 : 11, M.A. 10 : 1). Sometimes it is their religious faith which makes them worth saving. 'They believed in God and the Egyptians didn't,' says Alfred, aged 7 : 11 (M.A. 8 : 4), but Poppy goes much further, 'They are Christians. (Q) Maybe he just likes Christians. *Why?* I don't know. They pray to the proper God and not to idols' (age 8 : 3, M.A. 10 : 7). Robert puts it in another way, 'He didn't want them to work so hard. (Q) They were his

[1] See Appendix A, question S.2 : Q.4.

son's disciples' (age 9 : 6, M.A. 9 : 0). 'They hadn't done much harm. It was the Egyptians who'd done all the harm. God was angry that the King had broken his promise after giving his word,' says Sheena aged 9 : 9 (M.A. 13 : 0). Obedience is another characteristic, says Grace, 'They did everything Jesus (*sic*) told them to. He didn't want them to be killed. They were kind people' (age 10 : 1, M.A. 10 : 11). Some glimmering of a further purpose can be seen in Peggy's response. 'Most of them believed in God. If most Egyptians didn't believe in God and all the Israelites perished, there'd be hardly anyone left' (age 10 : 6, M.A. 13 : 5). The major characteristic of these answers is their inaccuracy, for it is evident that the Israelites were not good, nice, kind or helpful people, and the beginnings of Hebrew religion were only evident after the Exodus so that they could hardly be called God's followers before the Covenant. One child puts it very seriously, 'God was an Israelite himself.'

From about ten years on the pupils produce answers more accurately based, arising from God's sense of justice that no men should be slaves and all men should be equals. The insights are contained, however, within the specific situation and salvation is limited to this. Typical of this stage is Clive, aged 10 : 11 (M.A. 8 : 6). 'They were slaves, and the soldiers were cruel to them.' Eric mixes his reasons, 'They'd been slaves and made to do what they shouldn't. They belived in God and the Egyptians didn't so much' (age 11 : 2, M.A. 11 : 5). Brian aged 11 : 6 (M.A. 14 : 6) says, 'As slaves they led a poor life and God thought they should get away.' Sandra replies, 'They were being ill-treated. If people don't deserve it he doesn't like anyone to be ill-treated' (aged 12 : 2, M.A. 17 : 0). Many of these answers reflect concepts of a God who is concerned for all who are downtrodden in some way, but there is no sense of greater purpose than this expressed.

The next stage begins about 13 : 2 (M.A. 13 : 9) when a sense of chosenness appears, first of all in terms of reward for hard work or for suffering long endured, later as the fulfilment of a vague promise made in the past, and later still Israel is seen as saved for some divine purpose in the future. Only a few, and these are fifth and sixth formers, attain the idea of Israel's redemptive purpose as the cradle of Christianity. Echoes of the Promise can be heard in Robin's reply, 'Moses was going to lead them to another land. It was God's land. He'd promised them they'd go there because it was their land before they were slaves' (age 13 : 10, M.A. 11 : 5). Delia is not so certain, aged 14 : 3 (M.A. 15 : 4), 'Because he'd chosen them. *What for?* To be a nation of Christians. *Why did he choose them particularly?* He wanted to save them from being slaves and get them out of Egypt. *Why did he have to choose anyone at all?* I don't know.' 'They were his people,' says May, 'and he wanted to give them a better place to live in where they could be their own boss. *How do you mean they were his people?* They were started by Abraham, and God promised he'd always look after his people . . .' (age 14 : 9, M.A. 10 : 9). Hatty shows an interesting insight, 'He'd chosen them to be his followers. They didn't have a god of their own. They were so uncertain' (age 15 : 9, M.A. 19 : 3), but Harriet is still limited to 'Moses was leading them to a new land to start again. They hadn't had much of a chance in life being slaves' (age 16 : 4, M.A. 16 : 0).

Higher insights than this were rare and they perhaps only indicate in a phrase where understanding in depth is present. Patsy, for example, after saying the Israelites were chosen because they were good, adds, 'They were more in need of help than others.' The greater purpose is expressed by May, aged 14 : 10 (M.A. 19 : 11), 'Because they were the first to realise there was only one God. *Chosen for what?* Everything usually starts somewhere, like the mustard seed in the parable, believing in one God and spreading this throughout the world.' Dianne, aged 14 : 11 (M.A. 13 : 1) shows an interesting insight, 'He chose them to be his people and to found a new country. *Why?* Because they had to put up a struggle to get this thing if they really wanted it, then they'd show they really wanted this new life to become better people.' Jonathan aged 15 : 4 (M.A. 17 : 6) expresses the view that God had chosen them 'to become the founders of his religion. *Why?* He didn't choose them in the beginning, but they came together as nomads and grew in number and believed and produced a new race.'

The highest insights of all come from a small group of fifth and sixth formers. In general terms Frank is fairly typical, aged 16 : 10, 'They were his chosen people—they'd be a random choice. There have to be some leaders. He wanted one people to lead the world to come together. *Why choose the Israelites?* They might have been particularly good morally, but I'm not sure.' George too, aged 16 : 11, talks of a general purpose. 'God had chosen them as his nation, as an example to the world of what a nation could do, *even with shortcomings*, with God behind them. *Why choose Israel?* He chose Abraham and they were his seed. Abraham was the best man on earth to do it.' Others are more specific in terms of a Messiah, 'They were to be prepared for the coming of the Messiah. *Why them?* They already had an idea of one God. They were sensitive people and many of their prophets seemed near God.' 'He saved them to continue the Jewish nation and their faith with it, which later developed into the Christian faith.' 'They believed God could save them. He did have a plan for them. He could show how man had sinned and through Christ, save the world. *Why Israel?* He had some reason, but I can't see it.' Edward, aged 17 : 9, voices the view that Israel should be the receiver of Christ and tries to explain why they were chosen. 'Maybe they were better or more intelligent. I think some mental aspect of them, but I wouldn't know what it is.'

The four stages of concepts about the purpose of God in wishing to save Israel can be summarised as follows. Up to about 10 : 8 (M.A. 11 : 4), a non-conceptual level where answers are irrelevant or grossly inaccurate and the Israelites are credited with virtues and attributes they did not possess. Then comes the stage where concepts of elementary justice and desire for equality are the reasons for God's salvation, but salvation is seen only in terms of the immediate danger. A third stage beginning about 13 : 2 (M.A. 13 : 9) shows the pupils beginning to see the salvation not only in terms of reward, but also of promise. Only later in this stage does a long-term divine purpose begin to be seen. Finally a few adolescents see the purpose of saving Israel not only as a redemptive one, but also as the nation to whom Christ would come.

GENERAL COMMENTS ON GOD'S CONCERN FOR MEN CONCEPTS

The general picture that is formed from the data of the last two chapters indicates a number of serious limitations in the child's understanding, especially in relation to Old Testament material. We shall now explore what these limitations are and try to see what explanations are possible.

Children in Infant and Junior schools share fairly similar mis-understandings about God's concern for men up to about the age of ten to eleven years. These misunderstandings with younger children tend to be due to wrong cues or associations of thought and literal-isms, and with the older children in the Junior school, because of limitations set by emotional and social immaturity. God's love embracing all men is denied, because he cannot possibly love naughty people, or the universalism is accepted as a mere verbalism which breaks down in the case of the Egyptian army. Love, for the Primary school child, yields second place to vengeance and the child's view of the deity is clouded by the conviction that God is only concerned for retribution. He can be and is often unfair, because God can do any-thing; his behaviour is unpredictable and his punishment arbitrary. The child views the contenders in the Exodus story in terms of white and black, goodies and baddies, favoured and non-favoured, loved and unloved, worth saving and not worth saving. This simple division is made up to between eight and nine years, but continues as a domi-nant pattern in terms of group judgment into the secondary school before good and bad can be seen in both Egyptian and Israelite groups. In terms of why the Israelites should be saved, the Primary school child attributes belief, loyalty, goodness and many other virtues to them, long before the Covenant and in a manner which shows that God rescued them simply because they were his favourites. The reason for being his favourites is purely one of arbitrary choice.

Some of these concepts are characteristic of the pre-adolescent in the early stages of secondary schooling, but the universalism of God's love, with some of its implications, is grasped by this period. Punishment and love are seen as consistent, although divine justice is seen only through a glass darkly. Retributive punishment still continues, but there are reservations made, for example, in saying that the drowning of the Egyptians was necessary to prevent them doing further harm. This is also consistent with the view that God can be unfair, although he does not want to be, but may be compelled by circumstances to be unjust to foolish or wicked people. The early secondary school pupil still views the Egyptians as basically bad, but is beginning to differentiate between the majority who are evil and a few who are possibly not. He is still somewhat naïve about the overwhelming goodness of the Israelites. His judgments are partial and quantitative in that he still does not appear to understand the sinful condition of all men. Further, his concepts of God's reasons for salvation for Israel are still concerned with the immediate need to release them from slavery or escape cruel treatment, and no ultimate purpose appears to be in view.

Towards the end of the second year and often well into the third year of the secondary school, some of these limitations give way to higher insights, although many of the less able pupils retain their limitations for a longer period. The principle of universal love, now fully accepted, leads on to a concept of distributive justice, that God must treat all alike, and have no favourites. If punishment is required it must be in relation to the degree of guilt. Consistency now demands that God is always just, although sometimes he will seem to be unfair, simply because we cannot see the whole picture of the divine purpose. Realistic differentiation, in a qualitative manner (as opposed to a quantitative judgment) is beginning to be made about the Egyptians by thirteen years, although this does not occur in relation to the Israelites until a year after this, about the age of fourteen. About this time, and perhaps closely bound up with the foregoing concepts, some long term purpose is just beginning to be seen in the dramatic act of salvation at the time of the Exodus. Only the oldest and most able achieve any Messianic concept, but the nature of the questions asked did not allow a fuller exploration of these insights.

Naturally, the picture presented here is an over-simplification and ignores the numbers of pupils who achieve the various conceptual levels before the times suggested or long afterwards. What factors are at work with these many exceptions we cannot say. If, however, our general picture is on the whole an accurate one it raises several disturbing questions which we ought to recognise.

The first is that few of the pupils up to the middle of their secondary schooling appear to know how to think about the incident of the Exodus, except in terms of straight history. Much of the morality of the young child, of course, corresponds with the divine morality which is reflected if the Exodus narrative is accepted as literally true history. There appears to be an unconscious resistance among many teachers to informing their pupils that the Bible is not history, but a theological interpretation of history. It is obvious that to explain that some of the Bible is myth, legend, allegory and parable and that the stories are often theological interpretations of what really happened, is not only disturbing but probably beyond the intellectual level of many children. My view is that it is more disturbing to the adults concerned than for the children, since they feel they are tampering with the innocent faith of the young. If, however, we are not destroying their faith, but helping them to establish concepts which are not in contradiction to their later adolescent questions, we are providing a more realistic education. By failing to present Bible narrative as an interpretation we are probably prolonging and reinforcing childish moral views of God, which are bound to collapse under later critical examination. The second point about the child's intellectual problems in distinguishing between myth, legend, allegory, parable and interpreted history is not an insuperable problem if he is consistently introduced to these ideas, even before he can understand them. The sense of outrage or betrayal, which is often voiced by adolescents, can be avoided if children are introduced to non-literal approaches to Bible truth. At first these will be known only at a verbal level, but later, probably by the age of ten, there are indications that some understanding of these distinctions in biblical meaning are possible.

A further question provoked by the child's growing concepts of God's concern for men, is whether this story, or any of the Old Testament stories about the emergent nation Israel, should be introduced to pupils much before the middle of the secondary school. The reason for this is not only the immaturities of judgment displayed in the pupils' answers before this time but the fact that they are treating the stories they hear in comparative isolation. There is no apparent transfer of what they know from the New Testament to this story, and it is natural for them to isolate their judgments, so that they are contained within each story. I would suggest that systematic Old Testament teaching should be delayed until such time as comparative judgments can be made in the light of the New Testament, in order for pupils to see that the Bible is not all equally inspired, true or important. Either they will view God as having changed from an angry and unpredictable tyrant to the God of a loving father, or he is the same 'Yesterday, today and forever' but only partially known throughout the long search of man for truth, depicted in the pages of the Old Testament. There seems no choice beyond these two alternatives. I submit, therefore, that a major task of the religious educator is to equip his pupils to look at the Old Testament through New Testament spectacles, consciously comparing and judging it by what he knows to be Christian judgments and values. Until he can do this, until he has some realistic concepts of the Christ of the Gospels, then he should not be exposed to pre-Christian and often sub-Christian ideas which he will accept as authoritative.

The major import of all this is relevant especially to the Junior school. Are Bible stories, especially from the Old Testament, often selected for use with Juniors because they are full of action, stirring deeds and vigorous battles? The criterion in the selection of material for Juniors, as with all age levels, should be what is the level of understanding required and what are the residual effects of teaching such material, in the total picture of religion the child is formulating? We shall explore the implications of all this more fully in the final chapter.

Chapter Eleven

JESUS AND THE PROBLEM OF EVIL

JESUS CHRIST is the central and dominant person of the Bible, and it is a name with which children are familiar from a very early age. We have previously seen how the terms God and Jesus are frequently interchangeable in the child's thinking, and there is obviously little awareness until adolescence of the Jesus of history as distinct from the eternal Christ. The confusion between God and Jesus appears to be largely a verbal one, rather than due to an early recognition of the true nature of Christ. For the Primary school child the word Jesus tends to evoke a composite picture of the two, and the younger the child the more powerful, in a magical sense, the person of Jesus appears to be.

When we consider the central position which Jesus occupies in religious education, it is surprising that we know very little about the growing child's Christology. As in all other aspects of his religious thinking the child is always trying to make sense of many divergent details. From stories, hymns, celebrations of the Christian festivals and many other sources he is building up a conceptual structure of the kind of person Jesus is, the power he possesses and uses, the nature of his authority, the purpose of his ministry, crucifixion and resurrection, and the nature of the evil with which he had to contend. Several stories from the Gospels were explored to see which would most fruitfully evoke the pupils' concepts. Of these, one stood out more than the others as helping to reveal the pupils' thinking in this area and this was the story of the Temptations of Jesus. The story has two aspects. The first is to emphasise the humanity of Jesus, that he was 'in all points tempted as we are', and in a sense revealing this as a parable of everyman. The second aspect is the emphasis upon his divine mission, and the narrative may be viewed in this light as an allegory or parable of the dilemma of Christ in trying to divine what kind of Messiah he was to be. The three temptations can be described as the temptation to be an economic reformer by turning stones into bread; the temptation to be a Davidic type military leader, conquering all the kingdoms of the world; and the temptation to be a miracle worker, by jumping from the pinnacle of the temple. Most writers and commentators combine both emphases in exploring the meaning of the story. Discussion with pupils revealed interesting trends in thinking, even though the items were the most difficult to score in the whole test.

THE PERSON OF CHRIST

In the context of the temptation narrative discussion the pupils were asked, 'When Jesus was a man was he specially different from all other men?' They were then asked to give their reasons for their answers.[1] A scale was devised to see what insight into Christology the schoolchild had. The theological grading was based upon progress from crude to advanced, where little or no difference is seen in Christ from all other men, to the advanced theological view that Christ is unique both in his nature as part of the Godhead and unique in his mission and saving power. The sequences of thinking could be seen in roughly three stages. The highest concept of the first stage is that of Jesus as a good, helpful or devout man, the second that he was a unique person as a miracle worker, and the third where he is seen in terms of either his mission for the world or his nearness to God. In this final stage most pupils reflect concepts of saviourhood and divinity.

The first stage up to about 9 : 5 (M.A. 9 : 9) reveals a very wide variety of concepts ranging from the almost incomprehensible to the highest which sees him as a good man. At the confused level a typical example is Kathy aged 6 : 2 (M.A. 6 : 6), 'You can't see him. He was God', where the interchangeability of God and Jesus is mixed up. Others focus upon physical characteristics or other irrelevancies, and they are usually the younger and less able children, although not always so. Such answers are Leslie's, aged 6 : 1 (M.A. 5 : 6), 'Yes, He wore a big turban on his head. His shoes and hair were different. A difference in clothes satisfies Leona, aged 6 : 5 (M.A. 6 : 0), 'Yes, he had long short trousers and a little shirt on top of the trousers.' A comparison with modern men is made by Billy, aged 6 : 9 (M.A. 7 : 10), 'Yes, other men don't have long hair', ignoring the common biblical fashion. A few children call attention to the sandals Jesus wore, or his beard, 'Yes, Jesus had a beard and other men don't' (age 7 : 2, M.A. 7 : 11). Perhaps hearing in hymns or stories of the strength of Jesus, Tina aged 6 : 6 (M.A. 5 : 8) interprets it literally as, 'Yes, he was strong. He could lift things.' A curious answer is Leonard's (age 6 : 11, M.A. 5 : 9), 'Yes, he grew different. When he was a baby he was born with a different face, but then he grew (up) and he became magic. He flew off into the sky.' The latter being

---

[1] See Appendix A, question S.3 : Q.3D.

presumably a reference to the Ascension. A few, of which Lillian is typical, answer 'no' to the question 'because he was an ordinary man' (age 7 : 5, M.A. 9 : 2).

Many children still call attention to his clothes and other physical features, but also add qualities of goodness or some other characteristic. Denise, for example, aged 6 : 6 (M.A. 5 : 10) says, 'He wore different coloured clothes. He might be brown and old and have a different voice. He was a good man. He thought he'd like to be a good man and help people.' 'He was kind,' says Wallace, aged 6 : 7 (M.A. 7 : 8). 'He's a king,' says Tim, aged 7 : 9 (M.A. 9 : 4). 'He didn't kill men like others did,' says Godfrey (aged 8 : 1, M.A. 8 : 3), and Andrew aged 8 : 5 (M.A. 11 : 8) puts it, 'Yes, he was good. He didn't do any bad things.' Lora, aged 9 : 6 (M.A. 7 : 3) says, 'Yes, he had more holy spirit in him as he got older', whereas Massey, aged 7 : 8 (M.A. 6 : 1) shows mixed insights, 'Yes, they had jackets on and Jesus didn't . . . God was with him at every time. If they was both (?) in the dungeon, Jesus had God with him.' This latter part may reflect some confusion of identity with Saint Paul.

The most numerous answers in this first stage show Jesus not only as kind and good, but kinder, more devout and much more helpful and moral than other men. He is still a man, but the difference is one of greater degree. Joan says, 'Yes, he helps other people and he had disciples, followers who helped him' (age 7 : 9, M.A. 10 : 3). Desmond aged 8 : 9 (M.A. 7 : 5) replies, Yes. They wouldn't see the difference. He was different inside him, he was kinder and he loved men.' Dinah aged 8 : 11 (M.A. 8 : 6) has a similar view, 'He looked like others but he prayed and he'd help people not to rob or kill them.' Others, think of something particular Jesus did, such as Daisy, aged 8 : 9 (M.A. 10 : 3), 'Yes, He could tell stories to other people about believing in God. Other men didn't.' Others use the term 'Son of God' to describe how Jesus was different but were unable to explain what they meant. For many it was plainly a verbalism even if an adjective is added, for example, in Alfred's answer, 'Yes, he was holy. *How do you mean?* He was the Son of God. *Aren't we all God's children?* Yes, but he . . . I don't know.' For many of them a good or a holy man is equivalent to what they mean by 'the son of God'; such is Pat (age 8 : 7, M.A. 8 : 6), 'Yes, he went around to make people better. He was the son of God.' An occasional pupil describes him in terms of misunderstood kingship, 'Yes, he was king of Jerusalem. *How do you mean?* He was a real king with a crown' (age 7 : 10, M.A. 10 : 0).

After about 9 : 5 (M.A. 9 : 9) there comes an intermediate stage where Jesus is seen as different because of his miraculous powers. Some interesting examples are given by the pupils. 'Yes, it was his healing miracles,' says Harry, aged 9 : 8 (M.A. 11 : 11), 'He could walk on the water and vanish.' Sheena replies, 'He was the only man who could do miracles and parables' (age 9 : 9, M.A. 13 : 0). An additional question was put if the healing acts of Jesus were central to see how Jesus was different from doctors. For example, Norman aged 9 : 10 (M.A. 10 : 1), 'Yes, he believed, and had powers like healing the sick. *Was he different from doctors?* Yes, they couldn't heal all the things Jesus could heal.' Sara, aged 9 : 10 (M.A. 8 : 10), 'He could make cripples walk and the blind to see. *Doctors?* Yes. He could feed 5,000 people on one loaf.' Lesley maintains that 'Doctors took more time. Jesus could heal on the spot' (age 9 : 11, M.A. 13 : 5). Rodney aged 12 : 10 (M.A. 12 : 7) although much older, propounds exactly the same idea, 'Jesus could do it in a minute. Doctors take months. He also worked on the Sabbath day.' Sometimes the emphasis is upon the difficulties of healing, 'Jesus could heal leprosy and doctors gave up,' says Joel (aged 13 : 6, M.A. 12 : 11). This miraculous element is voiced at all ages; for example, Daisy aged 10 : 5 (M.A. 11 : 3), 'It wasn't in the clothes he wore. He went without food and drink for a long while. He had powers of miracle, and knew what stories to tell.' 'Other men can't do miracles like changing water into wine,' says Clive, aged 10 : 11 (M.A. 8 : 6). 'Yes. He had greater belief than others. He had the power to preach and do miracles', Daly aged 11 : 5 (M.A. 14 : 2). 'Yes, it was his preaching and teaching. *There were others who preached and taught?* Yes, but Jesus could work miracles. *Didn't Peter do miracles?* Yes. Jesus gave him power to do it' (12 : 7, M.A. 13 : 8).

A number at this intermediate stage try to discern his special status, in varying terms. Rose aged 9 : 11 (M.A. 10 : 0) says, 'He was great and people believed in him. He was God's son. *Aren't we all God's children?* Jesus was his real son. He was born to God and later went into heaven. *Don't we?* Yes, but Jesus was a real son. God had no others at that time.' 'Yes, He foretold the scriptures and only prophets can do that,' answers Barry, aged 11 : 6 (M.A. 12 : 5). But when asked if Jesus was different from the prophets he replied, 'He was God's son. The prophets only guessed but Jesus knew it was true.' Earlier Barry had said, 'He's God's only begotten son, as it says in the Bible. *Aren't we all God's children?* Yes, but he was only-begotten, his only real chosen son, or God wouldn't have sent the angels to tell Mary.' David explains the difference as, 'He was like God's secretary. God could tell him he was. He never did wrong. He prayed a lot on hillsides' (aged 11 : 8, M.A. 11 : 5). This special status is described by Harold as 'God helping him all the time, giving him greater knowledge' (age 12 : 1, M.A. 15 : 7). 'He was a King who could do miracles. He served his people. He wasn't an ordinary king.

I mean he didn't own a city or anything,' says Martha, aged 12 : 9 (M.A. 11 : 8).

From about the age of 13 : 8 (M.A. 14 : 6), the third stage of concepts begins to prevail. From this time Christ's special relationship to God is seen more clearly or his mission to the world is more apparent. Sometimes this is seen in terms of his Saviourhood or the view that he is part of the Godhead. Some express almost in terms of the previous stage, such as Robin, 'Yes, he could do miracles, heal the sick and the crippled. He was God's son. *Aren't we all God's children?* He was a special one sent to preach about God' (age 13 : 10, M.A. 11 : 5). His omniscience and sinlessness is expressed by Delia, 'He knew all about God and the scriptures. He knew the way he was going to die. He never did wrong. He was the only righteous person who lived on earth' (age 14 : 3, M.A. 15 : 4). Barry aged 14 : 5 (M.A. 17 : 6) says, 'Yes. He had powers to cure and he led the people to do righteousness. He was the son of God. *Aren't we all God's children?* God had sent him into the world to lead people into peace. If he'd failed God might have sent someone else.' Dianne states, 'He was God's son. *Aren't we all God's children?* Yes, but he was sent on a special mission. He came from where God is. He believed in his mission' (age 14 : 11, M.A. 13 : 1).

All those who express Jesus as the Christ at the highest level are Grammar school pupils. Jonathan, for example, aged 15 : 4, says, 'He was the direct son of God. That is, he was closer to God, part of God. We are his children, but not an actual part of him.' 'He was the son of God, divine,' says Owen, aged 15 : 10 in the science fifth. When asked did this make Jesus different from all God's children, he said: 'Yes, but he was God in human form. Our minds are not the same. *How do you mean?* Jesus had God's mind.' 'He was supposed to be the Incarnation of God,' says Edna, a future medical student, aged 16 : 10, 'He was God made man. He had a tremendous effect on all who knew him, and he was resurrected from the dead.' When asked to explain what she meant by 'Son of God', Deborah aged 17 : 11 said, 'We are reborn by the spirit. He was *originally* the son of God.' Edward, in the science sixth, says, 'He was the son of God and part of the Trinity, and as God is morally perfect, therefore he was morally perfect. *Are we all God's children?* Yes, but not in the same sense. Son here means very close to God. We are more subjects.'

Although this is an over-simplification, we can see from the previous descriptions that the sequence of concepts about the person of Christ starts with Jesus as a good man, then as a miracle worker, and finally as a saviour.

A previous question, 'When Jesus was a boy, was he specially different from all other boys?' was put to see what concepts the pupils had about the childhood of Jesus. The answers were so diverse that a straightforward evaluation was not possible, and the judgment of some twenty experts was sought. From this procedure no generalisations could be made about the concepts formed nor about the sequences of thinking, except to note that up to the age of eight years the children's answers were irrelevant, trivial or based upon physical aspects. The young children also tended to use theological terms such as 'He was God's son' or 'He was holy' which subsequent discussion revealed were used as verbalisms, with no understanding of what they meant. Typical of such a level of trivial answers were the following: 'Other boys were good and ran errands, but Jesus didn't. Many answers merely showed his clothes, his name or his appearance were different. Where clothes and appearance were concerned, it was plain that they imagined Jesus in Palestinian garb and all other children in modern clothes, such as they themselves wore. Quite a few children were concerned with the miraculous, and several said, 'He could do miracles, like change clay birds into real ones', or 'He could do all sorts of wonderful things.' The Christmas stories had left an important impression on others, 'He didn't live in a house, but in a stable', and 'All sorts of people came to see him, like kings and shepherds.' Typical of answers which emphasised the physical were, 'He had a better bearing than other boys', and 'He had a lovely face and a nice smile.' The verbalisms were 'He was God's son' or 'He was God's child' or 'He was holy' but how this made him different from other of God's children the pupils found it impossible to imagine. One child said that one difference was that Jesus 'got more attention from God'.

After eight years, the answers become very diverse as we have noted, and pupils of all ages gave answers which on the whole stressed a normal childhood. Let us take some ten year olds as examples. Grace aged 10 : 1 (M.A. 10 : 11) says, 'He was always kind to people, if they'd not done wrong', while Judy aged 10 : 4 (M.A. 10 : 9) sees no difference, 'He was an ordinary boy.' The accent on piety is fairly common. For example: Vera aged 10 : 3 (M.A. 9 : 1) is convinced 'He knew more prayers', and while stressing his normality Gordon supports the more pious emphasis, 'He was a boy just the same as anyone else. He was more religious than the others as the son of God' (age 10 5, M.A. 14 : 6). Peggy, aged 10 : 6 (M.A. 13 : 5), is similar in her views, 'Yes. He wanted to know about God and was eager to learn at school. When they wanted to do naughty things he'd say, 'Don't let's do that!' Rowena aged 10 : 7 (M.A. 12 : 3) puts it another way, 'No. He wasn't different. He'd go up the hill and play with them, but he did believe in his father, which other boys might laugh at.' Normality is stressed again by Alice, aged 10 : 11 (M.A. 15 : 8). 'He wouldn't know what his mission was then. He'd fight and play tricks but not do nasty things', and Alastair, 'No. He played like other boys did. He only changed when he became a man' (age 10 : 10, M.A. 12 : 7). Older pupils tended to emphasise greater intelligence and curiosity than piety, which the following answers illustrate. 'He seemed to be more inquisitive and to ask more questions' (age 14 : 11, M.A. 14 : 11). 'He was a normal boy, but when he was twelve he talked so wisely with the wise men in the temple' (14 : 11, M.A. 11 : 8). Those who answer from the pietistic viewpoint now tend to see it more realistically, as for example, Dianne, 'He was more gentle and persevering and patient' (14 : 11, M.A. 13 : 1). It is interesting in the last three answers to note that all three pupils are chronologically the same age. A sixth former expresses a concept of normality, which many of the older pupils also state in different words. 'God wanted it that way. If Jesus could believe in God as an ordinary boy, then everyone could.'

CONCEPTS OF CHRIST'S MORAL RIGHTEOUSNESS

To see the pupil's concepts of the person of Christ in greater depths two further questions were asked.[1] 'Did Jesus ever do wrong when he was a boy?' and 'Did Jesus ever do wrong when he was a man?' These questions followed on naturally from the temptation narrative. Unfortunately, the data defied several attempts to devise suitable criteria for scoring. The results set out below are merely descriptive in terms of chronological age, and are limited generalisations, since they are the subjective analysis of the investigator only. The pupils' responses can be divided into two types, those who see no moral imperfection in Christ and those who do. We will first summarise those answers where pupils conceive Christ to possess no moral imperfections either as a boy or as a man.

Most six, seven and eight year olds equate grown-ups with a Godlike nature (vide Bovet) and therefore once Jesus was grown up he could do no wrong, since he was a grown up. The general view at this age is naïve, frequently expressed as 'Jesus was brought up well, so he did no wrong.' Fear of consequences also is marked. 'Jesus was afraid of being whacked by his Dad,' as also 'He didn't do wrong as a man because he'd be afraid God would punish him.' One pupil suggested he would be unpopular and that no one would play with him, if he did wrong. Others advance reasons of status, for example,

---

[1] See Appendix A, question S.3; Q.3A and B.

'Jesus was a king, and kings do no wrong.' From nine years onwards more realistic views tend to appear and Jesus' sinlessness is linked with His mission—'He had to be a good example to others.' This latter appears more frequently with increasing age. During this period a sense of Christ's uniqueness appears to grow either as 'the Son of God' or in terms of his closeness to God. The term 'Son of God' is used earlier, probably more as a verbalism, but the idea of being close to God tends to be more emphasised after twelve years. About fourteen years childish reasons tend to recede sharply. The orthodox Christian view tends to be expressed after this age—'he is the only righteous person who ever lived', and 'If he had sinned, he couldn't be God nor make the necessary sacrifice for us in dying. He had to be a lamb without blemish.'

The frequency of those seeing no imperfection in Christ can be seen below:

THOSE WHO SEE NO MORAL IMPERFECTIONS IN CHRIST AS BOY AND MAN

Chronological Age	Number seeing no imperfection
6	19 out of 20
7	14 „
8	12 „
9	10 „
10	10 „
11	10 „
12	9 „
13	8 „
14	7 „
15	8 „
Totals	107

The decrease with chronological age of those who see no moral imperfections in Christ is obvious.

When we summarise these responses where pupils conceive of some moral imperfections in Christ as a boy, or as a man, or as both, some generalisations can be made, although with caution. Of those who saw Jesus doing 'wrong' as a boy, almost all saw the acts as mischievous boyish pranks and slight, but natural, disobedience to parents. A few feel he could have told lies, but 'small' lies only. A few cite the Temple incident as the only wrongdoing, since Jesus made his parents anxious by his absence when disputing with the scholars; they feel his intention was good, so it wasn't wicked. Only a very few allow that he would hurt another child or an animal.

Later, adolescents begin to see imperfection, not necessarily wickedness, since it is implicit in all childhood experience, and for Jesus to be human he would have to be a normal boy. These children only began after ten years of age to see that Jesus changed as a man by a conversion, a call or an 'adoption' experience. Even after this, many appear to think he became good just because he 'growed up'. They tend to assume that as he grew he simply learned what was right and wrong. The exercise of the will is not, on the whole, recognised as a problem. From eleven years onwards more pupils appear to achieve this insight. A few—sixteen pupils—see imperfections in Jesus as a man, but usually cite only one example and regard this as untypical. These incidents are various, such as anger when throwing over the money-changers' tables, the mistake of choosing Judas as his disciple, asking for the 'cup to pass from him' in Gethsemane, an imagined disobeying of God or forgetting to pray. On the whole, however, the view is expressed succinctly by seventeen year olds—'He was not perfect, but as near perfect as anyone can be. Perfection isn't possible.'

THOSE WHO CONCEIVE SOME MORAL IMPERFECTION IN CHRIST AS BOY, MAN OR BOTH

Chronological Age	As boy	As man	As boy and man	Totals
6	1	1	0	2
7	6	1	0	7
8	6	1	1	8
9	5	1	4	10
10	9	0	1	10
11	9	0	1	10
12	9	2	0	11
13	10	0	2	12
14	12	0	1	13
15+	12	0	0	12
Totals	79	6	10	95

Increase with chronological age is evident in thinking of Jesus as doing some wrong as a boy; this is also evident on total 'moral imperfection' numbers each year. (When the tables are compared it will be seen that 107 and 95 make a total of 202. The two extra are counted twice as ambiguities.)

To put some flesh on these statistical bones a few typical responses will provide useful illustrations. First, those who see no imperfections. A six year old: 'He was well brought up as a boy. He was obedient to Mary and Joseph to make him good. *As a man?* Some men are bad, but not if they are brought up to do good. Jesus is holy, like the bush.' Another six year old: 'No. He was the Son of God. Jesus and God can't do naughty things. *As a man?* No, most grown-ups don't do bad things.' A seven year old: 'God made him a good boy. He was God's son. *As a man?* My daddy don't do bad things. Some men do. *Why didn't Jesus?* Jesus had lots of friends. Bad men have no friends.' An eight year old: 'He'd know it was wrong, whatever it was, because God spoke inside him. *As a man?* He knew he should obey his father.' Nine years: 'He was God's son and could do no wrong. *Are we all God's children?* Yes, but God sent him specially to earth from heaven to teach people about God. *As a man?* He'd have to be good himself if he was to teach people about God.' Ten years old: 'Only in small things, mischievous things. *As a man?* When he was old enough to understand, Jesus knew he was from God and loved him, and didn't want to disobey him.' A twelve year old: 'He was the Son of God. (Q) He was protected from all evil by God. He was given special powers unlike us. *As a man?* He was a special chosen one to make more people believe in God. If he did wrong people wouldn't believe in him.' A fourteen year old: 'He was the Son of God, but he wouldn't know this as a boy. Children don't know what is right or wrong. *As a man?* He was son of God when he was baptised and he realised then that he wasn't ordinary, and had to keep to standards.' A seventeen year old: 'He had some sort of spiritual or mental capacity beyond a normal boy. He knew what he was about from an early age. *As a man?* He was the Son of God, part of the Trinity, therefore he was morally perfect. We are merely subjects; he was a son.'

Here, in contrast, are some responses from children who see some moral imperfections. A six year old: 'He might be disobedient to his mother. *As a man?* No, all men are good, they're grown up.' A seven year old: 'Yes, he could be disobedient and he might hurt someone by accident. *As a man?* No. He understood God more and what God said.' Eight years old: 'Yes, he might chop up his father's wood by mistake. *As a man?* No, Grown-ups know better.' A nine year old: 'Yes, in the temple, running away from his parents. *As a man?* No, he was holy then.' A ten year old: 'Yes, he'd get into mischief. He did get lost once, but that wasn't bad. He'd not go busting windows, or getting muddy. *As a man?* Yes, he was only tempted, and that isn't important.' Eleven years old: 'Yes, he was like every child. He'd steal cakes. God made him ordinary so no one would notice him. If they did, they'd kill him. *As a man?* No. At twelve in the Temple, God put things in his mind. They knew then he was different.' Twelve years old: 'No, he was the Son of God, nearer to him than we are. *As a man?* Yes, he overturned the tables in the Temple. It wasn't bad really because they were cheats.' At thirteen years: 'He'd tell fibs, pinch food, and maybe fight. He'd be a normal boy. *As a man?* No, when he grew up he worked for God.' Fourteen years: 'Yes, maybe disobey, and if he stole, it would be apples from an orchard. *As a man?* No, he'd matured. He realised he was the Son of God.' Fifteen years: 'Not much, perhaps greedy with his food. *As a man?* No, he changed when he was baptised and forgiven.' A seventeen year old: 'Yes, maybe he'd mix up his father's tools or be naughty. *As a man?* He wasn't perfect, but as near perfect as any man can be. Perfection isn't possible.' Another seventeen year old: 'He'd cry as a baby, maybe break some of his toys. But Jesus when he was old enough to realise was the perfect teenager. *As a man?* No, he was older and realised God sent him to show man how to be good.'

To summarise concepts of moral righteousness we can say that Christology on the whole tends to be primitive until thirteen or fourteen years, and also very confused, not surprising with such a difficult concept of relationships; God-man problem and other difficulties are resolved by many theologians. Christ's origins, special status, his function on earth and the implications of all these are seen only vaguely. These limitations appear to reflect the limitations of understanding both of the human situation and inter-personal relationships generally, restrictions inevitable with immaturity and inexperience. Few human beings really face the full human dilemma before mid-adolescence. There appears to be a marked tendency for children to supply their own contradictory reasons, often by holding idealised and unrealistic pictures of Christ, to sustain a taught theological idea only understood at a verbal level. Although practically all pupils (184) regard Jesus as a man, perfect in all moral matters, the boyhood of Christ provides an area of growing awareness, with pupils' increasing age, that childhood implies imperfection and a growing towards the truth. With increasing age, therefore, they appear to question former idyllic views of Christ's childhood. A few express doubts about the possibility of his perfect manhood.

THE TEMPTATIONS

We have already examined the reasons put forward by the pupils why Jesus would not turn the stone into bread, but this was an analysis of the methods of thinking used. In the context of understanding what children and adolescents think about Christ and the problem of evil, a study of the theological concepts raised by this question will be of some value. When we compare this with a later question about the role of God in the story of the temptation,[1] we shall see the sequences of thought in a fuller dimension.

[1] See Appendix A, question S.3: Q.4A and B.

Reasons why Jesus resisted the first temptation fall into three clear stages. First of all there are those responses which indicate misunderstanding due to crude literal interpretations, with some trivial and irrelevant observations. Then, at the next stage something vaguely wrong is seen in the devil's request, largely because it is the devil who asked it and it is God who commanded Jesus not to do it. No real insight into the situation or the problem posed by the story is yet evident. Finally we see associative and authoritarian concepts are left behind and the problems of obedience to God and misuse of power are beginning to be seen. But not until later in this third stage is the purpose of such a test or the problem of Messiahship recognised. Many older pupils do not achieve this higher level of thought. We could summarise the three stages as a non-conceptual stage, a stage of concepts of authoritarian obedience, and finally concepts of purpose and power.

The non-conceptual stage continues until about nine years (M.A. 9 : 4). A few answers are tautological or nonsensical such as, 'He didn't want to' (age 6 : 7, M.A. 7 : 8), or 'They wouldn't have bread in that country' (age 6 : 2, M.A. 5 : 3). Others, almost as nonsensical and irrelevant are: 'He didn't know the stone was magic and it could turn into bread' (age 6 : 6, M.A. 6 : 6). 'Something might have happened to the stone. It might have broke open and there'd be no bread again' (age 6 : 6, M.A. 5 :10) and 'because God was invisible' (age 7 : 1, M.A. 5 : 10). The vast majority of answers, however, are due to a literalistic interpretation of the phrase 'not by bread alone' which is variously thought to mean 'he had to eat something with it, like butter or jam or water' or 'there was no audience to see it happen'. Typical is Joan's reply, aged 7 : 11 (M.A. 10 : 1), 'God said that if you ate bread alone you wouldn't live. *How do you mean?* You should eat something else with it—butter.' Other answers reflect a child's limited experience. 'He didn't want to. *Why not?* Because he wasn't hungry' (age 8 : 10, M.A. 10 : 11), and 'He might have been so angry he wouldn't just do it, with the devil keep on asking him. The devil tired him out asking and Jesus got angry' (age 8 : 9, M.A. 6 : 5) are examples of this. One polite minded girl of seven said it was 'because the devil didn't say please'. Another felt 'the devil would grab it and eat it for himself' so it would be pointless for Jesus to do it. Yet another suggested Jesus 'had no magic left to do it. It was all used up.' Plainly no real concept of what the temptation meant is understood. Literalisms and materialistic considerations completely impede any insight.

The second stage where concepts of authoritarian obedience are evident rely upon the command of God not to obey the devil, or association of the devil with evil and therefore he is to be automatically refused. The deed itself is not the focus but the authority of God, or the converse. Examples of the authoritarian command of God are Allan's response: 'God wanted him to stay out in the wilderness for forty days and not eat. *Why not?* God, his father said he mustn't eat. *Why?* Because Jesus had a lot of work to do' (age 10 : 2, M.A. 9 :9), and Sophia's, 'He was told not to. *How do you mean?* By the Lord, by God. *Why?* Because that other man wanted to eat it.' Illustrations of aversion to the devil are Betty's reply: 'Jesus didn't believe in the devil, he didn't want to do it just for him. He's bad' (age 9 : 10, M.A. 10 : 11); Neville's, 'If he did he'd be doing what the devil told him. *What was wrong with that?* The devil's horrible!' (age 10 : 1, M.A. 8 : 10); and Teresa's, 'He knew the devil was tempting him. (Q) Once he had done one thing, the devil would try to make him do another' (age 11 : 5, M.A. 13 : 3). A few reflect a child's concern for showing off. Such is Claude's answer, 'He didn't want to show off his power. Anyway, the devil wasn't a nice man' (age 9 : 8, M.A. 13 : 6). A number also express the view that it was a trivial request, as for example, Alastair; 'Jesus didn't want to waste God's time. God must have more important things to attend to' (age 10 : 10, M.A. 12 : 7).

The final stage, with the growth of real insight, in concepts of the purpose and power involved in the first temptation, emerges about twelve years of age (M.A. about 12 : 4). Here some idea of the conflict of good and evil is seen, dimly at first, but more clearly later. Similarly misuse of power is an evident concern, not only in terms of 'wasting' it, but also in refusing to use it for an evil purpose. Only a very few, however, see Christ's refusal as a rejection of the possible role of Messiah as that of an economic and political leader, giving bread and security to the masses.

The conflict between good and evil is expressed at all ages and with varying degrees of insight. Here are some examples. Ray's answer, for example, is fairly simple, 'It wasn't God's will. *Why not?* Jesus shouldn't obey the devil, but God. God is the only one we should obey' (age 12 : 2, M.A. 11 : 5). 'He was obviously not going to be out-done by the devil,' says Polly, 'because it would show he was giving in to him. And if he gave in to the devil, it showed other people could do likewise' (age 13 : 5, M.A. 15 : 3). Robin sees it in terms of fasting. 'He was told to go for forty days without food . . . The devil was really trying to see if Jesus was honest, and if he'd obey God or the devil' (age 13 : 10, M.A. 11 : 5). It is this principle of choice which is expressed at this stage, put clearly by Jonathan, 'It was a case of good against evil. It would be a victory for evil against God if he did it' (age 15 : 4, M.A. 17 : 6). Two differing insights on the misuse of power come from Phyllis, aged 12 : 6 (M.A. 12 : 1); 'He didn't want to use his power on things like that. It was too trivial. He wanted to get people better and help them', and from Guy, 'Jesus didn't want to show he was Christ by doing miracles but by preaching, because this is what God intended him to do.'

The highest insights of all, expressed by older but necessarily more able pupils can be seen in the answers of Dianne, 'Because he said he was feeding on spiritual bread and he wanted his whole mind and body to be on God . . . Jesus wouldn't do miracles for the sake of it, only if he thought it would do any good' (age 14 : 11, M.A. 13 : 1) and of Delia, 'So that man should not eat bread alone; he lives by the word of God. If you have faith in him, he will provide all your needs' (age 14 : 3, M.A. 15 : 4). A sixth former aged seventeen says: 'Jesus didn't feel he had to prove anything. Jesus felt people should believe in him for what he was and not for what he could do in miracles.'

The whole point of the narrative of the temptations is seen more clearly when we press the questions, 'What was God doing?' and 'Why didn't he stop the devil tempting Jesus?' Answers range from crude and irrelevant statements to the view that the temptations were all part of Christ's preparation for his mission, and that God must stand aside and not interfere. This concept of a necessary test involves some very difficult ideas of human freedom. Unless the choice of Jesus was a human choice, between good and evil possibilities, and he had real freedom to decide, without extraneous divine protection or intervention, the story has no substance. It represents also a highly advanced concept of the nature of God and the nature of man, demanding propositional thinking, as well as a mature and permissive approach to human relationships. The tendency of children is to see those who have great power as using it. Self-restraint or self-limitation is not an attribute they would appear to comprehend until adolescence, although they practise both from an early age under the pressures of social demands. In scoring the answers the child's belief or views on a personal devil does not enter into our considerations, although it is inevitable that the lower scores will tend to reflect cruder views of the nature of evil.

Four stages are evident as sequences of thinking. First there is the trivial stage where inadequate and irrelevant answers are given up to about eight years of age. There follows a similar stage where serious misconceptions of the situations are made, often due to verbalism or tautological thinking. Up to this point extending to eleven years of age (M.A. 11 : 5) Jesus is regarded as so divinely powerful the temptation is no test, but a walk-over. From this point, however, the third stage indicates the beginnings of insight when a real test is felt to be basic to the story. Its significance is limited to the immediate situation and not really related to Christ's future mission. Finally, from fourteen years onwards (M.A. 15 : 0) the test is now recognised as related to Christ's role as saviour, to his humanity, sometimes to God's limitations of power, self-imposed in order to grant man true moral freedom.

Examples of the first stage are, 'God didn't know where Jesus was,' 'The devil might give away some plans and God could then capture people,' 'The devil was a kind man really,' 'Jesus wouldn't kill himself if he jumped,' 'God was frightened of the devil,' and 'God would let the devil wear himself out asking.' One or two fuller examples will be of interest. Massey, aged 7 : 8 (M.A. 6 : 1) says, 'God must have been with Jesus. *In what way?* He helped Jesus. He might be under the straw in the dungeon. He'd help Jesus out of the window. God would have a gun and shoot the devil. *Why didn't God stop the devil tempting?* God wasn't listening.' Joan aged 6 : 2 (M.A. 5 : 3) says: 'God'd tell the devil not to do it because Jesus was God's son. *Why didn't God stop him?* Because God was nice to people and the devil was people.' For Penelope, 'God was up in heaven and didn't know what was happening' (age 6 : 8, M.A. 6 : 4).

No real test is seen in the temptations at the second stage because 'God knew Jesus wouldn't give in,' 'Jesus had power like God and couldn't be harmed,' and 'God would only let the devil go so far, and then step in.' Fuller answers at this stage illustrate these limitations. Nicola gives a long explanation (age 8 : 3, M.A. 8 : 6): 'God was praying to Jesus and saying, "You won't be hurt, Jesus, and don't do anything the devil says." *Where was God at the time?* He was up in heaven. He prays and his voice would come down to Jesus. *Why didn't God stop the devil?* God knew he couldn't stop the devil. He wasn't like Jesus. He knew the devil wouldn't hurt Jesus in any way or touch him. He'd only tell Jesus bad things. *How do you mean, God couldn't stop him?* He didn't want the devil to stop. Jesus liked talking to him.' Claude puts the wearing-out-the-devil viewpoint. 'God was telling Jesus what to do, to resist the devil. *Why didn't he stop the devil?* God didn't want to. If he let him keep on he'd get tired and never come back to Jesus. Well, not for a long time anyway' (age 9 : 8, M.A. 13 : 6). A very mixed answer, with the beginnings of insight, is given by Rose aged 9 : 11 (M.A. 10 : 0), 'God wasn't there at the moment Jesus was tempted. He was healing someone. *Why didn't he stop the devil?* He maybe thought Jesus should fight his own battles, otherwise he'd look a proper baby.' Sophia at 10 : 7 (M.A. 9 : 9) says, 'God was just sitting down and listening, but not helping. *Why?* He knew Jesus wouldn't do it, he wouldn't kill himself. *Why not?* 'Cause Jesus had told God he wouldn't.'

The real watershed in conceptual thinking here is crossed about eleven years of age (M.A. 11 : 5) by most pupils when the idea of some choice in a test is expressed for the following reasons, 'to see if he'd obey God or the devil', 'to prove he was good,' 'to convince Jesus he could resist, and to give him confidence,' 'to see if he could sort himself out'. For one boy 'It was a demonstration rather than a test, to show how humans are tempted.' Fuller answers show more clearly the substance of these concepts. Martin aged 11 : 5 (M.A. 15 : 7) says, 'God was watching, but not helping. (Q) It was a test and it would mean defeat if God stopped it. *Why did God have to test him?* To see if he were the right person for his work.' Ray aged 12 : 2 (M.A. 11 : 5) feels God was there, 'telling Jesus not to do it. (Q) He could stop it but he wanted to test Jesus to see if he would obey. *Why was a test needed?* To see who Jesus believed in, God or the devil.' Larry, a very intelligent Grammar school boy, age 13 : 2 (M.A. 18 : 4) says, 'It was a test to give Jesus more heart, to make him feel stronger and more able to preach God's word.' And Audrey, aged 13 : 11 (M.A. 12 : 8) feels, 'God wanted to see what Jesus would do, if he'd stand up for himself. *Why was a test needed?* God wasn't sure at first. He wanted to see, as Jesus had been an ordinary boy when he was small, if he could trust Jesus, or if there was anything special about him.'

Higher insights break through for the adolescents after fourteen years (M.A. 15 : 0) when the purpose of the test is 'to prove he was good enough to be a saviour' (or able to do his father's work) and 'to be Christ he had to go through temptations without sin', and 'to be a saviour he had to be worthy of saving men'. One sixth former says, 'It was Jesus or God tempting himself. Everyone has to deal with his own desires.' A few fuller answers provide some further interesting details. 'It was a test to see Jesus' reactions,' says Ernest aged 14 : 5 (M.A. 14 : 10). 'It was a great temptation for anyone. He was the most important offspring of God, and Jesus had to prove his faith in God and himself.' May, aged 14 : 10 (M.A. 19 : 11), felt God would help Jesus to resist temptation but would not stop the devil tempting him, 'because Jesus had gone into the wilderness to prove himself strong enough to do the work he'd come to earth for. It was Jesus, in a way, testing himself. 'God couldn't stop it,' says Edna (a sixth former) flatly, 'because these were temptations all men have. He'd have to overcome the temptations in his conscience.' Another pupil, in the science sixth, says, 'God was Jesus, but the father was helping the Son, by giving him strength to resist. *Why didn't God stop the devil tempting Jesus?* That isn't his way. He doesn't stop temptation. He gives the strength to withstand it. *Why was God not sure of Jesus?* It was a test. Not a test arranged by God for Jesus. It just happened, but it was a test for Jesus.'

CONCEPTS OF EVIL

Concepts of Christ as Saviour involve the question of what he came to save men from (as well as the broader idea of salvation for a fuller life of love) and this in turn involves the problem of evil. The story of the temptation of Jesus involves concepts of evil, as personalised in the allegory of the devil. To ask the pupils, 'Who was the devil?'[1] may seem to be a weighted question, assuming the personal nature of evil and the devil as the inspiring genius behind every evil act of man. It was, however, the only form in which this question could be asked, especially in the context of Christ's temptations. 'What is the devil?' is equally weighted and is in contradiction to the vocabulary and assumptions apparently made in the story. Despite this problem of weighting the question either way in terms of a personalised devil or a depersonalised source of evil energy, a considerable number of pupils refuse to anthropomorphise the devil. In spite of the fact that they refer to 'him' and use the word 'he', discussion reveals that they basically conceive him in other terms, as we shall see. Concepts begin with crude and manlike quality and identity being attributed to a personal devil, proceed to a more spiritual idea of an evil force, which has an identity, to the final view that the devil is the name or symbol for every man's sinful nature, and a natural consequence of divinely given freedom of moral choice.

The stages suggested by the scoring are not quite so clear-cut as the last sentence might imply, but a threefold order of concepts is evidently present, as the following answers will illustrate. First, up to the age of about 10 : 8 (M.A. 11 : 0) the devil is seen as a fantasised or conventionalised man, visible and with physical attributes. The whole picture until this time is crudely anthropomorphic, almost in the identical age range of a similar concept of God.[2] After a few confused answers such as 'He was a good man,' 'He's a nice man' and 'Was he the King of Egypt?' children conceive the devil as 'a bad man,' 'A wicked man under the ground,' 'a naughty giant in the sky,' 'a bad animal, a dragon or a snake' or simply a bad man with often a conventional description 'red clothes and horns on his head', some kind of man-animal. Occasionally, he is thought of as a man with evil plans able to make himself invisible. Here is a fuller account of some typical examples. Leona says, 'He's a bad giant way up in the sky. *How did Jesus hear him?* The giant speaks out loud' (age 6 : 5, M.A. 6 : 0). 'The devil was nasty,' says Simon aged 6 : 6 (M.A. 6 : 6). 'He was a nasty man. (Q) A man who tells you nasty things and tries to make you do it. *Could Jesus see him?* Yes, He'd see him in a black cloak, a beard and black hair.' It is interesting, incidentally, to note

[1] See Appendix A, question S.3 : Q.2D.   [2] See Chapter Six.

how frequently children use black to symbolise the devil, whereas God is invariably seen to wear white clothes. The devil for Martha, aged 7 : 3 (M.A. 6 : 10), 'tries to make you do naughty things. He just likes naughty people and Jesus likes good people. (Q) He's a man, never smiling, but you can't see him. He lives up in heaven.' For Joan, aged 7 : 9 (M.A. 10 : 3) he is simply, 'a man with horns and things'. Slightly fuller answers can be seen, as for example in Andrea's suggestion that 'He's a bad man who kept asking people to do wrong things and then he'd tell other bad men to come and catch him. Jesus wouldn't see him. He'd hear a voice but the devil is magic' (age 7 : 7, M.A. 7 : 7). Joan, aged 7 : 11 (M.A. 10 : 1) expresses the man-animal concept, 'A horrible man, with horns coming out of his head.' For Desmond the devil is 'Satan, a bad person. Jesus would see an old man, ever so cheeky, who had a cheeky look on his face' (age 8 : 9, M.A. 7 : 5). Sara, aged 9 : 10 (M.A. 8 : 10) says, 'He isn't like God, nice and helpful. All the devil does is to make trouble. He's a kind of animal who could do just as he liked.' An interesting and typical answer at this stage is Gordon's (aged 10 : 5, M.A. 14 : 6), 'He causes all the bad things in the world. He works on people's minds. (Q) Yes, Jesus saw him. He'd be dressed in all black and be dirty and need a haircut—a horrible looking person.'

The second and intermediate stage shows some crude anthropomorphisms still present, but supernatural elements are added (as in concepts of God) to heighten the powerful and frightening nature of the devil. This stage continues for most pupils until about 12 : 8 (M.A. about 13 : 3), again showing a remarkable similarity to the child's concepts of God at that age. Sometimes the devil is seen impersonally as a power but having still a separate identity. There is still no concept of evil being part of every man's nature, but instead there is a curious objectivity of evil in man-spirit form. Catherine, for example: 'He's a person, a man, inside you who tells you to do evil things. That's why a naughty child is called, "a little devil". Jesus couldn't see him. He was inside Jesus. He's magic' (age 10 : 8, M.A. 10 : 6). Eric sees him dramatically as 'The God of thieves, murderers and robbers. The devil tempts men to rob' (age 11 : 2, M.A. 11 : 5). A vivid symbolic view of evil is supplied by Barry, aged 11 : 6 (M.A. 12 : 5), 'He's a black man, both on the outside and on the inside. He tempts everyone so they'll be naughty, then he'll be their ruler instead of God.' Halfway to a more spiritual view of evil, Roy envisaged the devil as a man, then goes on to say, 'It's your conscience, a bad conscience.'

The final stage shows through when the pupils' concepts leave anthropomorphisms behind. For some, evil may still have a separate identity as the evil spirit often spoken in opposite terms to 'the holy spirit'.

Most pupils, however, from the age of 12 : 8 onwards (M.A. 13 : 3) conceive evil as a propensity within every person and 'devil' is the symbol or name used to express this. Typical of the separate identity view is Mary, aged 12 : 8 (M.A. 16 : 10), 'He's a spirit, the opposite of God, an evil spirit. He came when the first person on earth did wrong. *Where from?* He came from somewhere under the earth, from a fiery furnace. (Q) No, he couldn't be seen. He was inside Jesus, speaking to him.' A similar answer is, 'He's some early King who'd done evil, and he became the evil spirit', and the fallen angel who disobeyed God and who was thrown out of heaven is often presented. Guy, aged 13 : 4 (M.A. 15 : 11) says, 'The devil is anti-God . . . he's not under the control of God. When Jesus was crucified he had all the sins of the world on him. Because he overcame Satan, God made him come alive again.' Glen suggests the devil is 'the spirit of evil, not outside God's control but nearly' (age 13 : 4, M.A. 12 : 4). In contrast, Patsy says, 'It's the evil spirit in us all. It has no real identity or separate being' (aged 14 : 5, M.A. 16 : 11). And Barry aged 14 : 5 (M.A. 17 : 6) is more explicit, 'It was his own mind trying to turn him to bad. (Q) It's in everyone, and it's not an independent power like God.' Dianne at 14 : 11 (M.A. 13 : 1) expresses a similar view, 'The devil is evil and wrong thoughts and deeds. He isn't a person, not a separate being. He's the darker side of everything.' Perhaps Michele expresses the subjective concept of evil most clearly when she says, 'He's almost a myth, which has grown up with God. God represents righteousness and the devil represents evil. He's only an idea or a name for badness. It may be a part of God, as creator, but his righteousness only we call God' (age 16 : 1, M.A. 18 : 3).

In brief then, we can say children's thinking goes through three conceptual stages in terms of understanding the nature of evil. First there is the objective-anthropomorphic stage, then an objective supernaturalised stage and lastly a subjectivised human view where evil is real because it is part of human nature.

GENERAL COMMENT ON CONCEPTS OF JESUS AND THE PROBLEM OF EVIL

The composite picture is not too clear when all the items discussed in this chapter are put together in terms of various ages. The one sure comment we can make is that until about nine years the child's view of Christ is extremely confused and the problem of evil is not being seen at all realistically until about twelve years onwards. Certain aspects, however, do stand out unmistakably and a characteristic rough conceptual profile of the pupils in stages is possible.

The characteristics of Infant children and early Juniors is one of great confusion due to God and Jesus being interchangeable terms. The boyhood of Jesus is seen unrealistically, and trivial and irrelevant details obscure their thinking. Very few feel Jesus could have done wrong and they view the boy Jesus as a model child who could never be naughty. 'God's son' is often used to describe him, but this is a verbalism accepted from adult language which they cannot understand. As a grown man Jesus is also perfect for the simple reason that all adults are good people and Jesus was no exception. Jesus is conceived as a simple good and devout man, who helped people. There is no concept of mission or divinity or saving power, simply because the problem of evil is still very vague and not thought of in personal terms. The devil is a real man, rather horrible, who tries to get Jesus and other people to be naughty. He is unsuccessful for variously trivial reasons and Jesus' refusal to turn stone into bread is completely misunderstood because of the irrelevant concern of the child with specific phrases such as 'not by bread alone' which is taken literally to mean, 'He wouldn't, because if he did he'd have no butter or jam to eat with it (alone).' God is unconcerned with temptation because he is not about, is not listening or is too busy to help. No real issues of good and evil are grasped.

The later Juniors and frequently the early Secondary school pupils are more realistic and less distracted by irrelevancies and misleading verbalisms. Jesus as a boy is seen in more normal terms by most of them and if he was different from other boys it was perhaps in terms of devoutness and interest in religious matters. He is, despite this, seen as capable of mischief and perhaps occasional disobedience just like other boys, although 'nothing serious' is sometimes stressed. As a grown man the major emphasis upon Christ's miracles and his helpfulness, although still mentioned, plainly gives way to a demonstration of power, not uninfluenced by awe of magic. Any wrong he did as a man, voiced by a few, are only mistakes with no evil intention, but for most he was perfect, untouched by the devil's temptation, simply because God commanded him to say 'No' and he was at all times obedient. For this reason, the temptations are not seen realistically because there was never the slightest chance that Jesus would obey the devil, since his magic power and his perfect obedience would prevent it. The devil is seen as a more menacing figure in the sense that he is more powerful as the objective source of evil, and the pupils are losing their crude anthropomorphic view of the devil and seeing him (or it) as a supernatural evil spirit.

In the second to third year of the Secondary school the composite picture changes to a considerably more realistic Christology and the major issues of good versus evil are beginning to be seen in personal terms. Jesus' boyhood is seen as a normal boyhood with the imperfections of learning from experience recognised as part of the normal powers of growing up. Most adolescents see Christ as perfect as a man, or as near perfection as any man can be and the focus of his significance moves from miracle to mission. The purpose of being sent to earth is to bring truth and love and to show men the way. In late adolescence this is seen in times of salvation from sin, but only a few attain such insights at the top of the Grammar school. Earlier than this, however, the point of the temptation is beginning to be seen as a real and necessary conflict. Since Jesus was human it is a necessary part of his humanity to be tempted, not by an objective power of evil, but by his own nature. Many pupils still continue to think of evil as some kind of objective power outside man, but most favour the subjective view. Thus the temptation is conceived by those over fourteen years as a real conflict of good and evil desires in Jesus, which he had to face, if he was to be worthy of his mission. God supports Jesus spiritually in such a conflict, as he does all men, not by intervening directly but by influence. God therefore, having granted freedom of moral choice, must observe sympathetically while that freedom is used. Turning stone into bread is rejected as a trivial misuse of power and incompatible with what his future work is to be. Not all achieve this level of insight but the older and more able adolescents are already attaining them in some measure.

Two aspects of Christology strike one on observing the thinking of the younger children. First, there is evidence that some of the unreal views of Christ's boyhood which they hold for a considerable period are due in part to the continual and persistent influence of the Nativity stories. Part of the misunderstanding is also probably due to the child's inexperience and inability to reflect upon what normal childhood is. But certainly the emphasis upon some of the myths surrounding the birth of Jesus appears to heighten the miraculous elements and to encourage a sense of unreality about what manner of man Jesus really was. The second aspect of concepts of Christ is the similar problem of miracle and magic in the late Junior years. It is apparent that the miraculous acts of Christ, both the healing and the nature miracles, attract a great deal of attention during late childhood. When one considers how Jesus himself rejected the temptation to be a miracle-worker and saw the dangers of impressing men by this means because it diverted attention from his true mission, one is constrained to ask if the same hazard is relevant for religious education? How we answer this, of course, depends upon what kind of Christology we wish to build in the child's conceptual structure. Yet whatever kind it is, we can see the risk of creating myths stronger than the original myths, which may in later life require such a radical demythologising that a true picture of Christ is then lost.

Chapter Twelve

CONCEPTS OF PRAYER

MOST children pray. They may do so regularly or spasmodically, with the encouragement of parents, or spontaneously. Some children pray, despite parental disapproval. One child with rather militantly agnostic parents, who had withdrawn her from Religious Education in her Primary school, confessed to praying occasionally, 'when Mummy isn't looking'. Rather pathetically she says, 'We pretend to pray, my sister and I, and we never know what to say.' This, of course, is an area of religious activity where it is easy to be misled by children, trying to please an adult by giving the right sort of expected answers. For this reason direct questioning of the pupils' personal ideas of prayer was not attempted, apart from the two brief questions about prayer, and 'Church Connections' at the end of the interview. Instead the picture of a child praying alone was shown, the child in the picture being the same sex and approximate age of the child being interviewed. Used as a projection device, this helped to produce unselfconscious answers about what 'the child in the picture' thought and felt about prayer.[1] The evidence indicates that there was a fairly good measure of projection and most children identified successfully with the child in the picture. When we allow for the tendency of some non-praying pupils to 'idealise' the child in the picture, that is to credit him with ideas and motives he does not himself possess, we do in fact gain a consistent picture of the growing child's developing prayer concepts.

Some of the questions were used as checks on other information and will not be dealt with here. Others have already been dealt with in terms of how God is visualised and the divine omnipresence.[2] One question designed to discover motives of prayer, 'Why do you think the boy or girl prays?' did not yield sufficiently varied answers to make scoring possible. We shall not, therefore, deal with this here. What we shall consider in some detail is what children pray about, their concepts of the efficacy of prayer, and their concepts of the non-efficacy of prayers.

[1] See Appendix A, Picture 2 and questions: P.2; Q.1, Q.2, Q.3, Q.4, Q.5, and Q.6.
[2] Questions P.2: Q.4 and P.2: Q.5.

177

TO WHOM ARE PRAYERS ADDRESSED?

It may be of some interest to know how pupils answered the question, 'To whom is the boy or girl praying?' More than 75 per cent of the pupils addressed their prayers to God, 15 per cent to God and/or Jesus, and just over 7 per cent to Jesus alone. One boy, an eight year old, addressed his prayers to 'God, Jesus and the Holy Spirit.' A sixth former preferred to address his prayers 'to a spiritual being whose presence is with him'. Seven and eight year olds have the greater tendency to pray to Jesus, a few also among the nines and tens, with occasional instances occurring afterwards. Among these there is no sex difference, although slightly more intelligent pupils tend to include Jesus as one to whom prayers should be addressed. While this tendency is seen more in the early years, we find one fifteen year old, a regular Church of England weekly attender, with an IQ of 140, and a Grammar school girl of seventeen years, with a similar level of intelligence, praying to Jesus. The general tendency, however, as we have pointed out, is to address God in prayer.

THE CONTENT OF PRAYERS

While we can be confident that by the projection device most children tell us what they themselves pray about, it is possible that a considerable minority include items they feel they ought to pray about, if ever they do pray. The test therefore does not necessarily reveal the actual prayers of all the pupils. Its value lies in the fact that it does tell us what children of varying ages, intelligence levels, church and non-church backgrounds think should be prayed about. Whether or not these reflect their own praying habits is, in a sense, irrelevant, for they do reveal what concepts the pupils have about what should be the composition of prayers. How the pupils have arrived at these ideas is largely a matter of imitation of prayers they have heard in public worship in church, in Sunday school or in the daily assembly in school.

The actual quantity of prayers can be seen in the table opposite.

This indicates a general trend of increasing number of prayers with age until about ten years, then levelling off to a fairly uniform frequency, sustained during early and mid-adolescence. It is consistent with the child's growing experience, his increasing social awareness, and perhaps, greater vocabulary. This, of course, tells us nothing about the quality or variety of prayers thought to be appropriate at given periods.

It is evident, from an analysis of answers that some children who pray regularly may lack a variety of prayers, and that some who pray infrequently may have a wider variety, or breadth of prayer content. In other words, frequency and quality in praying may not necessarily be related. The question may be asked what we mean by 'quality' of prayer? I attempted to score the pupils' prayers on the following qualitative basis; first, crude, materialistic and very egocentric prayers, then prayers less crude, materialistic and egocentric, and finally,

MEAN AVERAGE NUMBER OF PRAYERS PER CHILD FOR EACH YEAR AGE GROUP

Chron. Year Group	Mean average number of prayers for each child
6	5·8
7	6·2
8	6·4
9	7·8
10	8·3
11	8·2
12	7·9
13	8·1
14	8·0
15+	8·35

more refined, spiritual and altruistic prayers. Assessment of the prayers on this basis proved extremely difficult. For example, one child praying that his father should be protected from physical danger, may have a father who is a coal miner, in daily peril of a particular kind. Is his prayer to be classed as egocentric or altruistic? Despite these difficulties some twenty external assessors reached a surprising amount of agreement. When, however, the results were scaled no sequences of prayers, for example, from egocentric praying to altruistic praying would be discovered. Some trends, however, can be seen when we compare one age group with another. This is a comparatively crude statistical method but it nevertheless produces useful and interesting information. We shall review this information in terms of grouped categories of prayers, altruistic, self, protection or recovery prayers, and set prayers.

1. Altruistic Prayers

The following two tables indicate the number of prayers and the number of pupils praying altruistic prayers. There are twenty pupils in each chronological year.

INCIDENCE OF ALTRUISTIC PRAYERS
(summarised in year age groups)

| | Chronological Years | | | | | | | | | |
	6	7	8	9	10	11	12	13	14	15+
Altruistic										
Family and relatives	28	14	20	24	31	33	29	35	31	29
Friends	9	6	8	7	10	9	18	10	12	18
Others	15	30	33	32	21	30	28	35	27	35
Pets and animals	2	4	4	0	8	5	11	5	2	2
TOTALS	54	54	65	63	70	77	86	85	72	84

The incidence in the above table refers to the numbers of prayers suggested in the various categories in each year. The next table gives the same information in terms of the number of pupils in each year praying such prayers in each year.

NUMBER OF PUPILS SUGGESTING ALTRUISTIC PRAYERS
(summarised in year age groups)

| | Chronological Years | | | | | | | | | |
	6	7	8	9	10	11	12	13	14	15+
Altruistic										
Family and relatives	12	10	13	14	19	19	17	20	18	20
Friends	7	6	8	6	10	8	15	9	11	16
Others	11	16	16	13	12	10	13	14	12	16
Pets and animals	2	4	4	0	7	5	11	5	2	2
TOTALS	32	26	41	33	48	42	46	48	43	54

Altruistic prayers include all prayers for others in a widening social circle from the family outwards. Animals are included, since many children feel they should be included in their prayer content. The incidence of prayers for family and relatives shows an increase from 10 years on. The number of pupils, however, shows a steady increase up to 10 and a sharp increase at 11 years, maintained throughout adolescence. Friends, both in incidence and number of pupils, show increases at 12 and 15 years, the first possibly the time when passionate friendships are being formed and the second possibly when the true worth of friendship is more maturely recognised. Prayer for others is surprisingly uniform in incidence and number of pupils, except for years 6 and 10. Years 10, 11 and 12 seems the greatest time of concern for animals. Total results, on both tables, show a gradual increase in altruistic prayers with its highest point reached about the age of 12 and 13 years.

Not included here are prayers for other people, which look to be altruistic, but which are in effect only prayers for self. Children may pray for a friend 'to be a good friend to me' or for daddy 'to be a good daddy and take me swimming' or for grandma 'that she'll be nice and kind to the little girl'. These kinds of prayers are frequent and in keeping with the natural egocentricity of the young child.

2. Prayers for Self

Below the table shows the number of prayers made for self in each year age group.

INCIDENCE OF PRAYERS FOR SELF

	Chronological Years									
	6	7	8	9	10	11	12	13	14	15+
Self										
Thanks	5	13	10	17	20	9	7	6	10	7
Forgiveness & Confession	0	2	4	7	5	4	9	8	12	11
Better Behaviour	8	8	8	14	10	11	12	10	10	14
Material Gifts	13	8	4	2	5	5	2	3	5	3
School and Work	4	4	7	6	6	8	7	8	8	9
TOTALS	30	35	33	46	46	37	37	35	45	44

The next table gives the same information in terms of the number of pupils in each year age group.

NUMBER OF PUPILS SUGGESTING PRAYERS FOR SELF

	Chronological Years									
	6	7	8	9	10	11	12	13	14	15+
Self										
Thanks	4	6	8	9	12	7	6	5	8	7
Forgiveness & Confession	0	2	4	7	5	4	9	8	12	11
Better Behaviour	7	7	8	10	10	11	10	8	9	11
Material Gifts	7	4	4	2	5	4	1	3	4	3
School and Work	4	4	7	5	6	8	7	7	8	9
TOTALS	22	23	31	33	38	34	33	31	41	41

Prayers for self are not necessarily egocentric prayers, but prayers where the self is the recipient, or the bestower, as in prayers of thanks. This is a rough classification only, as will be seen by the various ingredients. Prayers of thanks show a peak of frequency about years 9 and 10 with a slow decline through later years. Prayers for forgiveness and confession show a very clear trend of increased concern

181

with age, with a marked increase from 12 years on. This would appear to coincide with puberty and with the onset of sex feelings and greater introspection. Prayers for better behaviour also show a tendency to increase with age, with a perceptible increase at 9 years onwards, which might indicate a greater awareness of growing moral demands by adult society and possibly greater pressures from peers. On 'incidence', prayers for material gifts are high at 6 and 7 years then markedly decline, as one would expect. Prayers for help with school work appear to increase about 8 years, declining slightly in years 9 and 10 and returning to the previous level at 11. Totals on prayers for self show a marked increase in incidence at years 9 and 10, and again from 14 onwards. This is not confirmed on numbers of pupils, since there appears to be a steady increase throughout the age range, slightly higher at age 10 and at its highest from 14 years on.

3. *Prayers in Illness and Physical Danger*

This type of prayer is fairly frequent and merits separate consideration. The first table following shows the incidence of these prayers made in each year age group.

INCIDENCE OF PRAYERS FOR PROTECTION AND RECOVERY

	Chronological Years									
	6	7	8	9	10	11	12	13	14	15+
Protection and Recovery Illness (self and others)	18	19	16	22	26	16	18	23	22	15
Physical Danger (self and others)	8	6	12	5	16	21	17	20	10	8
TOTALS	26	25	28	27	42	37	35	43	32	23

The second table, below, gives similar information about these prayers in terms of the number of pupils in each year age group.

NUMBER OF PUPILS MAKING PRAYERS FOR PROTECTION AND RECOVERY

	Chronological Years									
	6	7	8	9	10	11	12	13	14	15+
Protection and Recovery Illness (self and others)	11	12	14	14	15	11	13	16	11	9
Physical danger (self and others)	6	4	7	4	9	12	11	10	5	5
TOTALS	17	16	21	18	24	23	24	26	16	14

Prayers concerned with illness and physical danger include prayers for recovery and protection from danger, for both self and others. Apart from familial prayers these are the prayers of greatest incidence. The prayers concerning illness seem to show little pattern, but the incidence and number of pupils praying for physical protection increase steadily with age to a peak of concern at about 13 years. Combined totals of the two items, on 'incidence', partially show this increase, peak and decline at 14 years. Many adolescents at this later age tend to reject much of prayer as 'magic' and may therefore label prayers for physical health or safety in this way.

4. *Set Prayers*

By 'set prayers' we mean those learned by heart and repeated, and include the Lord's Prayer, the school prayer (such as the prayer of St. Iganatius Loyola), the General Confession and many others. Some younger children occasionally have a set prayer, culled from a children's book of prayers or one taught by a parent, such as 'Matthew, Mark and Luke or John, bless the bed that I lie on.'

INCIDENCE OF SET PRAYERS

	Chronological Years									
	6	7	8	9	10	11	12	13	14	15+
Set Prayers	13	14	15	21	20	27	20	24	25	20

NUMBER OF PUPILS PRAYING SET PRAYERS

	Chronological Years									
	6	7	8	9	10	11	12	13	14	15+
Set Prayers	12	11	13	15	15	19	16	17	17	18

Both in the number of set prayers used and the number of pupils suggesting set prayers, it is evident that there is an increase of learned prayers as appropriate for praying up to year 11. After this there appears to be a slight decline among adolescents who consider them not to be quite so appropriate content of prayers.

From this brief summary of results we can observe several factors which are consistent with what is known of changes occurring during childhood and adolescence, with greater moral pressures, widening social experience and growing self-awareness. Due to the stratified nature of the sample, however, these results must be seen only in the most general terms.

CONCEPTS OF EFFICACIOUS PRAYER

Children regard prayers as efficacious or successful in some way, or they would not engage in them. This was explicit in the children's discussion of prayers in almost every case. It was natural, therefore, to explore their reasons for feeling that prayer is a useful and rewarding activity. A preliminary question, 'Does what the child asks for in prayer, ever come true?' was asked. All but a few answered 'yes', the few answering 'always'. These were the very young and least able children who had no realistic ideas about prayer. Although the great majority gave a straight affirmative some qualified it by a 'sometimes' or 'if they are good prayers'. More importantly, the follow up question was, 'How does the child know they come true?'[1] designed to see how the pupil arrived at thinking some prayers are efficacious. Within the discussion of the child's reasons, a number of supplementary questions were asked to discover the real meaning behind some very general replies. For example, a popular answer was, 'Because ill people get well after they've been prayed for' and this was followed by the query (abbreviated in the text to Dr.?) 'How do we know it wasn't the Doctor who got him well, and not God?' Similarly, where examination success is cited the alternative explanation of 'hard work' is put to the child to test whether other factors are recognised.

Reasons for accepting prayer as efficacious show a very clear sequence of thinking in four conceptual stages. The first stage is the claim of immediate assurance from God or materialistic results appearing by magical power. These are magical concepts. Then follows a semi-magical conceptual stage, with argument by results employed, but the problems posed only result in confusion. Thirdly, more rational arguments by results are employed, with particular emphasis upon the spiritual results of prayer upon the person praying. This and the following stage we can depict as non-magical concepts. Lastly a few get to an advanced level of ideas in maintaining that no certain knowledge of the efficacy of prayer is available, only reasoning by probability, or by conviction and faith, is open to them. This sequence supports Theodor Reik's three stages of praying.[2]

Before these sequences are reviewed we should note that a few younger children aged 6 and 7 years simply could not understand the question or gave incomprehensible replies, such as, 'Once when he prays, his prayers get better and better. Sometimes he prays to Father Christmas and not to God.' The first magical stage of prayer shows two different types of answers, up to the age of about 9 : 4

---

[1]For these and the following questions, see Appendix A, questions P.2: Q.6A and B.

[2] See page 23.

(M.A. 9 : 9). The younger children tend to assume some immediate assurance from God, either spoken or in a dream or by some 'feeling'. 'If she was praying, she'd hear Jesus answering her and telling her it would come true.' 'God tells it in his mind. *How do you mean?* After he's succeeded, I suppose.' 'Probably someone comes and puts them behind his pillow, and he finds the things are true.' (An obvious association with Christmas, or sixpence for an old tooth). 'If he prays nice and gentle.' Here are some fuller examples in chronological order. Jean says, 'Because God makes them come true. *How does he?* Because he's up in heaven' (age 6 : 2, M.A. 5 : 3). Leona, aged 6 : 5 (M.A. 6 : 0) replies, 'God tells her. He's speaking when she's praying.' Simon gives the same reason (age 6 : 6, M.A. 6 : 6), ' 'Cause God tells him, just after the boy has prayed.' The authoritarian assurance is voiced by Noel, aged 7 : 0 (M.A. 7 : 2), 'His mummy would tell him it might come true.' Andrew, a bright boy, sees no problem at all (age 8 : 5, M.A. 11 : 8), 'Because they happen. (Q) They happen because he prayed.' Constance aged 8 : 10 (M.A. 7 : 11) says, 'She would dream about it.'

The second type of answer at this magical stage, usually by older children up to the age of nine years, is an irrational argument by results. No insight is evident that other factors may have caused an event to happen other than the prayer. It is confused but magical cause and effect thinking, such as that believed by the medicine man who puts on a green coat and dances round the totem tree, thus 'causing' a new coat of leaves to grow in the ensuing weeks. Clearly there are strong elements of magic here. Usually these children have crude materialistic prayers for toys, a bicycle, food, a doll or a pony and prayer is very much on a level with shouting one's requests up the chimney to Santa Claus. 'God makes them come true. *How do you mean?* God made me safe. *How?* If you do things right, like not stealing, He'll make you safe.' 'When he wakes in the morning. If it was Christmas and he asked God for his parents to bring a train set; if it came he'd know God had been listening. *Couldn't the parents alone have done it?* They could do if the boy had talked about it a lot. God would have done it somehow.' 'A doll. If it came God has answered. *How could she know that?* If she's prayed, the prayer has made it come.' 'If he's prayed to be safe, and if he's safe the next day.' 'He'd find out. *How?* If he prayed for a fine Guy Fawkes night and it was.' Here are some more typical examples, in chronological order. Andrea, aged 7 : 7 (M.A. 7 : 7): 'Yes. If she's a good girl, God makes her prayers come true. For example, if she asks for some things at Christmas. If she's been a good girl, her Mummy and Daddy would buy them for her.' Joan, aged 7 : 9 (M.A. 10 : 3): 'If poor people got food and she'd prayed this, she'd see it happening and know.' Lester

185

puts it vividly (age 8 : 2, M.A. 8 : 1), 'Yes, sometimes. (Q) When he wakes up in the morning he ain't dead. *How does that help him to know?* God has taken care of him.' Andy, aged 8 : 6 (M.A. 7 : 6): 'If he's been naughty, he'll know if his mother and father forgives him. He'd prayed for them to forgive him.'

These magical elements still persist into the second stage where knowledge by results is still the main argument, but a little insight is now present. The child is aware that other causative factors might exist, but when these are queried he may become undecided or confused. The results incidentally, are less now in terms of material benefits and more in terms of persons, but magical elements are seen. For this reason we can call this stage until about 12 : 3 (M.A. 12 : 2) the semi-magical stage of concepts. For example, 'He prayed for a friend to get well and she does. *Dr?* God has helped the doctor to make better medicine', and 'Like help with sums at school. *God do it?* She knows it was God in a special way; if she'd not got sums right before', and 'Next day . . . Like going across roads, nearly all people who get knocked over don't believe in God.' Here are some further illustrations set out in chronological order. Geoffrey aged 9 : 8 (M.A. 10 : 4), 'Yes, mostly they come true. (Q) If a friend got well again or if his father kept a good job. *Ill friend Dr?* God helps the doctor usually. *Would God help the doctor if the boy hadn't prayed?* Yes. *Well, how did his prayer make the friend get well?* Oh . . . I don't know.' Grace, aged 10 : 1 (M.A. 10 : 11), 'Yes. (Q) Because it's happened. *How do you mean?* If she'd prayed she'd been kept well. *How does she know it's God?* Because she'd prayed.' Judy aged 10 : 4 (M.A. 10 : 9), 'If she'd prayed to God to help her with her schoolwork, everything would be right in her schoolbooks. *Hard work?* Well, if she didn't try and it all came right automatically.' Peggy, aged 10 : 6 (M.A. 13 : 5), 'Yes, if Jesus thinks it's good for her. (Q) When it happens, like something special she'd asked for on her birthday and Jesus felt it was good for her. *How would she know it was God?* It must have been Jesus who put the idea in her mother's mind.' Petula, aged 11 : 4 (M.A. 15 : 0), 'Yes, I asked for a music stand and it came. It seems God would want me to play the violin. *How do you know it wasn't only your parents?* I wanted one. My mother and father knew I wanted one, and I already had a lot of clothes. Maybe mother and father decided, but God made them think of it as a present.' Barry, aged 11 : 6 (M.A. 12 : 5), 'If he wanted to get his strength back after being ill and he prayed, then beat a stronger boy who bullied him, then he'd know. *Couldn't it be good food which brought his strength back?* No, his mother might give him the same food every day.' Sandra, aged 12 : 2 (M.A. 17 : 0), 'Yes, if she prayed for a pet who is ill to be better and the pet recovers. *Wouldn't it be the vet who made it well?* No, it would just be because she believes in God.'

The third stage beginning at about twelve years, is the real conceptual dividing line when pupils move over to a non-magical, and specifically religious, conceptual level. Knowledge of the results of prayer still remain but now they are without magical elements. The results come from effort or faith on the part of the person who prays, or in illness prayer may help when medical help has failed. Often the results may be due to a change of attitude or a new confidence in the person praying. God is sometimes seen as the controller of all, and auto-suggestion is seen as part of the way God operates in human life. Thus, 'Yes, when his mother recovers when she was ill. *Dr?* If the doctor said his mother couldn't be helped, he'd know then it would be God. *What if it were an ordinary operation?* I don't know. He couldn't really tell', and 'Yes, when she's passed an exam after praying. *Hard work?* Well, she knows she's worked hard. God has helped her to work hard and understand a problem', and 'Getting over a pole vault. If he believed he'd get over he would. *Is it just his greater determination?* That's what it is. You become determined it can happen. It is auto-suggestion, whether it is assisted by God or not', and 'She prays for Jesus to come into her heart and she feels safe.'

Here are a few examples chosen at random and presented in chronological order. Mary aged 12 : 8 (M.A. 16 : 10): 'If she'd asked for her mother and father to get better then they've come true. *Dr?* God has given a knowledge of medicine to get her mother better. *Wouldn't the doctor cure her parents anyway?* She'd believe it was her prayer.' Guy, aged 13 : 4 (M.A. 15 : 11), 'Yes, if it's spiritual, not like asking for a new bicycle. (Q) It says in the Bible, "If you ask it will be given you." *Can you give an example?* If he prays to be a better boy, to stop him getting into arguments, he'd keep out of them. *Isn't that due to his own will-power?* Man can do nothing without God, it says in the Bible. God has given will-power.' Dennis, aged 14 : 4 (M.A. 19 : 2), 'Yes. (Q) Especially finding how to cure diseases. He'd pray for scientists to be successful. *If they were, wouldn't that be due to the scientists themselves?* The scientists may somehow have got to know what to look for and God had shown them in some way.' Ernest, aged 14 : 5 (M.A. 14 : 10) uses the passing of an examination as an example. *Isn't it his own hard work?* 'It's God partly and partly his own work. If he believes, God will have helped him work harder.' Dianne, aged 14 : 11 (M.A. 13 : 1) adds a personal note: 'Yes, my mother is deaf in one ear and I used to get irritable. I prayed to God to persevere and be patient and now I can be. *Was that God or yourself?* He created us. It's him who makes us work. He sorts of helps me decide and to carry it out.'

A few sixth formers reach the fourth stage of putting the main emphasis upon faith and the fact that one cannot know. Here are a few examples. 'Yes, because of his faith, he thinks it's come true, even if it's turned out different to his expectations.' 'Yes, when my sister was fourteen she was very ill and I prayed and she got better. *Dr?* One doesn't know. One may choose to believe it's God.' Another uses the same example and when asked whether it was the doctors who had done it, said: 'He wouldn't know, but he'd believe he'd been some help in a spiritual way.'

CONCEPTS OF UNANSWERED PRAYER

The obverse side of the previous question was explored by asking, 'Do some of the child's prayers not come true?' and a further query about the reasons for the answer given. These reasons could be assessed in terms of conceptual levels, which fell into three clearly defined stages of thinking about unanswered prayer. Incidentally, the terms 'unanswered' and 'answered' were not used since previous discussion with children revealed that their ideas of answering or not answering were confused by the expectation of a spoken voice. The three stages correspond fairly closely in age and content to the magical, semi-magical and non-magical stages of the previous questions. The first stage, is a moral conceptual stage, where failure in prayer is due to naughty behaviour or failure to ask in the right way. We might call the second a semi-moral stage, where unanswered prayer is not due to general naughtiness but due to stupid, materialistic, selfish or greedy prayers, sometimes because 'there is not enough to go round'. Finally, a stage of religious concepts, where unanswered prayer is the natural refusal of God to unnecessary, unsuitable insincere or unbelieving prayers. Later still at this stage, the age range is indefinable, God's will enters into the reasons. This concerns his willingness only to work at a spiritual level and to conform to his own spiritual laws.

Here are some typical answers of the first stage of moral concepts, which is normal up to about 9 : 5 (M.A. 9 : 9). A few answers are incomprehensible or unrealistic. 'No, all her prayers come true' and 'God forgets' and 'God is too tired (or too busy).' Most, however, have a moral connotation: 'She's been naughty,' 'He didn't ask politely enough', and 'He hasn't prayed hard enough.' Several children feel the child in the picture spoke too softly, and God simply couldn't hear the prayers. A series of full responses follow, taken at random and presented in chronological order. Kathy aged 6 : 2 (M.A. 6 : 6), 'No. All prayers come true.' Eve aged 6 : 5, M.A. 8 : 2, 'He might not hear them. The child might speak in too shy a voice.'

Nathan, aged 6 : 10 (M.A. 7 : 9), 'Yes, because he hasn't done a good deed.' Martha, aged 7 : 3 (M.A. 6 : 10), 'P'raps she's been naughty and if she doesn't like rain, he sends rain, when she's prayed for sunshine.' Henry, aged 8 : 3 (M.A. 6 : 8), 'Yes, God might not have heard those prayers. He may not have prayed loud enough.' Keith aged 8 : 11 (M.A. 10 : 0), 'Yes, maybe he had something else on his mind and didn't quite say it properly. He wasn't polite and got mixed up.' Mark aged 9 : 2 (M.A. 8 : 10), 'Sometimes when he is bad, he speaks to another person. *To whom?* He speaks to the devil. The prayers don't go to God.'

Some moral condemnation is implicit in many of the answers in the second stage. They do not involve general naughtiness but rather specific prayer selfishness, greediness and other errors in praying. We have called this a semi-moral stage from about nine to about 11 : 9 years (M.A. 12 : 4). Here are some typical examples. 'She's too greedy and wants too much.' 'They're selfish prayers.' 'Stupid prayers don't get answered, like asking for money or a bicycle.' 'Others may need it. God can't do everything and help everyone at the same time.' These and other types of answers can be seen in the following random selection, set out in chronological order. Harry, aged 9 : 8 (M.A. 11 : 11), 'God would choose the best ones which would be more useful. *How do you mean?* Say he was praying for a bow and arrow. It wouldn't be so useful as praying for sick people.' Betty aged 9 : 10 (M.A. 10 : 11): 'Yes. If everything happened, she might get spoilt.' Neville, aged 10 : 1 (M.A. 8 : 10): 'Yes, God might think he's being selfish. He shouldn't get more things than other boys.' Judy aged 10 : 4 (10 : 9), 'Yes. She prays and they are stupid prayers. Like she wants a horse and she hasn't enough money for one. You can't get a horse by just praying.' Rikki aged 10 : 7 (M.A. 10 : 3), 'Yes, it might be too much for God to give. He's to give things to other people.' Eric, aged 11 : 2 (M.A. 11 : 5). 'Yes, He might pray for himself. For example, if someone is ill he might pray for a new train set. God wouldn't be cross, but think he'd be better praying for something else.' Barry aged 11 : 6 (M.A. 12 : 5), 'Yes. If they're stupid ones, like for money. God don't give money, because if you're rich the Bible says you won't go to heaven, 'cause money can weigh you down. Or if he cursed God, God wouldn't give him his prayers, of course.'

While there are elements of insight at the preceding stage, it is not until the final stage is reached for most pupils at nearly twelve years (M.A. 12 : 4) that more spiritual, non-moral considerations occur in the responses. For this reason I have called from this age onwards the religious conceptual stage, although at first some of the answers are still immature. Answers include prayers which are unnecessary

189

or unsuitable for the child, 'Maybe she'll get it when she is older and ready for it', or insincere or unbelieving prayers. Later the unanswered prayers may be seen as inconsistent with God's nature and therefore contrary to his will, 'when the prayer has evil potential, like atomic energy and the boy doesn't know, but God does', and 'God only gives abstract things like love.' As before we shall now examine some fuller answers, selected at random and presented in chronological order. Sandra aged 12 : 2 (M.A. 17 : 0), 'Yes. Some take a long time to come true. They all come true eventually. *Why are some delayed?* Some may be better for the child to be delayed.' Hilda aged 12 : 7 (M.A. 15 : 7), 'God might think she shouldn't have them, because they wouldn't do her any good, like toys. Perhaps she's asked for too much recently and she might be better to wait.' Anis aged 13 : 1 (M.A. 14 : 1), 'Yes. If she was a person who was insincere God wouldn't help her in any way.' Guy has a curiously mixed answer, 'Maybe the wrong kind of thing he prays for, unspiritual, like ice cream' and goes on to a highly moral reply. 'And if his aunty never went to church and the boy asked to get her to come to church, God knows who is bad. If she is, He wouldn't get her to come. God is supposed to come again to sort out the good and the bad' (age 13 : 4, M.A. 15 : 11). Lucy, aged 13 : 7 (M.A. 13 : 6), 'If she got knocked over and she'd prayed for safety, it would be her carelessness.' Dennis aged 14 : 4 (M.A. 19 : 2), 'Yes, all of the prayers aren't right to ask for. It's up to him to put more effort into school work.' Dianne aged 14 : 11 (M.A. 13 : 1), 'Yes, the answer may be different to the one you expected. He always answers prayers. You maybe wanted something that wasn't right for you or fit for you, like praying to get through exams. It's mental capacity. If you're not good in a subject you won't get through however hard you pray.' Owen, aged 15 : 10 (M.A. 20 : 10), 'Yes. It's God's will. It may not be good for the boy.' Nancy, aged 17 : 2 (M.A. 19 : 1): 'Yes, they are not good —they're selfish prayers. They might affect others adversely. Maybe clothes your parents can't afford, and they'd have to do without things. And maybe they'd interfere with God's plans.' Deborah aged 17 : 11 (M.A. 18 : 8): 'Yes, if they are not in line with the will of God. *How do you mean?* If I'd pray for a new tennis racquet, something selfish. *Are all unselfish prayers answered?* Yes, unless God sees it isn't true yet. By waiting he may see there's more blessing.'

GENERAL COMMENTS ON CONCEPTS OF PRAYER

Profiles of the major stages of childhood and adolescence in terms of prayer are difficult to construct with clarity due to great diversity and problems of assessing the material. The following outlines presented are somewhat over-simplified, but the broad characteristics emerge from the material discussed in this and other chapters.

The Infant and young Junior child is increasingly aware that there are more things to pray about and the number of things about which he prays is probably multiplying. He addresses his prayers to God mainly, but to Jesus sometimes, as he sees God and Jesus interchangeably. Most prayers are thought to be appropriate for himself and although he does pray for others, many of these prayers are egocentric since he is praying for his friends, for example, to be better friends to him. Prayers for material gifts are fairly frequent and prayers of self-examination, such as for forgiveness or prayer of confession, are rare. Set prayers seem to be used least of all in this period, increasing in the late Junior years. God is visualised in prayer as a physically anthropomorphic being and when the child prays he is physically present or above him in heaven plugged in by wires so that he can hear. The child observes that his prayers come true for purely magical reasons, resulting in immediate verbal reassurance from God. Unanswered prayer is explained in moral terms because the child has not asked nicely enough or has been naughty, and refusal is God's means of punishing. These varying ideas and concepts of prayer are consistent with what we know of the natural needs, egocentricity and immaturities of children below the age of nine years.

The late Junior child and the pre-adolescent steadily increase the number and variety of prayers felt to be appropriate until about ten years, when they level off during adolescence. Up to and including ten years, we can assume a learning process encouraged by the child's widening experience and increasing verbal ability. There is a slightly greater possibility of addressing Jesus in his prayers although God is the one mainly addressed. There is a sharp increase in altruistic praying and prayers for self become more introspective, with a greater concern to be a better child. There is also a sharp increase in prayers for recovery and protection, as though awareness of dangers generates a desire for safety. Set prayers begin to be thought more appropriate in these years, as more memorised prayers are probably used in public worship, in school or in church. During this period at the end of the Junior school, the child will be moving from an anthropomorphic to a more superhuman and supernatural concept of the God to whom he prays, and a little later, as a pre-adolescent his physical ideas of God's presence in prayer will recede and be replaced by more spiritual ideas, expressed as feelings of peace or happiness or confidence. Prayers are seen as efficacious for semi-magical reasons, where argument by results is employed, but other factors are seen and cannot be resolved. Failure in prayer is thought of in largely semi-moral terms, due to selfish, greedy, materialistic or stupid prayers or to a shortage of what the prayer asks for. Again, we see in this period that these varied concepts are consistent with emerging social maturity, growing moral sensitivity and widening intellectual powers. What is interesting is that one of the limitations of these prayer concepts is probably due to concretistic elements (in the 'operational' sense), which begin to diminish towards the end of this period.

From twelve and thirteen years, with childhood on the whole left behind, prayer concepts take on a more realistic appearance. Numbers of prayers suggested tend to be similar to the previous level with a slight increase at fifteen years to the highest frequency. But variety and quality become more spiritual, in that materialistic elements almost disappear. Altruistic praying seems to reach its peak about twelve and thirteen years and maintains that level into adolescence, while prayers for self continue to be concerned with improvement of behaviour, with a marked increase in prayers of forgiveness and confession. From eleven years onwards there is an intensification of prayers for help in schoolwork as, no doubt, the demands of parents and the educational system are felt. The God to whom the adolescent prays is distinct from Jesus, and takes on symbolic and spiritual form. Faith and logic are indicators of God's presence in prayer as well as feelings of peace and fulfilment. While argument by results is advanced to explain the efficacy of prayers, there tends to be a realistic appraisal that other factors than prayer may have been responsible for these results. In the last resort, middle and later adolescents advance conviction and faith as the only guide to understanding prayer since no certain knowledge is available. Prayers remain unanswered now for the reasons of God's natural refusal, for the good of his children, to fulfil unnecessary, insincere, unbelieving prayers, or prayers which are unsuitable for those who pray. There is a clear recognition, that God must say 'no' or defer fulfilment until that person is spiritually ready for it. The later adolescent thinks more in terms of God's will and plans for the world, and that he only operates in prayer at the level of spiritual qualities. These concepts of prayer are again compatible with other known adolescent characteristics, such as sensitivity in personal and social behaviour, personal moral awareness and a capacity for dealing with abstractions at an operational level.

There is little here to comment on in terms of religious education for it is evident that children's prayers and their ideas of prayers will be limited in the ways we have outlined. We may note, however, how long childish patterns persist well into the Secondary school years until, for example, magical concepts and harsh moral judgments about prayer begin to disappear. It is possible that levels of worship designed to meet the needs of children and adolescents at their level of language, experience and conceptual capacity could exercise a profoundly educational influence upon the religious development of pupils. In worship, where the whole range from children to adults is encompassed, such specialised concern is not possible, but in schools, departments of church schools and Sunday schools, a reluctance to impose adult worship and a willingness to meet the needs of a particular age group would seem to be desirable. Even in church all-age worship there are other ways of meeting the needs of children. Certainly what emerges from the examination of concepts of the Church, in our next chapter, underlines this as an important area for concern.

Chapter Thirteen

CONCEPTS OF THE CHURCH

WE have now examined concepts of God, Jesus, Justice, Love the Bible and Prayer. This is fairly comprehensive but the picture is inadequate unless we include another important area in which religious understanding operates, namely, concepts of the Church. The church, or rather the churches (for this is how most children and adolescents think of the Church) is the visible and official 'religious' organisation of which all children have some experience, through attendance, through its clergy and ministers, or even if it is only an external acquaintance with buildings or services seen on television. Pupils who themselves attend church, and by this we include Sunday Schools, have slightly better concepts than those who do not attend, but the difference is not a significant one in our sample. On the other hand, pupils whose parents go to church with some regularity, even if it is only one parent and the child himself may not go often, have significantly higher church concepts than those whose parents have no active church connection. The relationship here is highly significant and probably indicates positive attitudes and an interest in the home towards the church and matters involving the church. This relationship between the pupil's religious activities and his religious conceptual development is something we shall explore in detail in the next chapter.

Because concepts of the church are affected by the attitudes of a child, positive and negative, some attempt was made to elicit likes and dislikes of the church, not in an attempt to scale attitudes, for this would have required a separately large research project in addition to the present one, but in order to focus upon those things which appear to help or impede the child's thinking about the church.

ASPECTS OF CHURCH LIKED AND DISLIKED

The assumption is made here that there is sufficient projection and identification made with the child in Picture 1[1] (The Child entering Church) to make it a valid reference that the pupils' responses are

---

[1] See Appendix A. Picture 1 and question P.1; Q.2A, B and C.

194

personal responses to the situation depicted in the picture. The picture is used as a device to secure rapport and to elicit concepts rather than attitudes, that is intellectual patterns of thought about the church. We are concerned not to devise means of measuring attitudes or 'degrees of feeling' in relation to a given person, object or situation. Our major concern in this item was to discern what particular aspects (not in any 'feeling' degree) of church life are most frequently liked and disliked, those aspects which can be intellectually recognised and expressed.

A sifting of answers revealed a wide variety of experiences liked and disliked. These were sorted out into categories; the positive 'likes' are set out below.

CATEGORIES OF LIKING CHURCH OR SUNDAY SCHOOL SERVICES

Worship Activities	Congregational singing. Praying. Offertory ('Putting pennies in the box'). Ceremonial—familiarity with it. Form of Matins or Evensong.
Special Worship	Harvest Festivals (when you say thank you to God). Holy Communion. Easter. Christenings. Weddings.
Intellectual Aspects	Bible Readings, reading Bible for oneself. Stories by teacher or priest. Stories about Christ and His teaching. The Sermon. Hearing a different view on a familiar story, especially modern examples. 'It's something to believe in.' Film strips. Doing work or drawing pictures.
Effects of Worship	Feeling of forgiveness. Being cleansed. A sense of feeling good at going to church. Being quiet for a time. Feeling of being near God, at peace. To be related to God, to think about Him.
Physical	The walk there (or home). The ride there in the car. It's nice and warm inside. ('Coming out' is really an inverted dislike.)
Social	Going with parents. It pleases father and mother. Meeting with peers. The friendly atmosphere. Seeing minister or priest—speaking with him afterwards. Christmas parties. Annual treats and outings. Meeting new people and old friends.
Aesthetic	Organ music. Choir singing. Looking at stained-glass windows or flowers. Pictures of Jesus round the walls. Special Service decorations—harvest display.
Irrelevant	Reading a comic or book. Doing some puzzles.

For each 'like' a point was given in the appropriate category. Since individual scores did not span the entire range of categories, and an aggregate score of all categories together would be meaningless, year age groups were combined for each category. The results are set out in the table below. Here the numbers indicate the number of 'like' responses in a given category made by pupils of one chronological year group. For example, at year 6, 16 responses (not necessarily pupils, since some make two responses) were made indicating what was enjoyed in terms of worship, seven in terms of intellectual enjoyment, three in terms of physical enjoyment and three aesthetic responses.

INCIDENCE OF 'LIKE' RESPONSES TO CHURCH

Chrono-logical Year		Categories of 'Likes'						
	Totals	Worship	Special Worship	Intel-lectual	Effects of Worship	Physical	Social	Aes-thetic
6	29	16	0	7	0	3	0	3
7	26	11	2	5	0	4	1	3
8	43	27	1	11	0	1	1	2
9	46	25	0	16	1	1	2	1
10	46	23	3	10	1	2	3	4
11	49	24	3	16	1	1	2	2
12	42	20	1	18	0	0	0	3
13	54	28	3	16	1	0	4	2
14	53	19	3	18	2	0	7	4
15+	55	30	3	10	2	0	7	3
TOTALS	433	223	19	127	8	12	27	27

These yearly groupings do not provide data for a precise statistical analysis. They do serve, however, as rough indicators of trends, as the following results indicate. Firstly, Worship is the dominant enjoyment, mostly expressed in music and hymn-singing; after seven years it is fairly constant, and highest with the 15–17 year olds. This supports Jahoda's finding (1951). Special worship, for example, Harvest or Easter services appears to be more appreciated in the later part of childhood and adolescence. Secondly, there appears to be a steady increase with age of the enjoyment of more intellectual aspects of church, with a peak from eleven to fourteen, as we would expect, as the age when 'church' language, which is largely difficult and abstract, is beginning to be understood more. The intellectual activities are Bible reading, stories told by teacher or preacher, and sermons. A few mention enjoyment in drawing pictures, and one looking at film strips. A sharp drop in intellectual enjoyment is visible with the fifteen to seventeen year olds.

Thirdly, effects of worship, for example, feeling forgiven, cleansed, good, peaceful, quiet or related to God, are only rarely mentioned, with a slight increase in adolescence. The reason for this may be that such effects are rarely felt or, although experienced, the pupils are too self-aware or self-conscious to express them. Physical pleasures such such as walking to church, the ride in the car, sitting down and resting, 'it's nice and warm inside', are obvious childish pleasures, expressed mostly between six and eight years and disappearing entirely by eleven years. Social pleasures—meeting with friends or friendly adults, with new or interesting people, accompanying parents (and including social events, such as parties and outings, organised by the church)—have only slight incidence before twelve years, with an increase at thirteen years and a sharp increase at fourteen to seventeen years. Earlier enjoyment is usually expressed in terms of parties and outings only. This result is consistent with what is known of the increasing social interests of adolescents. Totals of all enjoyments increase, on the whole, with age. We must beware of claiming too much for this result, since it may only reflect greater capacity for voicing enjoyment, which may have been previously experienced but not easily expressed, or even necessarily conscious. Contrary to this, however, we would expect this to operate similarly with negative feelings; yet negative feelings may be more readily expressed earlier than positive feelings, since they may be more obvious to the child.

A summary of items liked about church in order of frequency shows the following: Worship and Special Worship 242, Intellectual 127, Social 27, Aesthetic 27, Physical 12 and Effects of Worship 8.

A similar series of categories were arranged for 'dislikes' in the following manner:

CATEGORIES OF DISLIKING CHURCH OR SUNDAY SCHOOL SERVICES

Worship Activities	Lengthy Service. Long prayers ('hour after hour'). Long Bible readings. Notices after service. Singing hymns. Dull and dreary hymns. Formality, keeping to regulations of worship. Set responses boring. Too monotonous, same every week.
Intellectual	Long, dull, irrelevant or non-understood sermons. Talks too babyish and childish. People too passive, accepting things from preacher. If he disagrees with priest's views. Having doubts about God. Drawing pictures is boring.
Physical	Walking too far to church. Getting up too early to go. Going there in the rain. Wearing best clothes. Going every Sunday. Standing up and down a lot. Kneeling a long time ('It hurts my knees'). Sitting on hard seats. Sitting still a long time ('She can't'). Waiting long time for service to begin. Waiting and sitting down while people talk a long time.

Social	A bit nervous where lots of people are. No peers there. His friends don't approve of church going. Older people making you go to church. Don't like going alone. The clergyman's attitude. Moving around into different classes. Being told off by teacher.
Fears	Having to write or read ('I can't') or reading, aloud in front of class. Unfamiliar tunes or hymns. Losing the way in Service book. Frightening noise of changed prayer—or silence between prayers. Music loud ('it gives you earache'), ('Songs going round and round in your head, when you come out you feel dizzy'). It's strange there. Going new for first time.
Alternative Activities	Rather be out in open-air; playing; playing football; watching television.
Aesthetic	Building old-fashioned, dingy or dark. Colours of hymn book.
Irrelevant	Having to wipe feet on doormat.

Points were awarded on the same basis as 'likes', as the table below shows.

INCIDENCE OF 'DISLIKE' RESPONSES TO CHURCH

Chron. Year	Totals	Worship	Intel- lectual	Physical	Social	Fears	Alter- native Activity	Aes- thetic
6	16	2	0	6	2	5	0	1
7	17	5	1	6	1	3	0	1
8	21	2	2	13	2	2	0	0
9	15	6	4	2	1	0	1	1
10	31	6	9	8	3	3	2	0
11	22	8	8	3	1	2	1	0
12	22	7	8	3	1	1	1	0
13	24	7	10	2	2	3	0	0
14	26	7	11	3	2	2	1	0
15+	25	5	12	1	6	0	1	0
TOTALS	239	55	65	47	21	21	7	3

Again, although not statistically rigorous, these figures may serve as rough indicators of items most disliked by pupils. Firstly, certain aspects of worship are disliked by a considerable number of pupils, increasing slightly from the years nine to fourteen. These aspects are length of service, length of prayers and length of reading, dull and dreary hymns, too formal an atmosphere and the monotony of the same service weekly. The largest incidence of dislikes are intellectual, with the chief dislike being long, dull, irrelevant or incomprehensible sermons. This again supports the findings of Jahoda (1951) and

Hyde (1963). There is a marked increase in the incidence of these dislikes from about ten years onwards through adolescence. Thirdly, physical factors are disliked by the six to ten year olds especially, such as tiredness on a Sunday morning at having to rise early, the walk to church, in the service standing up or kneeling for a long period, sitting on hard seats ('I can't sit still long enough,' complained a six year old).

Social dislikes cover such items as 'no friends go', 'I don't like going alone', being made to go or personal dislike of a teacher or clergyman. This appears to have a low incidence until fifteen to seventeen years old when it increases. Finally, a separate category of 'fears' connected with church is tabulated since they are fairly frequently expressed by the six to seven year olds. Some younger children do have fears involving literacy; inability to read hymns or the Bible causes them to lose their way and become confused. Chanted prayers, loud organ music and the 'strangeness' of a church may frighten them.

A summary of items disliked about church in order of frequency shows the following: Intellectual 65, Worship 55, Physical 47, Social 21, Fears 21, Preference for Alternative Activity (playing football, watching television) 7, Asthetic 3. In concluding this section we must stress that no measurement of attitudes or 'intensity' of feeling is assessed, but merely the classifying of aspects of church life which are found to be enjoyable or contra. These serve as rough indicators of attitudes, but more importantly provide some insight into the pupil's thinking about the church, made clearer in the ensuing items.

THE NATURE OF THE CHURCH

We know that children's definitions of words and their use of them develop in a fairly predictable sequence. The word 'church' proved no exception. As this provides a framework for other concepts of church, a definition was sought from the children as they looked at the picture of the child entering a church doorway.[1] To the query, 'Is there anything special about a church?' all except a very few younger pupils replied in the affirmative and the follow-up question was 'What is special about it?'

The definition, or insight into the nature of the church, closely followed mental age rather than chronological age and three stages were evident. Firstly, irrelevant and physically external features of buildings, ceremonies or personnel which are seen to have some vaguely 'holy' association dominate the pupils' thinking. Then comes a stage where the spiritual function of the church is seen more

[1] See Appendix A, picture 1 and Question P.1 : Q.6.

clearly. Finally, corporate worship is seen as the major function of the church, the emphasis moving from the building to a believing group of people.

The first stage goes on to about ten years (about M.A. 10 : 4). The furniture, windows, spire, man in a white collar, christenings and weddings are frequent here. A few speak of it as a quiet place, but no religious significance is seen in this, and 'it's God's house' is quite a common response. This latter is interpreted as where God lives or some other anthropomorphic concept. One or two see it as a teaching centre 'where you learn about Jesus and God' but when questioned they see it in no different light from the day school where they do the same. Here is a random selection of answers, presented in ascending chronological age. Jean, aged 6 : 2 (M.A. 5 : 3), 'No, it's no different. They have a book they read songs out of.' Rosamund, aged 6 : 6 (M.A. 6 : 4) merely has an association with Christmas, 'A church is a stable. *How do you mean?* It's a house.' Tina, aged 6 : 6 (M.A. 5 : 8), 'No. It's different from a caravan. It's got the same things as a class at school. They teach you.' Leonard aged 6 : 11 (M.A. 5 : 9), 'Yes, it's got no doors there (pointing to the doorway in the picture). They go in with coats on and take them off inside.' Veronica, aged 7 : 4 (M.A. 7 : 1), 'Yes. It hasn't much furniture really.' Jenny, aged 7 : 1 (M.A. 5 : 10), 'It's writing there. It's got a round door. *Do they do anything special there?* They do some drawing and colouring. They learn singing.' Lillian aged 7 : 5 (M.A. 9 : 2), 'Yes, she learns things. *Is it different from school?* Yes, you don't play outside it. *Do you learn different things there?* No.' 'Yes,' says Kevan aged 7 : 7 (M.A. 6 : 5), 'It's got bells ringing, a church tower and flowers and gates.' Lester, aged 8 : 2 (M.A. 8 : 1), 'Yes. It's not a shaped door the same as a house. And a church is smaller than a house. *What about inside?* They pray. Jesus went to church.' Alec, aged 8 : 10 (M.A. 10 : 11), 'Yes. The disciples made it and it got bombed down, or shot down, when the Angles and Saxons came across,' a curiously garbled historical view. Keith aged 8 : 11 (M.A. 10 : 0), 'Yes, it's a place where you learn about God. *Different from school?* Well, no, it isn't.' Robert, aged 9 : 6 (M.A. 9 : 0), 'Yes, it's not noisy. It has an altar with a cross on it.' Cecil, aged 9 : 8 (M.A. 8 : 2), 'It's quiet. It has pictures of angels there.' A borderline view, showing differing levels, is by Rose, aged 9 : 11 (M.A. 10 : 0), 'It's got an altar. It's a place where people are christened. The altar is there to thank God and so they can ask for forgiveness. *What's christenings for?* So you're a Christian. *Why in a church?* It's a holy place. It's God's house. *How do you mean?* He gave strength so people made it.'

From ten onwards most pupils begin to see some spiritual function of the church. In all, over seventy pupils revealed concepts at this intermediate stage which continued to about fourteen years (M.A. 14 : 7). Some typical examples follow showing worship as the special significance of a church or some other activity, but some ambiguities and difficulties still remain. Allan, aged 10 : 2 (M.A. 9 : 9), 'Yes, you don't live in a church or sell things, as in a shop. You go there to sing prayers to God.' Rowenna, aged 10 : 7 (M.A. 12 : 3), 'Yes, it's a holy place and not meant for hooliganism and popular singing. It's really meant for prayer and worship and singing and to learn about God. *They do that in school.* Yes, but there's more teaching and explaining at school. At church it is read out of the Bible.' Josephine, aged 11 : 4 (M.A. 11 : 0), 'Yes, you go there to pray. *Can't people pray at home?* Yes, but there's loads of people there . . .' Barry, aged 11 : 6 (M.A. 12 : 5), 'Yes, it's got an organ and you have singing there. It's more silent there. You don't have loud cheers. *Why is that?* It's a house of God. God made it to be built and to be preached in.' Sandra aged 12 : 2 (M.A. 17 : 0), 'Yes, it's a holy place. *How do you mean?* You get the feeling God is specially near to you in church. *Why is that?* Because most of the people who go believe in God and they are friendly to the girl.' Mary, aged 12 : 8 (M.A. 16 : 10), 'Yes, it's God's house. *How do you mean?* Where people can pray to him in quiet. It's noisy everywhere else. *What about the top of a hill?* There's no altar there. *Is God in every church?* Yes. He's a spirit and can be everywhere at once.' Charles, aged 13 : 4 (M.A. 17 : 8), 'Yes, it's religious in there. *How do you mean?* It's ever so quiet and you get a feeling someone is there all the time. *Is there?* Not really, only God.'

A few answers from the final stage from fourteen and fifteen years onwards, illustrate the idea of a fellowship, which is often more important than the actual building. Dennis aged 14 : 4 (M.A. 19 : 2), 'Yes. It's a place regarded as reverent and holy. *How do you mean?* Churches are specially built as places of worship. *Why can't people worship anywhere?* They can, but it helps if there is communal worship, all doing it together.' Delia, aged 14 : 3 (M.A. 15 : 4), 'Yes, a place where God meets with people. *Can't he do this in other places?* Yes, but in the Bible it says, "Where two or three are together, there am I in the midst." *Suppose two or three are in a church or outside?* It's no different, really.' Ernest, aged 14 : 5 (M.A. 14 : 10), 'Yes, it's the house of God. *How do you mean?* The place where you can go with other people and worship the same God. *Why is that?* They all like to worship together and it's where God said you must worship.' Edna, aged 16 : 10 (M.A. 21 : 9), 'Yes. A building which has one purpose—the worship of God; but the Church in its broad sense is all who belong to it. As a place, it's peaceful and quiet. Most people are reverent there and whisper. They feel it's sacred, especially the chancel part round the altar.' Cecil, aged 17 : 5 (M.A. 19 : 1), 'Yes.

A place where you can worship God, which is dedicated for that purpose. They can do it at home, but they come together with others, they feel less self-conscious in church.'

We could designate the three stages roughly as dealing with physical concepts, functional concepts and fellowship concepts of the church.

ADULT MOTIVES FOR CHURCHGOING

In the picture of people entering a church, the pupils naturally assume that the two adults are the child's parents (with occasional variations of aunt or uncle) and so this provided an opportunity for seeing what insight the pupils revealed into the motives of adults attending church. Motives attributed to adults ranged from crude to advanced, from irrational to rational, and from egocentric to altruistic. Many children, especially the younger ones reflecting their own experience, answer that the grown-ups in the picture go 'to take the child'. In this case a further question was asked, 'What if the grown-ups have no children, why would they go to church then?' and only the answer to this supplementary question is evaluated.

Three stages of concepts of adult motivation are apparent from the answers. At first, children only see immediate ends or rewards as the reason, or religious duty, habit, worship and stories, for the pleasure they give are major reasons attributed to adults; but there is little apparent insight into the purpose of this. Some later reasons, at the second stage, are advanced in terms of personal help and 'learning more about God'. A final stage is discernible when pupils advance more spiritual, rational and altruistic reasons for churchgoing.

The first stage, apart from motives of immediate rewards also include a number 'to take the child' answers. Leslie, aged 6 : 1 (M.A. 5 : 6), for example, says, 'They help the little boy say his prayers. *Suppose they had no children?* No, they wouldn't go,' and Noel, aged 7 : 0 (M.A. 7 : 2) replies, 'To take the boy, because he might get lost. *No children?* Oh, I don't know what they'd do.' Many felt that the parents would go only to protect their children from the dangerous roads they have to cross. Here is a random selection of answers from other children up to ten years of age typical of this first stage. Penelope, aged 6 : 8 (M.A. 6 : 4), 'To get one of those square things, pictures of Jesus.' Leonard, aged 6 : 11 (M.A. 5 : 9), 'They like it. *Why do they like it?* Well, to let the boy do some puzzles.' Bob, aged 7 : 7 (M.A. 7 : 11), 'They like singing. *Couldn't they sing anywhere else?* Yes, but they want to pray and kneel down too.' Joan, aged 7 : 11 (M.A. 10 : 1), 'They like singing to God and praying to God. *They could do that in other places than a church.* Yes, but they like seeing flowers in a church.' Poppy, aged 8 : 3 (M.A. 10 : 7), 'To pray. *Couldn't they pray at home?* They like to sing hymns as well. They probably don't know the hymns and go because on Sunday it's God's day.' Constance 8 : 10 (M.A. 7 : 11), 'They like it. *Why do they like it?* To pray and sing hymns to God.' Keith aged 8 : 11 (M.A. 10 : 0), 'They might be teachers. *Suppose they weren't teachers?* Oh, they'd be going to see the children do a play, or maybe they are members and enjoy it.' Geoffrey aged 9 : 8 (M.A. 10 : 4), 'They like to go. *Why do they like it?* They hear about God and Jesus.' Lesley, aged 9 : 11 (M.A. 13 : 5), 'They enjoy going with the girl and encourage her to go. *Suppose they had no little girl?* Because *their* mothers, when they were children made them go. *How do you mean?* They grew up in the Church and liked it and went ever since.' Sara, aged 9 : 10 (M.A. 8 : 10), 'To be religious. *How do you mean?* To be like one of the Christians and go to church every Sunday.'

Simple pleasure, duty, habit and other lesser motives now give way to more religious motives, in a second stage beginning about 10 : 3 (M.A. 10 : 6), when personal help, learning about religion, praying to God for some specific help are the reasons attributed to adults for churchgoing. Some answers resemble answers towards the end of the first stage, but tend on the whole to be more specific in religious terms. Vera, aged 10 : 3 (M.A. 9 : 1), 'So they can learn prayers and pray to God.' Alice, aged 10 : 11 (M.A. 15 : 8), 'They are used to the place. *How did they begin going?* They were curious to know what it was like, then they enjoyed the sermons and they wanted their children to grow up in the church. They go because they want to get to know God, to understand him and get to know what he's doing for them.' Martin, aged 11 : 5 (M.A. 15 : 7), 'So they can know how to teach their boy. *Suppose they had no children?* To get closer to God.' Gerald, aged 11 : 8 (M.A. 11 : 4), 'To learn something like hymns and prayers. *Why?* So they could do it when they went to bed.' Tony, 12 : 2 (M.A. 12 : 2), 'To learn more about God than they do, and they might be in the choir.' Max, aged 12 : 6 (M.A. 14 : 6), 'To get the boy to be a holy person. *Suppose they had no boy?* To be holy themselves. *How do you mean?* To read the Bible often and sing hymns.' Roland, aged 12 : 7 (M.A. 12 : 4), 'They are religious. *How do you mean?* They want to learn more about the Bible.' These responses on the whole reflect a very conventional view of what is thought to be religion.

From almost thirteen years (M.A. 13 : 5) the motives attributed to adults in going to church become very varied, but the connection is made, either implicitly or explicitly, between churchgoing and belief, the one being an extension of the other. Sometimes this is expressed as a natural duty of being a believer, of praying for and with other people or other reasons. Here are a few examples. Janice, aged 12 : 11 (M.A. 11 : 6), 'They are good Christians. *Why should that make them want to go?* They believe in God.' Robin, aged 13 : 10 (M.A. 11 : 5), 'They go to pray. *Can't they pray at home?* Yes, but the church is a special place to go to pray. And they may have some sick friends they may want to get better.' Priscilla, aged 14 : 4 (M.A. 14 : 5), 'They might think it their duty or they believe in God and know they should go.' Patsy, aged 14 : 5 (M.A. 16 : 11), 'To offer themselves to God. *How do you mean?* To be prepared to do anything God wishes.' May, aged 14 : 10 (M.A. 19 : 11), 'They believe in God and Jesus. *How does that make them go to church?* So they can worship with others who believe.' Fellowship is also emphasised by Hatty, age 15 : 9 (M.A. 19 : 3), 'They join in with the rest of the parish and get to know everyone. And they go to pray. It's better to pray in a community, all together. *Why?* It's easier.' Deborah, aged 17 : 11 (M.A. 18 : 8), 'They may go out of habit. But more likely they are Christians and want to have fellowship with other Christian people, to learn about Christ.'

The three stages as outlined above can perhaps be summarised in a sequence of pleasurable concepts, conventional religion concepts, and concepts of churchgoing as an inevitable expression of belief. This latter stage develops about thirteen years of age.

THE HELPFULNESS OF CHURCHGOING

From the pupils' understanding of adult motivation in churchgoing, we pass naturally to how they regard the attendance of children in terms of its helpfulness in ordinary living. The initial question was, 'Does going to church or Sunday School help the child?' Reasons for the pupil's answer were then solicited and discussed. Some children found it difficult to understand the nature of the question, so for these younger ones alternative questions were, 'Does it help him in his everyday life?' or 'Does going on a Sunday help him on a Monday?'[1]

Answers were extremely varied and only two stages of thinking could be discerned with a dividing age about 10 : 8 (M.A. 11 : 3). Up to this time the younger children tend to think solely in terms of specific help, for example, in helping their skills of literacy; and older children up to this time see churchgoing as providing practice in religious activities or help with religious lessons at school. Sometimes help with general school work is seen as one result of churchgoing or divine protection by a few pupils. After the age of about 10 : 8 there is a tendency to be less specific and for pupils to see the relevance of

[1] See Appendix A, question P.1 : Q.5.

churchgoing to belief and behaviour. It makes one, the pupils suggest, more believing, calm and confident and perhaps morally a better person.

At the first 'specific help' stage, examples of help in literacy or other skills, are practically all from six and seven year olds. Leona, aged 6 : 5 (M.A. 6 : 0), 'Yes, it helps with singing. You sing better.' Leonard, aged 6 : 11 (M.A. 5 : 9), 'It learns him to play with his toys and when he goes back to school he does better writing.' Penelope, aged 6 : 8 (M.A. 6 :4), 'Yes, she learns how to sing and it helps her with sums.' Jenny, aged 7 : 1 (M.A. 5 : 10): 'Yes. In doing things like writing, 'cause they do it in Sunday School.' Shiela, aged 7 : 10 (M.A. 7 : 9), 'Yes, it helps her to read and to draw pictures. One eight year old, Godfrey, aged 8 : 1 (M.A. 8 : 3) gives a similar answer, 'Yes, it learns him to read more.' These are merely associative responses in that if one activity goes on in church or Sunday School, it helps with that activity elsewhere. All children who make these responses, including those whose answers are given above, are of average or below average ability.

Brighter and older children provide replies which might seem somewhat depressing to the sensitive teacher. Some are associative replies of a slightly better level, but most see it as helping provide better answers in the R.I. lesson next day at school or as helping one to be more devotional. These are rather circular arguments of the kind 'devotions help you to be more devotional', in a rather mechanical sense. Here are some examples. Patrick, aged 6 : 8 (M.A. 7 : 3), 'The hymns. It would help at school, learning the hymns in church.' Winifred, age 6 : 11 (M.A. 9 : 8), 'Yes, it helps her a bit about school. *How?* When they read books about Jesus at school it helps by practice with hard words.' Kevan, aged 7 : 7 (M.A. 6 : 5), 'Yes, it helps to sing about Jesus and God. *How?* Well, going to prayers at school, he'll know the hymns.' Poppy, aged 8 : 3 (M.A. 10 : 7), 'Yes, then you can say your own prayers, otherwise she'd forget to say them. She could write on Monday in her school news about going to church.' Alec, aged 8 : 10 (M.A. 10 : 11), 'Yes, sometimes people read stories from the Bible. If he gets stories at school, the same ones, he can tell the teacher all about it.' Robert, aged 9 : 6 (M.A. 9 : 0), 'Yes, it helps him with Religious Knowledge lessons at school, and it helps him to pray.' Sara, aged 9 : 10 (M.A. 8 : 10), 'Saying her prayers. She knew what to say every night in her prayers. And it would help her to sing better at school.'

A third type of answer at this first stage of thinking about the benefit derived from churchgoing expresses help in learning more about God and Jesus, or receiving some help in schoolwork or divine protection. Sometimes avoidance of wrongdoing is suggested as one of the fruits of churchgoing, but with no real positive assertion that it makes one a better person. Here are some examples. Rose aged 8 : 7 (M.A. 12 : 6), 'Yes, by reading and learning about Jesus. *How does that help her?* It would help her in lessons, the religious ones, at school.' Keith, aged 8 : 11 (M.A. 10 : 0), 'Yes, it makes him learn about God from the Bible. *How does that help him?* It learns him to say his prayers and then God helps him.' Harry, age 9 : 8 (M.A. 11 : 11), 'Yes, if he ever gets married he can tell his children and his grandchildren about Jesus. *How would it help him now?* In scripture lessons in school. He'll know more about it when writing essays. *Any other help?* Yes. It tells him not to steal or be violent.' Allan, aged 10 : 2 (M.A. 9 : 9), 'Yes, it helps God to be with him all day long and when he sleeps at night. *How does that help him?* It helps him to be out of danger.' Sophia, aged 10 : 7 (M.A. 9 : 9), 'Yes, by learning things about Jesus. *How does that help her?* It helps her at school to know the answers in Scripture.' The first responses in many of these answers appear to show some discernment but discussion reveals very limited insights.

From towards the end of the tenth year onwards most pupils achieve keener insights and higher concepts in that attention is focused upon becoming a better person, morally and spiritually. Some less able pupils still reproduce the previous type of answers but most achieve a breakthrough of understanding that what emerges from churchgoing is less tangible than answering scripture questions at school, but is much more important. At first then insights are mixed up with lower insights as with Annabel, 'Yes, when she grows up she might be a helper in Sunday School and she'd tell stories about Jesus. She could get her friends to go to church. And going to church might make her happier' (age 11 : 5, M.A. 10 : 7), and Sally, 'Yes, it helps her to be better and to help her mother more. It may help her to know more at school in religious lessons. It would help her to help her mother next day.' Two interesting examples at twelve years are Harold's, 'Yes, it helps him to be more truthful and to work harder at school' (age 12 : 1, M.A. 15 : 7) and Sandra's, 'Yes, the sermons help her to understand God is near all the time, and she'd realise she wasn't alone, if she had problems and difficulties' (age 12 : 2, M.A. 17 : 0). At thirteen, typical answers are Nina's, 'It helps her to live a better life . . . and she learns God shouldn't be confined to Sunday, but he's with her all the time. It would keep her good' (age 13 : 2, M.A. 16 : 6); and Guy's, 'Yes, he'll tell God of wrongs he's done and he'll ask for forgiveness. It helps him to be a better boy. And he learns all about Jesus and people of the Bible and missionaries. It may make him think of being a missionary.' Some fourteen year old replies are Fred's, 'Yes, it tells him what to do . . . to have better morals. He'd feel better and enjoy himself more' (age 14 : 5, M.A. 14 : 2); May's, 'She feels closer to God and it's easier to believe. It gives her strength, spiritual strength, to go through the next week' (age 14 : 10, M.A. 19 : 11); and Herbert's 'It helps him to understand people and their ways, to work much harder at school and not to hate people he doesn't like' (age 14 : 11, M.A. 13 : 4). Fairly typical of older pupils are George, aged 15 : 9 (M.A. 15 : 11), 'Confessing what he's done helps. He feels God will watch over him and see he doesn't do it again. It makes him a better person', and Nancy, aged 17 : 2 (M.A. 19 : 1), 'Yes, it helps to build up her faith. It gives a cleaner, fresher feeling inside and it would give strength to do her duties in school and home to think. Someone was interested in her and in looking after her.'

GENERAL COMMENTS ON CONCEPTS OF CHURCH

The Infant and young Junior child have a lesser enjoyment of the church than older children; the six year old especially, probably due to inexperience and other factors. Where the church is enjoyed it is the singing which is the most attractive feature, with physical and aesthetic feelings also enjoyed. Dislike of church in the very young include a number of fears such as loud organ music, at having to read and write, of having to sing unfamiliar hymns, and of losing their place in a service book. The younger children evince a dislike of the physical fatigue of sitting, kneeling or standing too long in a service, this dislike being at its highest at eight years of age. There are many expressions of boredom at listening to long talks, readings and prayers. Brevity of worship must be an important principle at this stage, if it is to remain an attractive religious activity. The church is regarded as a special building with some holy association, in which special furnishings, windows, spires, people and ceremonies are features, without their significance being seen. Although many voice the fact that it is 'God's house', this is either a verbalism not understood or interpreted as where God lives in a physical sense. The child at this stage tends to see the reasons for adults going to church for immediate ends, from habit and duty or for purely pleasurable reasons, not always very different from going to a play or a film. For the child himself the religious significance of church or Sunday School attendance is not seen or thought of only in terms of specific 'religious' help, such as helping with literacy skills, familiarising oneself with hymns or help in religious lessons at school. There appears to be no transfer seen from attending services to daily living.

This pattern continues until the late Junior years when ten to eleven years appears to be a crucial time when concepts of the church take on a new perspective. From this time on the spiritual purpose of the church is seen more clearly as distinct from its physical features, as the function of worship, although the child is still confused on many points. Duty and habit no longer account for adults going to church, and the child feels it must be because it helps them in some way, if only to learn more about God and Jesus. From nearly eleven years onwards he sees that children can be helped by churchgoing, not in trivial or extraneous matters, but to be a better person morally and spiritually. At this stage the moral aspect appears to be of the greater importance. The late Junior and pre-adolescent still enjoys church in terms of worship, and from nine years on intellectual enjoyment of stories, readings and sermons, is evidently increasing sharply. There is also an awareness, among some, of an enjoyable social occasion of meeting friends, and friendly adults. But dislikes increase at ten years of age and intellectual criticisms now begin to be voiced. Although the intellectual stimulation is enjoyed, long, dull, irrelevant and incomprehensible sermons are felt to be wearisome.

From thirteen years on concepts of the church continue to improve in insights. Adults are seen to attend church for reasons of belief and the church is also beginning to be seen in terms of a fellowship of believers more than a building or a functional institution, although this only becomes explicit at about fourteen years of age. Greater emphasis is placed upon churchgoing by adolescents as helpful in strengthening belief and making them more spiritual, although becoming better people morally is still an important consideration. From twelve onwards there is a sustained intellectual enjoyment of the church, but this dips sharply from fifteen years onwards. This trend is confirmed by growing intellectual criticisms of sermons during the adolescent years as dull, boring and often irrelevant. Social criticisms also increase in the fifteen to seventeen years group mainly in terms of social isolation; 'having no friend to go with', or personal dislikes of religious teachers or clergy are expressed.

These characteristics of the three stages of development are consistent with what we know of children and adolescents in relation to the church, and also with research by Jahoda (1951) and Hyde (1963). Again, we must face the realisation that as the growing person becomes more capable of finding more satisfying intellectual concepts of the church and the purpose of religion, he is also more prone to develop negative attitudes, which counteract and possibly cancel out his potential for greater religious insight.

Chapter Fourteen

THE INFLUENCE OF CHURCH, HOME AND OTHER FACTORS UPON RELIGIOUS THINKING

SINCE the findings of this volume are the results of a test of religious thinking, it is of interest to see what factors in the child's background may have affected their performance in the test. We have already noticed that mental age is a more important factor than chronological age in religious thinking, except in those questions requiring moral judgment. Here chronological age is more important, probably because of the factor of social experience and length of years in making a moral assessment of a situation. Apart from these moral judgments, the significance of mental age in all the other results appears to be that logical or operational thinking does play an important part in religious thinking.

Even where mental age is followed there are many exceptions, some of them remarkable. Occasionally a dull child will score much more highly than a bright child of the same age, and even surpass older children of greater ability. It is obvious in such a case that ability may be stimulated or depressed by the motivation of the child concerned. If he comes from a home where religion is practised actively by attendance at church, in the encouragement of private prayer and where the subject of religion is discussed from time to time, the motivation will probably be higher than if he came from a home where religion is treated with indifference. It is possible, of course, for children to react to their backgrounds. Homes where religion is actively discouraged may stimulate the child to take an inordinate interest in the subject, and homes where religion is felt to be an excessive pressure may produce a child bored with and even antagonistic to religion.

To assess how varying factors affect the religious thinking of individual is not possible with individual children, as we shall see when we examine a number of pupils later. The most we can do is to observe the factors present in all the children's backgrounds and put forward several hypotheses in an attempt to explain their significance. We can discern some of the influences at work on the children as a group by the device of correlation and other statistical procedures applied to the total results of all the pupils taking the test. In the discussion that follows the non-statistical may ignore the statistics given to support the conclusions arrived at, although the calculations involved are of a fairly elementary kind.

CHURCH OR SUNDAY SCHOOL ATTENDANCE

When we compared the frequency of attendance of pupils at church or Sunday School with the total score achieved in the test, the coefficient of correlation (product moment) was only 0·25. This shows a positive relationship between attendance at church or Sunday School and the level of religious insight achieved. The relationship, however, is a very low one and indicates that only some of the pupils who were regular attenders achieved high insights for their age. It also indicates that some regular attenders scored low, and that quite a number of non-attenders scored high. The balance is slightly in favour of attendance leading to better insights, but not significantly so. This result is compatible with both hypotheses advanced, one that motivation in relation to religious thinking may be increased when a pupil attends a church, and the other that some attenders may not be greatly motivated by their attendance. Interest on the one hand, and boredom on the other, may explain this diversity among attenders. Some non-attenders score expectedly low, but others score high in contrast to some regular attenders of their own age. It may be that in religious teaching non-attenders may not be exposed so frequently to a repetition of Bible stories, and they may escape some of the boredom which may occur with constant reiteration.

On a more specific question, insights into the church (seen in responses to Picture 1) were compared with the frequency of church or Sunday School attendance. The correlation coefficient (product moment) between these two factors was 0·33, which is sufficiently positive to indicate that attendance may help many, and non-attendance may hinder some, in their thinking about the church. The relationship again is not significantly high and allows for a considerable number of exceptions. Familiarity with church, Sunday School, services and church people may not necessarily result in higher religious insight into the nature and significance of the church in modern life.

It is also of interest to compare the likes and dislikes of children regarding the church with the pupils' frequency of church or Sunday School attendance. A simple count of likes and dislikes of church were compared with the number of attenders and non-attenders, and a significant difference was found between attenders and non-attenders in their likes and dislikes of some aspects of the church.

This produces the expected result that attenders had a greater number of likes and less dislikes of the church than non-attenders.[1]

PARENTAL SUPPORT

No frequency of parental attendance at church or intensity of support for religion was measured. Such an assessment of parental attitudes and habits would have meant a whole research project in itself. But from the slender information obtained, in terms of a simple plus or minus, it could be seen whether or not a parent attended church at all. Whether a parent attended church or not was taken as a demonstration of parental support for the child in religious matters, and a rough indication of interest shown in the home. When those children (eighty-five in number) who had some parental support in church attendance were compared with those who had no parental support (115 in number) the results were of interest. Their respective performances in the results of the test showed that those children who had some parental support achieved significantly higher religious insights than those who had not.[2] When the two groups of children were compared on the results of their respective performance in all the questions of Picture 1 (Concepts of the Church) we again see a highly significant relationship. Those children who had some parental support in church attendance, achieved significantly higher church concepts than those who had no parental support.[3] In other words, some church attendance of a parent tended to go with better insights of their children into the nature, purpose and function of the church. Finally, it was seen that when the two groups of children were compared in total results in Picture 2 (Concepts of Prayer), there was again a significant relationship. Those who had some parental support achieved higher prayer concepts than those who did not have any parental support although the significant difference is not as great as in the previous comparisons.[4]

We would assume from the results just reviewed that in homes where at least one parent attends church, there is a more positive attitude to thinking about religion, to the church and to such related subjects as Prayer, than in homes where neither of the parents attend church. These results agree with Hyde's (1963) conclusions about the relationship between interest in the home in religion, attitudes of

[1] A chi-square test was applied, giving a result of 5·956 at 1 d.f. yielding P=0·02, a significant difference of between 2 per cent and 1 per cent.
[2] A chi-square test yielded 14·47 at 4 d.f. and P=0·01 (1 per cent level).
[3] A chi-square test yielded 17·14 at 4 d.f. and P=0·01 (1 per cent level).
[4] A chi-square test yielded 10·547 at 4 d.f., this lay between P=0·05 and P=0·01 (between a 5 per cent and a 1 per cent level).

pupils from such homes and the level of religious concepts achieved by the children from such a background.

RELIGIOUS BEHAVIOUR

By 'religious behaviour' I mean the habits of the child in relation to three religious activities, namely, church or Sunday School attendance, Bible reading privately and private devotions of prayer. The frequency of these activities was ascertained from questions asked at the end of the test.[1] Each pupil had a total religious behaviour score assessed in terms of the frequency of these religious activities, plus the parental support they received at home. When we compare the pupils' total performance in the test with their total religious behaviour score, the coefficient of correlation (product moment) comes to 0·32. This means that there is a slight tendency for those who have regular habits of church attendance, praying and Bible-reading to have higher religious concepts than those who have irregular habits or none at all. This rather low positive relationship is not surprising since it accounts for some pupils who do not attend church or Sunday School, who still pray or read the Bible, and whose parents may go to church, even if their children do not.

When we come to consider some of the religious activities separately, the results are of interest; since we have already reviewed the activity of church or Sunday School attendance, we shall examine Bible reading and prayer habits. First, we can compare the pupils' frequence of reading the Bible alone with their total performance of insight into the three Bible stories. The resulting coefficient of correlation is 0·31. There appears from this result to be some positive relationship between frequency of reading the Bible and the level of insight achieved in religious thinking as applied to Bible stories. This is consistent with the fact that pupils choosing to read the Bible privately with some regularity will also tend to be more highly motivated about stories from the Bible. They will also tend to be children with good reading ability. Some of the positive relationship may, indeed, only reflect increased reading ability as pupils grow older and as they also achieve greater religious insight. The low coefficient of correlation of 0·31 would appear to support the view that reading the Bible itself, however frequently, will not necessarily improve insights into the experiences of which the Bible speaks. A similar finding results from a comparison of the frequences of pupils' Bible reading habits, and level of insights achieved in Picture 3 (Concepts of the Bible). The coefficient of correlation here is 0·35, a

[1] See Appendix A. 'Church Connections', questions 2, 3, 5, 10 and 11.

positive correlation showing some correspondence between frequency of Bible reading and insights into the nature and authorship of the Bible. The relationship may not be very high due to the fact, observed previously, that one can read the Bible regularly without necessarily acquiring a critical view of unity and authorship. Regular reading may, indeed, merely reinforce crude ideas about the Bible held by many children, unless it is supplemented by informed teaching.

Prayer activity has an even lower degree of relationship with insights into prayer. When we compare frequency of praying with total scores of Picture 2 (Concepts of Prayer), the coefficient of correlation is 0·19. This would appear to indicate that there is very little relationship between frequency of praying and insights both into prayer itself and into God's operational power in prayer. As in church attendance or in Bible reading habits, it may be that familiarity may help or hinder a pupil's motivation. Habits may inhibit new and creative thinking about problems not faced before. They may, in fact, inhibit a recognition that the problems exist at all. It was very evident in the prayer discussions that many of the problems posed by the questions were new to most Infants and Juniors.

SEX DIFFERENCES

The 100 girls and 100 boys who took the test were compared in terms of their total performance and their mean average scores achieved in the test. The difference between the mean average scores of each sex came to only 0·47 of a point, the average score for the test being 105·33 points (maximum being 180 and the lowest 21 points). For a total of 200 pupils this difference is of no significance. We can assume from this that there is no significant difference between the sexes in their levels of religious concepts and the quality of their religious insights. This difference is slightly in favour of the boys despite the facts that there is a small degree of more frequent church attendance evident among the girls, and that the boys have a slightly lower mean average IQ. This evidence does not appear to support the conclusions of other investigators such as Argyle (1958) and Hyde (1963), that girls are more highly motivated towards religion than boys and therefore will probably produce higher conceptual levels of religious thinking. However, the smaller size of my own sample may account for this discrepancy as compared with the results of other investigators.

FAMILIARITY WITH BIBLE MATERIAL

Some children had seen, before they took the religious thinking test, the film *The Ten Commandments* and also the television series *Jesus of Nazareth*, both of which depict the stories used in our investigation. Many children had seen neither, but some had seen both. There were also varying degrees of familiarity with the Bible material presented for discussion. Many of the younger children had not heard any of the stories before, some had heard one or two of them before, and a few had heard them all. Unfamiliarity with the stories, of course, declined with age. The two Old Testament stories were known in some form by practically all by the age of ten years, and the Temptations of Jesus by most pupils by the age of eleven years of age. This later familiarity with the Temptations of Jesus may account in part for a later development of concepts in connection with this story, although the level of difficulty is probably the major reason. Thirty-three pupils had seen the film *The Ten Commandments* and eighteen had seen the television series *Jesus of Nazareth*. Again, increasing age obviously increased the probability of a child seeing either programme. From fourteen years onwards more pupils had seen *The Ten Commandments* than in any previous year and more eleven year olds had seen *Jesus of Nazareth* than in any year.

Whether familiarity with story material appeared to exercise any influence upon the pupils' insights into that material is an almost imponderable question due to the small numbers involved in each year and the existence of other variables which cannot be isolated. Hence, no firm conclusions can be reached. Certain trends can be noted, however. With younger children, there appears to be a slightly better scoring with familiarity. This may be due to familiarity with words, names and situations rather than a help in obtaining insights, and should not be taken automatically to support the view that children should be made familiar with Bible stories as soon as possible.

Evidence is inadequate to comment upon the television series and its influence. There is, however, an indication that *The Ten Commandments* with its literal interpretation of the Exodus may have impeded some pupils' insights into the nature of both the Burning Bush and the Crossing of the Red Sea. The scores of the film viewers appear to be particularly revealing in the Exodus story. In conclusion, we can say that familiarity will often act as a motivating factor in the children's approach to biblical stories, unless they are familiar with them too young, hear them too frequently and become bored by them. There is no evidence from this study to indicate how the pupils in the sample have been motivated in this particular way.

SOME EXAMPLES OF INDIVIDUAL PUPILS

A summary of the influence of church, home and other factors upon the pupils' religious thinking is not possible to make without over-simplifying or distorting the results. Perhaps a better way of seeing the varying influences at work is to take some typical and exceptional pupils, and see their full performance in the test in terms of their religious insight against their backgrounds. The pupils discussed are presented in order of chronological age.

Tina is the lowest scorer of all. This girl is aged 6 : 6 with a mental age of 5 : 8 and an estimated IQ of 87. She is a regular weekly attender at a Church of England Sunday School, is a non-reader and so does not read the Bible privately. Neither of her parents go to church and she does not pray at home. In contrast, her twin sister *Rosamund* was also tested and with a similar background, identical frequency of Sunday School attendance and other religious behaviour she scores a little higher than her sister but is next but one to the lowest score. She is, however, more outgoing than Tina and also achieved a mental age of 6 : 4, which gives an estimated IQ of 97.

Denise, on the other hand, scores very highly for her mental age of 5 : 10. Her chronological age is 6 : 6 and her estimated IQ is 90. She is a regular weekly attender at a Gospel Sect Sunday School. She sometimes goes to a church service, where her mother plays the organ and is a regular attender. As a non-reader there is no Bible reading habit, but she prays occasionally at home. Compared with Rosamund, of higher mental ability, Denise achieves much higher insights. The factor here which appears to be important is that Denise has parental support from her mother.

Noel, a boy aged 7 : 0, with a mental age of 7 : 2 and estimated IQ of 102, is a non-attender who has never been to church or Sunday School, 'except with Mummy once to do the cleaning'. He never reads the Bible, never prays and neither parents ever go to church services, yet he scores as well as any of his contemporaries who do go to Sunday School.

Martha, aged 7 : 3, a mental age of 6 : 10, with an estimated IQ of 94, has been a regular weekly attender at a Church of England Sunday School for two years and even goes to morning service with a lady living near by. As a non-reader she does not read the Bible and prays occasionally. She achieves a much higher score than Noel, despite the fact that she has less ability and no parental support, since neither parent ever goes.

In contrast to Martha is *Lillian*, aged 7 : 5 with a mental age of 9 : 2, and an above average intellgience quotient of about 124. Yet she scores very much below her peers. She is a very marginal Church of England Sunday School attender, having last attended eight weeks prior to the test. Her mother and father go to church on alternate weeks, very regularly, and she has evening prayers with her mother at bedtime. Ability, parental support and encouragement is there, but the child appears to be poorly motivated towards religion.

Massey, a boy aged 7 : 8, with a mental age of 6 : 1 and an estimated IQ of 79, is just beginning to attend regularly at a Free Church Sunday School. He has gone for some time to their morning service with his older sister. Neither parents go. As a non-reader he has no Bible reading habits, but prays on average about once a week. His score is fourth from the lowest, possibly due to poor ability and lack of any parental interest.

Almost the same age as Massey, *June*, aged 7 : 5 with a mental age of 8 : 0 and an estimated IQ of 108, is of special interest. She is a non-attender at church and Sunday School, is withdrawn from school worship and religious education by her mother who is an agnostic, and all Bible-stories in the test were completely unfamiliar to her. About church attendance she says, 'I would like to go if I could but I don't believe in Jesus. Mummy doesn't believe in Jesus. She says when I'm sixteen or seventeen I can make up my mind if it's true.' There is no Bible reading and no praying at home although she confesses that occasionally 'My sister and I pretend to and we never know what to say.' Isolated from religious education as she is, one would expect a very low score. Yet in fact she scores better than average for her age, she is much superior in insights to all her other non-attending peers. She is also superior in score to most other children with no parental support, many of them regular weekly Sunday School attenders, who have parents presumably indifferent, but not hostile, to religion.

Sally, aged 7 : 8 , with a mental age of 8 : 7, yielded an estimated IQ of 112. She is a weekly attender at a Free Church Sunday School and morning service. Her mother takes the children, including Sally, to church regularly, 'while Daddy plays golf, but if it's raining he comes to church too'. Sally owns her own Bible and tries to read it but finds it too hard. She says her prayers every bedtime. This girl achieves a very high score far in excess of both her mental and chronological age.

Sidney, aged 7 : 8, with a mental age of 7 : 7 and an estimated IQ of 99, goes weekly to a Gospel Sect Sunday School with his two teenage sisters. Neither parent goes. He owns a Bible but cannot read it and never prays at home. Sidney scores very highly on the test, in excess of all before a mental age of 8 : 5. He is very interested in Bible stories, having heard all three stories at day and Sunday Schools.

Rose is aged 8 : 7, with a mental age of 12 : 6, and is obviously a

216

very bright child with an estimated IQ of 146. She is a regular weekly attender at a Free Church Sunday School with her sister aged five. She has her own Bible which she reads occasionally and prays at least once a week, but not every night. She has no parental support, since neither mother nor father ever attends a church. Despite her high intelligence her score is very low indeed, equivalent to the average seven year old. Her responses were extremely literal in both parts of the test, and she appeared to be content with this level of thinking. Lack of experience and lack of interest at home may be two reasons for this poor result.

Greta is aged 9 : 2, with a mental age of 9 : 1 and an estimated IQ of 99. She goes twice every Sunday to the Sunday School of a Gospel Sect, together with her older sisters and brother. She has a Bible of her own which she reads occasionally and she prays 'most evenings in bed'. There is no parental support. Despite this Greta scores the equivalent of those with a mental age of eleven years.

Cecil, aged 9 : 8 and a mental age of 8 : 2, has an estimated IQ of 84. He stopped attending a Church of England Sunday School when about seven years old, and goes to special services hardly ever, but when he goes he goes with his mother. This very marginal attendance is accompanied by an absence of Bible-reading and prayer habits. Although well below average in ability, and very marginal in religious activity, he scores almost as high as Greta.

We include *Geoffrey*, the same age, 9 : 8, as Cecil, by way of comparison. Geoffrey's mental age is 10 : 4 and has an estimated IQ of 107. He attends a Church of England Sunday School weekly and church once a month. Both parents are regular church attenders. He has his own Bible which he reads occasionally and he prays every night at bedtime. This boy is highly motivated and scores much higher than Cecil, and far in excess of most of his ability and age range.

Lesley is a very intelligent girl of 9 : 11, with a mental age of 13 : 5 yielding an IQ estimated at 135. She is a regular weekly attender at a Free Church Sunday School, although she goes occasionally with her mother to special services at a local Gospel sect church, where her mother attends regularly. She reads her Bible for ten minutes every night, but does not use any Bible reading scheme. She prays at nighttime at least once a week. Her total score is low for this girl's level of ability and the obvious religious support she receives from her mother. Resistance and boredom may be part of this child's pattern. There is some evidence of fundamentalist teaching here which appears to limit insights.

Alice, another highly intelligent girl, is aged 10 : 11, with a mental age of 15 : 8 and an estimated IQ of 144. Her parents are keen Free Church members and she goes regularly to Sunday School and to church with her parents on Sunday evenings. She has a Bible which she reads occasionally and says her prayers every day. The home is a Christian home and church matters are frequently discussed, since father holds office in the church. She achieves very high concepts, her score being equivalent to many sixteen year olds. She is highly motivated towards religion and her high intelligence combines with this to produce a remarkably high level of thinking.

Anabel is aged 11 : 5 with a mental age of 10 : 7, with an IQ estimated to be 93. She stopped going to a Gospel Sect Sunday School about nine years of age and still returns there occasionally for special services. She maintains she does not like going because she is ashamed of not having been christened. Both parents work on Sundays and do not go to church even when they are not working. There is no Bible reading but Anabel does pray every evening. She achieves the same total score as Geoffrey (aged 9 : 8). The factor of longer experience here may make up for less ability.

Max, aged 12 : 6, with a mental age of 14 : 6 is a non-attender with no home religious influence. He did go to a Sunday School once when about five years old and did not like it. He owns a Bible but never reads it and never prays. His score is about average for his chronological age but below that achieved by most others with his mental age. He has a literal approach to the Bible and is apparently not inclined to look at the Bible stories at all critically. He reveals a curious mixture of both crude and advanced concepts of God.

James, aged 12 : 10, with a mental age of 10 : 11, has an estimated IQ of 85. He is a Free Church monthly attender, preferring to go to church because Sunday School is 'now a bit childish' for him. He is an only child and mother goes with him to church. He occasionally reads his own Bible and prays every night. His total score is extremely high, and would still be even if he were of average intellectual ability. The type of answers he gave was more typical of fifteen year olds. Home influence and encouragement, leading to high motivation, might be a possible explanation.

Joseph is aged 13 : 6, with a mental age of 14 : 3, and has an estimated IQ of 107. Yet his score is far below James's by some 30 points. He, like James, is another solitary child in the family, going occasionally to a Free Church Sunday School. Both mother and father are regular attenders of the church. He reads his own Bible occasionally, but never prays privately. Motivation is probably fairly low here, despite parental interest and support.

Of well below average intelligence, *Meg* is aged 14 : 9, with a mental age of 10 : 9, and is a borderline E.S.N.[1] pupil with an estimated IQ

[1] Educationally sub-normal.

of 76. She is a monthly Church of England church attender, and an only child, with neither parent churchgoing. She reads her own Bible at least once a week, and prays at about the same frequency. Meg scores up to her chronological age, despite her mental backwardness and lack of home influence, showing occasional indications of high insight.

Hatty is a fifth-form Grammar school girl, aged 15 : 9, with an estimated IQ of 130. She attends a Church of England Bible Class every Sunday afternoon, and goes with her parents about once a month to church, which they attend reguarly. She is an occasional Bible reader and prays every day, morning or evening, and sometimes both. She is a high scorer for her chronological age but nevertheless a low scorer compared with those with similar ability.

Highly motivated is *George*, who wants to become a minister of the Gospel Sect to which he belongs. He attends a Bible class and services, in all three times each Sunday, and his parents are fervent members, attending with the same regularity. George is aged 16 : 11 with an IQ of 107 estimated. He studies his Bible every day systematically and engages in private and family prayers twice daily. It is not surprising that he scores almost the top score and despite a fundamentalist background is prepared to interpret the Bible for himself.

Similar to George is *Deborah*, aged 17 : 11, in the sixth form of a mixed Grammar school. Her IQ is estimated at 112. She is fervently evangelical and wishes to become a school-teacher. She now attends a Free Church twice on Sundays, after she claimed to be converted a few years previously. She studies the Bible each day systematically and prays privately every morning and evening. Her parents are non-church and one of her fervent desires is to see them converted to the Christian faith. It is not surprising that Deborah, very highly motivated, achieves the highest score of all pupils taking the test. Although she is the oldest pupil she is not among the older pupils with the greatest mental ability.

It is evident from these brief summaries outlined above why chronological and mental ages are only rough guides in following religious development. A considerable variety of factors appears to lie behind wide divergencies in the spread of ability in religious thinking, despite similarity of age and intelligence. The generalisations we have made in terms of 'most' pupils must be seen alongside the typical and atypical examples just cited. The generalisations are still valid as long as we allow for many deviations and for the importance of other factors beyond what is often narrowly conceived as education in a formal and institutional sense.

Chapter Fifteen

SOME IMPLICATIONS FOR RELIGIOUS EDUCATION

THE research procedure and results outlined in detail in this volume would seem to stress the limitations of children in understanding religion. This indeed has been one purpose of this study, but the intention and the result has been more far reaching than merely to underline the difficulties we already knew existed. Before the many problems can be faced and overcome in religious education they must be diagnosed in more specific terms. This is what the research has attempted to do in terms of some of the intellectual problems confronting children as they seek to understand religion. There are certainly other problems not discussed in this research, and not all the intellectual problems are touched upon. But there is sufficient evidence to provide a more realistic assessment of the pupils' intellectual difficulties, the implications of which provide positive pointers to the religious education suitable for the growing child. In this final chapter we shall first of all review the narrower implications and later the broader issues involved. In a later volume, *Readiness for Religion; a Guide for Child-Centred Religious Education*, the positive ideas resulting from this research will be set out in greater detail, and will deal with the more practical issues involved.

RELIGIOUS THINKING IN TERMS OF THE BIBLE STORIES USED

The specific concepts revealed and evaluated by our investigation, particularly in terms of the biblical narratives used, are useful indicators of the levels of religious understanding possible. First, we summarise the conceptual limits and possibilities evoked by the stories in terms of Infant, Junior and Secondary pupils.

Moses and the Burning Bush
Up to between eight and nine years gross misunderstanding due to verbal associations, irrelevancies and distortion, and limits set by logic and experience, are the major problems. Concepts central to

understanding the story in terms of its religious significance are many and complex, among them concepts of the holy, God's nature, His activity in the natural world, His methods of communication. These are so limited by concretistic thinking that C.A. 11 : 0 and M.A. 11 : 6 appears to be the time when possibilities exist for insights at a religious level, that is, when understanding of the narrative takes on spiritual meaning, and crudely physical, materialistic and other irrelevant factors cease to dominate the pupils' thinking. The conclusion is reached that this story is unsuitable for use in Infant and early Junior syllabuses because of the limitations of thinking outlined above. At a most conservative estimate the last year in Junior school for the most able pupils may be the earliest time when this story can be understood at a satisfactory level. It appears to be eminently suitable for an Old Testament course during secondary schooling.

The Crossing of the Red Sea

Trivialities, irrelevancies and tautological responses persist until later in this story than in the Burning Bush story. As an adventure-action story younger pupils may enjoy the narrative, but as a story told to reveal religious truths it appears to fail due to the limits of experience and undeveloped concepts of love, justice and historical purpose. The significance of the Exodus as a whole, and this part of the story included, is dependent upon understanding the historical continuity of the Old Testament, which in turn is dependent upon space-time concepts, only barely developing by the late Junior years. When we see how literal pupils are in their acceptance of Bible material, we may infer that the bald narration of the parting of the sea appears to supplement and reinforce the crude concepts already held by pupils, of God seen anthropomorphically, intervening personally and physically, and manipulating nature arbitrarily to serve His purpose. The major problems here are concretisation of thinking, of which anthropomorphic thinking about God is a part. For this reason we conclude that this story is quite unsuitable for Infants and Juniors and should only be used in Secondary schools after the second year, and even later with duller pupils. Since moral and emotional factors are evident in judgments of divine love and justice raised by this story, chronological age appears to be a surer guide than mental age in determining the age boundaries when maturer levels of understanding develop.

The Temptation of Jesus

Concepts in this story are complex, often involve philosophical problems, and emotionally appear to depend upon the personal and intense experience of adolescence before their significance is seen. The philosophical problems, which require propositional thinking, involve the issues of good and evil, and the question of human freedom. Added to this is the imaginative and parabolic form in which the story is set, and the three temptations must be understood as three possible ideas of kingship with which Jesus was tempted. We conclude that the limits of concretist thinking are so restricting and the possibilities of misunderstanding at a literal level are so great, that this story is most unsuited to children and will have its most educational impact about fourteen years of age, that is the last year in some Secondary Modern schools, and the third year of Grammar schools.

The point may be raised here that if children are to receive any religious education at all, these stories should be told to them before the ages we suggest. Is it necessary, it may be asked, that children apprehend the stories intellectually? Can they not understand at what may be termed an intuitive and emotional level, even if their operational levels of thought are limited? Is there not the need to be familiar with these central biblical stories from an early age? Since this investigation is concerned basically with religious thinking as reflected in the Bible passages selected, we only report what is evidently the minimum age at which understanding of the stories at a religious level begins. The evidence is here available. What we do with it in terms of a religious education policy or syllabuses is another matter I discuss elsewhere.

'They Must Know the Bible Argument'

Meanwhile, the problem of the desire of some teachers to familiarise children so that 'they may know and enjoy the Bible from their earliest years' remains. The view is held here, and the evidence appears to support it, that this results in such gross distortions of the three stories' meanings as to interfere with the normal and natural development of religious thinking. There are two dangers apparent in familiarising without understanding, in teaching these Bible stories. The first is the accretion in the child's mind of misconceptions, verbalisms and focus upon trivialities in the story, so that there may be in relation to the story a period of 'arrested development' in which the child is satisfied by his too simple explanation, his thinking is crystallised too soon and he sees no need to think further in relation to the story. 'Too much, too soon' is now regarded as a danger to a child's developing concepts of number, where similarly he can acquire a number vocabulary, counting skill and even computing facility without the necessary insights or growth of concepts to support them. This may not only waste a great deal of valuable educational time but may prolong childish thinking in relation to number. The parallel with religious education is obvious. There must be many for whom the freshness, pungency and simplicity of Christ's parables are lost for ever because they were taught them far too soon, and they crystallised misconceptions of their meaning, never penetrating to further insights.

A parallel is often made between telling Bible stories to the young as their religious heritage and the telling of the legends of man as part of the children's cultural heritage. If we dismiss Bible stories for the young it can be argued we should similarly dispense with Alfred and the Cakes, Bruce and the Spider, King Arthur and the Knights of the Round Table, the Greek legends and many fairy stories with their roots in legend. This argument would be a cogent one if it were not for one major difference. Bible stories, whether told with the intention or not, result from an early age in building up religious concepts about the nature of God and inevitable associated moral values with the people, incidents and situations depicted in the stories. And, as we have already seen, children attribute great authority to the Bible as a holy, inspired and literally true book. Teachers telling the legends of the race have no sense of guilt and no fears about disabusing children about the stories' literal truthfulness. And further, no theological judgments (although there are some moral ones) are attached to the characters of such stories. The child's faith is not imperilled by the knowledge that King Arthur may not have existed, and his vision of the ideals of noble knighthood portrayed in the Arthurian legend still continues. This is not so with, shall we say, the exploits of Joshua, a similar national hero to the Hebrews, who conducted a series of wars and did specific deeds apparently at the direct command of a national god. There is much of value in the story of Joshua, but not for a pupil unable to see Joshua in historical perspective, as a man of limited vision, going through a stage of only partially understanding God. To say that the child will 'grow out of his misunderstandings' is not an accurate statement, since all the evidence points to the fact that most children carry their misunderstandings through with them into early adolescence. They then find the crude ideas untenable, and because the alternative is not put before them or left until it is too late, they may then reject religion as intellectually untenable.

The second danger is not intellectual but emotional, in the sense that the motivation of the pupil may be affected by too early familiarity with a biblical story. Stories are essentially dramatic presentations of truth. But when a story becomes familiar, by constant retelling, the drama ceases to be dramatic. It no longer has the freshness, the element of surprise and the enjoyment it once had, and the child eventually becomes bored with it. This will directly affect the thinking power brought to bear upon it, for if the pupil is bored by a biblical story, he is not highly motivated in relation to it. Since he is most capable of dealing at an insightful level during his early or mid-adolescence with two of the stories ('The Crossing of the Red Sea' and 'The Temptations of Jesus') if he is familiar with them from an earlier age, not only is the freshness of its impact lost but also it is associated with a period of childishness. This also may seriously affect motivation in thinking of the story's meaning at a higher level.

THE MORE GENERAL IMPLICATIONS FOR RELIGIOUS EDUCATION

There is a danger in generalising about the whole field of religious education, and especially about the contents of Agreed Syllabuses, from data limited to three biblical stories and situational experiences evoked by the three pictures of Church, Prayer and Bible. There is some justification, however, in not confining our discussion of implications solely to this data for two reasons. First, while the questions and evaluation of answers in the items are related specifically to the individual story or picture, the reader will recollect that the items were selected as those most common to a much wider range of biblical and picture material. The biblical material, for example, was tested in preliminary discussions with pupils in relation to the Call of the Child Samuel, King Ahab and Naboth's Vineyard, Jesus in the Temple as a Boy, the Healing of the Blind Bartimaeus and the Resurrection Appearance on the Road to Emmaus, in addition to the stories finally selected. The original pictures included other church situations and also a figure of Christ, in addition to the three pictures finally selected. The immediate and specific results of the final items used may be rooted in the story or discussion context involved, but a review of the wider implications for the use of material similar to the data examined would appear to be legitimate. The second reason why we would be justified in extending our discussion to the wider field of religious education is that this research raised questions of a far-reaching kind in relation to the items in the test stories, but involving questions such as the authority, veracity and relevance of the Bible, the limits imposed by certain levels of operational thinking and other matters which can throw light on some of the pressing problems facing the teacher of religion.

The Need to Examine Concepts Involved in Understanding
Material Chosen for any Given Age Group
From an examination of our conclusions of related concepts earlier in this chapter, it is apparent that material chosen for any age group should be examined to see what concepts are central for the story,

biblical passage or other material, if it is to be understood at a satisfactory level. By 'satisfactory level', we mean where some measure of religious insight is attainable. This depends upon other aspects of the pupil's development, and the level attainable will vary with differing material, as is evident from the differing conceptual levels attained by the same child in the data from our three stories.

Whilst we cannot expose every part of a syllabus to such rigorous tests and analyses as have been carried out in this present research, it would appear both necessary and useful for those drawing up syllabuses to draw out from material what are considered to be the central and basic concepts that pupils must grasp in order to understand some part of the religious significance of what is taught. This would not only act as a guide to teachers in sharpening the aims of their teaching, but would also make them aware of the limits of thinking involved in apparently simple and often delightful stories. For syllabus-makers it would act as a rough and ready series of criteria by which to test the suitability of the material put forward.

We have previously mentioned the false assumptions apparent behind the design of some Agreed Syllabuses in relation to many biblical stories suggested for younger children. Parables are an example of this, and the more we know of children's thinking, the more we can see that not only concepts but the level of formal operations (or propositional thinking) demanded by the Parables of Jesus make them, on the whole, unsuitable for children. Another example is stories about babies or children of the Bible as suitable for young children, such as the Baby Jesus, Moses in the Bulrushes, and the Call of the Infant Samuel. This latter demands insights similar to those required for understanding the incident of the Burning Bush, especially in terms of grasping divine communication as internal, non-physical, without which the story does not make sense. We can say with some confidence, in relation to our three selected Bible stories, that many Agreed Syllabuses recommend them at far too early an age in most instances. Some analysis of the concepts involved in these stories, together with what is known about other aspects of child development, would have provided more realistic recommendations in terms of the ages for which they have been suggested.

Nevertheless, there would appear to be a pressing need for further research of a systematic nature into recommended biblical material to test out the suitability of the material recommended. The recommendation may have to be faced that very little biblical material is suitable before Secondary schooling.

The Limits of Understanding Imposed by the Levels of Operational Thinking

A general implication spreading beyond the biblical data examined by this test is the limits of understanding imposed by the various levels of operational thinking, evident at various stages of intellectual development. We have established (in Chapter Four) that these levels of thinking can be applied to religious thinking, and that the stage of formal operations or propositional, hypothetical thinking does not appear to develop before a mental age of 13 : 5 for most pupils, and with some stories this stage was only achieved after 14 : 0 (M.A.). This general age boundary approximately coincides with the fairly constant indications from our material that religious insight generally begins to develop between twelve and thirteen years of age, in that crude physical and materialistic considerations, which obscure the essential meaning of the stories, are beginning to be disregarded by pupils.

I have already cited Peel's (1961) contention that there is little evidence of children's capacity to set up possibilities to account for events in stories, as opposed to mere describing, before the age of 13 plus. Since the aim of telling religious stories should not be to make the children familiar with the stories at a descriptive level, but to provoke them to have insight into divine love, divine justice, the nature of God and other concepts, the implication is very plain. This finding is substantiated in our own results, that 'children appear in general to seize upon what content is available in the story and base their judgments solely upon this evidence even although, to the mature thinker, it is manifestly limited and insufficient' (Peel, 1962, p. 2). If our aim in religious education is to educate, rather than instruct, at the level of critical judgment, we must recognise the problem set by the limitations of pupils who have not yet attained the ability to think propositionally.

The major impediment, as is indicated by the last paragraph, is the dominance of concrete data, or to use another term to describe it, concretisation. Children still in the stage of concrete operations will be diverted in their thinking by the apparent importance of specific detail and are imprisoned, as it were, within the demands of thinking about concrete objects, actions and behaviour manifested by the main characters in a story. When this occurs constantly in relation to religious data, by its very nature, concretisation must lead to frequent distortion and misunderstanding. The truths to be gleaned from most biblical stories are generally abstract, are of a propositional nature and are dependent upon the capacity to see analogies from one situation to another and to understand the metaphors in which religious narratives abound. Concretisation,

226

however, will tend to restrict understanding in these terms, focusing attention upon the immediate objects and actions or images evoked by those objects and actions contained within a story. In this connection, it is of interest to see that anthropomorphic concepts tend to continue until about the time when propositional thinking begins and concrete operational thinking is on the decline. We are forced to the conclusion that religious concepts introduced too soon may lead to regressive thinking in religion, and not only retard later insights but may prevent them developing at all. Too much, too soon, too often is a danger for religious education as for other subjects. This supports E. Harms's (1944) findings, previously cited that rational and instructional ideas should be delayed because 'the entire religious development of the child has a much slower tempo than the development of any other field of his experience'.

No answer can be given to the theoretical problem of whether the limits are set by maturational capacity, by sheer lack of experience on the part of the child or simply by poor and confused teaching. In religious thinking it is probable that limits of conceptuality are due in differing measure to all three. The secondary nature of the data of religious thinking (see Chapter Two) implies that a child must spend a long apprenticeship in experiencing and understanding the data of life upon which religious thinking is based. It is not, therefore, surprising that the beginnings of real insights are delayed until some time in the secondary school. In our next section we shall explore the implications of this in relation to the religious needs of children and adolescents.

The Need for a More Child-Centred Religious Education

These limited findings lend support to the view that 'the Bible is not a children's book' and that the concepts demanded by the experiences described in our three Bible stories are only just beginning to be comprehended in early adolescence and are beyond the limitations of experience and thinking powers of all Infant and most Junior children. If our assumptions about religious thinking are correct this statement may very well apply to a great deal of biblical material. The question will then naturally be raised as to what shall be the content of religious education for children. While it was not at the outset the purpose of this study to suggest alternatives, certain implications may act as a guide for re-examining our work in the religious education of the young.

When we say that religious education needs to be more child-centred this is not to minimise the importance of the Bible. It is an observation based upon the demonstrable fact that the Bible itself, although not the ideas and persons of which it speaks, must be introduced in a systematic manner later in the child's development than has been previously been practised. Even the most ardent lover of the Bible must see that if the child is bored, confused or encouraged to make continual misjudgments about God by Bible-centred teaching it is better to seek other, more effective ways, which are more realistically rooted in the needs of the child at different levels of development.

There are two arguments I have so far encountered, both of which many teachers of religion feel give them implicit support for using extensive biblical material in the religious education of the young. The first, most frequently expressed, is what we might call the racial or anthropological argument. This is, briefly, the idea that children in their own religious and moral development recapitulate the growth of the human race and that it is natural for them to pass through an animistic stage, a crude anthropomorphic stage, and through violent group allegiances and punitive levels of morality. The racial recapitulation theory was propounded persuasively by G. Stanley Hall (1904), but it has quietly moved into the field of religious education and taken root over the last fifty years. There is, as we have seen from the research outlined in this book, some truth in this assertion and there is unmistakable evidence that in religious thinking children appear to pass through stages of concepts not unlike those of primitive man.

In very general terms the theology of much of Genesis does approximate to many Infant concepts, and Mosaic religion does correspond to certain aspects of Junior thinking. It is, however, quite another matter to suggest that these, and later, Bible episodes should be told to children because they meet their religious needs at certain stages of their development. If this were done then not only would the children's development be incredibly slow, but may, as we have seen, be arrested at an extremely childish level. The true aim of developmental education is to satisfy the child's deeper needs for security, significance and standards which create the conditions for growth. Society in practice recognises natural desires of a deep-seated racial character, but insists rightly upon some restraint, while allowing expression of them in fantasy and play. It is possible, as William Golding portrays so vividly in 'The Lord of the Flies', that children are natural cannibals, but we do not condone cannibalism in them. If we are wise we allow children to fantasise in play on such matters, as a necessary release for their emotional health. It is quite another matter to tell stories or relate Bible incidents of a primitive nature which appear to the child to have the full authority and approval of the adult world. We must let the child fantasise about religion, as a necessary aid to growth, in his own terms, without the authority of adults to keep him at such a level, and without the mass of religious verbalisms which distort and malform his future understanding. It may be, for example, that the 'black and white' clear-cut morality of parts of the Exodus story appeals to Juniors at their own level of morality. As Ruth Batten (1963) says, 'In telling this story Christians want children to learn that God acted in love to save. They also want children to learn that this is universally true. But can this be done by telling a story of this kind? Is it not possible that such a story, which children will accept literally and authoritatively because it is a story about God, may hinder moral development by reinforcing the strong ideas of vengeance which children's morality still retains? Should not teaching about God's love and saving acts be presented in material in which the moral values are Christian? Should not stories, which because of their antiquity retain primitive ideas of God, be delayed until children are mature enough and have sufficient historical sense to understand how man has learned about God?' We shall return shortly to the role of fantasy in religious education.

The second argument for using Bible stories, especially from the Old Testament, with children is that many of these same stories were used in the religious education of Jesus himself as a boy. This appears to be a very persuasive argument and is often used to justify the inclusion in syllabuses for Infants of a series under the title: 'Stories Jesus heard as a boy.' Now while it is true that the boy Jesus was probably nourished on many of these stories as part of his religious education, there are two distinct differences between the education of a Jewish boy of that time and a modern child. The first clear distinction is that such a Jewish child lived in a pre-scientific age and in a society where religious precepts were accepted as basic. The universe of the Hebrew child was a three layer universe in which supernatural explanations were acceptable and certain parts of the Old Testament, which formed the Bible of Jesus, conveyed no such intellectual tensions which a modern child, especially the adolescent, must face. The second difference is that these scriptures, despite the pre-scientific limitations we have mentioned, were probably not regarded nor taught literally. They were recognised for what they were as theological and poetic interpretations of the nature of God. I may appear to be arguing here for an earlier sophisticated approach to the Scriptures than in fact existed. It is true that in pre-Christian Judaism there had always been contending factions between those who interpreted the scriptures literally and narrowly and those who felt the spirit more important than the words. We have evidence for this although, of course, no evidence for the statements about the education of Jesus. But what is our response when we are confronted by the stark question, 'Was Jesus a scriptural literalist?' or put in cruder terms, 'Was Jesus a fundamentalist?' Many attempts have been made by interested parties to prove that he was, by reference to his comments about Jonah (there is a distinct parallel between Jonah as the symbol of the nation in exile and Jesus' time of exile in death before the resurrection) and other textual devices. These attempts miss the point of Christ's struggle with the powerful conservative elements of Israel and simply sidestep the massive objection that if Jesus had been a literalist in a scriptural sense he could neither have been the Christ nor been the inspiration of a *New* Testament. Rather than contributing to an obscurantist literal view of Scripture Jesus both spoke of it and interpreted it poetically. F. H. Hilliard (1963) puts it in clear terms: 'There is more poetry in the Bible—even, paradoxically enough, in many of its prose passages—than the matter-of-fact, literal-minded European has sometimes realised. Those who had the misfortune to be educated in their youth, into a literalistic method of understanding the Bible, and have later learned, probably not without some anguish, to value it rather for the religious truth it expresses, can look back and perceive now that the transition has meant, for them, something like the cultivation of a symbolic, a poetic appreciation of the Old and New Testaments.'

Bible-centred religious education emphasises that the Bible must be taught because it *is* the Bible. Child-centred religious education, however, focuses upon the fact that it is the child as a growing person who should be our central concern. Where some parts of the Bible may answer his needs at a certain stage of his development these should be used. But if much of it is detrimental to his growth then much of the Bible must be introduced at a later date when he is capable of dealing with it in poetic rather than in literal terms. Child centred religious education must attempt to satisfy the basic needs of developing children at any given time but at the same time throw intellectual bridges forward into the future so that developing religious concepts can cross over into adolescence. Religion can then be seen to be all of a piece with former learning and not in contradiction to what has been previously accepted. What this means in more practical terms we shall now explore.

THE RELIGIOUS CHARACTERISTICS OF THE YOUNG CHILD

By the 'young child' we shall think of Infant and lower Junior children, roughly five to nine years, since even those aged eight to nine years have similar characteristics to the younger ones. By 'religious characteristics' we shall refer mainly to the intellectual and conceptual patterns of thought dominant at this time, which can act as a guide to a programme of religious education.

God at this stage of development is conceived in physical, anthropomorphic terms, as an old man in Palestinian clothes, with a physical voice and presence, living in heaven, which is situated in the sky, making occasional visits in person to the earth. His visitations are rare nowadays as compared with Bible times. He is unpredictable in his actions, rather like a touchy, powerful adult and sometimes vindictive to those who are naughty. His powers are akin to those of a magician and he is to be feared for this reason. This is the stage of mythological artificialism where natural events can only be explained in terms of human or divine intervention. As Ruth Batten (1963) says, it is 'a world of strange logic, where laws of natural causation were not recognised and anything could happen'. Although most young children pay lip service to God's love for all men, there is no eternal principle of love recognised at the heart of the universe. Since God can do anything, not only can anything happen, but he can be unfair if he wants to be. Vengeance is a paramount concern with God as thought of at this age. Naughty people are not only unloved but vehemently punished, and God divides people into those good and bad, loved and unloved, favoured and non-favoured, worth saving and not worth saving. The Bible itself is one source of these crude ideas, being a book of magical and holy veneration, written by God himself, or of one powerful holy person and therefore incapable of being at fault. If it is in the Bible it must be accepted as true. Jesus and God are frequently confused and there is no clear identity of Jesus. The children tend to have a sentimental pietistic view of Jesus as an angelic boy, and perfect as a man because all grown-ups are perfect. Jesus is seen as a mixture of a simple, good, holy man and a magician. There is no insight into the problem of evil of a realistic kind. The devil is the black antithesis to God, but singularly ineffective except with thieves and murderers. The power of Jesus is so great the devil is wasting his time trying to tempt him, and God is too busily occupied somewhere else to be concerned.

This younger child prays to God, sometimes to Jesus, and his view of prayer is largely egocentric, even when he conceives prayers for other people. The younger he is the more prayers for material gifts are made, and the fewer prayers of self-examination occur. The child feels his prayers come true for magical reasons, or they don't come true because he has been naughty or impolite. He enjoys church to a limited degree, especially the singing, but experiences some fears about it, as well as physical fatigue. The church for him is a holy building with special holy physical features, to which adults go for pleasurable reasons, out of duty or habit, and children might go for immediate help in learning to sing, to do religion better in day school or have practice in reading. There appears to be no transfer made from church or Sunday School to daily living.

We cannot say what proportion of these characteristics are due to the natural limitations of the child and how much to experience, in which teaching is included. Some measure of these restrictions is undoubtedly due to the intuitive or pre-operational mode of thought used by the child. Some will have arrived at a concrete operational level in relation to religious thinking by the end of their eighth year, but some are still borderliners in logical terms, and easily regress.

RELIGIOUS EDUCATION WITH YOUNGER CHILDREN

The major task of religious education of the younger child is to feed the child's crude deity concepts and his physical anthropomorphisms in such a way that he refines his crudities of religious thinking as far as his limits of experience and ability allow. While with J. J. Smith (1941) 'we must expect an infant's religion to be infantile' it is important to avoid the use of material which only tends to reinforce crudities rather than disperse them. Since anthropomorphic confusions abound in the child's mind between God and Jesus, they can perhaps be refined by constant focus upon Jesus, as an example of God come to earth, and as the incarnation of love. While the Christmas story should be retained, it is Jesus the man who should be the focus rather than the helpless Babe of Bethlehem.

The greatest danger for the Infant pupil is that of acquiring a religious vocabulary which has no conceptual substance, comparable to possessing a number vocabulary without number insights. For this reason and in the light of our evidence of gross distortion in terms of verbal misunderstanding, emphasis in Infant schools (and in the first two years or more in Junior schools) should be increasingly in terms of influence rather than instruction. This offers a particularly vital opportunity to the Primary school teacher often able to use a nature table as a natural worship centre in her own classroom. There is possible the slow building of experience as the basis of religious experience, as well as the communication of attitudes. Where a teacher shows attitudes of reverence for the wonderful and mysterious world of Nature, shares enjoyment of simple pleasures, appreciates the work of people who help us and naturally shows her own dependence upon God, all this must considerably affect the child and begin to create a frame of reference, even if it is primarily emotional. The Bible itself can be seen as one of the important books the teacher uses and respects, from which the occasional verse may be read, but Bible teaching as such would appear to be wasteful and inappropriate with these younger children. Rather emphasis should be upon exploring and clarifying those experiences, which later religious language and story will illumine, because the experience which forms the basis of it has been known and encountered with some understanding. Themes such as Our Home, People who help us, People who put things right (doctors, builders, gardeners), Friends, Farm animals and the farmer, are some examples of what might be attempted at the top end of the Infant school. This will be an enlargement of general experience with perhaps the occasional 'religious' focus, but would not necessarily come under a narrow 'religious knowledge' label on the time-table.

Since intellectual comprehension is extremely limited, many children still being at a stage of pre-operational thinking, feeling and fantasy will be the natural methods of exploration for them. More conscious attempts may be made through music, dancing, painting and creative work to help children to fantasise their way into religion. Harms suggests that the young child should approach religion 'not rationally, but playfully'. Simple experiences can be explored and known at depth, not perhaps verbally and rationally, but in feeling expressed physically. As Ruth Batten (1963) writes: 'We should remember that fantasy is not most naturally expressed in words. The children interviewed (in the Religious Thinking Test) discussed their ideas with evident enjoyment, but only because they were prompted. In most cases it is unlikely that such ideas would have emerged verbally in a class situation, but this does not exclude the possibility that some such thoughts might have been expressed had provision for dramatic play, movement, creative work and music been available. Children may grow out of many misunderstandings, but daily contact with perceptive teachers in all the activities of the classroom could help them in this process of adjusting fantasy to actuality. . . . The process of adjustment implies for teachers the challenging task of trying to understand what children mean by what they say and do, for only then can suitable provision for the next stage of learning be made.' Miss Batten continues, 'Sensitive teachers would find that in a rich environment many questions arise which have a theological and religious significance and open possibilities for thinking and learning. These would provide clues for further stimulation in the form of pictures, stories, music, poems (some from the Bible) and expression in all the forms available.' In other words, to formalise religious education in terms of religious instruction at this stage is to force the child to formulate his ideas too much in words which too easily crystallise into inflexible concepts. Activities, on the other hand, help fantasised ideas to be expressed and explored and then discarded for the next stage of thinking to occur.

Feeling being so dominant, as we know for example from the young child's egocentric thinking, worship can be used to stimulate and satisfy the young child's religious needs. If the language and experience invoked lies within the compass of young children, worship may be a sharing with and focusing upon God naturally, especially if elements of 'news time', when normal events of a child's real world form the data. This worship, of far greater importance than any set lesson, should be brief, colourful, beautiful, enjoyable, and intimate. Language should be concrete and non-theological and as most worship is the sharing of experiences with God, it would seem appropriate to worship not at the beginning of the school day, but at other times, after the children have shared something together. Since the sense of awe, or the feeling of the 'numinous' of the young child is strong, although still in a primitive form, this natural sense of mystery should be respected. While the God who cares and guides and is our friend is mediated continually through the life of Jesus, the 'otherness' of God must not be glossed over by intimate and sentimental assumptions.

We may characterise this stage from about five to nine years (to the end of the eighth year), with others such as Yeaxlee (1939), as the years of fantasised religion, and the major task of education is to stimulate and realise such ideas in fantasised form to be explored, but left flexibly within a secure framework of ideas, simply and frequently expressed, of a God who loves us and cares for us, who has provided for us in this earthly home and who is always with us.

THE RELIGIOUS CHARACTERISTICS OF THE LATE JUNIOR AND PRE-ADOLESCENT

By 'late Junior and pre-adolescent' we are thinking roughly of the child aged nine to twelve or thirteen years of age. In some ways this is not a homogeneous group intellectually because certain concepts appear to advance significantly about the age of ten or eleven. We can generalise, however, with some accuracy in saying that this is the time between fantasy and adult logic, when some confusion is apparent and a great deal of intellectual activity is taking place. In religious terms, the picture is something like the following.

Cruder anthropomorphic ideas of God are receding and the emphasis is much more upon supernatural than superhuman concepts of the deity. Some limiting human elements still persist in that God still has a human voice of physical quality and possesses power seen in physical and magical terms. There is a great deal of confusion as the child tries to think his way through these problems. For example, God if present must still be present himself in person, and concepts of omnipresence are still uncertain. The difficulties are seen but not resolved with most pupils until about thirteen years of age. This is the time from nine to thirteen years when a dualistic way of looking at God's activity in the natural world begins, one theological and one scientific. He holds strongly to many of his infantile ideas in thinking of God intervening in the world in an arbitrary fashion, but his growing awareness of scientific matters begins to create a divergence in thinking. At nine this is only beginning but by the age of thirteen it has been organised into a dualistic system of thought. Thus Miss Batten: 'Many of the children interviewed seemed able to hold incompatible ideas in mind but if, when conflict arises, the teacher's authority insists that belief in miracles is a necessary part of the truth of the Bible, only two alternatives remain for the children, to accept and stop thinking or to reject a great deal of what they have been taught.' The evidence is that the great majority accept it and resolve their tension by keeping the supernatural and the natural world in separate compartments.

The child's relationship with the God of the supernatural world is tinged with awe, as someone who invokes feelings of guilt for specific wrongs done. God is the possessor of the 'holy' which is still conveyed as a power by physical means. He continues as an avenging God to the Junior but the pre-adolescent is in a stage of hesitation about God loving all men. He knows it should be so, but cannot overcome the problem of evil people. He is on the borderline of recognising that love and justice may be compatible. God is seen as occasionally unfair, but only reluctantly, as though the child recognises the problem that God ought always to be just, but he cannot resolve the problems. Since this is an area of uncertainty his concepts of group judgments are moderating in relation to bad people; they are no longer seen as an undifferentiated whole. But he is still quite uncritical of the Israelites, since they are God's obvious favourites and God wants their immediate release from slavery and cruelty. No greater divine purpose is discerned for them than this.

On the human aspect of Jesus, late Juniors and pre-adolescents are becoming more realistic and his boyhood is seen in more normal terms. Jesus is regarded as a normal boy, with normal mischievous actions and disobedience of parents, but there is nothing really grave since he would be interested in religion and a rather serious-minded boy. The emphasis upon the significance of Jesus as a grown man is placed upon his miracles. This is clearly conceived in magical terms, and there is still no real contest with the devil in the temptations because his magic power and his special status protect Jesus from harm. Even so, the devil is seen as more menacing than in the previous stage, as though the child is become more aware of the fact of evil, and it is interesting that he ceases to be as anthropomorphic and becomes more supernatural in thinking about the devil, as he does about the deity. The devil is *the* evil spirit and the master-mind behind all evil actions done by men.

As the source of Truth the Bible is still revered because it is an ancient book, appealed to by teachers, and because it tells stories about God and Jesus it cannot therefore be untrue in any sense. It is an authority in a literal verbal manner, but its multiple authorship is being recognised and a few minor mistakes 'due to the writing down' are sometimes allowed. A few are beginning to see that the Bible deals with matters relevant for today and that the God of which the Bible speaks is still active.

Prayers increase at this period and they can be equally addressed to God or Jesus who are present, but not in a physical presence. True altruism in prayer is apparent and more prayers of self-examination occur. There are more prayers expressing desires to be a better person, in a moral sense, and there is an interesting emphasis upon prayers for protection in danger and recovery in illness, no doubt as he becomes more aware of the frailty of human life and the facts of physical suffering. Learned or set prayers are now at their highest level. Prayers are known to come true in semi-magical terms, the child using arguments by result, and the failure of some prayers is due to semi-moral reasons of greed or selfishness or plain stupidity. Ideas of the church begin to change from infantile concepts towards the concept of a place of worship where adults go to learn about God and Jesus, and where the church helps the child to be a better person. While he is beginning to enjoy the more intellectual aspects of a service of worship criticisms are beginning to increase, especially in pre-adolescence.

The move forward from the early stage of fantasy is assisted greatly by the growth of operational thought and it is characteristic of this period that the child is concerned with concrete situations, actions and people. This liberates him from the triviality of so much childish thought but also limits him at a new level to thinking in terms of specifics. He is not interested in principles but in fact, and one can see the intensive accumulation of real facts serving as a bridge to the later reflective sifting of the facts in adolescence. It is natural that children who are abandoning fantasy as a method of exploration, but have not attained the power of real logic, should prefer correct, factual information. Perhaps this is the emphasis to make in a programme of religious education in terms of the child's religious needs.

RELIGIOUS EDUCATION OF LATE JUNIORS AND PRE-ADOLESCENTS

The period we are considering spans roughly both the last two years of the Junior school and the first two years of secondary schooling. To suggest a similar emphasis of religious education for both groups seems too generalised, but the needs of the pupils are fairly similar. It is noticeable that pupils in the first years of secondary schooling still resemble Junior school children, not only physically, but psychologically in their attitudes to work, to teachers and their more open approach to personal relationships. There are rarely behaviour problems with the lower forms of secondary schools, the characteristics of these pupils being eagerness to please and to accumulate interesting facts.

It is about nine years of age that themes involving the real world of the child's experiences can be extended so that real things can be seen in a religious perspective. Projects which cut across the narrow divisions of the time-table are common enough in Junior schools today, but rarely does religion play an important part in such projects, unless the exploration has to do with a church or a similar 'religious' object. Yet the growth of Science in the Junior school provides many opportunities for seeing life, and seeing it whole, within a religious framework. To explore light and darkness, sound and silence, shapes and symbols, air and earth, law and order is to confront a child with the immensities of creation in the concrete facts which face him day by day. In these themes alone, to mention only a few, the Bible speaks in poetic and in factual terms, not as a scientific text book but theologically, of God as the maker of it all, the abiding presence within it and the heart of which is love. Such themes may not appeal to unimaginative teachers and it is certainly more demanding than a straight account of biblical history, in a tidy historical sequence. From the child's viewpoint, of course, such imaginative themes in terms of his experience make sense and meet his basic needs.

While the Bible can be used as a quarry for helping forward such themes by providing illustrations incidentally, the factual quest of the Junior and pre-adolescent child can be utilised to provide background information about Bible times. Even though a historical sense is as yet undeveloped many ideas of how people lived in Bible times, how and why they dressed the way they did, their customs, their homes and their essential needs can be appreciated. Too much attention should not be focused upon the strange, the exotic or the novel differences between Bible and modern times, but a steady focus upon the similarities of the human condition, then as now, expressed in differing

237

manners and customs, will prepare the child for a right attitude towards the Bible as a book relevant for today.

Up to this time Jesus will have featured, although not in great detail, in the child's learning about religion, if not in direct teaching in school then at least in the celebrations of the great Christian festivals. From about nine years onwards a more systematic, simple narrative of the life of Jesus in the form of stories could profitably be used provided that Jesus as 'the best man who ever lived' is the emphasis and little stress is made upon the miracles, lest concepts of 'the master magician' replace ideas of 'the master'. Incidents illustrating his love, his strength, his thoughtfulness, his friendship, his influence over people, with the Crucifixion mentioned but not dealt with in detail and the focus at Easter time centring upon the Resurrection, seem most appropriate for this age. Where the Nativity narratives are concerned there is no reason why they should not be simply and consistently introduced to the children from this age as stories men used to express the wonder and joy that so good a man was born. The term 'myth' might very well be employed and explained, and the poetic rather than the historic emphasised, even though the pupils will find it hard to understand this at first. In so doing, teachers are throwing bridges forward into adolescence and avoiding the later charge of dishonesty and betrayal. Some teachers may feel reluctant to introduce such ideas, but the evidence indicates that if it is delayed until entry into secondary school, or even later, the religious commitment of the pupils will be seriously affected. At the beginning of the secondary school this outline could be filled out with a more systematic exploration of the Gospel of Mark or Luke but not slavishly following the text verse by verse and chapter by chapter.

Alongside this introduction to the Jesus of history from nine onwards, there is an obvious need to begin to see the Bible for what it is, a library of inspired literature by many authors, tracing how a nation encountered God through revelation and experience. Its magical holiness should be minimised and its value for the ideas it relates should be stressed. If already the child is beginning to be introduced to the land of the Bible and its peoples, the last year of Junior school or the first year of secondary would seem to be the best time to show what kind of book is the Bible (and what it is not). Since concrete modes of thought are dominant, factual information about sources, institutions and people in the Christian faith provide a vast amount of appropriate material. Exploring a church as a distinct project, or as part of a study of the locality, has immense possibilities. The lives of Christian heroes, men and women of all times from the first century to the twentieth, and the background material to the Bible of which we have spoken, are suitable for this age group. Some material from the Old Testament, such as carefully selected songs from the Psalms, introduced as poetry and hymns, or stories of individual justice, such as Naboth's Vineyard, may be used, but most of the Old Testament still contains too many intellectual problems to be overcome. The emphasis in all these suggested materials should be fact and accuracy, which the children can check for themselves. In an honest introduction to myth and a project exploring 'What kind of book is the Bible?' the child would be prepared for a critical but reverent approach to the Bible and stimulated to the less passive and more questioning attitude, which is his normal method of thinking in areas other than religion at this time.

It is an interesting reflection that the time given to religious education at different ages is in fact the opposite weighting to what is required in terms of the pupils' maturing concepts and growing understanding. In the Primary school, due to intellectual limitations there should perhaps be less time devoted to direct religious education, and in secondary school, as more and more material can be dealt with at a greater level of understanding, more time could be profitably given to it.

THE RELIGIOUS CHARACTERISTICS OF ADOLESCENTS

By 'adolescents' here we mean pupils approximately from twelve or thirteen years onwards, rather than those who have attained puberty. Adolescence is used in age rather than physiological terms, although by thirteen years many of our modern youngsters have become adolescents in the physical sense. The characteristics which we shall outline are mainly intellectual, especially in terms of conceptual levels of thinking, but we cannot ignore the pressing question of changing attitudes.

About the age of thirteen represents a marked watershed in religious thinking. Although fully formal operational thinking does not obviously occur until a little later most pupils have attained an intermediate stage enough to begin to think in terms of propositions and to break with concrete modes of thought. This coincides, not surprisingly, with the ability to conceive of God in symbolic, abstract and spiritualised ideas. There are still some anthropomorphic traces evident in adolescent thinking, especially with the less able pupils, but God is essentially thought of as a spirit, unseen and unseeable. When physical human terms are used by the adolescent, they are clearly seen as analogies, as for example, a 'voice' describes 'God speaking', but divine communication is clearly mental, internal and subjective. God as a spirit is unimpeded by physical limitations and he is therefore omnipresent in his creation. The Natural and the Supernatural worlds are still separate, especially in early adolescence, and there is evident conflict about miracle. This is a characteristic which may be changed considerably by a more positive programme of religious education, beginning in the Junior school and continuing into secondary school in encouraging critical and creative thinking in relation to religion. As Loukes (1961) has shown, there is a later tendency to see much of previous teaching as 'childish' and to reject it at that level because the authoritarian literalism of the Junior child is unacceptable and no coherent alternative has been presented. The Bible, for example, is seen at this time in a truer light, although some cling to concepts of the Bible as infallible due to misconceptions of childhood still persisting. Perhaps for this reason very little poetic insight into the Scriptures is seen even towards the fifteenth year.

Higher concepts are also expressed in thinking of the holiness of God, and the deity's relationship with man, in a more spiritual manner. Man is in awe of God because his holiness is an indication of his moral purity and his almightiness. He loves all men, including evil men, which incidentally later pupils take to include all men, and divine justice is seen distributively (that is, God must be just equally to all). Punishment is now related to degrees of guilt and God is always just, although he may appear to be unjust to those who cannot see the whole picture. Groups are not now so readily condemned as evil, but group judgments about Israel are not too realistic until fourteen years of age. Some developing purpose in Israel's destiny is now beginning to be seen. A realistic Christology is also evident, where a normal boyhood of Jesus is recognised with normal childhood imperfections as necessary if Jesus was to have been truly man. Jesus is now identified with his mission and the Jesus of history is seen as the incarnation of the Christ. For these pupils the Temptations were seen as a real ordeal, with no foregone conclusion, and they are thought of in a subjective manner as a conflict of good and evil desires. God does not intervene because he has granted humans freedom of moral choice.

During adolescence, prayers conceptually take on a different texture and from thirteen to seventeen attain a greater degree of altruism. There is a sharp increase in the appropriateness of prayers of confession and forgiveness, and an increased desire to be helped with school work is noticeable. God is felt to be present in prayer in a sense of peace or calm or joy, and faith and logic are indications of the power of prayer. Failure in prayers is due to them being contrary to God's will. The church is now apprehended as a fellowship of believers and churchgoing for adults and adolescents is seen as a natural expression of belief and a means of making one a better person, spiritually as well as morally.

The greater number of criticisms of the church are indications of more negative attitudes to religion which Hyde (1963) reveals as increasing during this time. Wright (1962) and Daines (1962) both support this in relation to brighter pupils who have attained the sixth form. They reveal also that although these later adolescents are very critical and often disillusioned about religion there is an expressed hunger for spiritual truth. There are many complaints of 'childishness' about religious teaching during the adolescent years. For many of them the subject never came alive until the freedom of sixth form discussion was experienced. The picture of pupils in the fifth and sixth forms of Grammar schools appears to be, as Wright says, 'one of unrealised potential'. It is curious, as we have noted before, that at a time when real religious insights become possible there is a strong tendency for negative attitudes to occur. It is interesting that this is particularly true of less able pupils, who are obviously less equipped to wrestle with the intellectual difficulties, posed by the need to move from a childish to an adult framework of religious belief. For many of them the easiest solution is not to wrestle with the problems at all, but to give them up and retreat into indifference or hostility.

THE RELIGIOUS EDUCATION OF ADOLESCENTS

From the second or third years of secondary schooling the change in the quality of religious thinking presents great opportunities to the teacher. 'In other words,' writes Dr. Hilliard (1963), 'the teacher now has to begin deliberately and consistently to help his pupils to explore the inner meaning of stories, incidents, history in the Old Testament, and of parables, miracles and overt teaching in the New Testament. This does not, of course, imply that he can afford to ignore the difficulty of helping adolescents to see why these profound religious truths are sometimes conveyed, in the Bible, in terms which no longer make sense in the twentieth century. Myth, magic and miracle (in the sense of a suspension of "natural law") angels, evil spirits and heavenly voices, all these phenomena must be discussed in terms which a thoughtful adolescent can accept as aspects of the thought-worlds of the Hebrews and the early Christians. Accept that is, for what they once meant, but mean no longer. But he must be shown, at the same time, how to keep for himself and how to clothe in a more acceptable framework of thought, the profound truths about God, man, the world and man's salvation, which men of old expressed in their own way.'

Such a task of reinterpretation, so well expressed by Dr. Hilliard, is the core of religious education in the secondary school. The pupil in the age group we are considering has the conceptual and intellectual ability to begin such a task but four major intellectual problems must be faced. Although we have discussed them in part before we must see them now in relation to our older pupils.

(1) *The Problem of Literalism and Authoritarianism*

This problem is reflected in the results stemming from items on the nature, veracity and authority of the Bible. It is evident that a basic literalist stage exists until about 12 : 11 chronologically, until which time most pupils tend to see the Bible narrative as literally true. It carries with it not only the prestige of the printed word, but also, to the child, the authority of the adult world. It is true because it is old and venerated, and it is true in a literal manner.

Pupils must be helped to pass through this stage and weaned towards a more critical view of the Bible. A prerequisite for any course which involves the use of biblical material with older children would appear to be some systematic examination, exploration and discussion of such questions as 'What is the Bible?', 'How did the Bible begin?', 'In what way is the Bible true?', 'Can we trust the Bible?', and others. As concepts of what is the nature and inspiration of the Bible affect all other concepts of what it contains, a new emphasis appears to be necessary. Lessons of this nature need not be abstract theological talk but active exploration and research into the text to provoke the important questions such as, 'Is this true?', 'Can it be true in more ways than one?', 'What do we mean by true?' These are continuing questions which must be encouraged throughout secondary schooling.

(2) *The Problem of 'Two Worlds'*

We have already pointed out the separate existence in the child's mind of two worlds, or rather two modes of looking at the world, one theologically and the other logically-scientifically, each held in isolation from the other. With the beginnings of formal operational thinking there is the danger that logical-scientific thinking will dominate in middle adolescence. There is an equal danger for the few that they will be dominated by a still literal theological way of looking at the world, minimising as far as possible their logical scientific frame of reference. Some pupils appear to carry on this dual frame of reference until well into adolescence. We have evidence to support the view that at some period many adolescents jettison their theological framework as childish, and because it cannot apparently be reconciled with science, and it is one hypothesis which seems to account for the loss of many pupils to the Christian faith.

242

A major task appears to be to refine the theological world of the ten to fifteen year old in such a way as to break down the wall between his two worlds. It may be that his theological thinking must become more logical and scientific, just as his scientific thinking must become more theological. This means, on the theological side new concepts of Bible inspiration and authority, a recognition that the Bible is not a scientific textbook, and that scientific and religious views of the world are far from incompatible. This does not mean, as it might appear to imply, courses in 'Science and Religion' early in the secondary school syllabus, since most pupils will have an insufficient experience of science to profit from what should properly be a Grammar school sixth-form course. Rather, it is a thoroughgoing critical, rational and yet reverent way by which a teacher of religion will teach his subject.

(3) The Problem of Old Testament Teaching

We have already discussed one aspect of this problem in relation to the story of the Exodus. We have suggested that the Old Testament should be introduced and examined critically, after some sustained New Testament teaching, in the light of the New Testament ethos. Current theological writings emphasise the unity of the Bible, and urge us to remember that when we teach any part of the Bible we must teach 'all of the Bible'. By this is meant that we must always enlighten any portion of Scripture by comparative judgment of the full revelation of Scripture, namely the Incarnation of God in the person, mission and salvation of Jesus Christ. This, however, is not a task confined to trained theologians, but is a necessary way of looking whole at the Bible by all who read it. When, with older pupils, we study the Old Testament we must, to coin a phrase, train them to read 'through New Testament spectacles'. If this is done the problems posed by such incidents from the Exodus narrative as we have discussed, can be honestly faced in the light of the Christian revelation of divine love and justice. What some have called vividly 'the Rape of Palestine' by the Israelites can be seen for what it is, a misguided view of the deity as a war god, but nevertheless showing partial insights of faith, courage and devotion to the fierce God they followed. What can be more rewarding from a study of the later prophets than to see the struggle of ideas between the universalist and particularist views of Isaiah and Ezekiel, foreshadowing the struggle between Jesus and the official Judaism of his day? This approach to the Old Testament is not destructive, as some would assert, but is positive, consistent and more satisfying to the querying adolescent.

(4) The Problem of Biblical Relevance

Earlier we examined the delayed 'isolation-time' view present in the thinking of many pupils, who would relegate much of the significance of scripture to a holy place, with holy people, at a holy period in history; we also saw how this view was resolved completely by most pupils from about a mental age of thirteen. The problem is a serious one to which teachers should address themselves, since vestiges of this view linger on long beyond the age boundary mentioned.

There is no easy solution to the problem of presenting biblical material as relevant to today, such as the producing of a moral at the end of a lesson or even attempts to convey a modern parallel. Part of the problem is overcome if the material to be taught has been selected wisely at the level of the thinking and experience of the age group taught. Religious truth cannot be seen as relevant if it deals with experience foreign to the person to whom it is to be communicated. Personal experience and relevance must go hand in hand. It is best seen when eternal elements of a religious truth are presented, common to both ancient and modern men, and speaking to the condition of teacher and taught. As H. A. Hamilton (1963) writes of the adolescent, 'It is in the real world of his everyday life that he must be able to recognize the truth of what he is taught. No knowledge of obscure periods of history or stories of far-off events can avail, unless he is helped to come to terms with his own experiences.' And, 'So, again, formal teaching is the holding together of the given word and the given person. The past and the present must be seen to be continuous or the past has no authority in that world of here and now in which every child lives.'

(5) Practical Implications for the Secondary School

Faced by these four problems what practical steps can we take to help the adolescent overcome them? If in late Junior years and pre-adolescence the pupil has been taught in terms of suggestions outlined previously he will have been prepared in some measure to make the intellectual transition required during adolescence, and his attitude to religion in general and the Bible in particular will be changing to a healthily critical one. He will be disposed to look at the Scriptures as truthful in a non-literal manner; the two worlds will be the same world seen at different levels; the Old Testament can be the source of an exciting discovery of how men grew in their understanding of God; he will be constantly encouraged to try to evaluate the experience of people in the Bible in terms of his own experience and relevant to his day and age.

To ensure that this wholesome trend continues will depend upon a programme designed to meet the adolescent's changing intellectual and emotional needs. In terms of formal material, from thirteen years on an exploration of the major ideas of the Bible can be explored, not by means of a detailed and dull sequence of Old Testament history but by means of wide sweeps, using selected material, to see how from Patriarchial times to the great revelation in Christ man grappled with Suffering, Sin and Salvation, with Death, with Love and Justice, and the many questions posed in the Scriptures. This type of material still does not teach 'the Bible' but teaches from the Bible selectively and is fruitful only so long as the ideas used are comparable in some way to the experience of the adolescent. When one considers that for the Secondary Modern pupil from thirteen years on there may be less than two years before he leaves school, it would be fatal to try to cram into this period a complete chronological account of both Old and New Testaments. In sheer quantity the material is far too much, even if it were desirable to teach it. It is not desirable to teach it since for most of our pupils the wood could not be seen for the trees and the Word would be lost in the words. It is the grand theme of the Bible followed through the great ideas, and seen through the key people as they wrestled with the mysteries of life and death, which must be understood, and which must not be buried beneath the dead weight of so much 'Scripture Knowledge' of a historical, chronological and factual kind.

This type of material, as the content of religious education, should be dealt with also by means of more than an instructional method. Not only must the adolescent's intellectual needs be satisfied, but his emotional involvement secured. From the surveys mentioned previously the common complaint of adolescents about religious teaching in secondary school is that they are still subjected to non-adult forms of teaching, that too much thinking is done for them and the need for greater freedom to express and explore their religious ideas is not answered. Harold Loukes in *Teenage Religion* illustrates this vividly from comments by pupils. One says, 'Most scripture lessons at the lower end of the school are given by the teacher doing all the work, and the class just sitting back and relaxing', while another says, 'I like a Scripture lesson when you are at ease with the teacher, when you argue and have it out with the teacher about certain points. I like to have debates about unexplainable things to get nearer to the truth.' Loukes himself argues for the use of at least the final year in terms of a 'problem-method' religious education, once a three year course of the great themes of the Bible has been covered. This has much to commend it and clearly Agreed Syllabuses need revising in this direction in addition to a drastic reform of syllabuses for the Primary school. The problem of most existing syllabuses is not only the content recommended, and the amount of Old Testament material suggested is considerable, but that in putting forward Bible content in such a manner they are encouraging the unimaginative and theologically untrained teacher to teach by means of an instruction method to the exclusion of all other approaches.

More specific comments and suggestions, however, are beyond the scope of this present book, and will be discussed in a later volume. It has been the intention of this present work to outline the major changes in developing religious thought as the child grows forward into adolescence, the more clearly to diagnose the intellectual problems he faces. For the teacher, it is hoped that this provides a realistic picture of his pupils' development which will enable him to help the young achieve a deeper understanding of the Christian faith and a belief in God which is intellectually satisfying.

APPENDIX A

THE PICTURE AND STORY RELIGIOUS THINKING TEST

(Administration and Interview Blank)   Number......

Boy/Girl

Name...

Type of School..

Name of School.......................................

Form and stream......................................

C.A. at time of test...................................

Estimated M.A. at time of test........................

Estimated I.Q..

Estimate of Ability:

Type of Intelligence Test

1............. Date............. Score.............

2............. Date............. Score.............

3............. Date............. Score.............

4............. Date............. Score.............

School attainments

ADMINISTRATION PROCEDURE

Each pupil, once selected, was sent for by the head teacher of the school, introduced to the investigator and told, 'This is a gentleman from the University who would like you to help him.' The pupil was then taken by the investigator to the interview room where the following standard procedure was carried out with a slight variation according to the age of the child.

Introduction for 6, 7 and 8 years old

The younger children were asked to bring their reading books and the investigator spent some time getting the children to talk about the pictures in their books. When it was felt that the child was sufficiently responsive the investigator said: 'I have some pictures here you might like to see and later some stories you might like to hear. Would you like that? First, I'll show you some pictures and we'll talk about them. Then we're going to hear some stories from the Bible and we'll talk about each one. I think you'll like it. Remember when I ask you questions just tell me what you think. There are no right or wrong answers. This isn't an exam of any kind. Just tell me what you really think. Let's look at the pictures now, shall we?'

Introduction for 9, 10 and 11 years old

'Do you like looking at pictures and listening to stories? Good, so do I. That is what we are going to do today.

'First, I am going to show you some pictures and we'll talk about each one. Then we are going to hear some stories from the Bible, and we'll talk about them. I think you'll enjoy it.

'When I ask you questions just tell me what you think. There are no right and wrong answers—it isn't an exam of any kind. Just tell me what you really think.

'Let's look at the pictures now.'

Introduction for Secondary School Pupils

'Perhaps you are wondering what this is all about. Well, I am interested in what Secondary school pupils think about certain pictures and stories. It might help teachers to make their religious knowledge lessons more interesting. I wonder if you would help me in this?

'First, I want to show you some pictures, and I want you to feel perfectly free to answer my questions about them. There are no right and wrong answers—this isn't an exam of any kind. I just want to know what you really think about the pictures you see—and later—what you think of the stories.

'Let's look at the pictures now.'

Following this the same procedure was adopted for all ages.

P.1. *Family going to Church*

'The first picture here shows a mother and a father going to Church with their son (daughter). The son looks as though he might be about your age. As you can see, the family is just about to enter the Church to attend service.

'Look carefully at the picture. Now, can you tell me . . .' (follow question sheet).

P.2. *Boy or Girl at Prayer*

'Here is a picture of a boy/girl praying beside his bed. He is all alone in his own bedroom praying privately.

'Look carefully at the picture. Now, can you tell me . . .' (follow question sheet).

P.3. *Boy or Girl looking at Mutilated Bible*

'This next picture is of a boy/girl looking at a Bible, one of those big family Bibles. His young brother or sister has torn it and scribbled on it and made rather a mess of it, hasn't he?

1

2

3

'Look carefully at the picture. Now can you tell me . . .' (follow question sheet).

. . .

'Now I am going to let you hear some stories from the Bible on this tape recorder. You may have heard some of them before, but listen carefully just the same.

'After each story I am going to ask you some questions. Remember, there are no right and wrong answers to these questions. It isn't an exam of any kind. All I want to know is what you really think.

'Here is the first story.'

S.1. *Moses and the Burning Bush* (Exodus iii, 1–6)
'Have you followed the story? Good, here are some questions . . .
'Here is the next Bible story . . .'

S.2. *Crossing the Red Sea* (Exodus xiv)
'Have you followed the story? Good, here are some questions . . .
'Let's hear another story, shall we?'

S.3. *The Temptations of Jesus* (Matt. iv, 1–11 ; Luke iv, 1–13)
'Have you followed the story? Good, here are the questions . . .

Church Questionnaire
'Just before we finish, I wonder if you could tell me about yourself? For example, what is your father's job . . .'

Care was taken only to continue the interview as long as the children seemed interested and involved. At the first sign of fatigue the completion of the discussion was left to another session. Most Infant pupils required three periods, most Juniors required two, and most top Juniors and Secondary school pupils could sustain the one session. Total time for completing an interview was approximately 80 minutes, but this varied considerably from pupil to pupil. The investigator was friendly and interested but neutral, encouraging and praising effort throughout.

It should be noted that details concerning home and personal religious habits and other matters were left to the very last in order to establish a good relationship and not destroy rapport at the outset. This was felt to be most important where adolescents were interviewed, even though it meant that some interviews were wasted and not used in the final sample.

PICTURE 1. FAMILY ENTERING CHURCH

How often do you think they go there?	P.1	Q.1

    1. Once a week?
    2. Once a month?
    3. Occasionally for special services?
    4. Hardly ever?

A. Does the son/daughter like going there?	Yes	P.1.	Q.2
	No		
	d.k.		
	not sure		

B. What does he enjoy about it?
C. What does he *not* enjoy about it?

Why do you think the father and mother go to church?		P.1	Q.3
Does the son/daughter believe in God?	Yes	P.1.	Q.4
	No		
	d.k.		
	Not sure		

Does going to church or Sunday School help the child? How?	P.1.	Q.5

(Does it help in his everyday life?)
(Does going on a Sunday help him on a Monday?)

Is there anything special about a church? What?	P.1.	Q.6

(How is a church different from other places?)

PICTURE 2. CHILD PRAYING ALONE

How often do you think the boy/girl prays in private?	P.2	Q.1

    1. Every day?
    2. At least every week?
    3. Occasionally?
    4. Hardly ever?

A. To whom is the boy/girl praying?	P.2.	Q.2

B. What does the boy/girl pray about?
    i. Spontaneous:
    ii. Prompt:
    For *himself*? What does he pray for himself?
    For *others*? What does he pray for others?
    Is there anything else he prays?
    Are there any favourite prayers he says each time he
        prays?

Why do you think the boy/girl prays?	P.2	Q.3

You say the boy/girl is praying to God/Jesus/Spirit P.2   Q.4
Now, most people when they pray have a picture or an
    idea, of . . . . in their minds.
        What is the picture or idea of . . . . this boy/girl
        has when he is praying?

A. Is God/Jesus/Spirit . . . . there in the room with   P.2   Q.5
    the boy/girl?
B. If He is, how does the boy/girl know He is there?
    Can he hear God's voice? (Ext/Int)
    Can he see God in any way? (Ext/Int)
    Can he feel God in any way? (Ext/Int)

Does what the boy/girl asks for in prayer ever come true?   P.2   Q.6
A. How does he know they do come true?
Do some of his prayers not come true? Yes. No. d.k. Unsure.
B. Why do you think some don't come true?

PICTURE 3. CHILD AND MUTILATED BIBLE

What do you think the boy/girl is thinking?   P.3   Q.1
        Anger
        Shock
        Disgust
        Regret
        It's naughty
        It's wicked

Does he think this because the Bible is different from other   P.3   Q.2
    books?
What is so different about the Bible, what's so special about
    it, that he should think this way?

You can see from the picture it's called 'Holy Bible' (or you   P.3   Q.3
    yourself called it holy).
What is holy about it? What makes it holy?

How did the Bible come to be written?   P.3   Q.4

THE STORY TEXTS
(Heard by each pupil on a tape recording)

STORY 1: MOSES AND THE BURNING BUSH
(Exodus iii, 1–6)

A man called Moses was one day looking after a flock of sheep in a rather lonely place, close to a mountain.

Suddenly an angel appeared to Moses in a flame of fire, out of the middle of a bush. The curious thing was that the fire was burning away, but the bush itself wasn't burnt.

Moses said to himself: 'I must go and look at it closer, to see why the bush isn't burned.' Now when God saw Moses come nearer to the bush, God called out from the middle of the bush, 'Moses! Moses!' And Moses, not knowing who it was calling, said, 'Here I am.'

And God said: 'Come no closer and take off your shoes. You are standing on holy ground.' Then God spoke again and said, 'I am your father's God, and the God of great men like Abraham and Isaac and Jacob.'

Then Moses hid his face, for he was afraid to look at God.

STORY 2: CROSSING THE RED SEA
(Exodus xiv)

Once, long ago, there lived in Egypt a people who were called Israelites, and they were made to work as slaves by the Egyptians. The Israelites were treated very cruelly, until their leader—Moses—persuaded the Egyptian King to let the slaves go free.

Then Moses led the Israelites out of Egypt, across the desert for many miles, until at last they camped on the shore of the Red Sea.

Meanwhile the king of Egypt had changed his mind, and was very angry that he had let the slaves go free. So he came after them with his army of six hundred chariots. Now when the Israelites saw the army coming after them they were afraid, but Moses said that God would save them.

Then God told Moses to stretch his hand over the sea. And at that very moment the waters parted, and the Israelites went across the sea on dry land to the other side.

When they were safely across, the Egyptian chariots started to come after them, but God told Moses to stretch his hand over the sea again. And at that moment the waters came together and the entire Egyptian army was drowned. And when the Israelites saw that they were saved, they feared God and believed in Him and in Moses His servant.

STORY 3: THE TEMPTATIONS OF JESUS
(Matt. iv, 1–11; Luke iv, 1–13)

When he was thirty years old, Jesus was led by the Spirit into the desert to spend forty days, where he was tempted by the devil. He ate nothing during that time and felt very faint and hungry.

Then the devil came to him and said, 'If you really are the son of God, tell this stone to turn into a loaf of bread.' Jesus answered, 'The Scriptures say, Man shall not live by bread alone.'

Then the devil took him up and showed him all the kingdoms of the world, and said to Jesus, 'I will give you all this power and wealth that you see, if you will only fall down and worship me.' Jesus replied, 'It is written in Scripture, You shall worship the Lord your God and Him only shall you serve.'

Finally, the devil took him to Jerusalem, right to the top of the highest tower of the temple, and said, 'If you really are the son of God, throw yourself down from here, for it says in Scripture that angels will take care of you.' To this Jesus replied, 'It is also written in Scripture, You shall not tempt the Lord your God.'

And when he had tried every kind of temptation on Jesus, the devil went away for a time.

STORY 1. MOSES AND THE BURNING BUSH

Have you heard this story before? Yes/No/d.k./unsure.	S.1	Q.1

It says at the end of the story that Moses hid his face because he was afraid to look at God. A. Why do you think Moses was afraid to look at God? Any other reason(s)? B. Should he have been afraid to look at God? Yes/No/d.k. 　Why?/Why not? C. Would you have been afraid? Yes/No/d.k. 　Why?/Why not?	S.1	Q.2

Supposing Moses had got over his fear and looked at God. 　What do you think he would have seen? What sort of man 　　　　face 　　　expression 　　　　light 　　　　fire 　　　angel	S.1	Q.3

A. Why do you think the ground upon which Moses stood was holy?   S.1   Q.4
B. Is God everywhere? Yes/No/d.k./unsure.
Then is everywhere holy, or just special places?
C. Is this ground holy? Yes/No/d.k./unsure. Why? Why not?

How would you explain the bush burning, and yet not being burnt? (How do you think such a thing could happen?)   S.1   Q.5

A. If Moses had been deaf, do you think he would have heard God calling him?   S.1   Q.6
Why?/Why not?
B. If there had been other people near, would they have heard God calling Moses?
Why?/Why not?

Do you think this story really happened?   S.1   Q.7
A. All of it or part of it? What part didn't happen?
B. What makes you think so?

A. If I told you this story as though it had happened to me yesterday, would you believe it had happened?   S.1   Q.8
Yes/No/d.k./unsure.
Why?/Why not?
B. If it happened in Bible times could it happen now?
Why?/Why not?

STORY 2. THE CROSSING OF THE RED SEA

Have you heard this story before? Yes/No/d.k./unsure   S.2   Q.1
Have you seen it in a film or on T.V.?

Does God love everyone in the world? Yes/No/d.k./unsure   S.2   Q.2
A. Did He love the men in the Egyptian army? Yes/No/d.k.
Why?/Why not?
B. Why was it that He allowed all the men in the Egyptian army to be drowned?
(How could He love them and let them drown?)

A. Was it fair that all the men in the Egyptian army   S.2   Q.3
    should be drowned? Yes/No/d.k./unsure
    Why do you think it fair/unfair?
B. Were all the Egyptian soldiers bad?
    What makes you think so?
C. Were all the slaves—the Israelites—good?
    What makes you think so?
D. Can God treat people unfairly? Yes/No/d.k./Unsure.
    What makes you think so?

STORY 2. THE CROSSING OF THE RED SEA
(*continued*)

Why did God want to save the Israelites?   S.2   Q.4

How would you explain the dividing of the waters of the   S.2   Q.5
    Red Sea? (How do you think such a thing could happen?)
(With a 'natural' explanation: Did God do it? How?)

Do you think this story really happened?   S.2   Q.6
A. All of it or part of it? What part didn't happen?
B. What makes you think so?

A. Is it true because it is in the Bible?   S.2   Q.7
B. Is everything in the Bible true? Yes/No/d.k./unsure
    (If Yes) Why?
    (If No) How can we tell what is true and not true in the
      Bible?

A. Could this story happen today in real life? Yes/No/d.k.   S.2   Q.8
    unsure
    What makes you think so?
B. (If No) Why did it happen in Bible times and not now?

STORY 3. THE TEMPTATIONS OF JESUS

Have you heard this story before? Yes/No/d.k./unsure   S.3   Q.1
Have you seen it on T.V. or film?

A. If He was hungry, why didn't Jesus turn the stone into   S.3   Q.2
    bread?

B. Could Jesus have turned the stone into bread if he had
    wanted to? Yes/No/d.k./unsure
    How?
    Didn't he turn water into wine once? What was different
    about that? Why did he do that but not stone into
    bread?

C. What was wrong in doing what the devil said?

D. Who was the devil?
    Could Jesus see him? (If Yes) what did he look like?
    (If no) How would Jesus know the devil was there?

A. Did Jesus ever do wrong when he was a boy?   S.3   Q.3
    (If Yes) What sort of things?
    (If No) Why not?

B. Did Jesus ever do wrong when he was a man?
    (If Yes) What sort of things?
    (If No) Why not?

C. When Jesus was a boy, was he specially different from
    all other boys? (If Yes) How? (If No) Why not?

D. When Jesus was a man, was he specially different from
    all other men? (If Yes) How? (If No) Why not?

A. What was God doing when Jesus was talking with the   S.3   Q.4
    devil?
    (How would God help Jesus?)

B. Why didn't God stop the devil tempting Jesus?
    (If 'It was a test') Why was God not sure of Jesus?

A. Is the devil still about today telling people to do wrong?   S.3   Q.5

B. (If Yes) How does he work?
    (If No) If he was about in Bible times, why isn't he now?

C. (If Yes) Can he be seen?
    What does he look like?

STORY 3. THE TEMPTATIONS OF JESUS
(*continued*)

Do you think this story really happened?   S.3   Q.6

A. All of it or part of it? What part didn't happen?

B. What makes you think so?

CHURCH CONNECTIONS

	Item	Score

What is your father's work?........................ 1.
  Job, trade, profession? ....

Do you attend (*a*) Sunday School? 2.
  (*b*) Bible Class?
  (*c*) Junior Church?
  (*d*) Children's Church?
  (*e*) Anything similar?

If you attend any of these, do you go 3.
  (*a*) Once a week?
  (*b*) Once a month?
  (*c*) Occasionally for special services?
  (*d*) Hardly ever?

Did you go once and stop going? .... 4.
If so, when did you stop going regularly? ....
Why didn't you want to continue?

Do you go to grown-up (adult) Church services? If so 5.
  (*a*) Once a Sunday?
  (*b*) Once a month?
  (*c*) Occasionally for special services?
  (*d*) Hardly ever?

(Secondary only) Are you, or do you intend to become, a 6.
Church member, or confirmed, etc.?
  Yes. No. d.k. Unsure. Already done so.

Do your parents go to church regularly? Mother 7.
  Father
  Both m. & f.
  Neither

What is the name of the Church or Sunday School, which 8.
you attend?

Would you call yourself: 9.
  (*a*) Church of England?
  (*b*) Roman Catholic?
  (*c*) Methodist, Baptist, Congregational, Presbyterian,
    Friend?
  (*d*) Salvation Army, Pentecostal, Gospel, Brethren?
  (*e*) Jewish?
  (*f*) Anything else? ....
  (*g*) Nothing?

Do you own your own Bible? Yes. No. N.T. only 10.
Do you read the Bible privately at home?
  (*a*) Every day?
  (*b*) At least once a week?
  (*c*) Occasionally?
  (*d*) Never?

Do you use a Bible reading scheme? Which? ....

Item *Score*

Do you say your prayers—by yourself? 11.
               —with others in the family?
If by yourself—Every day?
           At least once a week?
           Occasionally?
           Hardly ever?
           Never?

APPENDIX B

A BRIEF DESCRIPTION OF THE GUTTMAN SCALOGRAM METHOD APPLIED TO THE EVALUATION OF PUPILS' RESPONSES

Once the independent assessments of pupils' responses had been made, mostly upon a 7-point scale, some discrepancies of scoring were to be seen between the assessors on specific items. To fix a final score, the average score between assessors on any one item was taken where there was only a one-point difference, then in all cases the higher score was taken. This led to a slight inflation of the scoring, but its effect was very slight. When the final scores were made on this basis all items were scaled. Some description of the method used might be of use to the statistically interested reader.

Since each year age group is limited to twenty in number, this is found to be too small to reflect a yearly series of steps, in terms of distribution of scores. If a sequence of thinking or an improvement in 'levels of understanding' is to be seen, the mean average scores for each year will move from lower to higher scores in an orderly progression. Such a neat and predictable pattern is difficult to achieve in mental testing, for the curve of distribution for any given item may not be normal, but also if the spread of scores is fairly wide the curve may not be contained within a single given year or even two years. In a few items where other statistical methods do not apply I have used yearly mean average scores but for the reasons enumerated above they are regarded as far from satisfactory.

The sample of 200 subjects and the items of the test were so arranged that scale analysis could be applied to the data. The technique of scale analysis can be used with qualitative data and has been applied, in the main, to the measurement of attitudes and opinions. Guttman's scalogram analysis—Stouffer and Guttman (1950)—may be useful when applied as a suitable technique to other areas of research. Guttman himself suggests that they may be applied to 'the measurement of human intelligence and abilities' (p. 61). Peel (1959), suggests that Guttman's scalogram analysis can be used to express the discrimination of the Piaget schemata in the case of logical judgments, as a coefficient of reproducibility taking chronological age, mental age and total level as criteria. A single item may be evaluated in this way, or any number of items may be combined, to see whether they form a single scalable universe. The technique has been described by Guttman (1944 and 1947), Stouffer and Guttman (1950), and Peel (1959) has clearly outlined how it may be used to evaluate sequences of thought in relation to Piagetian-type data. There is no need, therefore, for other than the briefest description here of how it is applied to the data of religious thinking.

Once scores are allocated on a 7-point scale (0–6) they may be set out in various ways. One way is to arrange the scores in seven category columns in order of increasing or decreasing rank. This is used, for example, by Coltham (1960) in evaluating children's understanding of historical terms. Where, however, a wide age range of pupil's responses is involved as in Lodwick's study (1958) and in this present research, the scores can also be arranged in order of chronological age, mental age or in order of total scores (total rank order).

We would expect that if levels of insight are related to mental age the scores would move gradually from left to right, i.e. from lower scores to higher scores, so that the familiar parallelogram of scores would occur. With a perfect parallelogram of scores the reproducibility would be perfect and be expressed as 100 per cent. Such reproducibility, however, rarely occurs. Some brighter children may not score so highly, or some duller children score fairly well.

To improve reproducibility it is legitimate to combine categories of scores. Guttman (1947) elaborates the reasons for this:

'It has seldom been found that an item with four or five categories is regarded as distinct. One reason for this is the verbal habits of people . . . (they may) have essentially the same position in the basic continuum, but differ on an extraneous factor of verbal habits. By combining categories, minor extraneous variables of this kind can be minimised.'

For example, scores 0, 1 and 2 may combine to form category 1
„ 3 and 4 „ „ „ 2
„ 5 and 6 „ „ „ 3

Cutting lines are then inserted according to the frequency of each category. It will then be seen that in each category there are some displacements or errors.

Category 1 may have 11 errors in a frequency of 32 responses
„ 2 „ „ 24 „ „ „ 118 „
„ 3 „ „ 14 „ „ „ 50 „

Total No. of errors 49   Total frequency 200

The coefficient of reproducibility is then found by the formula:

$$\text{Coeff. of Reproc.} = 100\left(\frac{\text{Total No. of errors}}{1 - \text{No. of items} \times \text{No. of subjects}}\right)\%$$
$$= 100(1 - 200)\%$$
$$= 100(1 - \cdot245)\%$$
$$= 100 \times \cdot755\%$$
$$= 75\cdot5\%$$

Guttman in scaling attitude questionnaires, says Peel (1959) 'insisted upon a minimum of 85 per cent. Guttman's condition is very stringent and not often met, and in this work (scaling logical judgments) we might say that 75 per cent is a reasonable figure to take' (p. 94). The view is taken here that any coefficient of reproducibility which approaches or meets Peel's 75 per cent requirement is sufficient to justify the existence of sequences in thinking, based upon the scoring criteria given.

The 75 per cent requirement is particularly appropriate in this investigation, since no attempt has been made to move the cutting lines up and down, ignoring the marginal frequencies, as is permissible in attitude scaling. The coefficients of reproducibility reported are obtained from a very rigorous application of scaling techniques and tend therefore to be on the conservative side.

In evaluating responses in this investigation, several simple rules have been observed, in addition to the above-mentioned observations, based upon Guttman's criteria.

(i) No category shall have more error in it than non-error. (Guttman, 1947, p. 260.)

(ii) To avoid spuriously high coefficients of reproducibility due to very high frequency in one category, only those coefficients are regarded as satisfactory which have the best distribution of marginal frequences. (Guttman, 1947, p. 260.)

(iii) When less than ten items are used and combined 'it may not be safe to assume that the universe is scalable if all the items must be dichotomised in order to obtain high reproducibility; at least some should be retainable in trichotomised form in order to make the inference plausible.' (Stouffer, 1950, p. 117.)

(iv) Where items are combined, and some are trichotomised and some dichotomised, some dichotomies should have marginals close to 50:50 to avoid spuriously high reproducibility.

In the evaluation of the five operational items the problem of dichotomous items does not occur. It does occur, however, with some frequency when the theological items are being evaluated. Where an item cannot be trichotomised, a dichotomous arrangement of categories is tried, and where this meets the 75 per cent requirement it is assumed that a two stage sequence of thinking exists, with a change in thinking occurring roughly where the cutting line between the dichotomously arranged categories falls.

A NOTE ON THE RELIABILITY OF THE TEST

The effort has been made to maintain uniform interview conditions by ensuring standardised administration, privacy, good rapport and other details; by this, the investigator aimed at reducing error variance and at producing reliable test scores.

In an investigation of this type, involving a lengthy interview, and a large sample, re-test reliability would not only be difficult, but would also be of doubtful value, due to the factor of practice. Due also to the nature of the test, no equivalent form reliability is available. Split-half coefficients of reliability were not obtained, but several other methods of obtaining indications of reliability were felt to be satisfactory.

First, on the five ' Operational thinking' items, when scaled against the criterion of Total Score (scores arranged from least to best scores in total performance), the coefficients of reproducibility are 84, 70, 72, 78 and 76 per cent. When the Total Score on all five items was used as data and scaled against the criterion of mental age, the coefficient of reproducibility is 75 per cent. Both of these coefficients indicate a suitable level of reliability or item consistency, for taking the score on any one item we can then reproduce with some 75 per cent accuracy a pupil's performance in all other items.

Second, on the thirty-three theological items, taking Total Score scaled against the criterion of mental age in trichotomised categories, the coefficient of reproducibility is as high as 80 per cent. Even the criterion of chronological age yields a coefficient of 78 per cent. Here again, this is regarded as a suitable indication of reliability.

Third, as is indicated in a previous section—'Methods of Assessing Individual Responses'—high scorer reliability has been achieved, with the exception of three slightly suspect items already noted. These general results are sufficiently high to claim suitable examiner-scorer consistency.

A NOTE ON THE VALIDITY OF THE TEST

Are the results of this test valid, in the sense that they indicate a universe of religious thinking? If we take the definition of religious thinking as previously indicated to mean 'thinking directed towards religion', face validity would assure us that all items are within the area of experience we normally call religion. Religion, of course, is so vast a topic that no test can claim to cover the entire field, or even a balanced series of items covering most aspects of it. An inspection of the items included in the test, however, will show the wide variety chosen. The justification for the selection of these items is discussed in Chapter Three.

A discussion of the danger of merely testing language facility, verbal fluency and other variables, is to be found elsewhere at the end of Chapter Three.

Because this type of investigation is comparatively new in the field of religious thinking, no methods of factorial validity are possible, since other estimates or measurements of religious thinking are not available for the wide age range tested. Some correlation coefficients which are presented in our final chapter have been found, which substantiate what is known from other investigations. An example of this is the high relationship which is known to exist between parental attitudes to religion and their children's attitudes. Details gained from 'Church Connections' (see Appendix A) also appear to correlate suitably with certain parts of pupils' test performance.

It could also be pointed out that if our definition of religious thinking is a valid one, the final scores on the five items assessed by psychologists on Piagetian 'Operational' criteria, and the same five items assessed by theologians on 'Theological' criteria, should show a high degree of correspondence. This is evident from the product-moment coefficients of correlation between the two scores, Operational and Theological, which are 0·80, 0·79, 0·78, 0·79 and 0·86.

APPENDIX C

A GLOSSARY OF TERMS FOR AMERICAN READERS

NOTE. Most words used in this book will be familiar to both British and American readers. Social and educational differences between the two countries, however, make the explanation of a few terms necessary, to those unfamiliar with the educational system of England and Wales.

Agreed Syllabus: the content of a religious education programme suggested for the state schools in England and Wales, drawn up in consultation together and agreed jointly by the Protestant churches, the teachers and the local education authority of an area. There is no one national Agreed Syllabus, but many regional syllabuses. Each local education authority has devised its own Agreed Syllabus or agreed to use that of another area.

Church of England: the state church in England (but not in Wales or Scotland) of the episcopalian tradition. It has no special privileges in state schools, but has a number of its own schools, where it has the freedom to teach its own church doctrines.

Education Act of 1944: the religious settlement clauses of this Act state that state schools must begin their day with a corporate act of worship, and that the teaching of religion, according to the Agreed Syllabus, shall be compulsory. Parents may withdraw their children from these requirements, but in practice very few do so. Teachers may not be subject to any religious test on appointment and may not be compelled to teach the subject of religion.

Fifth Formers: pupils in Secondary schools, mostly studying in academic or pre-college courses, prior to entering the Sixth form. Usually 15–16 years of age and above, the equivalent of 10th grade or beyond.

Free Churches: Protestant Churches of an established tradition, such as Baptist, Congregational, Methodist or Presbyterian. The term implies freedom from state connections, in contrast to the establishment of the Church of England.

Gospel Sects: Pentecostal, salvationist or similar type bodies, as distinct from the older established churches.

Infant Schools: compulsory schooling begins at five years old. Infant schools extend from five years to between the 7th and 8th year. Top Infants would therefore approximate to the 1st and 2nd grades.

Junior Schools: these continue where Infant schools finish, and go on to about the age of 11 to 12 years. They cover the equivalent range of 3rd through 6th grade. Lower Juniors is a term used for eight and nine year olds, and Top Juniors for 10 and 11 year olds.

Primary Schools: the range of Infant and Junior schools together.

Secondary Grammar Schools: although some Comprehensive Secondary schools exist in England and Wales, which are similar in some ways to the American High School, children in most areas tend to be selected for differing types of secondary education between the 11th and 12th year. Grammar schools are for the academically more able and provide approximately 20 per cent of Secondary school places.

Secondary Modern Schools: schools for those not so academically able as to merit a Grammar school place. The exact dividing line of ability between those allocated to Grammar and Modern schools is difficult to define and has led to some controversy. Upwards of 70 per cent of pupils after 11 years old, go to a Secondary Modern school.

Sixth Formers: pupils in Grammar schools, 16 years old and above, staying on usually to take college or university or professional entrance examinations. In age only, they are the rough equivalent of 11th grade onwards, and are of usually higher ability. The Science Sixth is the section of the Sixth form specialising in Science subjects.

Sunday Schools: the religious education departments of the churches, usually held on a Sunday. Although this term is often used in the United States, many prefer the term 'Church Schools', which has a different connotation in Britain.

BIBLIOGRAPHY

ACLAND, R. (1963), *We Teach Them Wrong: Religion and the Young*, Gollancz, London.

AINSWORTH, D. (1961), *A Study of some Aspects of the Growth of Religious Understanding of Children aged between 5 and 11 years*, unpublished dip. ed. dissertation, University of Manchester.

ALLPORT, G. W. (1951), *The Individual and His Religion*, Constable, London.

ANASTASI, A. (1955), *Psychological Testing*, Macmillan, New York.

ANTHONY, S. (1940), *The Child's Discovery of Death*, Kegan Paul, Trench and Trubner, London.

ARGYLE, M. (1958), *Religious Behaviour*, Routledge & Kegan Paul, London.

BATTEN, R. (1963), Symposium on 'Readiness for Religion' in *Learning for Living*, May 1963.

BARTLETT, F. (1958), *Thinking*, Allen and Unwin, London.

BEARD, R. M. (1960), 'An Investigation of Concept Formation among Infant School-children', unpublished Ph.D. thesis, University of London.

BEISWANGER, G. W. (1930), 'The Character Value of the Old Testament stories', *University of Iowa Studies in Character*, Vol. III, No. 3, pp. 63f.

BELL, J. E. (1948), *Projective Techniques*, Longmans Green, New York.

BELLAK, L. (1951), *A Guide to the Interpretation of the Thematic Apperception Test*, The Psychological Association, New York.

BERLYNE, D. (1957), 'Recent Developments in Piaget's Work', *Brit. J. Ed. Psych.* 27, 1–12.

BOSE, R. G. (1959), 'Religious Concepts of Children', *Religious Education* 24, 831–7.

BOVET, P. (1928), *The Child's Religion* (trans. G. M. Green), Dent, London.

BOWLEY, A. H., and TOWNROE, M. (1953), *The Spiritual Development of the Child*, Livingstone Press, London.

BRADSHAW, J. (1949), 'A Psychological Study of the Development of Religious Beliefs among children and young people', unpublished M.Sc. dissertation, University of London.

BRISTOL (1960), *The Bristol Agreed Syllabus for Religious Education*.

BRUNER, J. S., GOODNOW, J. J., and AUSTIN, G. A. (1956), *A Study of Thinking*, John Wiley, New York.

CAMBRIDGESHIRE (1949), *The Cambridgeshire Syllabus: Religious Teaching for Schools*, Cambridge University Press.

CARLISLE, CUMBERLAND and WESTMORLAND (1951), *Agreed Syllabus*.

CATTELL, R. B. (1938), *Psychology and the Religious Quest*, Nelson, London.

CHESSER, E. (1956), *The Sexual, Marital and Family Relationships of The English Woman*, Hutchinson, London.

CHURCHILL, E. M. (1958), 'The Number Concepts of Young Children', *Research and Studies*, University of Leeds Institute of Education, 17 and 18.

COLTHAM, J. B. (1960), 'Junior School Children's Understanding of Some Terms commonly used in the Teaching of History', unpublished Ph.D. thesis, University of Manchester.

COLQUHON, F. (1955), *Harringay Story*, Hodder & Stoughton, London.

DAINES, J. W. (1949), 'A Psychological Study of the Attitudes of Adolescents to Religion and Religious Instruction', unpublished Ph.D. thesis, University of London.

DAINES, J. W. (1962), *An Enquiry into the methods and effects of Religious Education in Sixth Forms*, University of Nottingham Institute of Education.

DAWES, R. S. (1954), 'The Concepts of God among Secondary School Children', unpublished M.A. thesis, University of London.

DEUTSCHE, J. M. (1943), 'The Developments of Children's Concepts of Causal Relationships', in Barker, Kounin and Wright, *Child Behaviour and Development*, MacGraw-Hill, New York.

DURHAM (1946), *Agreed Syllabus of Religious Education*, University of London Press.

FLUGEL, J. C. (1945), *Man, Morals and Society*, Duckworth Press, London.

GERKIN, C. B., and COX, D. G. (1953), 'The Religious Story Test', *Journal of Pastoral Care*, VII, 2.

GESELL, A., and ILG, F. L. (1946), *The Child from Five to Ten*, Hamish Hamilton, London.

GLASSEY, W. (1945), 'The Attitude of Grammar School Pupils and their Parents to Education, Religion and Sport', *Brit. J. Ed. Psych.* 15.

GOLDMAN, R. J. (1959), 'What is Religious Knowledge?', *National Froebel Foundation Bulletin*, No. 117.

GOLDMAN, R. J. (1963), 'Children's Spiritual Development', in *Studies in Education: First Years in School*, published for the University of London Institute of Education by Evans Bros., London.

GOLDMAN, R. J. (1963), in 'Readiness for Religion', symposium in *Learning for Living*, May, 1963.

GORER, G. (1955), *Exploring English Character*, Cresset, London.

GRIFFITHS, R. (1935), *Imagination in Early Childhood*, Routledge and Kegan Paul, London.

GUILFORD, J. P. (1956), *Fundamental Statistics in Psychology and Education*, MacGraw-Hill, London.

GUTTMAN, L. (1944), 'A Basis for Scaling Qualitative Data', *Am. Soc. Review*, Vol. 9, 2, 139-50.

GUTTMAN, L. (1947), 'The Cornell Technique for Scale and Intensity Analysis', *Educat. and Psych. Measurement*, Vol. 7, 247-80.

HALL, G. S. (1904), *Adolescence: Its Psychology & Its Relation to Physiology, Anthropology, Sociology, Sex, Crime, Religion and Education*, D. Appleton Co., New York.

HAMILTON, H. A. (1963), *The Religious needs of Children in Care*, National Children's Home, London.

HARMS, E. (1944), 'The Development of Religious Experience in Children', *Am. J. of Soc.*, Vol. 50, No. 2, 112–22.

HAVIGHURST, R. J. (1953), *Human Development and Education*, Longmans Green, London.

HAZLITT, V. (1930), 'Children's Thinking', *Brit. J. Ed. Psych.*, XX, 4, 354–61.

HEBB, D. O. (1948), *The Organisation of Behaviour*, Wiley, New York.

HEBRON, M. E. (1957), 'The Research into the Teaching of Religious Knowledge', *Studies in Education*, University of Hull.

HEIDBREDER, E. (1946), 'The Attainment of Concepts', *J. Gen. Psych.*, 35, 173–223.

HEWITT, G. (1963), in Symposium on 'Readiness for Religion', in *Learning for Living*, May 1963.

HILLIARD, F. H. (1959), 'The Influence of Religious Education upon the Development of Children's Moral Ideas', *Brit. J. Ed. Psych.*, 29, 50–9.

HILLIARD, F. H. (1959), 'Ideas of God among Secondary School Children', *Religion in Education*, Vol. XXVII, No. 1.

HILLIARD, F. H. (1963), Symposium on 'Readiness for Religion', in *Learning for Living*, May 1963.

HOLLINGWORTH, L. S. (1933), 'The Adolescent Child', in Murchison, *A handbook of Child Psychology*, Clark University Press.

HUBERY, D. S. (1960), *The Experiential Approach to Christian Education*, National Sunday School Union.

HULL, C. L. (1920), 'Quantitative Aspects of the Evolution of Concepts', *Psych. Monographs*, 38.

HUMPHREY, G. (1952), 'Abstraction and Generalisation', Chapter 9 in *Thinking: an Introduction to Experimental Psychology*, Methuen, London.

HUNT, J. McV. (1961), *Intelligence and Experience*, The Ronald Press Co., New York.

HUNTER, W. S., and BARTLETT, S. C. (1948), 'Double Alternation Behaviour in Young Children', *J. Exper. Psych.*, 38.

HURLOCK, E. B. (1956), *Child Development*, McGraw-Hill, New York.

HYDE, K. E. (1963), 'Religious Concepts and Religious Attitudes', *Educational Review*, February and June 1963.

HYDE, et al. (1956), *Sunday Schools Today*, Free Church Federal Council.

INHELDER, B., and PIAGET, J. (1958), *The Growth of Logical Thinking*, Routledge & Kegan Paul, London.

INSTITUTE OF CHRISTIAN EDUCATION, *Religious Education of Pupils* (series).

ISAACS, S. (1945), *Intellectual Growth in Young Children*, G. Routledge & Son, London.

JACKSON, L. (1952), *A Test of Family Attitudes*, Methuen, London.

JAHODA, G. (1951), 'Development of Unfavourable Attitudes towards Religion', *Brit. Psych. Society Quarterly Bulletin*, 2.

JAHODA, G. (1963), 'Children's Concepts of Time and History', *Educational Review*, Vol. 15, 2.

JAMES, W. (1902), *The Varieties of Religious Experience*, Longmans Green, London.

JEFFREYS, M. V. C. (1955), *Glaucon*, Pitman, London.

JOHNSON, J. E. (1961), 'An Enquiry into some of the Religious Ideas of 6 year old children', unpublished dip. ed. dissertation, University of Birmingham.

JOHNSON, P. E. (1957), *Personality and Religion*, Abingdon Press, New York.

KENWRICK, J. G. (1949), 'The Training of the Religious Sentiment', unpublished Ph.D. thesis, University of London.

KENWRICK, J. G. (1955), *The Religious Quest*, S.P.C.K., London.

KUENNE, M. R. (1946), 'An Experimental Investigation of the Relation of Language and Transposition, Behaviour in Young Children', *J. Exper. Psych.*, 36, 471–90.

KUHLEN, R. G., and ARNOLD, J. (1944), 'Age differences in Religious Beliefs and Problems during Adolescence', *J. Gen. Psych.*, 65.

KUPKY, O. (1928), *The Religious Development of Adolescents*, Macmillan, New York.

LEUBA, J. H. (1925), *The Psychology of Religious Mysticism*, Kegan Paul, London, and (1921), *Belief in God and Immortality*.

LODWICK, A. R. (1958), 'Inferences drawn in History compared with Piaget's stages of mental development', unpublished dip. ed. dissertation, University of Birmingham.

LOOMBA, M. (1944), 'The Religious Development of Children', *Psychol. Abstracts*, 345, 35.

LOVELL, K. (1961), *The Growth of Basic Mathematical and Scientific Concepts in Children*, University of London Press.

LOUKES, H. (1961), *Teenage Religion*, S.C.M. Press, London.

LUNZER, E. A., 'Recent Studies in Britain based upon the work of Jean Piaget', *Occasional Publication No. 4*, National Foundation for Educational Research.

McKEEFENY, W. J. (1949), 'A Critical Analysis of Quantitative Studies of Religious Awakening', unpublished Ph.D. thesis, Union Theological Seminary, New York.

MANCHESTER (1957), *Agreed Syllabus of Religious Education*.

MATHIAS, D. (1943), 'Ideas of God and Conduct', unpublished Ph.D. thesis, Teacher's College, University of Columbia.

MORETON, F. E. (1944), 'Attitudes to religion among adolescents and adults', *Brit. J. Ed. Psych.* 14, 69–79.

MORETON, F. E. (1931), 'A Brief Consideration of religious Experience', unpublished Ph.D. thesis, University of Birmingham.

MURRAY, H. A. (1943), *The Thematic Apperception Test Manual*, Harvard University Press, Cambridge, Mass.

NAGLE, U. (1934), *An Empirical Study of the Development of Religious Thinking in Boys from 12 to 16 years old*, The Catholic University Press of America.

NEWCOMBE, T. M., and SVEHLA, G. (1937), 'Intra-family relationships in attitudes', *Sociometry*, 1, 180–205.

OAKDEN, E. C., and STURT, M. (1922), 'The Development of the Knowledge of Time in Children', *Brit. J. Psych.*, 12, 309–36.

OTTO, R. (1950), *The Idea of the Holy*, Oxford University Press.

PEEL, E. A. (1959), 'Experimental Examination of Piaget's Schemata Concerning Children's Perception and Thinking, and a Discussion of their Educational Significance', *Brit. J. Ed. Psych.*, xxix, Part 2, 89–103.

PEEL, E. A. (1960), *The Pupil's Thinking*, Oldbourne Press, London.

PEEL, E. A. (1961), 'The Growth of Pupils' Judgments—Thinking Comprehension', unpublished account of research at Princeton, New Jersey.

PIAGET, J. (1929), *The Child's Conception of the World*, Routledge & Kegan Paul, London.

PIAGET, J. (1930), *The Child's Conception of Causality*, Routledge & Kegan Paul, London.

PIAGET, J. (1932), *The Moral Judgment of the Child*, Routledge & Kegan Paul, London.

PIAGET, J. (1952), *The Child's Conception of Number*, Routledge & Kegan Paul, London.

PIAGET, J. (1953), *Logic and Psychology*, University of Manchester Press.

REICHARD, R., SCHNEIDER, S., and RAPAPORT, D. (1944), 'The Development of Concept Formation in Children', *Am. J. of Ortho-psychiatry*, 14.

REIK, T. (1955), 'From Spell to Prayer', *Pscyhoanalysis*, 3, 4.

RIXON, L. D. (1959), 'An Experimental and Critical Study of the Teaching of Scripture in Secondary Schools', unpublished Ph.D. thesis, University of London.

RUSSELL, D. H. (1956), *Children's Thinking*, Ginn, London.

RUSSELL, R. W., and DENNIS, W. (1939), 'Studies in Animism', *J. of Gen. Psych.*, 55.

SERRA, M. C. (1952), *How to develop Concepts and their Verbal Representations*, Elem. School J.53.

SMITH, J. J. (1941), 'The Religious Development of Children', in Skinner and Harrison, *Child Psychology*, Macmillan, New York.

SMITH, J. W. D. (1949), *An Introduction to Scripture Teaching*, Nelson, London.

SMITH, J. W. D. (1953), *Psychology and Religion in Early Childhood*, S.C.M. Press.

SMOKE, K. L. (1935), 'The Experimental Approach to Concept learning', *Psych. Review*, Vol. 42, 274–9.

STARBUCK, E. D. (1899), *The Psychology of Religion*, Walter Scott, London.

STOUFFER, S. A., and GUTTMAN, L. (1950), 'Measurement and Prediction', in *Studies of Social Psychology in World War II*, Vol. 1, Princeton University Press.

STURT, M. (1925), *The Psychology of Time*, Kegan Paul, Trench, Trubner and Co., London.

SUNDERLAND (1944), *Agreed Religious Education Syllabus*.

SURREY (1947), *Agreed Syllabus of Religious Instruction*, Surrey County Council.

SYMONDS, P. M. (1948), *Manual for the Symonds Picture-Story Test*, Bur. of Publications, Teachers College, University of Columbia, New York.

BIBLIOGRAPHY

THORBURN, M. (1946), *The Spirit of the Child*, Allen and Unwin, London.

THURSTONE, L. L., and CHAVE, E. C. (1929), *The Measurement of Attitudes*, University of Chicago Press.

UNION COLLEGE CHARACTER RESEARCH PROJECT (1959), *Children's Religious Concepts*, Schnectady, New York.

UNIVERSITY OF SHEFFIELD INSTITUTE OF EDUCATION (1961), *Religious Education in Secondary Schools*, Nelson, London.

VINACKE, W. E. (1951), 'The Investigation of Concept Formation', *Psych. Bulletin*, 48, No. 1.

VINACKE, W. E. (1952), *The Psychology of Thinking*, McGraw-Hill, New York.

WALKER, D. J. C. (1950), 'A Study of Children's Conceptions of God', unpublished Ed.B. thesis, University of Glasgow.

WEST RIDING (1947), *Agreed Syllabus of Religious Education*.

WRIGHT, D. S. (1962), 'A Study of Religious Belief in Sixth Form Boys', in *Research and Studies*, No. 24, October 1962.

YEAXLEE, B. (1939), *Religion and the Growing Mind*, Nisbet, London.

INDEX OF SUBJECTS

abstraction, 12
abstract thinking, 12, 21; religious, 60–2
accommodation, 47
aesthetic development, 18
age divisions, 49
agnostics, 40, 65, 177
Agreed Syllabus, 5–7, 36, 49, 224–5, 245; revision of, 7
allegory, 103, 154
analogy, 15, 47, 63
animisms, 25–6, 27
anthropomorphisms, 28, 29, 87–8
artificialism, 26–7, 113–15
assessors of material, 48, 179, 199
assimilation, 47
attitudes, 31–2
authority, 135
authoritarianism, 242

beliefs, *see* attitudes
Bible, as infallible, 68, 77–8; as true, 68, 75–6; authority of, 78–9; author ship, 71–5; -centred teaching, 222–224, 228, 230; criticism of, 80; familiarity with, 214; inspired, 68; isolation in time, 82; kind of book, 69–70, 84; reading of, 212–13; relevance of, 80–4, 244
biblical stories used, 37–9
Burning Bush, *see* Moses

cannibalism, 228
child-centred religious education, 227, 230
children's names, 49
cinema, 39, 214
chosen nation, 128, 133, 149–51
Christ, *see* Jesus
Christmas, 161, 200
church, aspects liked and disliked, 194–9; attendance, 42–3, 210–12; concepts of, 194, 207–8; connections, 258; & fatigue, 207; fears of, 207; fellowship, 201; nature of, 199–201; social attractions, 197, 199
churchgoing, helpfulness of, 204; motives for, 203–4, 208; parental, 211

Church of England, 42, 66, 215, 217, 219
coefficients of reproducibility, 48, 62, 206–3
communication, divine, 93–5, 97, 100
concepts, of church, 194, 207–8; formation of, 11–13; of God, 15–17, 24, 28, 56; of prayer, 177; space-time, 22; of the Holy, 123, 126–7
concrete operations, 20, 55; thinking, 55–6, 58–9
concretisation, 21, 226–7
constraint, 135
Crucifixion, the, 82, 238

death, child's discovery of, 26
depth psychologists, 8
development, aesthetic, 18; moral, 18
devil, 167–71, 172–4, 175
dichotomized items, 262
divine communications, 93–5, 97, 100; immanence, 88, 123; justice, 128, 135–9, 153; love, 128–35, 153; presence, 95–99
dualistic systems, 114

egocentricity, 21, 30, 181
emotions, 3, 30
ethical monotheism, 116
evil, problem of, 172–5
Existentialist writers, 3
Exodus, 154–5

films, 39, 214
formal operations, *see* abstract thinking
Free Church, 42, 66, 216, 217–19

generalisation, 12
Gestalt school of psychology, 30
God, activity in natural world, 102–4; as king, 24; awe of, 120; belief in, 28; concepts of, 15–17, 24, 28, 56; concern for men, 152; confusion with Jesus, 88, 100, 156; fairness of, 140–2; Fatherhood of, 24; fear of looking on, 117–9; identity of, 28, 98–100; obedience to, 167; omnipresence of, 95–8, 100, 124–7;

omnipotence of, 95, 133; omniscience of, 97; pictures of, 24; relationship to Jesus, 165; visualized, 88–92, 100; see also Old Testament, New Testament.
Gospel sect, 42, 215–19
group halo effect, 148–9
group moral judgements, 126, 128–9, 135, 143–8, 152

holy, concepts of the, 123, 126–7
holy ground, 56, 98, 121–3
Holy Spirit, 174, 178

imagination, 25
immanence, divine, 88, 123
implications for religious education, 25, 67, 85, 114–15, 154–5, 220–46
Incarnation, the, 160
individual differences, 64–6, 215
intellect, role of the, 2
intelligence tests, 42
interview methods, 35–6, 39, 247–50

Jesus, as Messiah, 156, 167–8; as Saviour, 160; boyhood of, 161–2; confusion with God, 88, 100, 156; incarnation of God, 160; miracles of, 159, 176; mission of, 160; moral imperfections of, 163, 165; moral righteousness of, 162, 166; nature of, 156–7; relationship to God, 165; Son of God, 158–9, 163; uniqueness of, 157; see also Temptations.
Jews, 40
judgement, of Egyptians, 146–8; of Israelites, 147–8
justice, distributive, 135, 137–8; divine, 128, 135–9, 153; retributive, 135–6

legends, 223
literalism, 52, 70, 76–80, 85, 103, 242, 299–30
logical thought, 66–7
love divine, 128–35, 153

magic, 23, 27, 53, 104, 108, 176, 184
Messiah, the, 149
metaphor, 15, 47, 63
miracles, 159, 176
miraculous, the, 53, 59
moral development, 18
Moses, and the Burning Bush, 37–8, 52, 54, 56, 60–1, 81, 91, 97, 104–7, 117–19, 220, 253; deafness of, 93–4
motivation, 31
mystics, 14
mythological artificialism, 26–7, 114

Nativity myths, 176
nature, God's activity in, 102–4
negroes, 40
New Testament, 29, 74–5, 79, 85, 128, 135, 142–3, 154–5, 230
numinous, 105, 116, 125

obedience to God, 167
Old Testament, 7, 23, 49, 74, 75, 79, 85, 127, 142–3, 152, 154–5, 229
operational thinking, 21, 27, 226–7

parables, 6, 23
parents, religious practices of, 32, 211–12
percepts, 11, 17
personality differences, 215
physical causality, 26
picture projection, 36, 37, 44–5
prayer; addressee of, 178, 191; altruistic, 179–81, 191–2; comments on, 191–3; concepts of, 177; content of, 178–83; developing view of, 23; efficacious, 184, 191; for self, 181, 191; frequency of, 179, 213; in illness, 182; & magic, 185; motives for, 177; & physical danger, 183; quality of, 179; set, 183; unanswered, 188, 191–2; variety of, 179
progressive revelation, 49, 88
Psalm XXIII, 14
psychology of religion, 8

racial recapitulation, 228
rapport, 35, 41, 46
readiness for religion, 64
redemptive purpose, 150
Red Sea, the Crossing of, 37–8, 53, 55, 57, 59, 61, 81, 107–12, 136–9, 221, 253
relationships, 23–4
religion, definition of, 4; ignorance of, 29; psychology of, 8; revealed, 68; stages of, 24
religious behaviour, 212–13
religious characteristics of young child, 230–4; of adolescents, 239–246; of pre-adolescents, 234–9
religious literature, 14, 63
religious teaching, content of, 5–7; implications for, 25, 67, 85, 114–5, 154–5, 220–46
religious thinking, abilities in, 22–30; materials of, 13–18; motives for, 31–3; nature of, 3–5, 10; process of, 22; stages of, 24
research and religion, 8–9
responsibility, corporate, 143; individual, 143

Resurrection, the, 238
Roman Catholics, 29, 40

salvation, 38, 83, 107, 152
sampling, 34, 39–43
Samuel, 37, 38
scalogram method, 260–3
school, religious influence of, 32, 43
science, influence of, 27, 242
scientific laws, 103
sensori-motor intelligence, 19
sequences of thought, 62
sex differences, 213
socio-economic status of home, 43
Sunday School attendance, 32, 42, 195, 204–6, 207, 210–12

technical artificialism, 26, 14
television, 39, 214
Temptations of Jesus, 37–8, 54–5, 57, 59, 61, 81, 112–3, 221–2, 156, 166–171, 173–5, 254, 256–7

test administration procedure, 247–250; objectivity of, 48; reliability of, 45, 262, scoring methods of, 48–9; validity of, 45, 263
Thematic Apperception test, 44
theological thinking, 66–7
thinking, abilities in, 19–22; concrete, 19; intuitive, 19–20, 52–4; materials of, 10, 11–13; motives for, 10, 30; pre-operational, 20, 52–4; processes of, 10, 19–22; propositional, 19, 21–2, 58; regressions in, 21; sequences of, 62; transductive, 52, 54; uni-directional, 21, 30

universal love, 130, 153

vengeance, 143, 152
verbalising, 15
verbalisms, 18, 46
vicarious experience, 14

worship, 25, 193, 201

INDEX OF NAMES

Acland, R., 86
Agreed Syllabus, 5, 36, 49, 224–5, 245
  Berkshire, 38
  Bristol, 38
  Cambridge, 5–6, 38
  Carlisle, 38
  Cumberland, 38
  Durham, 6
  L.C.C., 38
  Manchester, 38
  Middlesex, 38
  Sheffield, 38
  Surrey, 38
  West Riding, 6, 38
  Westmorland, 38
Ainsworth, D., 23
Allport, G. W., 8
Anastasi, A., 44
Anthony, S., 26
Argyle, M., 8, 9, 29, 42, 213
Arnold, J., 29
Austin, G. A., 11

Bartlett, F. C., 12, 47
Batten, R., 229, 231, 233, 235
Beard, R., 47
Beiswanger, G. W., 23
Bell, J. E., 44
Bellack, L., 44
Berlyne, D., 19
Blyton, E., 73
Bose, R. G., 28
Bovet, P., 6, 87, 162
Bradshaw, J., 29
Bruner, J. S., 11, 13
Buber, M., 23

Chave, E. J., 32
Chesser, E., 32
Churchill, E. M., 15, 21
Coltham, J. B., 22, 36, 261

Daines, J. W., 7, 32, 241
Dawes, R. S., 28

Flugel, J. C., 8
Freud, S., 8

Gesell, A., 1, 25
Gestalt, school of psychology, 30
Glassey, W., 32

Golding, W., 228
Gorer, G., 32
Griffiths, R., 25, 27
Guttman, L., 260–2

Hall, G. S., 228
Hamilton, H. A., 244
Harms, E., 24, 25, 36, 227, 233
Havighurst, R. J., 13, 14, 19
Hazlitt, V., 21
Hebb, D. O., 11
Hebron, M. E., 23
Heidbreder, E., 11, 47
Hewitt, G., 7
Hilliard, F. H., 29, 230, 241–2
Hull, C. L., 47
Hunt, J. McV., 64
Hunter, W. S., 47
Hurlock, E. B., 11, 13, 19
Hyde, K., 7, 29, 32, 42, 115, 199, 208, 211, 213, 241

Ilg, F. L., 1, 25
Inhelder, B., 19, 21
Isaacs, S., 64

Jackson, L., 45
Jahoda, M., 22, 23, 196, 198, 208
James, W., 4, 14
Jeffreys, M. V. C., 80
Johnson, J. E., 24, 36
Johnson, P. E., 23
Jung, 8

Kenwrick, J. G., 23
Kuenne, M. R., 47
Kuhlen, R. G., 29
Kupky, O., 28, 92

Leuba, J. H., 8
Lodwick, A, R.. 21, 22, 23, 64, 261
Loomba, R. M., 25
Loukes, H., 7, 80, 240, 245
Lovell, K., 21
Loyola, St. Ignatius, 183
Lunzer, E. A., 21

Malting House School, 64
Mathias, D., 28, 48
Moray House Intelligence Test, 42

Moreton, F. E., 27
Murray, H. A., 44

Nagle, U., 29
National Foundation of Educational Research, 42
Newcomb, T. M., 32

Otto, R., 116

Peel, E. A., 10, 19, 21, 22, 23, 48, 63, 226, 260, 261
Piaget, J., 2, 6, 19, 20, 21, 22, 23, 26, 27, 30, 36, 46, 47, 48, 51, 60, 62, 63, 87, 114, 135, 136, 139, 260

Rapaport, D., 13
Reichard, S., 13
Reik, T., 23, 184
Rixon, L. D., 32
Rorschach Test, 45
Russell, D. H., 10, 11–12, 13, 19

Schneider, S., 13
Serra, M. C., 15
Sheffield University Institute of Education, 7, 29
Sleight Non-Verbal Intelligence Test, 42
Smith, J. J., 4
Smith, J. W. D., 15
Smoke, K. L., 11, 47
Spearman, C., 23
Stouffer, S. A., 260
Svehla, G., 32

Thorburn, M., 6
Thurstone, L. L., 32

Vinacke, W. E., 12–13, 15, 16, 18

Walker, D. J. C., 28
Wright, D. S., 7, 32, 241

Yale Clinic of Child Development, 26
Yeaxlee, B., 4, 25, 234